TURGENEV

the man,
his art
and
his age

Avrahm
Yarmolinsky

TURGENEV

the man,
his art
and
his age

THE ORION PRESS

New York

PREFACE

For years Turgenev held a place among the world's greatest masters of the craft of fiction. Henry James was not alone in being inclined to pronounce him "the first novelist of his time." True, even in the nineteenth century there were dissenting voices, but on the whole his reputation with the cultivated British public, and even more with the Americans, was extraordinary. More recently, the towering figures of Tolstoy and Dostoevsky, as also the achievements of such probers and experimenters as Proust and Joyce, have cast a shadow over his performance. He lacks the massiveness and scope of these writers, neither diving as deep nor soaring as high as they do. The present generation is apt to find Turgenev's realism not searching enough and his reliance on "the homeopathy of science and civilization" somewhat naive. Nevertheless, he continues to be regarded with respect and affection. To an apprentice writer who wanted a reading list Hemingway recommended individual works by a score of authors, and all of Turgenev. At home his books, for all his outspoken Western sympathies, were not suppressed even when the orgy of anti-Westernism was at its height. To judge by the size of the Soviet editions of Turgenev, his popularity there was growing in the postwar period. The appearance within the last few years of half a dozen new English translations of his major works points to a revived interest in him elsewhere. Perhaps public favor is swinging in his direction again.

Certainly there is much in his writings to engage the emotions and feed the mind. The reader who first encounters him or who returns to his work soon realizes that he is in the company of a clear-eyed, sensitive observer, a humane and free spirit. Here is a lucid, self-disciplined writer with an immense curiosity about men and women, young and old; kin, neighbors, friends, enemies. His stories and novels show a fine economy and an architecture, based on contrast, which delights with its simplicity and formal elegance. His numerous and various characters, whether carefully portrayed or merely sketched in, are done to the life. Their personal histories unfold in an atmosphere created in part by the authentic social setting, in part by the background of earth and sky. One of Turgenev's gifts is the ability to conjure up the genius of a place, generally a rural one: the autumnal forest familiar to the hunter; a riverside meadow with its lime tree in the fragrance and radiance of summer; a timeworn yet sturdy manor in its imperturbable peace. He commands a prose that moves with an unselfconscious grace.

Turgenev does not ignore the evil in the human heart, but his forte is the projection of high-minded if generally ineffectual men and of women equally idealistic but of greater fortitude and moral stature. The pathos, the tragedy of the human condition was never quite absent from his thoughts. His pages are deeply tinged with melancholy and haunted by nostalgia, yet the melancholy alternates with elation, and the nostalgia is countered by expectancy. Hence Virginia Woolf could speak of his "generalized and balanced view of life" as a source of his profundity. Happiness, he implies, is evanescent, but that only renders its moments the more precious. The existence of the individual is a brief interval, threaded with mystery, between two nullities. There is nothing in the natural world, he suspects, to insure the things that sustain the soul: goodness, courage, beauty, love. All the more, then, did he prize these, and it is the virtue of his art that he presented them compellingly.

His propensity was for such themes as the blossoming of young love, the misery of unrequited passion. But he was writing in the middle decades of the nineteenth century, when the Russian public expected the novelist to confront the political issues of the day. Turgenev responded by seeking to become the chronicler of his age, a perceptive witness, testifying, sometimes with sardonic humor, against the extremists on both the right and left. He was abjectly modest about his gifts, yet he did express pride in having striven after "impartiality and integral truth." His novels are, in a sense, chapters from the history of the Russian middle class during the troubled period when the country was shifting from a serf economy to one founded on free labor, while the autocratic regime remained intact. In diverse ways his work sheds light on "the strangest and most amazing people in the world," as he once characterized his compatriots. He was not himself a remarkably strange or amazing man, but his lifelong devotion to Mme. Viardot, which was so fateful for him, makes his personal history extraordinary. The historian and statesman, Paul Milukov, justly observed of Turgenev: "He will always attract people wishing to understand our past." It is a truism that such an understanding is essential to the comprehension of contemporary Russia.

The present work attempts to comprehend the novelist himself and to chronicle his days and works. It is a completely revised version of the book published in 1926. Of course, I have taken advantage of the new material that has come to light in the interim. I have also re-examined some of the sources used originally. A large proportion of the text has been rewritten. Chapters VI and VII are now combined and the division into parts has been abandoned. Needless to say, such factual errors as I have been able to discover have been corrected. There are two new features here: a chronological table of important events in Turgenev's life and a brief bibliographical note.

My thanks are due to Professor Leon Edel, the biographer of Henry James, for giving me certain bibliographical information and particularly for his graciousness in making available to me the passages relating to Turgenev in his transcripts of the unpublished correspondence of Henry James. Grateful acknowledgment is hereby made to Professor William A. Jackson and the Houghton Library of Harvard University for permission to quote two passages from as many unpublished letters of Henry James and a phrase from a third. To Miss Isabelle C. Holland I am under obligation for a number of suggestions. I am deeply indebted to my wife, Babette Deutsch, for her help at every stage of the revision.

August, 1958   A.Y.

PREFACE TO

THE FIRST EDITION

As the statements of fact in this narrative derive chiefly from sources which, being in Russian, are inaccessible to Western readers, and as the works drawn upon run into the hundreds, the author deemed it unnecessary to burden the book with references. His researches, begun in the New York Public Library, took him to the Staatsbibliothek in Berlin, the Bibliothèque Nationale, and the British Museum, as well as to the great libraries of Leningrad (Petersburg) and Moscow. He recalls with special pleasure the long hours spent during the winter of 1923-24 in the cold reading-room of the Pushkin House, not far from the ice-blocked Neva, and in the Leningrad Public Library, whose more clement atmosphere allowed him to shed his overcoat while he worked. To the administration of these two institutions, as also to that of the Library of the Russian Academy of Sciences and of the Historical Museum in Moscow, he is obligated for access to much manuscript material which yielded data presented here for the first time.

He wishes to thank the following: Professor Nikolay Leontyevich Brodsky, of Moscow, for the use of his private library and for permission to read the manuscript of a volume of the novelist's unpublished correspondence; Mr. Mikhail Veniaminovich Portugalov, curator of the Turgenev Museum at Oryol, for help in procuring unpublished pictorial material; Mr. Ivan Ivanovich Lebedev, an archivist of the same city, for unpublished information relating to Turgenev's forebears; Mr. Modest Hoffmann, of Paris, for permission to read his transcripts of unpublished documents from the collection of the late A. F. Onegin, a friend of the novelist's; Mr. Anatoly Fyodorovich Koni, of the Russian Academy, one of the few surviving acquaintances of Turgenev's, for his interest; and Professor André Mazon, of the Collège de France, chiefly for intelligence concerning Turgenev's literary remains contained in the papers of the Viardot family, upon which he has been at work since 1914. His catalogue of this material has been completed but not yet published. Some of the documents have, however, already appeared in print. They furnish evidence that the gestation of Turgenev's major compositions covered a longer period than has been believed, and that the plots were elaborated years before the novels were actually executed, a circumstance which allowed him to keep several works on the stocks at the same time. They further emphasize the novelist's reliance upon living models. The published catalogue, as Professor Mazon has been good enough to indicate in a letter received as this book goes to press, will contain a reprint of a hitherto unknown plan for an unwritten novel. The kindness of the late Henry Holt, in permitting him to read a personal letter addressed to the publisher by Turgenev, is gratefully remembered by the author. Above all, he is heavily indebted to Miss Babette Deutsch for her persistent encouragement, for the stimulus of many fertile suggestions, and for guidance in the treacherous ways of a language to which he was not born.

August 31, 1926   A.Y.

CONTENTS

ILLUSTRATIONS

TURGENEV

the man,
his art
and
his age

1

IN WHICH A RUSSIAN

IS SCRATCHED

"On Monday, October 28th, 1818, son Ivan—21 inches Long was Born at Oryol in my own house, at twelve of the clock in the Morning." When Turgenev's mother made this entry in her tiny memorandum-book she was a woman of thirty. Her figure was small and neat, but stooping; her fine eyes were set in a sallow, coarse-skinned, pockmarked face, above a broad nose, which was to turn blue with time, and a determined chin. It was her tragedy to be passionate without being lovable. Though capable of generosity and kindness, she was given to outbursts of spite and willful brutality that kept the household in a state of terror. Her son suffered too much from her ogreish disposition to appreciate that shrewd response to the minutiae of experience which she bequeathed to him. Inordinately arrogant and overbearing, she wore her ego like a hoopskirt, taking it for granted that people would get out of her way. In her meager person she combined a *grande dame* and a barbaric matriarch. One sees her, during her placid moments, moving about her drawing room, her delicate hands hovering over her Sèvres, her *bibelots,* her flowers, her bird cages, and alighting upon her *Imitation de Jésus Christ*—herself carefully bonneted and ruched, as she always was to everyone but her maid.

Varvara Petrovna, to refer to Mme. Turgeneva in the Russian manner by her given name and patronymic, always mentioned her forebears with unction. Her family pride was part of the small, rigid set of traditions to which she was born. Not that she could have traced her ancestry back further than the beginning of the eighteenth century, when these Lutovinovs began to accumulate their lands and their wealth.

They did not distinguish themselves as soldiers, scholars or gentlemen. What they possessed was a violent energy, a gross self-will, rooted in generations of insolent authority. Their lettered descendant took pleasure in privately vilifying these homespun Borgias. He once remarked that his ancestors were probably as ugly as goats and stank like monkeys.

Some of the bones of the family skeletons are to be found in Turgenev's writings. The "Reckless Character" who gives the title to his last story but one is a cousin of his, an alcoholic become a derelict. (In a letter the novelist described another relative on his father's side as "the biggest son-of-a-bitch and robber.") Ivan Andreyevich, the first Lutovinov on record, retired from the army with the rank of "brigadier," superior to that of colonel. He had five daughters and three sons: Pyotr, Alexey, and Ivan. The conscienceless, cold-hearted, diabolically clever reprobate who is the villain in "Three Portraits" has been identified as either Alexey or Ivan. In this story the young gentleman seduces his foster sister and, finding her with child, lays the blame to her betrothed and kills that honest simpleton in a framed-up duel. The author confided to a friend that in reality the murderer was also guilty of incest, since the girl in the case was his blood sister. The father, who is pictured as a harsh, miserly old man, re-appears in "Freeholder Ovsyannikov." He boldly possesses himself of the land of a peasant freeholder, and when the wronged man complains to the court, has him flogged into submission.

A gruesome story attaches to the novelist's maternal grand-mother. In her old age, Turgenev told a German friend, Ludwig Pietsch, she was paralyzed, but on one occasion in a fit of temper she worked up sufficient energy to knock unconscious with a chunk of wood the little serf boy who at-tended her, and then suffocate him with a pillow. A variant of this story figures in "The Brigadier." Varvara Petrovna filially remembered the old lady's virtues. Her mother, she told Ivan, was so far ahead of her time that she read books, held opinions on politics and business, and was "infinitely more entertaining" than his paternal grandmother. His ma-ternal grandfather was Ivan Andreyevich Lutovinov's eldest son, Pyotr. He was remembered for having taught his peasants to graft sprigs of orchard trees on the wild apple and pear trees growing in the woods that encroached upon his fields. A peasant boy, owned and picked for schooling by Varvara Petrovna, wrote in later life of having munched these forest fruits. Pyotr died before Varvara, his only child, was born—on October 30, 1787.* With her mother's second marriage the girl's unhappiness began. She grew up a homely, gawky creature, the ugly duckling among her pretty stepsisters, and warped by her mother's odd dislike and her stepfather's brutality. He humiliated her and beat her when he was drunk, but in due time began to show an interest in her of an unmistakable kind. Many years afterward, Varvara Petrovna took Bibi (Varvara), her little foster daughter who had been received into the household as an infant, to visit the old mansion which had been the scene of her own bitter girlhood. The house was deserted and the door leading to her stepfather's rooms was boarded over. "No sooner did I run up to it," writes Bibi in her reminiscences, "and touch the ancient copper padlock which stuck through the boards, than Varvara Petrovna seized my arm: 'Don't touch it! You mustn't! There is a curse on these rooms!' Never shall I forget her voice and the way her face looked at that moment. They expressed so much fear and hatred and rage."

It is told that after her mother's death her stepfather tried to rape her. She fled the house and walked for miles to seek refuge at Spasskoye, the estate of her only remaining uncle, Ivan Ivanovich Lutovinov. It was to him that the family possessions had fallen. The relations between the bachelor uncle and his niece are a matter of conjecture. She lived under his tutelage for about a decade. Though a miser like his father, he liked to keep open house, and there was no scarcity of entertainment for man and beast. It may have been in the rough male society which his hospitality provided that the girl developed her masculine tastes. She preferred horseback riding, hunting, and target shooting to knitting

---

* *"Généalogie de la famille Loutovinoff"* in J. Mourier, *Tourguéneff à Spasskoe,* p. 113. The inscription on her tombstone (Grand Duke Nikolay Mikhailovich, *Moskovsky nekropol,* v. 3, p. 232) implies that she was born in 1780.

bead bags and embroidering on canvas. In later years she could beat her sons at billiards. Obviously she was no dainty goose. To judge by her letters, her uncle must have offered her the advantages of the female education of the day. It is known that she attended a boarding school for a time, and that she was an avid reader, chiefly of French novels and travel books.

According to one account, Ivan Lutovinov died of grief at the news that Moscow had succumbed to the French. His great-uncle's patriotism was to be held up as a reproach to Turgenev, who ultimately settled in France and, indeed, expended his last breath there. It is a matter of record, however, that the old man died in 1813, the year after Napoleon's invasion. His estate comprised about twenty villages scattered through three provinces, and a vast amount of personal property. His silverware alone is said to have weighed two thousand pounds. Turgenev's mother inherited all this wealth, as she had inherited the eccentricities and savageries of her race.

Now that she could do as she pleased, the heiress spent part of the year at Spasskoye and part in the neighboring city of Oryol. She was anxious to find a husband. It was in keeping with her virile character that she should make no bones about it. One young man whom she wooed too vigorously was literally forced to flee her importunities. According to his own story, she had lured him from town to her estate, where she provided him with lavish entertainment, and on the occasion of his name day presented him with the deed to one of her properties to which were attached five hundred souls. But Varvara Petrovna saw her deed torn up by the very hands into which she gave it, and that night the young man secretly left Spasskoye.

It was in Oryol that she may have met the handsome young officer of the Cuirassiers who was to become the father of the novelist. He owned about one hundred souls and an unprofitable little property in the neighborhood of the Lutovinov estate. The mistress of Spasskoye was plain-looking, albeit possessed of spirit and of a vivid intelligence. Moreover, she was of a ripe age, being indeed six years older than her suitor. But she owned five thousand "souls" (male serfs) and many thousands of acres. It is reported, plausibly enough, that the lady made the advances, and the lieutenant's father had to intervene to bring the young man into line. A more theatrical and less credible tale runs thus: Lieutenant Turgenev visited Varvara Petrovna to negotiate the purchase of some horses for the army; the young woman liked the fascinating officer, and with the free hospitality of those days invited him to join her in a game of cards, the winner to claim whatever he chose; the cavalier won, and demanded the loser's hand in marriage. He followed up his victory with another the next day which enabled him to name the date of the wedding.

Under the portrait of the novelist's father at Spasskoye hung a picture of his family tree. Its branches reach into four centuries of Russian history. The Turgenevs derive from a Tartar Khan named Turga, who left the Golden Horde, accepted baptism, and entered the service of Grand Duke Vasily the Blind in the fifteenth century. The golden star on the azure field and the silver crescent above it in the family's coat of arms refer to the Tartar origin and the Mohammedan faith of their ancestors. Thus the maxim ascribed to Napoleon fits Turgenev literally. On one occasion he referred to his Tartar blood to account for the nomadic strain in his make-up.

The Turgenevs, who belonged to the middle nobility, served their czars faithfully and not without honor as soldiers or administrators. One Turgenev was beheaded by Pseudo-Demetrius for his devotion to the lawful dynasty and is revered by the Church as a martyr. Two Turgenevs perished in the *jacquerie* headed by Stepan Razin in the seventeenth century. Several of them were among the gentry whom Peter the Great forced to learn the business of war from the bottom up, and one was killed in his service. Another held an important post under Empress Anna. Romance enters the family chronicle with the novelist's great-grandfather, who was taken prisoner in one of the Turkish wars and became a slave in the sultan's harem. There, the tradition goes, a sultana was charmed by his appearance and helped him escape. A legend makes one of his sons a lover of Empress Elizabeth.

This Turgenev's second son, Sergey, born in 1793, was the

novelist's father. In him the heritage of good looks was stamped with a strange femininity. A portrait of him which hung at Spasskoye has been described thus:

In spite of astonishing dark eyes, daring and manly, it seems that this is not a man, but a woman, or better still, a demimondaine, arrayed in the white uniform of the Guards and wearing a neckerchief which, without a knot or a bow, is twisted about her white, swanlike throat. The glance is a mermaid's, calm and enigmatic, the lips are sensuous and curved with a scarcely perceptible smile.

In the "mermaid's" features his wife found, in his middle years, a resemblance to Voltaire. Lieutenant Turgenev's grace went with an athletic build: he was a tall, broad-shouldered man, and his distinguished son contended that he inherited the giant frame of his father and the vitals of his lean, sickly mother.

On Friday, January 14, 1816, Varvara Petrovna Lutovinova, at the age of twenty-nine, was joined in matrimony to Sergey Nikolayevich Turgenev, who was twenty-three, in the name of the Father, the Son, and the Holy Ghost. In after years she warned her young friends not to marry on Friday, because the day was fatal to married happiness.

2

"SHADES OF THE

PRISON-HOUSE"

The newly married pair remained in the city of Oryol for some time, and there the eldest child, Nikolay, and the second son, Ivan, were born. The third and last child, Sergey, who arrived when his parents were married five years, was an epileptic, who died at the age of eighteen. Strangely enough, there is no mention of him in the letters nor allusion to him in the works of his brother, the novelist. In 1821 the father retired with the rank of colonel, and it was then that the family settled definitely in the country, at Spasskoye, a village on the fringe of the province of Oryol, lying about two hundred miles southwest of Moscow, in the heart of central Russia. They made, however, extensive and frequent trips abroad—in the early years for pleasure, and later for the sake of the colonel's impaired health. The journey was sometimes made, at least in part, in a huge lumbering *dormeuse* of Viennese make, which had dining and sleeping compartments, and which was drawn by ten horses. As a boy of four Ivan saw Germany, France, and Switzerland, on a trip made in the company of the entire family, and also of a young Russian doctor. At Bern the boy's career nearly came to an abrupt end when he all but tumbled into the famous bear pit.

His early recollections fasten like lichens to the oaken walls of the wooden manor house at Spasskoye, to the wayside chapel, and to the cemetery that lured and scared him. Every part of the great gardens was as familiar to him as the inhabitants of his green bird cage or the nurse who had him in charge. The boy could wander from the big house, past the rookeries in the birches, into the depths of the park, down the shelving slope to the pond where the fish rose to feed from his hand

and where the children had a little boat to themselves, or over to the orchard where the trees stood heavy with cherries or plums or apples. In the autumn he might startle the snipe that flocked toward the reddening rowans, or watch the partridge and wild duck that were later to prove his game. Squirrels, kestrels, orioles, and hedge-sparrows, violets and gooseberries—these will make a noise and a fragrance in his pages. "Oh, my garden!" exclaims, in a mood of reminiscence, the hero of one of his early stories. "Oh, the overgrown paths by the shallow pond! Oh, the little sandy spot below the tumble-down dike where I used to catch gudgeons!" And he proceeds to evoke such sights and sounds and smells as must continually have flowed in upon the senses of the young Ivan: the dark track of the wind as it moved over the golden meadow grass; the forlorn song of a peasant broken by the jolting of his cart; the humble chime of the cracked church bell; the pungent bitterness of wormwood; the sweetness of freshly mown buckwheat on the summer air.

Naturally, most of the crowded frescos of this outdoor world that were painted on the walls of his young mind flaked off with time. These few endured until death erased them forever: the patch from which he used to steal sun-warmed strawberries; the tree from whose bough he shot his first crow; the spot where he found a mushroom of prodigious size; above all, the place where he watched, spellbound, the duel between an adder and a toad. This last horrid spectacle made the child doubt for the first time the goodness of Providence. And no amount of metaphysics from his professors later, nor earnest arguments from his devout friends, could do more than film over that subversive picture.

The boy lived in the country until he was nine years old and found there plenty of nourishment for his growing curiosity. He had a particular fondness for pulling off the petals of a rosebud and trying to discover the core of it. It always irritated him to find that the innermost sheaths were so thin and delicate that he could not tear them off. Perhaps this practice taught the novelist to content himself with the exquisite epidermis of reality, to draw, as George Moore said of him, only the skin from his subject.

When winter came, and the snow weighted the branches

of the pines, humped itself over the low hills, and blunted the edges of the ravines, there remained a house of forty rooms in which to lose oneself. It seemed as big as a town to Ivan. He would walk around the heavy oak tables, vast settees upholstered in yellow leather, cabinets filled with foreign bric-a-brac, arm-chairs whose ebony backs were decorated with bronze cupids leading lions on leashes of flowers. From one corner in every room the boy would be regarded gravely by icons dark with age, before which dim lamps were kept steadily burning. In some such setting one pictures him playing lotto with Nikolay on a checkerboard whereof the central square was "The Temple of Happiness," or, as he grew older, composing the geography and history of the imaginary island kingdoms over which he and his brothers ruled. At night he would sometimes try to keep awake in order to see the house sprites (*domovye*). His father was afraid of them. The novelist was to recall how, by flickering candlelight, he would follow his father and the priest summoned to exorcise them by sprinkling the corners of the rooms with holy water.

The spacious, rather homely mansion was connected by galleries with two wings, one of which comprised the offices, the other being reserved for guests. If Ivan might explore the house and grounds, always under the eye of some servant, it was probably a much rarer thing for him to find the way to what one might describe as the back door of the estate. Here were the icehouses and the smokehouse, the dairies and the wine cellar, the pigs and chickens, the barns and stables, and at a little distance the quarters of the house serfs, which hummed and clanged with the work of milling and tanning, churning and weaving. Spasskoye was virtually a self-sufficient economic unit, not unlike a medieval manor, producing all that the family ate and drank, most of its clothes, and some of its furniture. It is curious to note that another of the Turgenevs' estates housed a paper factory which supplied the young author with the foolscap on which his first stories were written.

The Turgenevs lived hospitably, commanding a hierarchy of domestic serfs as well as the hangers-on that were to be found in every manor house, and providing for relays of guests the pleasures of both the country and the town. The day that began with a fox-hunt might end with a masquerade, with private theatricals, or with a grand ball for which Mme. Turgeneva would gown herself in some imported confection of *tulle illusion* in which she had danced in Paris. The tendency to ape court etiquette, which gives an anecdotal touch to her widowhood, must have shown itself in an earlier devotion to pomp and circumstance.

Colonel Turgenev was allowed no hand in the management of the estates, but he seems to have had his way in affairs of the heart. His appreciation of feminine charm, even in his wife's serfs, led him to break his marital vows with a fine contempt for class differences. We have it on his son's authority that he had a knowledge of women which made him irresistible, and it was as a tribute to this quality that the novelist called his father "a mighty hunter before the Lord."

In the story "First Love" Turgenev, if we choose to believe him, drew upon his reminiscences of the family life of his parents. The self-contained, elegantly groomed gentleman of the tale, with his spasmodically affectionate manner toward his family, his excellent horsemanship, and his epicurean tastes was modeled upon the author's father. Certain episodes, such as a domestic scene over his interest in a beautiful girl, and his ungallant reference to his wife's age, serve to corroborate Turgenev's assertion.

Varvara Petrovna's attachment to her husband, although deep and sincere, was another expression of her egotism. As for him, he was dependent on his homely, eccentric wife for the money he spent on his pleasures. He treated her, one must suppose, except in times of an open breach, with the consideration which his position required, and she interpreted his attitude to suit herself. Being sticklers for the proprieties, both were interested in having their children believe the decorous myth of their conjugal felicity—a myth which Varvara Petrovna elaborated when she became a widow.

To the bitterness of a dissatisfied wife, the mistress of Spasskoye added the slave-owner's habits of mind and an inherited disposition toward cruelty. The combination was not likely to contribute to the happiness of her inferiors—her serfs or her sons. They lived in an atmosphere of feudalism not tempered by the chivalric ideal of the West. It is true that her paternalistic attitude toward the "souls" she owned, coupled with a managerial ability, assured the peasants a good living. At the same time she felt herself authorized to inflict anything on them, from a flogging to a forced marriage. The walls of Spasskoye witnessed not infrequent acts of revolting despotism.

At least one such scene so impressed itself upon the memory of a small boy that half a century later he incorporated it into one of his stories. Two young peasants who were working in the park neglected to bow to Varvara Petrovna as she passed them—an offense for which she at once ordered them deported to Siberia. "Here is the window at which my mother sat," Turgenev once remarked to a visitor at Spasskoye. "It was summer, and the window was open, and I was a witness to how the two men, on the eve of their deportation, approached the window with bared, bowed heads to take leave of her."

Looking back at his childhood from the vantage point of his seventeen years, Ivan wrote: "About my childish years I know that I was a spoiled darling, but very homely, and that at the age of four I nearly died, and that I was then brought to life by old Hungarian wine—perhaps that's why I like wine," adding, "although I don't drink much," and then crossing it out. As an old man, however, he spoke of having been flogged nearly every day. Sitting at dinner with friends in Paris, Turgenev is carried back to his childhood by a remark of Flaubert's to the effect that in a youthful drama of his, he made the people complain to Louis XI that they were forced to season their vegetables with the salt of their tears. Turgenev recalled how, because of some slight misdeed, he would be first lectured by his tutor, then whipped, then deprived of his dinner, finally wandering out, hungry and sore, into the park, and "drinking with a kind of bitter pleasure the salt water which streamed from his eyes down his cheeks into his mouth." He was inclined to exaggerate, but it is certain that his mother believed in the rod and used it readily. Once when giving her eldest son ten strokes she nearly fainted, and she liked to relate afterward how he stood before her with bare little buttocks, shouting, "Water, water for Mummy!" Apparently the father made no attempt to shield the children from their mother's sadism.

Ivan, outraged by an unjust punishment, on one occasion decided to run away from home. His German tutor discovered him stealing out of the house in the dead of night, persuaded him to return, and managed to heal the sprained filial bond. The hatred of injustice which warms so many of his pages must have been kindled again and again in the heart of a tormented and furious boy, who not only suffered himself, but constantly saw his brothers and his playmates, the familiar house serfs, undergoing disproportionate punishments for trivial misdemeanors. In retrospect Varvara Petrovna flattered herself that she had treated her sons fairly. "When you were children," she wrote to Ivan years later, "you were flogged, but not oppressed. You entered the room noisily, without fear." It would seem that the mother deceived herself. The whole course of her second son's life was to bear witness to the crushing effect of her overbearing manner. It sapped his initiative in the conduct of his affairs, and his dislike of her self-assertiveness made him incapable of standing up for his own rights.

Such anecdotes as have come down to us about the active little boy with the large brow seem to show that he kept a child's fresh point of view and on occasion wagged a child's free tongue. Upon being presented by an awed mother to an aged princess, the child, inspecting her soberly, observed with penetration: "You look just like a monkey!" This early aptness of simile was of course rewarded with a whipping. At another time the boy was made to recite a fable of Dmitriev's before the author himself, a venerable old man and a third-rate writer, who was visiting the house. Not content with the role of performer, Ivan assumed that of critic, and remarked to Dmitriev point-blank: "Your fables are good, but Krylov's are much better." In recounting the story later Turgenev said: "My mother got so angry that she flogged me, and thereby fixed in my mind the memory of my first meeting with a Russian writer."

Dmitriev, like not a few of his mother's friends, belonged to the age of the great Catherine. Indeed, representatives of that formally courteous, suavely cynical period were not infrequently to be seen at Spasskoye, and Ivan was also being reminded of it by the ladies and gentlemen whose portraits stared at him from the walls of home. The exquisites and the skeptics of the eighteenth century fitted the Russian scene no better than a paste buckle does a bast shoe, and they themselves must have known it. This picturesque incongruity of crinolines, powdered wigs, patches, and quizzical eyebrows with coarse native rusticity, impressed itself on the boy indelibly.

The flabbiness of will which afflicted Turgenev to the end of his life may have been in part due to the cramping atmosphere of arbitrary authority which prevailed in the household, quite aside from the treatment he received at his mother's hands. So strong was her passion for regulating and labeling that her house was run with the strictness of a military establishment. She insisted upon certain formalities of speech and gesture in the children's approach to their parents and their Deity. In later years, apparently feeling that the Lord would prefer to be addressed in a civilized tongue, she made Bibi start the day by reciting the following prayer: *"Seigneur, donnez-moi la force pour résister, la patience pour souffrir, et la constance pour persévérer."* In addition there was the matutinal duty of reading a chapter from *L'Imitation de Jésus Christ*. Mme. Tugeneva could hardly have been less exacting in the religious education of her own children. A Spartan discipline was the educational vogue of the time, and Turgenev later asserted that his parents were influenced by the fashion in this matter. Coupled with the authoritarian spirit was the corollary sense of caste. The little masters played with the children of the serfs, but the latter were not allowed to presume upon their privileges. Turgenev tells the story of a pillow fight with a serf boy during which the latter was caught by Varvara Petrovna in the act of throwing a pillow at her son. The little serf, who was Ivan's best friend, was immediately sent to be flogged. Ivan's protests availed nothing. The succession of Fräuleins and Messieurs who were hired to instruct the children were treated with scarcely more civility than were the servants.

Varvara Petrovna herself had a hand in her sons' education. Her notebook for 1823 contains an outline, in the form of questions and answers, of lessons for the eldest boy. The temperamental lady had the intelligence to relate some of the questions to the child's experience on their trip abroad: "What did you see in Bern? Live reindeer, wild goats, and four bears. Where did you live in Paris? Rue de la Paix." The answer she made up for one of her questions suggests from whom her literary son inherited his sensitive eye: "What is the color of the Rhine? The color of green grapes."

French was in common use in the household and the main subject of instruction, but as the boys grew older Russian received a measure of attention. Colonel Turgenev in ill-spelled letters enjoined upon his sons the desirability of improving their knowledge of the native tongue. He also urged them to write their diaries in Russian at least twice a week, alternating with French and German; and it was he who asked Ivan's opinion about the correctness of a Russian phrase, "because," he said, "you [children] know the grammar better than we do." Like Pushkin, and so many other masters of Russian, Turgenev owed his knowledge of the vernacular chiefly to contact with the serfs. It was probably a domestic who taught him to read and write the language.

He certainly had one of the servants to thank for his introduction to the native poetry. He was about eight years old when one night, in collusion with this young serf who had an unschooled passion for verse and was himself something of a rhymester, Ivan broke open one of the heavy old black bookcases in the nursery, and standing on the shoulders of his accomplice, drew out two enormous eighteenth century tomes, smelling of dust and mice. One of them, entitled *Symbols and Emblems,* contained puzzling pictures accompanied by equally puzzling explanations of their significance in five languages, including English. The impressionable child, having spent the next day over this curious volume, which had been adapted from the Dutch by order of Peter the Great, went to bed half-delirious: "Unicorns, negroes, kings, suns, pyramids, swords, snakes," he recalled later, "whirled through my poor head; I was an emblem myself. I 'signified,' I was lighted by the sun, I was hurled into darkness, I sat upon a tree, I sat in a pit, I sat on clouds, I sat on a belfry. . . ."

The other stolen volume that Ivan's friend appropriated was that grandiloquent, lumbering epic, *Rossiad,* Kheraskov's unhappy attempt at a Russian Iliad. The two naïve readers found this book a wellspring of pure delight. The fascination of those summer hours, when in some green and secret place the child listened to the man thundering out these lapidary dactyls, is written down in one of Turgenev's late stories, "Punin and Baburin." The narrator is clearly Turgenev himself, and Punin has some of the lineaments of the serf who initiated him into his native literature:

It is impossible to convey an idea of the feeling I experienced, when, seizing upon a convenient moment, suddenly, like a hermit out of a fairy-tale or a benevolent spirit, he [Punin] would appear before me, with a ponderous book under his arm, and stealthily beckoning with his long crooked finger, and winking mysteriously, he would point with his hand, his eyebrows, his shoulders, his whole body to the deepest thickets of the garden, whither no one could follow and where it was impossible to find us. And now we have succeeded in getting away unnoticed, now we have safely reached one of our secret nooks, now we are sitting side by side and the book is being slowly opened, emitting a pungent odor, then inexpressibly sweet to me, of mildew and age. With what a thrill, with what an agitated and mute expectancy I gaze at the face, at the lips of Punin, —the lips from which in a moment a stream of delicious words is to flow! At last, the first sounds of the reading ring out. Everything round about vanishes. . . . No one knows where we are, what we are about, while with us is poetry, we saturate, intoxicate ourselves with it; we are involved in a weighty, grand, mysterious process. . . . Punin preferred sonorous, thunderous verse; he was ready to lay down his life for it! He did not read, he shouted the verses out solemnly, in a flowing, rolling outpour, through his nose, like a man intoxicated, like one beside himself with ecstasy, like a Pythian priestess. . . .

3

"THE AMERICAN"

When Ivan was nine years old the family moved to Moscow, where they bought a house and settled down to the usual life of the gentry who wintered in town. It was customary to come into the city for the Christmas festivities, preceded by a string of carts loaded with domestics and with the carcases of pigs, geese, and ducks which were to provide the household with viands until the third week in Lent. It was then time to be thinking about a return to the country, before the spring thaws had erased the roads.

Ivan was placed in a boarding school run by one Weydenhammer. In those days the government schools were held in contempt by the nobility, and a gentleman's son was either tutored at home or attended a private academy. On one occasion the authorities were actually forced to close a public high school for want of pupils. That the private schools left much to be desired may be inferred from the fact that the Government, alarmed by the low standard of instruction there, opened, in connection with the high schools, special classes for the nobility, and in 1833 forbade the establishment of new boarding schools.

The shades of Weydenhammer and his assistants dwell in the limbo of unremembered schoolmasters. Virtually the only recollection of this period which Turgenev set down is one of those puerile savageries inevitable among children. He imagined that his brain was covered only with skin and hair, and when he was tapped on the head he came near fainting —a weakness which his schoolmates were not slow to discover. He always believed that his fontanels failed to close, and joked, in later years, about bequeathing his freakish skull to the Academy of Sciences. One guesses that the two years which Turgenev spent under Weydenhammer's tutelage were made up of a regimen of French irregular verbs and German vocables, a little mild fagging, and probably several violent friendships.

He seems to have recorded one such boyish attachment of his in the story, "Yakov Pasynkov," substituting suggestively Winterkeller's boarding school for Weydenhammer's. The narrator, palpably Turgenev himself drawing upon memories of his schooldays, exhibits a mixture of youthful snobbishness and romantic affections which rise above considerations of caste. The object of his passion is an older boy, an abandoned orphan, who was kept at school out of charity and was passed over at dessert on weekdays. Poetry drew the two together. Schiller's facile raptures fell from the lips of the elder into the open heart of the younger. They would desert their beds for a spring lilac bush, and, in its fragrant shadow, talk till dawn. It is possible that in this story we have reminiscences of a somewhat later period projected upon a background of boarding school years.

In the summer of 1829, Ivan, together with his brother Nikolay, was transferred to the so-called Armenian Boarding School, one of the best private schools in the city, which later became the Lazarev Institute of Oriental Languages. He stayed there only about two months. It was during this period that he started the study of English, and laid the foundation for his later enjoyment of Shakespeare, Shelley, Keats, Byron, Bulwer-Lytton, Dickens. It was also here perhaps that Turgenev thrilled to Zagoskin's novel, *Yuri Miloslavsky,* which was read aloud by an instructor. The book is a historical romance of ancient Russia in the style of a third-rate Walter Scott. The boy was so fascinated by "this miracle of perfection," as he described it later, that he hit out at a schoolfellow who dared to interrupt the story. It was his misfortune, a year or two afterward, to meet Zagoskin as a daily visitor at his father's house: a little gargoyle of a man, with a head like a squashed pudding, bulging bespectacled eyes, and a cleft chin—prodigal of grotesque gestures and mangled French, and cherishing the delusion that he was a Samson in strength and a Don Juan in love. Thus early Turgenev discovered that an author may be the least heroic of the characters whose lives he has to live. The three years following Ivan's unexplained withdrawal from the Armenian Boarding School were spent at home preparing under private tutors for entrance to the university. Some rough sketches of them have come down to us in their pupil's hand. There was the instructor in literature with his purple nose who was always, as the French say, "between two wines." He held the boys to a strict classic diet, having a thorough dislike of that flighty young recreant, Pushkin, "the snake with a nightingale's voice," whom Ivan, with the rest of Russian youth, already idolized. There was the German tutor, a lachrymose fellow, who could not read Schiller without crying, and who kept a common crow in a cage as his pet. Discovered to be an uneducated saddle-maker, he was replaced by a fellow-countryman. There was the teacher of history, a student by the name of Ivan Klushnikov who wrote verse and had a penchant for German metaphysics, which was then just beginning to be in vogue. The boy also had a swimming master, a Prussian, who would shout at him: *"La bouche hors de l'eau, Schwere Not."*

Five Russian letters, the earliest known from Ivan's pen, forming a diary for a fortnight in the spring of 1831, have recently come to light. It appears from them that he had a French tutor for whom he wrote compositions under such titles as *"L'ambition," "L'homme vaniteux,"* and who had him read a speech by Mirabeau which delighted the boy. He was also taking dancing lessons and being tutored in Latin, arithmetic, geometry, geography, "philosophy." Then, too, he had a drawing master who set him to sketching, among other things, a hand holding a bunch of grapes. These pages are sprinkled with quotations from Derzhavin, Zhukovsky, Pushkin, and there are two lines from an attempt to describe in verse of his own the break-up of ice on the Moskva River. The writing is not without crude grammatical errors. One entry records "the unutterable agitation and upheaval in the entire interior" caused the diarist by a passage in a tale of Marlinsky's (for years that purveyor of thrillers was to remain the idol of young Turgenev—he kissed Marlinsky's name on the title pages of magazines). Another entry offers a glimpse of an evening *en famille*: Ivan is writing his letter, Nikolinka, his elder brother, is munching dried apricots and thumbing an almanac, the boys' governor is reading a "Mythology" and

Maman is at her desk, studying German vocables (Papa is in Petersburg).

The letters are addressed to Ivan's paternal uncle, Nikolay. The thirteen-year-old boy phrases his affection for him in the most extravagant terms: "I love you inexpressibly, I love you to infinity." He writes like a love-sick girl: "If I had wings, I would fly there (to Spasskoye). I would press you to my breast strongly, strongly, and kiss you again and again." And in another letter: "When I know that you are well, I study better, I play more happily, I sleep more soundly." Receiving a letter from Uncle Nikolay, he keeps it as a talisman.

Before Ivan left the hands of his tutors for the arms of his alma mater he passed through an obscure crisis, such as is not uncommon in early adolescence. His own account of it years later, set down by a friend who had caught him in a reminiscent mood, appears to be an unequal mixture of truth and fictive memory. "Until the age of fourteen," Turgenev recalled, "I was of small stature, obstinate, morose, evil-tempered, and fond of mathematics. At the age of fourteen I fell dangerously ill, was in bed for several months, and when I got up I was almost as tall as you see me now. The doctors asserted that I was ill because of too rapid growth. At that time I underwent a complete change: I became soft, weak-willed, fond of verses, literature, and inclined to dreaminess."

When Ivan matriculated at the University of Moscow he was a stout, slightly stooping boy within a month of his fifteenth birthday. It was no sign of precocity that he entered so young, for in those days the university in its non-professional departments was really little more than a secondary school. The entrance requirements recall the recipes in an old-fashioned cookbook. They stipulate "a sufficient knowledge of one or two foreign languages in common use," added to a "grounding in history, geography, arithmetic and geometry," as well as the knowledge of the native tongue. The requirements had been raised, however, two years before Ivan's matriculation.

Having satisfied the faculty as to his eligibility, he was duly enrolled. A friend of the family gave his bond that Ivan would always appear in the proper uniform while in the university and that he would conduct himself fittingly, and Ivan himself signed a paper stating that he did not belong to, nor would he join, any Masonic lodge or secret society. The year he entered there were twenty-two students and auditors in the medical and thirty-six in the ethico-political faculty. Ivan was admitted to the faculty of history and philosophy. His class consisted of thirteen students and auditors, fewer than half of whom were to be promoted.

The boy was good at his lessons. Diligently he parsed his Livy, read his manuals, and attended his lectures. Such mental stimulation as he received seems to have come from the one teacher who was less interested in cramming the memories of his hearers than in stirring their minds. Nominally professor of physics, he taught his students Schelling's *Naturphilosophie*. The Russian university aimed, however feebly, to pattern itself on the German model, but lacked altogether the latter's freedom of teaching. It was dominated by the narrow spirit of an establishment created essentially for the purpose of training bureaucrats. And yet the University of Moscow was one of the few democratic institutions in a country of caste and privilege, admission at that time being open to all comers, serfs excepted.

Looking back on this period, Turgenev recalled that his own professed democratic sympathies and his enthusiasm for the United States had won for him the nickname of "the American." In the semi-autobiographical tale "Punin and Baburin" he declares that as an undergraduate he was a good republican, and hung lithographed portraits of Fouquier-Tinville and Chalier over his desk. His fellow students in Moscow, especially the seniors, lived in an atmosphere of intellectual excitement. Ivan must have been influenced by it, although there is no evidence that he made contacts with the upper classmen among whom were men who were to leave their impress on Russian culture. A few years later, when he found himself in their company in the lecture rooms of the University of Berlin, some of them became his close friends.

The boy was to get no more than a taste of the academic life of Moscow. And yet the flavor of it lingered with him and is to be sensed in his writings. When he had passed his examinations at the end of the first year he was temporarily transferred to his third boarding school. His brother Nikolay was then in Petersburg. His mother was preparing to visit Germany to take the waters, and his father, who was ill, was getting ready to leave Moscow for the capital. In their comings and goings and scatterings the Turgenevs were then leading the life of a twentieth-century family, and Ivan had an opportunity early to acquire the habit of travel which he never lost.

In the autumn of 1834 Ivan also went to Petersburg and entered the university there. The young man, coming from Moscow, must have felt—whether contributing to his refreshment or his disturbance—the ascendancy of a new *genius loci*. The contrast between the two cities was even then a stock theme for wits and wiseacres. Peter's city, in its beginnings a murky dockyard on a Finnish swamp, within a hundred and thirty years had outdone in growth the seven-century-old Muscovite capital. If Moscow was idealistic, slovenly, old-fashioned, Petersburg was practical, trim, fresh as paint. It was kept stiffly aware of the proximity of the monarch, like a roomful of schoolboys next to the principal's office. The very promenaders whom Ivan passed on the Nevsky, which was then still lined with lime trees, marched in such regular formation that a sharp-tongued critic said that they could be mistaken for detachments of police. There was a severe angularity about the geometrically patterned streets, about the stern buildings, the very color of whose fronts was prescribed, about the thin chilly gardens and the massive palaces.

The stamp of officialdom was heavy upon the barrack-like buildings of the University of Petersburg where Ivan spent three rather ineffectual years. Painted the dull red of most of the palaces and public buildings of the capital, it looks out on the Neva with a façade like a narrow face on a lanky prostrate body. The corridor above the arcade where the students loaf during recesses is so long that to stand at one end is literally to lose the other in the haze of distance. Discipline was stricter here than in Moscow. The rector was given to scrutinizing the students' uniforms with the eyes of a sergeant inspecting his men. Allegedly a former secretary of Robespierre, he had fled from the guillotine only to pursue carelessly accoutred boys and personally escort them out of the portals of the university building.

Intellectually the place did not differ much from the Moscow institution of learning. There were the same academic fossils who read off their lectures from manuals that they prudently concealed from their students and made them commit certain passages to memory. Some of the foreign instructors were better equipped, but, not knowing enough Russian, they delivered their lectures in Latin, which their hearers scarcely understood. One of these professors taught the elements of Kantianism with the aid of a text arranged in the form of a catechism. At this time literature rather than philosophy attracted Turgenev, and he derived some stimulation from his contacts, both in and out of the classroom, with his professor of Russian literature who was a friend of prominent writers, including Pushkin. The last year of Turgenev's attendance saw new blood infused into the instruction. Courses were offered by several young Russians fresh from the hands of professors in Berlin or Göttingen. One of these men, a teacher of political economy, did not last long. He was so bold as to appear in the auditorium wearing a turnover collar and a knotted tie with flapping ends. Such a sartorial vagary must have raised the hair on the rector's scalp.

There were in the capital, as elsewhere, student cliques: *kruzhki* (circles). Turgenev must have belonged to one or more. A story of his, "The Hamlet of the Shchigry District," contains a diatribe against them:

A circle substitutes arguments for conversation, it accustoms you to fruitless chatter, distracts you from solitary, beneficial work, infects you with the literary itch; in fine, it deprives you of freshness and virginal strength of soul. A circle—why, it is vulgarity and boredom under the name of brotherhood and friendship, a chain of misunderstandings and pretensions under the pretext of frankness and sympathy. . . . In a circle people watch each other like police officers.

Socially speaking, the student body was a mixed company. Sons of princes came to the classrooms attended by their *gouverneurs* who sometimes interrupted the lecturer with a snore. They rubbed elbows with impecunious attic dwellers. A classmate of Ivan's tells the story of how one such student became the talk of the town. Unable to pay his rent and evicted by his landlady, he took his books and his poor sticks of furniture and piled them in the middle of the Semenov

Square, attaching a placard which read: "A Student's Apartment." In spite of the severity of academic regulations, here, as in Moscow, Ivan breathed a democratic air, but these young men's interest was in pleasure rather than in philosophy. He tasted something suggestive of the German *Burschenschaft* in the escapades, the lady-killing, the drinking parties enlivened by *"Gaudeamus igitur"* and *"Edite, bibite, collegiales"* sung with a strong Russian accent.

4

ADOLESCENCE

Close upon Ivan's arrival in Petersburg his father died, after years of invalidism. Morning and evening Ivan and his elder brother, Nikolay, had been obliged to come to his bedside to kiss his limp hand. A summons to the sickroom at any other hour filled the boys with fear. When the end finally came, Varvara Petrovna was in Italy, taking a cure, and the children became the charge of Uncle Nikolay.

After Varvara Petrovna returned, a visitor who met her at her mother-in-law's had this to say about her: "She is the same eccentric, and is not at all unhappy. She has brought no end of dresses from abroad and flaunts them." Above all, the widow outraged her mother-in-law's visitor by what that old lady interpreted as designs upon her son, absurd enough in any case, but intolerable in a woman on the shady side of forty "and with such a hideous phiz." Whatever impression Mme. Turgeneva gave her neighbors at the time, four years later she was writing to Ivan: "This [his father's study] is my grave, here I pray for your father, and talk to him mentally. Here I work, here I live in the past, on memories. It is only at the Smolensky Cemetery [where the colonel was buried] that I am happier."

Such of Colonel Turgenev's letters as have come down to us—they were addressed to Nikolay—show him to be a solicitous, sententious parent, eager to see his son grow into *"un jeune homme comme il faut."* He was sufficiently concerned for the education of his children to make a special trip to Switzerland in order to engage a tutor for them. His son Ivan paints him, on the contrary, as a cold, courteous *viveur* and "a well-known Don Juan." Whichever picture is true, certainly the affection that he aroused in Ivan was insufficient

nourishment for filial piety. In later years Turgenev spoke
of his father with a disrespect which savored of malice. In
the confessedly autobiographical story "First Love," the boy's
admiring worship of his father is met by a fitful affection
which alternates with long periods of chilling indifference.
"I used to stand and scrutinize his clever, handsome, brilliant face . . . and my heart would begin to quiver, and my
whole being would yearn toward him . . . and he would seem
to feel what was going on within me, and would pat me on
the cheek in passing—and either go away, or begin to occupy
himself with something, or suddenly freeze all over, as he
alone knew how to freeze; and I would immediately shrivel
up and grow frigid also." It is difficult to say to what extent
imagination has distorted memory in this picture, but the
novelist is firm on the point that the situation upon which
"First Love" is built—that of an adolescent in love with his
father's mistress—was his personal experience.

The object of this early passion was the daughter of an
impoverished princess who lived in the neighborhood. There
are vague references to other boyish amours, no less intense for
being platonic. But Ivan must have been tutored in love, as
he had been in literature, by domestic serfs. Even in the town
house there was a constant coming and going of women servants, all of whom were at the beck and call of the young
master, and some of whom were pretty.

On a January day in 1878, Turgenev was dining with some
French *littérateurs* and the conversation with which they sea-
soned their entrée began bawdily. He received the spicy
stories with what the Goncourts' *Journal* describes as "the
somewhat *médusé* astonishment of a barbarian who makes love
very naturally." When they began matching their sharpest
sexual experiences, Turgenev racked his memory to produce
the following:

I was only a boy, and virginal, with the desire which one has at
fifteen. My mother had a pretty chambermaid with a stupid look,
but you know there are some faces to which stupidity lends nobility.
It was a soft, humid, rainy day, one of those erotic days which Daudet
has just painted. Dusk was beginning to fall. I was strolling in the
garden. Suddenly I see the girl coming straight toward me and she
takes me (I was her master and she—she was just a slave) by the

hair on my nape, saying: "Come!" What followed was a sensation not unlike the sensations which we have all experienced. But this gentle seizing of my hair with this single word sometimes comes back to me, and the bare thought of it makes me happy.

Thus, if we are to believe the *Journal,* Turgenev, in his first amorous adventure, rejoiced to play a passive role. That toward the close of his life he should declare this incident to have been so keen a delight is a clue to his temperament.

The pricking of the senses was accompanied for Ivan, as for most adolescents, by an atrabilious complexion of the spirit. Sixteen is a melancholy, metaphysical age, and if there was a little dalliance in the garden, there was much vexation in the closet. One may readily believe, however, that he sucked on the thought of suicide as a small boy does on a lemon-stick, and that he played with transcendental platitudes concerning the use of life and the meaning of death as he used to play with new puppies. A youth of his feminine temper and at his age is defenceless against the atmosphere and the influence of romantic poetry. But where another might be content to mouth the sonorous syllables and the vehement sentiments, Ivan must blunt his pens imitating his idols.

The literary itch had seized him before there was down on his lip. His earlier known compositions which are in verse are inscribed in a slim notebook entitled "Prayerbook," its thick paper covered with idle drawings in ink and pencil, notes on assigned lessons, Latin words with their German equivalents, and some sentences in cipher. The poems are puerile efforts: stanzas for an album, a disquisition on the sorrows attendant upon the seven ages of man, a ballad on a maiden thrust by an assassin into the sea, a patriotic ode, and, a curious item: an imitation of a native folk song. A later and more ambitious work is a dramatic poem in three acts, with epigraphs from *Manfred* and *Timon of Athens.* It is a sophomoric piece, mimicking Byron's impatience with the social and divine order and showing the lineaments of its author's mind as in a quaint, indistinct daguerreotype.

Steno, the protagonist, who gives his name to the piece, is discovered on a moonlit night in the Coliseum, soliloquizing on the transience of things and the emptiness of life. These meditations overwhelm the youth, who is found in a swoon by Giulia and Giacoppo, her brother. They bear him off to their mean cabin and the girl forthwith falls in love with him. Himself the victim of unhappy love, Steno has little tenderness for the sufferings of others. To her passionate entreaty "Oh, my Steno, love me!" he replies with a harsh "Ha, ha, ha!" Within a few days Giulia dies of a broken heart, and her brother, mad with grief, kills her physician and rushes off to avenge her. But his intended victim, Steno, had in the meantime committed suicide. The lesser members of the cast are a pale, blood-stained demon, a pious monk, two airy Voices.

"Steno" was begun on September 21 and finished on October 13, 1834. Its sixteen-year-old author was not a little proud of his composition, and even pressed it upon the attention of his professor of Russian literature. Undiscouraged by the man's strictures, he went on scribbling, and in the next three years wrote two long narratives in verse, about a hundred lyrics, and started another drama. He also translated *Manfred,* part of *Othello* and *King Lear* ("with large omissions"). He was so dissatisfied with the last two renderings that he destroyed them. Nor has the rest of these juvenilia been preserved, except for two poems written in 1837 and published the following year. In one of them the author laments the fact that "not a single creature is capable of knowing the mysteries of being." The other hymns Venus, "the captivating testament of bygone days," and declares that "to *us* the language of love and passion is inaudible: our souls have withered."

He was as imitative as an infant, and as serious about the business. In 1835 he started an autobiography thus:

I turned seventeen a week ago. I want to write down all I know about myself, my entire life. Why do I do it? For two reasons. First, I have recently read *Les Confessions de Jean Jacques Rousseau* and so I conceived the idea of writing my own confessions. Secondly, having described my life now, I shall not touch this notebook till the age of fifty (if I live that long), and then it will certainly give me pleasure to recall what I thought and dreamed of at the time when I was writing these lines. And so, having made the exordium, which is always necessary, I begin.

Unfortunately, he gave himself only one unfinished paragraph to reread at the age of fifty; at least, that is the sole page of his "confessions" that has come down to us.

He was as eager as any literary aspirant to hear the voice and touch the hand of the great. The briefest personal contacts with men of letters which he made during his university years remained enduringly fresh in his memory. A few days before Pushkin's romantic death, Ivan sighted him at a concert and stared so hard at "the demigod" that after thirty years he still recalled the "small swarthy face, the African lips, the grin of large white teeth, the pendulous whiskers, the dark bilious eyes under a high forehead all but bare of eyebrows, the curly hair." Gogol, Ivan knew in the unhappy capacity of professor of universal history at the University of Petersburg. He sat under him during those lectures to which Gogol brought Cyrano's nose, but not his eloquence. "He was born to instruct his contemporaries," Turgenev was to write, "but not *ex cathedra*." A year later, in 1836, Ivan applauded the première of *The Inspector General* without having grasped, as he afterwards confessed, the import of the comedy. He packed off Koltzov, the Russian Bobby Burns, in his own sleigh, and drove him home after an evening at the house of his professor of literature, the man who wept in the classroom at the news of Pushkin's death. The drawing rooms to which Ivan had entrance may even at this time have afforded him a glimpse of the fabulist Krylov, sitting placidly, like a Buddha, his eyes alone moving now and then under his beetling eyebrows and his paunch attesting to his celebrated passion for suckling pig with horseradish.

Mme. Turgeneva did not entirely share her son's literary sympathies, but she made an exception of Zhukovsky, the ballad writer, who, family tradition had it, had visited Spasskoye when she was a girl. Besides, he held the post of tutor to the Czarevich. At his mother's instance, Ivan went to pay his respects to the poet on his saint's day, carrying him a present of a cushion on which was embroidered a maiden in medieval costume with a parrot on her shoulder. The boy wandered through the dreary corridors of the Winter Palace, stumbling upon motionless sentinels, and when he finally found himself in the great man's presence he was in such an agony of embarrassment that he thrust the cushion at Zhukovsky without being able to produce a syllable.

On his own account Ivan paid a call upon Yelizaveta Shakhova, the youngest poet in Russia, to whom, he was pleased to discover, he was distantly related. The girl, who looked less than her sixteen years and still wore her hair in curls down her back, had just had her first book, *Essay in Verse,* printed at the expense of the Russian Academy. Having armed himself with a commission from one of his aunts, and having, probably, draped himself in one of the wide Spanish capes which were then fashionable, Turgenev presented himself to the mother of the prodigy, as the maid explained to him that her mistress insisted on being the first to receive her daughter's callers. The lady was unfortunately blind and so she could not fall a victim to the outward and visible charms of the tall young man whose eyes looked very blue behind his colored spectacles. She consented, however, to let him see her daughter, the success of whose talent he "wished to promote." The mother received these advances coldly. She frowned upon the idea of a literary career for Liza as a danger to the child's religious welfare. The visitor hotly assured his newly found relative that it was sinful to deprive society of the fruits of genius. Before this bold championship Yelizaveta dropped her eyes to her black silk apron. But Ivan was not asked to call again. And the young poetess in due time became a nun, like Liza in *A Nest of Gentlefolk,* of whom she is said to have been the prototype.

At home, life went on with no grave disturbances. The last years of her husband's life were difficult for a woman who was impatient of invalidism and whose conjugal affection was not as strong as her self-love. Varvara Petrovna must have felt the colonel's death to be in the nature of a release. Thereafter she built up her whole emotional life upon her children, especially Ivan. There was, indeed, something morbidly exaggerated about her maternal passion.

The widow, who wore her weeds with a certain coquettishness, was a harsher and more eccentric woman than the wife. Mme. Turgeneva was reputed to have called the page who handled her mail her Minister of the Post, and to have designated her butler as Minister of the Court. One of his duties was to announce her sons to her. She had her own police force on her estates, and with a feudal contempt for officers of the Government consented to see only the highest local officials. According to an anecdote, reminiscent of the French seigneur who ordered his vassals to silence the frogs that interfered with his slumbers, Varvara Petrovna had her serfs divert the course of a stream which, in forming a waterfall, disturbed her night's sleep on a visit to one of her villages. A scarcely more credible story has it that she insisted that since her porridge was most palatably cooked in a village ten miles away, it should be brought to her hot by a relay of horsemen. It is impossible to prove that these, and many similar stories told about Varvara Petrovna, are untrue. The young democrat must have been continually offended by his mother's despotism and her affection of feudal pretensions. Yet he was fond of her in a mild way. Unequal to the task of combating her severities and vagaries, he simply withdrew, an attitude which sorely vexed her.

Neither his mother's conduct, distasteful as it was to him, nor yet his fits of *Weltschmerz,* seem, however, to have seriously affected Ivan's youthful buoyancy. He had a histrionic streak that he never lost, and a strong liking for fun and mystification. We catch a glimpse of the grown boy teaching his small foster sister what he called "frog Greek." Standing her on a table in a classic pose, he makes her repeat the chorus from *The Frogs*: *"Co-ax, co-ax, co-ax, Brekekekex co-ax,"* first in the solemn accents of tragedy and then in a high, thin, rapid voice. The performance ends in a burst of laughter which brings Varvara Petrovna to the scene, full of reproaches for such *"rire bourgeois!"*

5

THE IMMACULATELY

CONCEIVED

"I was convinced," wrote Turgenev in his *Reminiscences,* "that in Russia it was possible to get only preparatory instruction and that the source of real knowledge was abroad. Among my teachers at the University of Petersburg there was no one who could shake this conviction." Accordingly, in May, 1838, less than a year after he received the degree of "candidate," amounting to the baccalaureate, he went to Berlin, the new Athens, to finish his studies. His mother consented to part from him because she flattered herself that he would thus prepare to play in public life a role befitting a descendant of the Lutovinovs. She filled the mooncalf's purse with rubles and his ears with injunctions, warning him above all not to touch cards, a command which was the first he disregarded. On the morning of his departure the whole family went to the Kazan Cathedral where a mass was said for the safety of the traveler. During the entire ceremony Varvara Petrovna, sitting on a folding chair, wept bitterly, and on her return from seeing him off indulged in a swoon.

It was customary in those days to go to Germany by sea. The young man therefore embarked for Lübeck on the good ship *Nicholas I,* accompanied by a retainer who enjoyed Varvara Petrovna's complete confidence, and who is said to have been a bastard of her husband's. This Porfiry resembled Ivan in feature and was of an even more generous stature. When the vessel was off the port of Travemünde it took fire. Forty-five years later Turgenev set down an account of the affair with a wealth of detail which bears witness to his prodigious memery. He states that in his fright he promised one of the sailors, in his mother's name, ten thousand rubles if the man would save his life. When the first panic was over, he perched on a stairway from which he could easily have jumped into the water. He had decided that drowning was preferable to frying. While he was sitting there, looking at the flame-lit foam, listening to the roar of the fire and pitying himself because he must die so young, a simple old woman, thinking he planned suicide, begged him to give up his intention, saying that he would be punished for it in after-life. The romantic notion of suicide so appealed to him that he made several pretences of leaping into the waves. But he soon became ashamed, and desisted. He noted that the women behaved more bravely than the men, and for the rest of his life he was to embroider on the theme of woman's larger courage and greater stamina.

His account of the disaster gives the impression that he recovered his nerve quickly, and in fact was something of a hero, helping four women escape from the blazing ship. The rumors which reached Petersburg at the time, however, had the bulky young gentleman cut an inglorious figure. It was drawing room gossip that the captain had to restrain him in his dash for the lifeboats, and that he cried out in a thin voice surprising in one so corpulent, lamenting his untimely end. His mother wrote to him quoting reproachfully the reports concerning *"ce gros M. Tourgénieff qui se lamentoit tant, qui se disoit mourir si jeune."* Thirty years later he denied, in print, a story circulated by a fellow passenger to the effect that he had cried: "Save me, I am my mother's only son!" The fire destroyed the ship, but Ivan sustained no more serious injury than this blemish upon his reputation.

He spent some three years abroad, with an interval of several months at home in the winter of 1839-40. He matriculated at the University of Berlin. Moscow and Petersburg had scarcely done their duty by the young student. While he was taking Roman Antiquities with Zumpt and History of Greek Literature with Böckh, he was cramming Greek and Latin paradigms in the privacy of his room. He notes with nice precision that the voice of the geographer Ritter contrasted pleasantly for him with the bird-like whistle of Ranke the historian, with Zumpt's antediluvian bellow and Böckh's lisping purr. To the soothing noise made by the last-named lecturer he wrote letters, appropriately enough in hexameters, about a friend's love affair with a pretty charwoman. His chief intellectual interest was in philosophy. One of his notebooks shows clearly the trend of his studies in that subject. While Boehme and Schelling get one and a half and one page respectively, Bacon is accorded half a page and Hobbes a single line. The German philosophy of the day was dominated by Hegel's system. The person chiefly responsible for initiating Turgenev into its mysteries was a young professor by the name of Karl Werder. Something of a poet and a playwright, he was able to give body and substance to the abstractions of the great metaphysician whom he regarded as his master. Hegelianism, according to his interpretation, bordered on a religion and demanded complete moral dedication. A fervent and inspiring lecturer, he was idolized by his students, among whom were several Russians. Turgenev, too, came under the spell of his magnetic personality and was soon drawn into the study of Hegel.

He would break away from the *Phänomenologie des Geistes,* however, to train his dog to catch rats, an absorbing occupation in which he was assisted by his attendant, Porfiry. Or one might discover Ivan teasing a kitten by tying paper to its tail, or again, with the faithful Porfiry, engrossed in playing at cardboard soldiers. Porfiry was a person of voracious appetite—he was not uncommonly served with two dinners—and amorous disposition, and Ivan would employ his German in writing love missives for his smitten servant. Indeed, the man was more of a companion than a valet to the student—a relation which elicited Varvara Petrovna's reproaches.

Among Ivan's more expensive amusements the theater and the opera played a large part. Like his mother, he had a passion for music and the stage. The hero of his story "Faust," speaking of student days in Berlin, recalls Fräulein Clara Stich, and Karl Seidelmann in the part of Mephistopheles— celebrities of the day whom Ivan himself often went to hear. These, as well as two rival prima donnas, especially Löwe, received the young man's noisy ovations, which he mentioned to his mother, who wrote back with more force than elegance: "Do not yell in the theaters the way you brag about!" Then there were the farces at the Königstadt Theater, the excitement of masked balls, the excitement after them, the stir and color of town festivals. In one of his stories ("Asya") he describes a student fraternity carousal such as he must himself have witnessed.

There are always ways for young men to spend money, and Ivan was quick at discovering them. The letters which Varvara Petrovna addressed to her son contained repeated references to his spendthrift habits, which were the chief theme of his brother's letters as well. His mother begged him to keep some account of what moneys he had left at the end of each month. She preferred to learn about his balance rather than about the height of the Strasbourg Cathedral. In 1838 he cost his mother fifteen thousand rubles. The following year she cut his allowance, yet in three months he managed to spend nine thousand rubles. In 1840 there was a terrible famine in Russia, and the previous year had witnessed a ruinous fire at Spasskoye. This led his mother to declare that she could not keep him abroad any longer, but he did receive 11,000 rubles from home. When he left Berlin to go home in 1841 he owed one hundred and fifty *écus* to a German banker and three hundred to the Russian ambassador in Berlin.

To her warnings and reproaches his mother added the weighty burden of her passionate affection. "You are my star," she writes. "My life depends on you. . . . Like a thread in a needle—where the needle goes the thread must follow." Varvara Petrovna tries to convey the painful intensity of her feeling for her two sons by the homeliest metaphor! "I love you both passionately, but differently. You, [Ivan] especially wound me. . . . If my hand is squeezed it hurts, but if my bunion is stepped on, it is intolerable." In 1839 she makes the following entry in her journal, as usual, in French "Jean is my very own sun. I see nothing but him, and when he is in eclipse I can't see any more. I don't know where I am any more."

There is a touch of more than eccentricity in her expressions of tenderness. On one occasion she addresses Ivan as *"ma chère fille, ma Jeanette,"* and goes on writing: *"Vous êtes ma favorite*—Ssh! for Heaven's sake, let nobody hear it." Again, she refers to herself as his "most tender father and friend." Her maternal absorption in Ivan leads her to a flat denial of any intrusive paternity as far as his procreation was concerned: "I alone conceived you," she writes on May 6, 1839, "all that I am, you are."

She gives him the news of the household. Bibi is growing into a real little English girl, the type Ivan dislikes: neither shy, pale, nervous, nor languid, but "gay as the April sun." She is such a good little girl that "you couldn't have made a better one out of wax." His dog Napol "looks as much as his own father as your brother looks like his or you like me. Fine comparisons!" The queen bee was caught in the rain and dried by the drones. "She stretched her legs with an air of dignity, played the coquette, feigned extreme fatigue. Oh, woman," adds Varvara Petrovna, "you are the same in all creation, loving to please and to be admired."

As one reads these ill-spelled, pithy, opinionated epistles sprinkled with French phrases and redolent of an acrid personality, one comes to believe that the novelist inherited his talent from this shrewd termagant, who latinizes for the sake of her son and enters into trenchant discussions with him on books, ideas, amours. He did not hesitate to confide certain intimate matters to his mother. She reproaches him for treating her, rather than his brother or his uncle, to these confidences, only to declare in a subsequent letter that she is his proper confidante and has always been a comrade as well as a mother to him. One brief affair of his is discussed in their correspondence. The object of his affection was a Mme. Tyutcheva.* She was well past her first youth, a fact that delighted Varvara Petrovna, who had just been reading *La Femme de Quarante Ans* by Charles de Bernard. In this novel, which she pressed upon her son's attention, a young man of twenty, coming from the provinces, is introduced by his uncle to a woman of forty, that she may annex him and make a man of him. The uncle believed, and Varvara Petrovna with him, that such a woman, with a good social position and a distinction of mind and manners, offers all the

---

* There is a remote possibility that this was the first wife, Eleonora, of the well-known poet, Fyodor Tyutchev. With her three daughters, she was Ivan's fellow passenger on the ill-starred trip to Lübeck. She was on her way to Turin to join her husband, and died there on September 9, 1838.

guarantees demanded of one to whom a parent confides a child. A younger woman, he argues, would have made the boy commit many follies, an older one would have rendered him ridiculous; with a bourgeoise he would have lost the tradition of good society; with a courtesan he would have wasted his substance. On the other hand, the lady is rewarded for educating him by the temporary happiness which he gives her.

Mme. Turgeneva writes to her son on December 16, 1838:

> Speaking of sugar, let's talk of something sweeter. . . . Of the end of your letter, of your little love affairs, of Tyu——va . . . That's news. . . . . I read it in your heart before you did, and I began to write to you myself. . . . Am I a mother like others? . . . . I am always with you, and all for you, and all yours. Well, thank goodness, I am not fat. . . . It seems to me that you wouldn't love even your mother if she were fat.

She continues pointedly:

> And sometimes it seems to me that as your first love was naturally your mother, pale, sallow, nervous, so you are accustomed to love sallow women. This is all right for little love intrigues, but a sallow wife is not very savory.

She goes on at great length about the distinction between love and coquetry, and the inequalities in love, adding that the balance of happiness is on the side of the lover rather than that of the beloved, and candidly concluding: "Although this agrees entirely with my own thoughts, it is taken from *Eynerley,* by Alphonse Karr." Varvara Petrovna was given to quotations and allusions no less than her literary son.

The affair came to an abrupt end with the death of Mme. Tyutcheva. Varvara Petrovna, condoling with Ivan on the event, writes:

> I have always wished you the love of an experienced, middle-aged woman. It is such women that educate the young. It is a mutual advantage. The woman is flattered and the man has the benefit of her experience. I am sorry for the Tyutcheva woman. She must have been intelligent. You wouldn't have cared for a fool.

The mother cannot resist the opportunity of indicating that she wants Ivan to give her a daughter-in-law who will be not only young and obedient, but beautiful as well, for the sake of the honor of the house and of the race. She adds that she would find no fault with the girl, as long as she reciprocated his love and made him happy. On another occasion she writes:

> You are an egoist of egoists. . . . I know your character better than you do yourself. I prophesy: your wife will not love you. You do not know how to love. This is, you will love not the woman but your own pleasure.

His mother eagerly follows his travels, recalling her own experiences abroad and chiding him for his blindness to the fine details of the European scene. "You are like a Government courier dashing along toward his destination." When Ivan is in Switzerland Varvara Petrovna exclaims over his not being impressed by the mountains and his failure to mention the Swiss cream, the white veal, the cheese: "I do not recognize my son or his gastronomy." And she adds serenely: "Your uncle is afraid that while in Bern you may commit *de l'inceste*. When he stayed in Bern he was very friendly with the girls there, and that was sixteen years ago." She keeps an eye on Ivan's studies, but she frequently reminds him that she sent him abroad not only to get learning but also to acquire social polish. She insists on knowing the status of his friends and laments his failure to make connections with the right people.

Ivan's share in the correspondence with his family has not been preserved, but one gathers from the letters which he received from home that generally speaking he wrote when he was in need of money. Toward the end of his stay in Berlin his mother heard from him so rarely that she was reduced to the ignominy of inquiring about him of his friends. He was a slothful boy; he was absorbed by new interests and contacts; he was at an age when one's family seems to be little else than a nuisance. Although at first he complained of loneliness and strange faces, he could not have been sorry that so many hundreds of miles separated him from the domestic complex.

Uncle Nikolay was a storm center. He was managing the estate of his widowed sister-in-law, who one day protested that she loved him as her soul, since he reminded her of her deceased husband, and the next denounced him as her enemy.

Ivan, though siding with his uncle, had no desire to come home to take his part. There were periodic invasions of Spasskoye by Mme. Tugeneva's relatives-in-law, who ate and drank, and worried her to such a degree that she said she would have preferred to stay alone and see her shadow on every wall. She complained to Ivan that they tried to wean his brother away from her by all sorts of insinuations, especially about the maternity of her foster daughter, Bibi, adding that they were dealing in a pack of lies, and that her sons could say of her, "as the Lutovinovs said of their mother: 'a sainted woman was our mother.' "

The young man's attitude was aptly characterized by his brother in a letter in which he imagines Ivan apostrophizing the family thus: " 'Cruel fate has decreed that I should be born a man of 1941, but live in 1841. The people with whom I have to associate, that is, my near and dear, are therefore just one century behind me. And so I say: 'Good-bye. Keep well and happy, but don't forget my twelve thousand a year. Farewell, farewell!' "—concluding with a bar of music.

Sometimes Ivan used his verse as a substitute for letters, a procedure which his mother resented. The vanity of the young poet had to suffer, for she was an opinionated critic with old-fashioned tastes, who didn't mince words: "You, my friend, are like a deaf man singing mass. I cannot understand poems without rhymes." Here was an unappreciative family. When Ivan, being ill, wrote home that he was hesitating between Paris and Italy, his brother replied: "That a sick man goes to Paris for treatment is intelligible, but tell me, please, what do you want to go to Italy for? Are you a musician or a poet? I don't understand it."

The demand for some word from the callous Ivan is never absent from his mother's letters. Frequently they read like those of a neglected and importunate mistress. She threatens to whip a foster child for her son's failure to write to her. "It is a pity," she adds. "He is a dear, good boy, and I teach him, and he is clever at his lessons. But what's to be done? The poor boy will have to suffer. . . . So do not bring me to this injustice." Provoked by Ivan's inattention, she writes, "If philosophy chills us and makes us careless of our sacred duties, you'd better not study it." She had once wanted to see in him nothing but perfection. Now she is more modest. "Be like the others," she writes. "Limp with the lame."

What Varvara Petrovna especially clamored for was a chatty letter, such as she herself well knew how to write. On one occasion she gives him a detailed account of her day, retailing how, on awaking, she washes her eyes with a mixture of rum and tea, how she makes her devotions and follows these by telling fortunes with cards between two cups brewed from the Chinese weed, and more gossip of the same sort. She continues:

> Here I am, sitting in the drawing-room all dressed, eye to eye with my second son. You do not know him. He is a great rascal, is too lazy to write to me, and when he does write, it is as though only to fulfil his duty toward his mother. . . . I know him as I do my own self. . . . He has the kindest of hearts, but the passions, the passions are ready to get hold of him and he yields to them, although if he wished he could master them better than a cold-blooded man.

The portrait which Varvara Petrovna kept on her desk was a water color made in Berlin in 1838 or 1839. It shows a romantic, well-fed young man. The brooding, melancholy eyes dominate the round, mild, handsome face, with its broad brow and soft, thick hair parted on the side—the somewhat lax, almost feminine face of a youth accustomed to the sheltered life of the privileged.

6

"THE SPHERE OF
THE IDEAL"

Some of Turgenev's fellow students in Berlin had been upper classmen when he was attending the University of Moscow. At the time there were two tiny coteries there: one was grouped around Nikolay Stankevich, the other around Alexander Herzen. The members of the first were engaged in a philosophical quest for spiritual illumination; the members of the second were concerned with more mundane matters, such as the lamentable material conditions in their country, and they regarded themselves as heirs of the rebels who had stained the snow on the Senate Square in the capital with their blood on December 14, 1825. While the callow politicals sought intellectual nourishment in the writings of French socialists, the young philosophers found it in German metaphysics. During the early thirties they embraced Schelling's pietistic and transcendental idealism. Later in the decade they were offering Hegel the uncritical homage that a subsequent generation was to accord Marx. Such was the case with the volcanic Mikhail Bakunin, Michel to his friends, the future founder of international anarchism. Having given up an army commission to study philosophy, he began by exploring Kant, Fichte, and Schelling, and ended by passionately embracing Hegelianism. The young Muscovites had few and lean newspapers to read and no serious weeklies; there were no political parties to engage their attention, no clubs to join, no cafés in which to loiter. And so they spent their long leisure in letter-writing and talking, and they philosophized with the utmost seriousness. Abstruse metaphysical speculations provided sensitive souls with an escape from crass reality.

The following passage from Turgenev's first novel is apparently an attempt to evoke the atmosphere that prevailed at the meetings of the Stankevich circle, of which he had indirect knowledge, probably through his tutor, Klushnikov, who belonged to the group.

Philosophy, art, science, life itself were all just words to us—even mere concepts, if you like—alluring, beautiful, but scattered and disconnected. We had not been aware of any bond uniting these concepts, we didn't sense any common law of the universe, although we talked about it vaguely and tried to form some idea of it . . . Listening to Rudin, it seemed to us that for the first time we had grasped it, that common bond, that the curtain had at last been lifted! . . . Order and harmony entered into all that we knew, whatever was scattered suddenly assembled and composed itself into a whole, grew formed with spirit. . . . Nothing remained meaningless, fortuitous, like an edifice before our eyes. Everything was illuminated and in everything expressed rational necessity and beauty; everything acquired a clear and yet mysterious significance; every separate phenomenon of life sounded like a chord of music; and we ourselves, filled with a kind of sacred awe and shaken by a sweet emotion, felt ourselves, as it were, living vessels of eternal truth, called to achieve something great. . . .

Turgenev happened to fall in with some members of the Stankevich group, who, like himself, had come to Berlin to drink *ex ipso fonte* (this city was still the source for Hegelians, although the master himself had been dead some half a dozen years). There was Granovsky, the future historian, Katkov, who was to become the novelist's publisher, the "heavenly" Stankevich. He had been in Berlin a year when Turgenev arrived there, and the two soon came to know each other. There was something extraordinarily attractive about this white-faced, weak-chested young man, with his child-like naïveté, his ready laughter, his complete sincerity. He had a conviction of being right that tended to make him didactic, but this was not resented, since there was no trace of self-regard in it. Years later Turgenev was to recall vividly the way his black hair was tossed back from the slanting brow, the delicate, twitching nostrils of the Roman nose, the large, gnarled, old man's hands on his stick, his native grace and distinction, "as of a king's son ignorant of his origin." He regarded the man, who was five years his senior, with a respect verging on awe. Looking back, he attributed this attitude to a consciousness of his own "unworthiness and mendacity." Stankevich, for his part, rather cold-shouldered "the fatty with the complexion of old linen," as Turgenev described himself. The younger man may have innocently aroused his jealousy, by showing attention to a certain pretty German girl of easy morals. Though "chaste at heart," in Turgenev's words, the immaculate idealist was no ascetic.

During his first winter in Berlin Ivan was taken ill. "Is it something venereal?" his brother Nikolay asked in a letter. "If so, it isn't dangerous, and there is no need to alarm *Maman.*" Wondering if it might be gonorrhea, he added: "What young man hasn't been through this?" *Maman* did learn that her darling was out of health when word came from Porfiry, in mid-January, 1839, that his master was suffering from a urinary complaint. Varvara Petrovna, like the rest of the family, was inclined to take lightly what she called "man's disease." Nevertheless she wrote to him in March: "Oh, my God! Why didn't I show you, when you were leaving, the lines that your father wrote *d'une main égarée avec ses larmes* the very day he was paralyzed: 'My son take care that you do not infect your blood, take care that you do not poison your body!'?" What made her really anxious was the thought that Ivan might have gallstones, his father's illness. He seems to have informed her that he intended to go to Paris to be operated on, since he suspected that it was gallstones. This was a false alarm. His brother fancied that it was just a stratagem to give him a chance to amuse himself in Paris. In any event, nothing further was heard of the matter.

Exalted ideas about human worth, the nobility of womanhood, the divine essence of love, lived in closed compartments in the heads of Turgenev and his friends side by side with the reflections of the average sensual man. Their moral ideas were so impossibly high as to be out of sight as far as the conduct of some of their affairs were concerned. In fine, they were lusty young men and lived as young men have done since Adam's fall. Turgenev's unpublished correspondence includes two scrawls in ill-spelled German addressed "To my dear friend Turgenev—Well-born, from his Lina." In one of them she writes that she would like to wander by his

side all her life, but that he does not even give her a thought.
She goes on to say that she is deep in debt, and has been
forgotten "by you all." She had once refused a kindness which
he offered, but now she makes a claim on his good will, and
remains his "dear friend," Lina or Carolina Foerster. In the
second letter she says that she called upon Turgenev but did
not find him at home, that she is "no merry little Lina any
more," and that he should please tell her when she may come
to him.

It is presumably the same Lina who figures in a letter to
Turgenev from a fellow student, dated Berlin, October 7,
1840. Ivan was then in Dresden. He had come there from
Marienbad, where he had been laid up apparently with
"man's disease." He had not yet recovered, and was inveighing against his fate, which he described neatly as a ghastly
old hag with a bulbous nose and a cudgel in her fist, constantly
moping in a corner with a threatening air. His correspondent,
after mentioning that he has written a dissertation dedicated
to the memory of Boehme, that he has lost a book to Bakunin
in a game of cards, and that "the fierce Bohemian of Krausen-
strasse" has laid another friend low, goes on to speak of news
"more terrible than Napier's invasion," namely, that he is
reported to be the author of Lina's pregnancy. He denies the
charge vividly, and confesses horror at the prospect of paying
the mother three thalers a month for fourteen years: "with
that money one could put up a magnificent cross to Börne
[a baptised Jew], or build a small charitable institution." The
victim of the fierce Bohemian writes to Turgenev about
another common acquaintance, one Bertha, and projects an
affair with a fourth young woman, named Amalia, while yet
another friend mentions "the three graces" and a certain
Mariechen into the bargain.

The latter part of 1839 Turgenev spent at home. A friend
in Berlin kept him informed of events there: the latest plays
and operas, a new statue on the Museum Square, a torchlight
procession commemorating the Reformation. In January of
the following year he left Russia and by March was in Rome.
Here he again met Stankevich. An intimacy sprang up between them, although the elder of the two, impatient with his
friend's "frivolity," showed some condescension toward him.

Those Roman days were caught in the amber of Turgenev's memory. Accompanied by a couple of other young Russians, they "did" the city together, with the aid of Nibby, the Baedeker of the day. They wandered through the galleries, Turgenev quoting appropriate passages from the Russian poets, and Stankevich admiring the art of the ancients and regretting that they did not ask beauty to be more spiritual. They visited the Villa Borghese, where Turgenev chased lizards. They drove out to pay their respects to dignified ruins, and one evening as they passed an ivy-covered heap of stones on their way from Albino, Turgenev made Stankevich pale by summoning the ghost of the divine Cæsar with a shout.

There was music, too, a young Pole, an accomplished pianist who was a friend of Liszt's, being of the company, and, since the smell of paint was in the air, drawing lessons, which Turgenev turned to account by making caricatures of his friends. For a while painting was the stock subject of his conversation. Finally, there was the sixteen-year-old Chou-chou Khovrina, who was stopping with her parents at 57 Via dei Pontifici. Stankevich played duets with her and Turgenev wrote poems to her, one of which he was to incorporate in *A Nest of Gentlefolk* twenty years later.

With Stankevich, whom he saw daily, Turgenev would talk endlessly, not only of love, which the former held the fullest and noblest mode of being, belonging to the religious order of experience, but also of art, of antiquity, often of death. He was just then at the mercy of formless reveries and conflicts, in a mood, which was to grow increasingly familiar to him, of unrest and dissatisfaction with himself. Stankevich, on the contrary, approached the serenity of an Eastern mystic, though his lawgiver was not Buddha but Hegel. He offered Turgenev the peace that the latter needed.

By the end of May the traveler was back in Berlin. Before he reached the capital he touched at Leghorn, Pisa, Genoa, sailed on Lago Maggiore, traveled to St. Gotthard in a sleigh, visited Lucerne, Basel, Mannheim, Mainz, Frankfort and Leipzig, all within thirteen days. In the same period he managed to lose an umbrella, a cloak, a box, a walking stick, an opera glass, a hat, a pillow, a pen knife, a purse, three towels, two neckerchiefs, two shirts, and, for a short time, his heart.

On May 17 he wrote a brief, spirited account of this hectic trip to a friend in Wiesbaden from a Frankfort café, to the thunder of billiard balls and under the influence of a bottle of Altmanshauser.

On June 24 Stankevich, on his way to Lake Como, died in a small Italian town. Turgenev passed the sad news on to Karl Werder by letter, not having the heart to face him with it. In one of his last messages to Ivan the deceased had written: "Tell Werder that his friendship will always be sacred and dear to me and that everything decent in me is inextricably bound up with it." When Turgenev finally met the professor he said: "A part of you has died with him." Werder agreed, calling Stankevich one of his best pupils, one of his "apostles." Then, choking back his tears, he read to Turgenev a threnody he had composed on the occasion. Turgenev's own grief was no less genuine for being expressed in voluble prose. In apprising Granovsky of Stankevich's death he wrote:

We have lost a man whom we loved, in whom we believed, who was our pride and hope. . . . The cold hand of death fell upon his head, and a whole world perished. . . . Who of our generation can make good the loss? . . . But no, we must not be dejected and resigned. Let us come together, join hands, stand closer. One of us, perhaps the best, has fallen, but others are arising and will continue to arise. God's hand does not cease to sow seeds of great strivings, and sooner or later light will conquer darkness.

Writing on September 8 from the birch woods of Marienbad, Turgenev dispatched a letter to friends. The communication, which is entitled *Turgenevii ad amicos Berolinenses epistola quinta* and which mixes German and Russian, turgid philosophy and genuine wit, holds the following passage:

How significant the year 1840 has been for me! How much I have lived through these nine months! Imagine: early in January a young man dashes across the snows of Russia in a sledge. The ferment has scarcely started in him, vague thoughts agitate him, he is timid and barrenly pensive. . . . The young man spends ten days in the fat capital of Austria and proceeds to Italy. In Rome I find Stankevich. Do you understand the transformation or rather the beginning of the development of my soul? How eagerly I listened to him—I, destined to be his last comrade, whom he initiated into the service of truth by his example, the poetry of his life, his words. . . . He enriched me with silence, the gift of fulness, me, the still unworthy one. . . . Without remorse I could indulge in quiet contemplation of the world of art: Nature smiled to me. I have always keenly felt its fascination, the breath of God in it. But in its splendor it had seemed to reproach me, poor, blind, and full of futile doubts as I was. Now I joyfully stretched out my arms to it and before the altar of the soul I pledged myself to be worthy of life. . . . One thing renders a man defenseless: his own weakness or if his spiritual powers are at war. . . . But now my enemies have left my breast and, feeling myself a whole man, I am joyfully ready to fight them. Stankevich, to you I owe my rebirth, you offered me your hand and showed me the goal. . . .

Stankevich had a way of drawing those with whom he came in touch into "the sphere of the Ideal," as Turgenev later phrased it. He affected them not by any writings, but by the enchantment of his personality and the strength and purity of his philosophic convictions. Spirit and reason prevail in the universe; the world is the emanation of the divine Idea, attaining in man to the supreme state of self-consciousness; art, philosophy, science, and particularly religion offer glimpses of the grand cosmic pattern. Such was Stankevich's credo, and he demanded the utmost of himself by way of deepening his intuitions, expanding his knowledge, refining his moral sensibility, governing his conduct by the same high principles that, he believed, governed all creation. His concern was with wisdom and virtue and inner freedom. It appears, however, that the young idealist was not entirely unaware of life's imperfections, at least as far as his own country was concerned. Absorption in self-cultivation, he held, far from being egotistical, was a sure way to social melioration. With a naive optimism, born of the Hegelian view of the State as the embodiment of reason, he felt certain that, once the Russian people had matured intellectually, the authorities would take the initiative in abolishing serfdom and enacting other reforms. And it is reported that he made several of his comrades, including Turgenev, solemnly promise to devote their energies to the cause of spreading popular education.

The Berlin friends to whom the epistle quoted above was addressed included Bakunin. A feeling that he was in need of deepening his insights into metaphysics had brought him to Germany. "I need baptism," he wrote; "I expect my regeneration from it in Berlin." His task, he declared, was not "to amass useful knowledge like a pedant," but to attain nothing less than the absolute truth by an effort of his entire being. Least of all was he, or any other Russian Hegelian, interested in pure ratiocination. He had no head for abstract thinking. Philosophy was an equivalent of religion, a way of life for him. The death of Stankevich dealt him a painful blow. It was "a noble revelation of immortality," he wrote home. "The holy middleman between us and truth, the link between us and heaven," was his description of his departed comrade.

Turgenev met Bakunin the very day he arrived in Berlin in the summer of 1840. The two Hegelians struck up a friendship at first sight and were soon on terms of intimacy. Throughout the next academic year they shared living quarters. Turgenev gave Bakunin—who was four years his senior—not the reverent admiration he had accorded Stankevich but the warmer affection of an equal. In the epistle quoted in the previous chapter Ivan was writing to Michel:

> Stankevich united us, and death will not divide us. . . . I see a man, at first timidly, then with faith and joy, going up a steep mountain crowned with eternal light. With him goes a comrade, and they press onward, leaning upon each other, and from the sky a quiet moon shines upon him. . . . On the title page of my encyclopedia [Hegel's *Encyklopädie der philosophischen Wissenschaften in Grundrisse*] I wrote: "Stankevich died on the 24th of June, 1840." and below: "I made the acquaintance of Bakunin on the 25th of July, 1840." Out of all my former life I wish to retain no other memories.

On the margin of the other pages are the addresses of several Berlin cafés.

As though guessing that the season of 1840–41 was to end his career as a student, Turgenev filled it with lectures and music, debates and books. There were late vigils in his room, where he clung to the stove and Bakunin to the divan. Deciding that their life was too abstract, the two would plunge into reality by paying calls together, the plump Ivan wearing his green velvet "Don Juan" waistcoat and the lanky Michel a lavender one. They must have swum, occasionally, through the clouds of tobacco smoke that thickened the air of Hippel's famous *Weinstube* on Friedrichstrasse, seen its lights reflected on the high forehead of Max Stirner, and mouthed the names of the two Bauer brothers and the other Left Hegelians who frequented the place. For these radicals the master's dynamic conception of history sanctioned rebellion.

After a Beethoven symphony they would drop in to see Michel's sister Vareñka, whom Stankevich had loved and in whose arms he had died. It was to her that Ivan presented on New Year's Day, 1841, eight neatly copied poems by Lermontov, the poet of the hour. At Vareñka's they discussed things great and small over smoked tongue, Russian tea, and sandwiches, from which butter dripped like tallow from the candles whose sputtering Ivan imitated to the full satisfaction of the company. There, one Sunday night in December, Professor Werder helped celebrate his own birthday by reciting the prologue and first act of his poetic drama, *Christopher Columbus*. And then there was the biweekly gathering of the Russian contingent, either in the third-floor chamber which Ivan shared with Michel, or in the room of another friend, where they would sit till the small hours of the morning, filling their stomachs with cold meat and their ears with hot arguments.

At this time Turgenev had moments of proud anticipation which recurred more infrequently as his achievements solidified. The preceding year he had written to Michel, in the *epistola quinta* quoted above, mentioning a friend who had died: "But you will live and I shall live, and perhaps both of us not for naught." Bakunin lived to be a flea in the ear of the established order, a life of sound and fury. Turgenev lived the receptive, responsive, inward life of the artist, who alters his environment with what little permanency it permits.

The influence of both Stankevich and Bakunin on Turgenev was in keeping with the philosophy that he was being taught at the university. Since the middle thirties Hegel's system had been undergoing revision by some of its expositors, who were intent on giving it less of a quietist character. Karl Werder was, with some reservations, an orthodox Hegelian. Nevertheless, not being of a conservative temperament, in expounding the master's doctrine to his students he stressed the negative phase of the dialectic process and was at particular pains to drive home the precept that complete spiritual freedom inhered in philosophic meditation as a consequence of the dogma of divine liberty.

The idea of freedom on the material plane was in the air at the time. The ferment of liberalism was then at work in every department of German life. Turgenev did not remain untouched by it. During his first year in Berlin he, like Stankevich, was an habitué at the Frolovs'. Nikolay Frolov was an earnest student of geography, married to a homely, highly cultivated and very charming invalid of a somewhat skeptical and realistic disposition. Their drawing room was something of a salon which attracted people of distinction. Although the hostess was, according to her young compatriot, *"un peu de l'ancien régime,"* the house was frequented by several Berliners with liberal leanings.

At these gatherings, to which Turgenev came "to gape and to listen," as he wrote later, he may have heard the great naturalist, Alexander von Humboldt, air his unconventional ideas about marriage, and Varnhagen von Ense, editor of a Hegelian journal, express sympathy with the principles of 1789. (He was to hail the February Revolution as "a radiant dawn," to judge by an entry in his diary). Turgenev, no doubt, hung on the words of another guest, a lady on the shady side of fifty who dyed her hair: Bettina von Arnim. He wrote her name on the flyleaves of his books, as he was wont to do with the names of his idols, and in his first novel the leading character reads Bettina to the heroine. An alleged intimate of Goethe's, she wore for Turgenev a romantic halo, but he may also have been impressed by her enthusiasm for such causes as freedom of the press and constitutional government. His daily contacts with the Germans, not only fellow students, must also have fed the democratic and libertarian sympathies of the youthful Hegelian once nicknamed "the American." His newly acquired interest in esoteric metaphysics was skin-deep; the idea of freedom as man's natural right will become part of the very texture of his thinking.

7

LOVE, CARNAL
AND SPIRITUAL

Ivan had been abroad hardly four months before he was confronted with the possibility that the letters from home might be supplanted by the presence of his mother. Almost every envelope he opened contained the threat of an imminent descent upon him. Early in 1839, having heard that he was ill, Varvara Petrovna wrote: "Whether you like it or not, I leave Spasskoye and I go abroad on the seventh of May. Wherever you are I'll find you and I'll go back with you. You'll bring me back to Russia alive or dead, and I'll bring you back into the family alive or dead, and deliver you into your brother's hands."

This visit, like others, was postponed, but she could not give up the notion of meeting her son abroad, pouring tea for him from the samovar she would bring with her, going under his escort to the theater, spending a spring with him in Italy, and then triumphantly bringing him back to Russia to settle down. In the end, however, she did not go, and Ivan finally paid a reluctant visit to his importunate parent, starting for home in October. By January, 1840, as has been stated, he was again off for foreign parts, and again his mother renewed her cry of "Come back, come back!" mindless of his protest that in summoning him home she wanted to pluck an unripe fruit.

While Ivan was in Rome with Stankevich, one of his friends, who had a brother in Moscow, sent the latter this injunction: "If you see Mme. Turgeneva . . . give her my compliments, but keep her from going to Italy." She was willing to give up her home for the deserts of Arabia, if she could but meet Ivan in them. Her lamentations are not astonishing in view of the fact that sometimes she did not hear from the wanderer for two months together. On one occasion she was forced to send a servant to the Bakunins to inquire about him. In consequence one of the sisters wrote to Michel to tell Ivan that he must be more filial. In the autumn of 1840, hearing that her darling was again ill, Varvara Petrovna conceived the idea of having her elder son resign from the army and go to Berlin "to sweeten Ivan Sergeyevich's life." Nikolay used the phrase in a letter to Ivan, requesting him to reassure *Maman* and tell her that he had no need for the solace of his brother's company. This Ivan apparently did, and the plan was abandoned. In January 1841 his mother wrote: "If you don't come in May, I shall die of grief in June." Her untimely end was averted by the prodigal's return on the twenty-first of May.

At Spasskoye Ivan found great changes. With the exception of one wing, the old wooden manor-house had gone up in smoke. A letter from home had told him how it started. One of the women in charge of the cattle had fumigated a sick cow by burning certain roots in an old bast shoe. In accordance with the prescribed magic practice, she had buried the shoe full of hot ashes under the threshold of a barn. It is not known whether or not the cure was effected, but the structure caught fire and the flames spread to the manor-house itself. "We have lost everything," his mother had written to him, "save honor."

Ivan's home-coming to what was left of his mother's house occasioned a general holiday. Varvara Petrovna busied herself thinking up ways of spoiling her learned son. The menu was arranged with due regard for his preferences, such as tripe soup; and great jars of currant jam, of which he was fond, were sent up to his room. For his part, "Jean" was affectionate and attentive.

After the bright, lively, less restricted life of Western Europe the home scene was depressing. But at first he must have rather enjoyed the familiar sights of manorial Russia: the sleepy ponds with their lazy swans, the bonneted grannies skimming caldrons of jelly under the trees, the spacious white mansions with their classic columns, the fat poodles, the old servitors, the drowsy flies, the general air of imperturbable placidity and leisure to eat and sleep in order to eat again. And the environs of the estate offered him a chance to indulge in his favorite sport of shooting woodcock and other feathered game.

A young, pretty seamstress in his mother's employ afforded him other pleasures. The affair was of brief duration and lasting consequences. He gave her some money and dismissed her from his mind. In due time he discovered that on April 26, 1842, he had become the father of a girl, who was baptized Pelageya. The mother, as soon as her condition had become apparent, had been shipped back to her native Moscow, and for a time neither Ivan nor the mistress of Spasskoye took any interest in the baby. Inasmuch as he was content to leave it a strictly private matter, Varvara Petrovna was not at all distressed to find that her shiftless "Jean" had sown a wild oat.

This was neither the first nor the last of the young man's affairs with women beneath his caste. One such relation with a serf girl preceded his departure to Berlin. While he was abroad he learned that she had been sent away from Spasskoye. Fearing that she was being persecuted, he wrote home, in February, 1839, asking that she be given some money and her freedom. He was assured that she had been packed off to her family simply to keep a certain Vaska (who had made another girl pregnant) from marrying her. "What a funny one you are, Ivan!" wrote his mother. "Why should I reward and free an old girl who bore children both before and after? A few rubles are enough for her. It isn't as though she had presented you with her virginity. That's my opinion. . . . I didn't see any guilt in it, either on your part or hers. It's merely physical passion. . . . You sinner, you've made me sin, too. Such stuff I'm writing the first Monday in Lent!"

At the end of the summer Ivan left for Moscow. Varvara Petrovna gave him a list of fourteen relatives and friends there, as well as a thumbnail character sketch and instructions on how to behave with each. One woman she called his "old flame," of a certain matron she wrote: "Flirting with her is permitted." He must be sure to pay his respects to Marya Vasilyevna: "If she says you're all right, everyone else will

say you're a wonder." And not to call on the Nebalsins—
relatives—is to be a boor.

Turgenev paid the prescribed visits, appeared at balls, and
on the whole produced a favorable impression. Naturally,
he formed connections on his own. While in Berlin he had
been eager to know the Bakunins. And so when, in May,
1841, he was preparing to go home, he commanded Michel
to give him an introduction to the family. "Tell them nothing
about me," he said, "but that I love you." Michel sent an
encyclical to his brothers and sisters—eight of them were then
in Russia—telling them about this great friend of his, with
whom he had worked all winter long and who had shared
both joy and grief with him and Vareñka. The latter, for
her part, loved Ivan as a brother. Michel recommended him
further as a master story-teller and as a person who would
act on them all as a cordial. Varvara herself in an earlier
letter had spoken of Ivan as "a pure, bright, gentle soul."

It was not until October that Turgenev visited the Bakunins
at Premukhino, their estate, near the town of Torzhok. He
stayed there nearly a week and enchanted the family. Every
one of those days, he is reported to have said ecstatically,
"contained an eternity." Subsequently he met the two youngest Bakunin boys in Moscow. They spent glorious evenings
together. "In his presence," Alexey, one of the youths, wrote
home, "all the capacities of the spirit are quickened as by a
living fire." Ivan splendidly sustained his reputation as a
raconteur, thrilling his audience with such tales as that of
a moonlit night spent in the ruins of a castle crowning the
famed Drachenfels on the Rhine in the sole company of a
bottle of Rhine wine. In addition to talk there were wrestling
matches. On one occasion he was thrown, making the floor
quake; on another he was twice the victor, which pleased him
hugely. The Bakunins adopted him as their "brother." He
called them "my children" and felt for them an affection
slightly tinged with superiority.

"On Thursday, December 18," Alexey wrote home glee-
fully, "two Bakunins, one Turgenev, one dog and the Moon
will proceed from Moscow to Torzhok." Ivan had promised
his mother to return no later than Christmas Eve, but, as
was not unusual with him, did not keep his word. She was

outraged. He had chosen to spend the holiday, for which she had eagerly waited, with total strangers, as she put it, 200 versts away from home! "What have I done to deserve such slaps in the face from you?" she demanded bitterly. "If you become a stranger to me, will the Bakunins console you?" She did not know, being no longer in his confidences, that the visit to the Bakunins was in a sense a sentimental journey.

It seemed to be the fate of Michel's friends to become enamoured of one or more of his four sisters. There was Stankevich, who had been temporarily affianced to Lubov and had subsequently returned the passion of Varvara. There were Belinsky and Botkin, both destined to become Ivan's intimates, who lost their hearts to Alexandra. There were Turgenev and Tatyana.

On first meeting her, Belinsky had written: "I looked at her, spoke to her—and was angry at myself for speaking. I should just have looked, loved, and prayed." Michel himself, devoted to all his sisters, singled her out for adoration. "I love you more than anyone in the world," he wrote to her; "you are my sole, my only idol." So unbrotherly was his feeling that for a time any suspicion that she took an interest in a man threw him into a tormenting fit of jealousy. On one such occasion he asked her if she had fallen in love. She replied that the man she could love existed solely in her imagination and that she would perhaps meet him only in heaven. She met him under her paternal roof in the person of Turgenev. Tatyana was then a frail, highstrung bluestocking of twenty-six, who lived in a state of rapture fed by Fichtean metaphysics.

She fell in love with Ivan at first sight. For a while she tasted the pure bliss of believing her passion reciprocated. Recalling the miracle of those days, she wrote to her brother Pavel after nearly a decade: "I lived with my whole soul, my whole heart, every little nerve in me trembled with life, and everything around me was suddenly transfigured, as it were. . . . For a woman there is no greater happiness than such love." Her ecstasy was short-lived. She was soon overcome with doubts of the strength and sincerity of Ivan's feeling for her. This was unendurable. She was literally lovesick. By the middle of November her condition was so alarming that there was talk of taking her to Moscow for medical treatment. Turgenev's visit in December did not improve matters. It was not until mid-January that Tatyana was in Moscow. Ivan called on her now and then, and, although they were in the same city, they engaged in an active correspondence. Retrospectively she spoke of his "touching, agitated letters." (Few of them have been preserved.) They must, however, have been noncommital. The more she saw of "her Christ," as she used to call him, the less she felt able to trust the genuineness of the love that his glances and words had seemed to promise her in the beginning. Her health worsened. Night after night of crying brought on vomiting spells. It seems that early in March, at her request, he returned her letters. Not that she was afraid of being compromised. "Go tell everyone you please that I love you," she wrote, "that I humiliated myself by laying at your feet my unbidden, unwanted love . . ." She had merely wished to free him from every memento that could call forth sorrow or regret, for her desire was to surround him with all that was "beautiful, holy, great." As for *his* letters, they would be with her while she lived, which would not be long, since she would soon joyously meet her death.

At the end of March, Turgenev departed for the northern capital. He could not leave Moscow, he wrote, without saying a "heartfelt word" to her. He admitted that they had become strangers to each other and that he wished to forget everything in the past, except her gaze, in which he read forgiveness and reconciliation, but spoke of the strange bond between them that was part of his very being. He went on:

> I feel that we do not part forever. I shall see you again, my good, wonderful sister. . . . Listen, I swear by God that I am speaking the truth, I am saying what I think, what I know: I never loved any woman more than you, though I don't love even you with a complete and steadfast love. . . . For you alone I would wish to be a poet, for you with whom my soul is bound in an inexpressibly wondrous way. . . . Oh, if at least once on a spring morning we could walk under a long, long row of lime trees, if I could hold your hand in mine and feel that our souls were mingling, and everything alien and morbid was vanishing, everything crafty was melting

away—and forever! Yes, you possess all the love of my soul, and if
I could only speak my mind before you, we would not be in such
a painful situation . . . and I would know how I love you.

He ends this ambiguous declaration by telling her, in German,
that she, "his best, his only friend," is his Muse, and that she
may still build on him as on a rock, "within whose innermost
heart true love and emotion lie locked."

Tatyana was not content with the role of Egeria. After his
departure he kept receiving hysterical, wordy, trilingual epistles from her, innocent of punctuation and written at such
hours as midnight and dawn, sometimes to the accompaniment of a storm. About ten of them have come down to
us. She tosses between serenity and despair, between surrender
to her fate and rebellion against its ingloriousness, between
avowals of undemanding sisterly affection or limitless maternal
tenderness and protestations of a deathless passion. She worships him, she hates him for the power he has over her. He
is a child, a playboy, a pleasure-seeking trifler, he is one of
God's elect, destined for a glorious future. Christ was her
first love, he will be her last, "everlastingly true, everlastingly
holy."

Habituated though Turgenev was to the overheated romantic atmosphere, these ravings must have made him uncomfortable. Nevertheless, he seems to have found it titillating
to encourage them. In April he encloses a song from "The
Temptation of Saint Anthony," a play on which he is working, with a letter to the Bakunin boys, directing them to
show it to Tatyana. "She will say at once if it is good or
bad. I trust her." He inquires about her health, adding that
he thinks of her "very often." He sends Tatyana a poem of
his, dated June 2, 1842, in which he declares, presumably
to his correspondent, that they will yet live through "eternal
moments" together. The sickening cerebral romance did not
actually come to a close until the summer of 1843. In the
letter to her brother Pavel cited above, Tatyana stated that
it had all been "the figment of a fevered imagination, in
which the heart could not help playing a part." On the margin of Ivan's last letter to her she scribbled self-righteously:
"Strange how some people can imagine anything they please,

how the most sacred things are a toy to them, and how they don't hesitate to ruin another's life. Why can't they ever be honest, earnest and simple with themselves and with others? Have they no notion of truth and love?"

The affair was naturally an open secret in a circle which was given to discussing at great length the feelings, the views, the actions of its members. A young woman who was a close friend of the Bakunins was at pains to write to Michel about what had passed between Tatyana and Ivan, and intimated that there was cause for Michel's breaking with Turgenev. Michel balked at that. Hadn't he, in his message to his sister, greeting the New Year 1842, recommended Turgenev to her especially? "Let him be a brother and friend to you all," he had written; "that is my blessing for you and my New Year's gift, and you must accept it because I have always been your spiritual father." Surely, he couldn't have been so mistaken about the man. He received an account of the affair, by word of mouth, from Ivan; by letter, apparently, from Tatyana. Writing to her in April, 1843, he expressed satisfaction in finding his first informant had been mistaken. He must cease to believe in a man before he was willing to break with him. He was no slave of the conventional ideas that rule the world. He loved Turgenev. He knew Turgenev. If the man had weaknesses, they were due to his extreme youth.

Immaturity alone is not enough to explain Turgenev's behavior. He had been drawn to Tatyana because of the aura that clung to her philosophical family. But the aura soon faded. Reaction against the ecstatic unrealities that had bewitched him in his Berlin coterie was bound to assert itself with the sobering effect of the Russian scene, and with them went his "theoretical" romance. Perhaps what contributed to his defection was the fact that the girl was three years his senior and that her admirers, in paying her extravagant homage, dwelt only on the beauty of her dark-blue eyes and her soul. The difficulty was that he did not recognize soon enough how discarnate and how spurious the relationship was and that he did not have the courage to make a clean break. In January, 1845, he was writing to Alexey Bakunin that in every respect it was all a thing of the past for him, and that he had abandoned the realm of fantasy and begun to live in the world as it is.

Vague echoes of his metaphysical entanglement are discernible in the verse that he wrote at the time. His first story, printed in 1844, is a plea for pitiless honesty and clarity between lovers. An old maid who falls in love with a student is sketched into the background of "Tatyana Borisovna and Her Nephew," a story he wrote several years later.

She at once rushed into an ardent and active correspondence with him; in her epistles, as was fitting, she consecrated him to a noble and beautiful life, offered "the whole of herself" as a sacrifice, demanded only the name of sister, elaborated descriptions of nature, mentioned Goethe, Schiller, Bettina and German philosophy, and finally drove the young man to blackest despair. But youth asserted itself: one fine morning he woke up with such a ferocious hatred for "his sister and best friend" that in his passion he nearly gave a thrashing to his valet, and for a long time afterward all but bit whoever alluded even slightly to "exalted and disinterested love."

It has been suggested, plausibly enough, that this is a simplified and soured version of the author's affair with Tatyana Bakunina. Her love-sickness, by the way, did not prove fatal. She died, a spinster, at fifty-six.

8

THE POET

In Berlin Turgenev had at times played with the idea that his studies might lead him to a chair of philosophy. The notion tickled his mother's vanity. Her Ivan a professor—why, that would be "the height of bliss" for her, she wrote to him on November 30, 1840. In March, 1842, as the first step toward the realization of his plan, he requested the University of Moscow to examine him for the degree of Master of Philosophy. The chair of philosophy being vacant there at the time, he went to Petersburg to take his examination at his alma mater.

His brother was then living in the capital with his wife, a former chambermaid of Varvara Petrovna's, whom he had secretly married the previous year, and the several weeks Ivan stayed in their apartment were some of the smoothest his life was to hold. He had a fine room, with a fireplace, three armchairs, quantities of pillows, and a desk with a lamp. The days began well with excellent tea, sipped out of large English breakfast cups, and delicious rolls. They wore on through placid hours, in which he lounged and crammed, warmed by the open fire, lulled by the dancing snowflakes outside, vaguely exhilarated by the profundities and promises of his texts. "Yesterday," he writes to the Bakunins on April 9, 1842, "I swallowed at one sitting Descartes, Spinoza, and Leibniz. Leibniz is still growling in my stomach. But without waiting I gobbled down Kant, and now I am getting my teeth into Fichte, and as this man is somewhat dry, I am putting him aside to write to you."

He goes on to note his train of thought as he sits, book on knee, before the fire: he reads a line of his philosopher, decides that the fire needs wood, puts it on, reads another line, suddenly recalls a verse of Lermontov; he yawns, paces over to the window, hums a sonata, watches the falling snow for ten minutes, imagines himself a cabinet minister, then returns to his Fichte, and for five minutes stares smiling into the fire. "Oh, the joy of leisured, studious solitude!"

His examinations were in philosophy and classical philology. In writing his Latin theme, which had to do with the influence of Greek literature on that of the Romans, he was so carried away by his enthusiasm for Homer that he felt it necessary to append an apology to his examiners for his unconventional manner. He owed the German university a perdurable taste for the classics. His paper in philosophy had Pantheism for its subject and its target. The candidate's attitude was that of his teachers, who were all conservative, "right" Hegelians. Pantheism, he stated, was essentially a materialistic doctrine, denying the living, personal God, and therefore, utterly false. He found a form of pantheism in Schelling's teachings, and he sharply rejected those theories, which, like Feuerbach's, admitted Revelation but saw its source in the human self. The true religion of the spirit, founded on both faith and reason, he declared, was Christianity. There can be no discord between it and either philosophy or science: "Already many are beginning to believe that man must depend lovingly on God, and that only in this relationship is it possible to find truth and freedom of thought and happiness."

It is doubtful if Turgenev had preserved the naive faith, such as enabled his mother to make an intimate and counselor of Jesus. "I dare not even think of offering prayers to God," she wrote to her son. "But Christ—he had been a human being. He is so kind." Varvara Petrovna called Him "Emmanuel Osipovich Kristofovich," she told Ivan in confidence, and she queried her son if Christ had black hair, as she had dreamed when she was small and as the Italians painted Him, or if He had golden hair, as she had recently read. Yet at this time Turgenev could sincerely argue for a personal God. Belief in such a Deity was current in his circle. There exists a yellowed sheet without a date, bearing on the margin the pencilled words: "Turgenev in his youth. Wanted to tear up." Inscribed on it in his handwriting are two conventional orisons, presumably offered by him on unknown occasions.

One is entitled "A Prayer in Time of Suffering." The other, "A Prayer in Time of Relief," opens with the words: "Gracious Lord, I thank Thee from the depths of my heart for the relief from my illness." Writing in April of that year, he attributed the unhappiness of the Bakunin brood to lack of "deep religious feeling," resulting in a half-hearted compromise with reality on the basis of "some measly moral sentiment or principle." Eventually he will be able to resign his faith without much pain, though his comfortless spirit will be visited by recurrent regrets for its loss. He continued to use the terminology of faith freely even after its substance was gone.

He came through his examinations with flying colors. To the Bakunins he confessed that all he had done was to rattle off a string of high-sounding phrases. He was sure real scholars must despise him and his philosophy. He would despise them if they didn't. The young man was scarcely suited for an academic career. At the time he was taken up with "a drama in one act," entitled "The Temptation of Saint Anthony." The heroine of this piece, which has remained a fragment, is a mistress of the devil, answering to the name of Annunziata.

The only thing that now stood between him and his degree, since he had passed both the oral and written tests, was the public defense of a dissertation. But he returned to Moscow when the examinations were over, with no further interest in pursuing the matter. Not even his mother's offer, two years later, of two thousand rubles if he would write a dissertation, will be enough to revive it. Not long before, a young man of very good family had received his master's degree and, as Varvara Petrovna naïvely confessed to Ivan, she had dreamed of the same honor for him ever since. But in vain.

During the summer he spent a week or two at Spasskoye, hunting. In August he went back to Germany to consult an oculist. There was a reunion with Michel Bakunin in Dresden. Ivan's unhappy relationship with Tatyana was not the only thing they talked about. Michel had just passed through a severe ideological crisis. He had reached the conclusion that inner freedom without external liberty was "an empty phantom," as he phrased it. As a result he gave up his metaphysical quest, and decided to expatriate himself so that he might devote his life to the cause of revolution. A born proselytizer, he must have gone out of his way to convert his friend to his new faith, but Ivan was not one to be moved by his arguments. He could no more become a political agitator than he could walk on his head. They parted amicably, however, Turgenev promising to send Bakunin 2,000 thalers to placate some of his more pressing creditors. Bakunin, who had come to Germany on Herzen's money in the first place, had a habit—which he was never to outgrow—of piling up debts with a childish unconcern about paying them off. He sent several letters after Turgenev, the last of which, dated November 20, 1842, concludes thus:

> We go two entirely different, opposite ways. Do not forget me. I shall never forget you. Never, never shall I cease really, concretely to love and trust you. When you forget me, I will think you dead. It's well we've seen each other again. We have come to know each other and I am certain that no matter where or under what circumstances we meet, we will shake hands . . . I am certain that we shall live humanly—that's the chief thing, that's our duty.

Ivan's mother was not concerned about his living "humanly." What she craved above all was that this giddy-head should settle down. If an academic career did not appeal to him, a position in the civil service would befit his station. She writes to him:

> Ivan, if you were to tell me: "*Maman,* my career in the civil service has begun well, I am satisfied, and people are satisfied with me," then without a moment's thought I give my orders and am taken to you. I make a home for you; you shall have your pocket money. You come home, everything is ready: the table, the goodies, and a loving word. As usual, every one waits for a glance from you, to take Ivan Sergeyevich's orders. When my Ivan is with me in the winter, that's my fur coat, and I'm warm; in summer, I'm kept cool and comfortable. Without you, I suffocate and am miserable.

She does not insist on a bureaucratic career; she is content to see her son a gentleman of leisure:

> You don't want to serve? God bless you, don't serve. Live quietly, where you please and how you please. You have an excuse which everyone will approve of: "*Maman* is very ill; how can I leave her to strangers?" . . . I do not demand that you should serve. Why should you? You like to write, to promenade, to hunt, to travel. Who interferes with you? Spend the winter in Petersburg. Amuse yourself.

Go to the theatre. . . . In springtime come back to the country. . . .
The summer we shall spend traveling. In the autumn you can do
your hunting. Live, and let us live near you. That's why I beg you:
begin your dissertation. Work on it a year, two years. . . . Then
you're a Master. Maybe you will even try for a doctorate. . . . You
hold the happiness of the family in your hands, but your laziness and
indifference are the cause of everybody's wretchedness. Sound your
tuning fork, put it to your ear, give voice, and we shall all chime in.

On his return from abroad early in December Turgenev
settled in Petersburg and in January, 1843, applied for a
post in the Ministry of the Interior. He took this step, yielding, no doubt, to his mother's importunities. Apparently in
support of his application he submitted to the authorities a
memorandum in which he set down some remarks on Russian
economy and the Russian peasant. It is the work of a right-
thinking, loyal subject. "Russia," he writes, "even more than
Prussia, owes everything to its sovereigns." He is proud of
the might, the monolithic quality, the unique character of
his country, which has been "so wondrously guided by Providence," but warns against "blind worship" of everything
Russian and "ungrateful" attacks on the West. The national
economy, he holds must rest on the unshakable foundation
of agriculture, and any attempt to industrialize and mechanize
the latter is both "foolhardy and immoral." He admits that
Russian farming suffers from many weaknesses. "We must
part with much, perfect much, acquire much." Above all,
it is necessary to liquidate "the outdated institutions bequeathed by the patriarchal order." Communal land tenure
is among them, but the author does not state explicitly that
serfdom is such an institution. He is no abolitionist. His chief
desideratum is that the relations between the landowning
gentry and the peasantry should be regulated by exact laws
firmly adhered to. This would eliminate the master's arbitrary authority, and hence "what is called slavery," a condition which cannot exist in a Christian state. It would also
enable the muzhik to become a full-fledged citizen. Moreover,
all changes must be effected "slowly, gradually." Turgenev
will eventually traffic in ideas of a more clearly liberal cast,
but will always remain a prophet within the law, a moderate,
looking for reforms from the constituted authorities.

It was summer before he actually assumed the duties of a

minor official with the rank of "collegiate secretary." The story goes that he came to the office every morning to sit down to the business of reading George Sand's romances and writing verse. He had just published his first long narrative poem and lyrics flowed from his pen.

The easy-going young man, being of good family and the heir to a large estate, had the entrée to some of the best drawing rooms of the two capitals. Society in those years carried on in an atmosphere of imperturbable gaiety. The chief excitements were the introduction of the polonaise in 1844, and, at about the same time, the inauguration of a new card game, called "preference." The dance took the ballrooms by storm, and hearts not stirred by the music were agreeably agitated by the game. In the theatres the audience was stiffly seated in accordance with the official Table of Ranks, but the stage was dedicated to the lightest forms of entertainment. A few prescient spirits may have heard far-off rumblings of disaster, but the general public, believing that their world rested securely on its foundations of autocracy and serfdom, faced life serenely enough.

Turgenev's mode of living was rather expensive. Besides, there was his obligation to satisfy some of Bakunin's creditors. He did not perform all he had promised Michel, as the latter discovered to his distress, but he did, after some prevarication, remit a thousand rubles. Bakunin, though in desperate circumstances, excused him on the ground that his intentions had been honorable. Aside from his salary, which was a mere pittance, Turgenev was dependent on Varvara Petrovna. The correspondence between mother and son centered on money matters. To keep him in funds, she wrote on one occasion, was like trying to fill a bottomless tub. In vain she pleaded with him to reveal the total amount of his debts. He would receive sums from her with which to buy bonnets and fashion magazines for her, but before he found time to carry out her commissions, the money seemed to leak out of his pocket. When, in July, 1843, three hundred rubles that she had sent him for the purchase of a cape disappeared in this manner, she commented briefly: "That's stealing!" It was rather carelessness and unfilial irresponsibility, of the kind that caused him to mislay his university diploma and lose

the prescription against toothache given him by Nikolay for
the benefit of their mother's sexagenarian teeth. These failings of her Vanichka did not lessen her passionate attachment to him. "I myself blush when I think of how very
precious you are to me," she wrote to him in June, 1843,
"maybe, it's a sin."

On a visit to Moscow in March, 1844, Turgenev contracted pneumonia and was not back at his desk until May.
During the summer he stayed in a suburb, leading a placid
existence, drinking Kreuzbrunnen, promenading, a green
shade over his eyes, which were not strong, and writing
verse. The following February he took a two months' leave
of absence from the Ministry, and was not seen there again.
During his year and a half in service he was repeatedly
reprimanded for tardiness and negligence. He never forgot
one instance of the latter: because of a slip of his pen a poor
devil of a thief received thirty lashes with the knout instead
of with the whip.

He had closed the door on his bureaucratic career. This
drew down upon him a letter full of maternal pain and
pleading, and he was treated to an objective review of what
he had done with himself since his return to Russia. By his
mother's account it amounted to nothing more than idling,
traveling for his health, and applauding "a damn Gipsy,"
as she called a foreign prima donna of whom more will be
heard. Varvara Petrovna was disgusted with her son.

Her first-born caused her an even more grievous disappointment. She had little affection for him, finding him can-
tankerous, lecherous, cowardly, the kind of person who is
only happy when he is unhappy. It has been indicated that
he had married his mother's chambermaid, a woman of
German stock who hailed from Riga. The marriage was kept
from Varvara Petrovna, but the report had reached her that
he was living openly with a strumpet, to the scandal of
friends and relatives. This was a painful blow to her pride.
What galled her was the publicity of the outrageous liaison.
She asked Ivan to tell his brother that you don't bare your
bottom in public, or make a show of your chamber pot, even
if it is a silver one—hers, like Trimalchio's *matella,* was of that
metal. She considered it a shame, she wrote to Ivan on

February 25, 1843, to give Nikolay money "to keep whores." Accordingly, she stopped his allowance, so that he had to take a clerkship to support himself and his wife.

Varvara Petrovna may have suspected that Nikolay had actually married the woman. She pleaded with the wretch "not to count on the promises of the passions," adding: "If there is still time, renounce a weakness that can only bring about your ruin." At the approach of the ninth anniversary of her husband's death (October 30, 1843) she commissioned Ivan to take his brother to their father's grave and kneel down with him—in the mud, if necessary—not to rise until he swore to give up his disgraceful alliance. If he agreed, Ivan was to hand him his father's watch. "If he says that it would kill him, as he had written me," she concluded, "then I would rather see him dead and pure than alive and sullied. "

It is not known if Turgenev carried out this injunction, but several months later his mother claimed that Nikolay had given her his word to tell his "mam'selle": "I love you dearly, but I love my mother even more," and that he would never see her again. If he made this promise, he did not keep it. When in 1845 Varvara Petrovna finally had to face the fact that her son was married, she disowned him. Some time later she conceived a desire to see her grandchildren. As she would not have them in her house, she looked at them through her lorgnette as they were led past her windows.

After his retirement from the service Turgenev continued to live in the capital. Now and then his mother, saying she could not live without him, would threaten to join him there. She divided her time between Moscow and the country. In 1846 he made a long stay at Spasskoye, chiefly for the sake of the shooting. On his hunting trips he was usually accompanied by Afanasy Alifanov, a peasant who was owned by a neighbor of Varvara Petrovna's. He figures in one of Turgenev's stories under the name of Yermolay. These excursions afforded the huntsman a chance to gather the impressions that went to the making of the first book to bring him fame.

Home was becoming a more and more distasteful place. Age added to Varvara Petrovna's piety, without improving her disposition. Both sons had failed her lamentably, and she had other vexations. She expended her anger and resentment by tormenting those around her with a kind of idle sadism. She did not suffer any independent opinion or interest on their part. When her brother-in-law, who was managing her estates, took a wife, she regarded this as a sign of disloyalty to her and dismissed him. She did, however, agree to bring up little Anna (Asya), his illegitimate daughter by a serf. Holding that she alone had a claim to the devotion of her "subjects," she deprived a married couple, her trusted servants, of their children. Her brutal treatment of the dumb giant who was her porter afforded her son material for his "Moomoo," which Carlyle is said to have called the most pathetic story in existence, and which made Herzen tremble with fury.

On one occasion she enacted a little farce, such as might well have been imagined by Molière. When, in 1845, Ivan's nameday came round, in spite of his absence the event was celebrated at Spasskoye with a dinner of traditional pork, roast goose, pies and vodka for the entire household. As a domestic in charge of the linen had been permitted to observe her own nameday festively the same afternoon, a good deal of liquor was consumed by the servants. At nine o'clock in the evening the news ran through the house that the mistress was dying. The priest, hurriedly summoned, confessed the stricken woman. Before receiving the sacrament she called for the portraits of her sons and repeated in a faint voice: "*Adieu, Jean! Adieu, Nicolas! Adieu, mes enfants!*" Then she blessed her foster daughter with an icon of the Holy Virgin of Vladimir. Finally, she indicated her desire to take leave of all the servants. While her private physician, a serf of hers, stood by with a vial of medicine, and her favorite maid was fanning her witih a cloth dipped in vinegar, dozens of men and women filed by her bedside, each bowing down to the ground and kissing her hand. But then she seemed to rally, demanded tea, and proceeded to mete out punishment to those who had failed to appear for the leave-taking ceremony or who had come in tipsy.

The same year she abolished Easter for her domestic establishment. During Holy Week she fasted and was moved to grant pardon to her steward whom she had literally almost killed for having concealed Nikolay's marriage from her. But on Easter Sunday she rose in the worst of bad tempers. She ordered the church bells silenced and the day treated as any other. Since there was no Easter for her, she declared, there should be none for anyone near her. She brooked no dictation even in her relations with her God. She is said to have forced a young priest to confess her in the presence of all her domestics, in flagrant violation of church statutes.

Turgenev faced no serious opposition from his mother as far as his literary preoccupation was concerned. She was delighted when, at Easter, 1843, he brought her a copy of his first book, *Parasha,* named after its heroine, and she kept the thin pink brochure on her drawing room table. She was proud of him, and suggested that he take her maiden name as his *nom de plume.* Indeed, he did sign some of his early work "T.L." for Turgenev-Lutovinov. "I do not know if it was difficult for you to give birth to a daughter," she wrote him, "but, thank Heaven, you came through it beautifully. I am putting the amount of the Eleanora debt under my first granddaughter's pillow. That's over and above your allowance." She thus accorded the child of Ivan's brain the recognition she was unwilling to bestow on the child of his loins. She was inclined to encourage the young author: "Do not stop writing. . . . No, no, our *Parasha* is not without merits." A line therein, to the effect that cider is not served in the best houses, deprived his mother's guests of it permanently. His uncle's enthusiasm was even greater than his mother's. The man dubbed everything he loved "Parasha," from a new-born calf to Bibi. Yet Varvara Petrovna could hardly consider writing a serious occupation for a gentleman. She saw little difference between an author and a clerk, since, as she remarked in a moment of irritation, both were only soiling paper for money. Further, an author was liable to suffer various indignities. She watched the reviews jealously and said of criticism, *"Cela purge,"* but when Ivan proudly announced that his work had been noticed, she burst into tears at the thought that some priest's brat had criticized a Turgenev.

The budding author was welcomed by the *literati* of the capital. A noteworthy circle was dominated by the critic Vissarion Belinsky. Wine and cards were a matter of course at the gatherings of the coterie, as was good talk. The company would amuse itself with skits and occasionally with the obscene inspirations from the pen of Mikhail Longinov, a bibliographer who had a taste for pornography. Turgenev himself perpetrated a bawdy narrative in verse, belonging with such contributions to erotica as Pushkin's "Gavriliad." He was also a good hand at tossing off epigrams. The target of one of these shafts, which he composed in collaboration with another literary tyro, Nikolay Nekrasov, was a shy, morbidly thin-skinned young writer, whom Belinsky had just dragged into the limelight and who some thirty years later was to write *The Brothers Karamazov*. The group often met at the Panayevs'. Ivan Panayev was a minor writer married to a young and beautiful woman with literary ambitions who eventually became Nekrasov's mistress. She maintained a kind of salon, where Turgenev was often seen. During the season he would come to her Saturdays from some fashionable drawing room, immaculate in his blue swallowtail with gold lion's head buttons and light checkered trousers, his white vest enlivened by a colored tie, and his hair worn à la Liszt.

Half a century later his hostess was to roll upon her malicious tongue various choice morsels about the young Turgenev. She made him out a good deal of a snob, avid of aristocratic connections, boasting of his successes in society and no more reticent about his affairs of the heart, inclined also to treat truth rather cavalierly. His friend Annenkov, too—they met in the autumn of 1843—spoke of what he called Turgenev's "poetic lies," attributing them to a desire to produce "a literary effect." The young man gave the impression of completely lacking sincerity and candor. What he appeared to abhor above all, was the disgrace of being like everyone else. To avoid it he ascribed to himself all manner of impossible traits and even vices of which he was incapable. He would assure his hearers that in the presence of a great work of art the hollow of his knees itched and his calves turned triangular. Annenkov found something feminine in his disposition. Practical jokes of an outrageous kind

delighted him. He irritated people by his poses, trying on
the roles of a Don Juan, a Manfred, an Onegin, a frivolous
dandy, an acrid skeptic.

He shed these masks and dropped these affectations when
he took up his pen. It is noteworthy that in spite of his various
distractions he managed to produce a considerable body of
writing during this period. In addition to *Parasha* he published a second long narrative poem in 1845 and two more
the following year. His last long poem, composed in 1847
and left unfinished, celebrates a Florentine who fights the
tyrannical rule of the Medici and commits suicide in prison.
The fragment ends on a cheerless note: the earth absorbs
blood poured out in a righteous cause as indifferently as it
does dew, no avenger arises from the martyr's bones and
oblivion is his lot. Between 1838 and 1846 Turgenev also
published some thirty lyrics. In after years he conceived a
strong distaste, "almost physical," as he put it, for his verse.
A poem, he said, is like an oyster: if it is not excellent, it
is worthless. This did not prevent him from writing an occasional epigram or letter in rhyme and tossing off an im-
promptu quatrain for an after-dinner speech. In the sixties
he wrote a number of lyrics that were set to music, and as
late as 1876 he spent a wakeful night composing a political
poem. At eighteen he broke into print with a prose piece:
a review of a book of travel in the Holy Land, contributed to
an issue of the *Journal of the Ministry of Education*. At rare
intervals he again tried his hand at reviewing. In 1843 a one-
acter of his was printed. His first story, "Andrey Kolosov,"
appeared a year later. Two more were published in 1846.

All these writings are the work of a gifted apprentice, still
lacking his own way and following, not without distinction,
in the footsteps of Pushkin, Lermontov, Gogol. Some of his
lyrics are trite and heavy-handed exercises in the treatment
of the stock themes of love and nature and the transience
of things. Elsewhere the light touch, the tone of irony and
badinage predominate, save when (as in his dramatic poem,
"Conversation") he stigmatizes his own generation as pre-
maturely old, hollow, without desires or faith. With one
exception, the background is the native scene: provincial or
manorial Russia, seen as a world of hopeless stagnation and

stifling vulgarity. Early in Turgenev's work, it is characteristic that women, rather than men, dream of escape from
this philistine world, or, indeed, have the strength and will
to defy it. At the same time, the young author is impatient
with those who contemn or merely tolerate ordinary people.
He is at pains to discredit the Byronic type as an individual
locked within himself and divorced from life. Both the passions and the sorrows of the romantic hero are shown to be
spurious, artificial, unreal. Turning against the phantasmal
and fevered idealism of his Berlin days, Turgenev exalts simplicity, sobriety, naturalness, the emotions not sicklied o'er by
sterile self-analysis and hypertrophied cerebration. Furthermore, a few of these pages adumbrate an awareness of the
writer's duty to commit himself to the cause of social justice.

9

BELINSKY'S DISCIPLE

It was during the second winter after Turgenev's return from Germany that he became acquainted with Belinsky. "Fierce Vissarion" had a maternal tenderness for fledgling talents. He greeted *Parasha* with an enthusiastic review. Its author, he wrote, was "the child of our time, carrying within his breast all its sorrows and problems." Turgenev spent the summer of 1844 as Belinsky's neighbor in a suburb of the capital, and the two became close friends.

They met almost daily. In the pungent twilight of the pine grove the tall, bulky figure might be seen marching beside the slight, stoop-shouldered one, or both would curl up on the moss to finger the dry needles and talk and talk. Turgenev was keyed up by the excited voice, the gestures of the small, fine hands. He was proud to be able to satisfy the hungry curiosity of his companion, who could learn the last word on German metaphysics only by report. Belinsky was a critic of letters, though obliquely also a critic of life. Turgenev, even if only the author of certain slight lyrics and a solider narrative in verse, was a literary aspirant. It is hard to imagine that they failed to talk shop. One must be a craftsman, of course; one must remember that literature is as autonomous as the other arts and, like them, the domain of spontaneity and freedom. And yet one must ask of every literary work to what extent it speaks for its age and what it contributes, however indirectly, to the solution of contemporary problems. Turgenev, as he watched his friend's features grow a pale blur in the dusk, adored his stern mind, felt himself poor, unworthy, unaccomplished, dreamed of turning a new leaf. Those were the days when he wanted each moment of his life to be "significant," as he admitted later, adding: "A daring and hardly sinless desire!"

Turgenev's long poem, *Conversation,* which followed *Parasha,* also found favor in Belinsky's eyes. He praised it for mirroring a disease of the age: "the apathy of feeling and will combined with the devouring activity of thought." The young man's further efforts in verse somewhat cooled Belinsky's enthusiasm, and eventually the critic declared that he lacked the authentic lyrical gift. Their friendship, however, did not suffer. Belinsky overlooked Ivan's irritating mannerisms and delighted in his observing eye, his lively mimicry, his wicked sarcasm. He may also have enjoyed playing the mentor to the young man, eight years his junior. As for Turgenev, he was won emotionally and intellectually. Belinsky replaced Stankevich in his affections. Like Stankevich, the critic was a man with a weak body and a strong devotion to the things of the spirit; an intense and disinterested soul, shy among people and ferocious in dealing with ideas. Turgenev relished Belinsky's fervor and forthrightness, his earnestness and good sense, his intellectual honesty and independence, and that candid obscenity which spots his published correspondence with blank spaces. How could he but admire one who was so well served by such learning as he had? For whatever Belinsky knew, and there were great gaps in his knowledge, was not dead ballast but a very wind in his sails.

The critic had once been as ardent an Hegelian as any. Misinterpreting the philosopher's dictum that everything real was reasonable, he had even extolled in print the Romanov monarchy. But by the time Turgenev became acquainted with him he had repudiated with his customary vehemence the sanctified standpattism sponsored by Hegel, and developed a strong animus against religion. He was now storming at the insults that the existing order heaped on his intelligence and his sense of decency and justice. He declared his enthusiasm for the United States of America because of its "ideal" government. What he cared about was the dignity and physical well-being of the individual man, woman, and child, here and now.

Since his return from Germany Turgenev, like most members of the old Stankevich set, was undergoing a change of heart. He continued to cherish the values that he had learned to revere during his formative years: truth, reason, art, humanity, freedom above all. A vein of idealism will run through his work, but deprived of its mystical and optimistic tinge. He was emerging from the clouds of metaphysical abstractions and turning his attention to the phenomenal world about him—more concretely, to what was going on among the uncouth, abused people of his own country. When formal instruction stopped for him, a new phase of his education began. His commerce was now with men, rather than ideas. Association with Belinsky—a crucial experience—encouraged this process of sobering and maturing. It must have led him to think of the public good in terms of the welfare of separate persons. In one respect he was at variance with the critic. The latter was an extremist. "To make even a small fraction of mankind happy," he wrote to a friend, "I am perhaps ready to destroy the rest by fire and sword." Turgenev, on the other hand, was a moderate who abhorred force and violence. He was in duty bound, he felt, to do his part to help the human race advance toward the light, but he knew that such progress must be as slow and gradual as that of a sprout pushing up through the darkness of the soil.

The attempt to grapple with social problems divided the intelligentsia. By the mid-forties there were two small hostile camps. One went by the name of Slavophils. The other, under Belinsky's generalship, was known as Westernist. Here Turgenev naturally found himself. He ascribed his life-long Westernism to the fact that he had dived into "the German sea." Neither side had as yet climbed down from the peaks of theory onto the plain of performance. The nearest approach to it was the adoption by certain brave Slavophils of an archaic costume so historically correct that it looked foreign to the natives. What could any reform movement be in the reign of Nicholas I except a pious wish? The prevailing frame of mind under this régime was such that a man felt he had achieved the utmost by taking thought. Ideas were regarded not as the blueprints of action but as the very sum of architecture.

Moscow was the chief scene of the combat between the two factions. Turgenev, making his home in Petersburg, and coming only rarely to the old Russian capital, may not have been present at the verbal tourneys that went on there from dinner time until nearly dawn. But he was undoubtedly abreast of the matters that were being debated no longer in the salons only, but now even in the public prints. His verse narrative, "The Landed Gentleman," published in 1846, contains a biting caricature of Konstantin Aksakov, a pillar of Slavophilism. Not for nothing had Turgenev won the nickname "gamin" from Belinsky, who soon after the beginning of their acquaintance wrote to a friend: "There is malice, gall, humor in him. He understands Moscow deeply, and mimicks it so that I get drunk with pleasure." Of course, the battle had but a secondary interest for Turgenev. His writings showed clearly that his concern was not with social theories but with the social scene. Yet there was no mistaking his sympathies.

For many years the two orientations, long anonymous, had striven for supremacy, but it was only now that the conflict was raised to the level of elaborate ideology. The Slavophils took over the old nationalist faith, and, not without the help of imported philosophy, namely Schelling's ideas, made it flourish like a new evangel. They held that Russian culture rested on a religious foundation and so was different from and superior to that of the West, with its legalism and materialism. Believing that Peter the Great had deflected Russian history from its true course by his reforms, they advocated a return to the ways of the Muscovite past. Yet, at least during the forties, these traditionalists and pietists were not complete reactionaries. They looked askance at the Petersburg administration and indeed shared their opponents' desire to see the serfs emancipated. They spoke up for civil liberties, although their main concern was with spiritual freedom, the gift of Orthodox Christianity. The native customs and folkways were very much in their minds and affections. They prized particularly the institution of common land tenure (*obshchina*) in the Great Russian villages (condemned by Turgenev in his memorandum on the Russian economy), taking it as evidence that the peasantry, unlike the educated classes, had preserved in its purity the Orthodox faith, with its spirit of brotherhood and equality, to which Western individualism was so foreign.

Their opponents were a humbler and more realistically-minded lot. The Westernists saw Russia as the stepchild of history, but, however neglected, a born member of the family of European nations. In order to realize its potentialities, the country, they maintained, must follow in the footsteps of the West. Culturally, they were inspired by the humanist ideal, fostered in Europe by the Renaissance and the Age of Reason, both of which Russia had been denied. Politically, Westernism ranged from a radicalism that dreamed of achieving happiness for all by a socialist revolution to a moderate liberalism that favored representative government and free enterprise. The Westernists dismissed with scorn the bizarre Utopia projected by the Slavophils into a fictive past, a Utopia in which the lion of autocracy would lie down beside the lamb of the plebs in the shade of a theocratic Church. They submitted that in practice their adversaries' stand meant support of the existing order.

With few exceptions, the men on both sides belonged, like Turgenev, to the gentry. But whereas the program of the Westernists expressed some of the aspirations of the third estate, that of the other faction embodied the attitude of a feudal class looking back to a patriarchal golden age.

After the summer in which his intimacy with Belinsky began, Turgenev became a regular visitor at the shabby rooms that the critic occupied with his wife, a homely, sickly school teacher, no longer young, and their baby daughter. The host would pace up and down, or sit huddled in his gray, cotton-lined jacket, tapping his snuffbox with his frail fingers, his blue, gold-flecked eyes widening with animation as the talk went on. The interchanges continued even when the consumptive Belinsky was in distress, and Turgenev, much to the invalid's displeasure, was usually the first to suggest breaking off the discussion for some more sustaining occupation. "We haven't yet settled the question of the existence of God," Belinsky once reproached him, "and you want to eat!"

Recalling those evenings, after the lapse of a quarter of a century, Turgenev wrote:

Here is what meets your gaze as you look round: bribery flourishes; serfdom stands firm as a rock; barracks are in the foreground; justice is non-existent; it is rumored that the universities are to be closed, and indeed soon the complement of students is reduced to three hundred; foreign travel is becoming impossible; no decent book can be ordered from abroad; a dark cloud hangs over the department of learning and literature, so-called, and informers hiss all around you; there is no common bond among the young people, nor have they any common interests, fear and servility dominate them. Well, you make your way to Belinsky's flat, one or two friends turn up, conversation gets under way, and you feel better.

He added that the talk was on philosophical, literary, perhaps social subjects, but that it seldom touched on history, and there were no political discussions, their futility being too obvious to everyone.

Young Turgenev's capacity for exalting some individual who won his respect and affection is evidenced in his relations with Belinsky, as it had been in his friendship with Stankevich. He always spoke of Belinsky with boundless admiration. Two decades after the man's death—it occurred in May, 1848—Turgenev called him a truly "good" man, a "great" critic, endowed with impeccable taste and a profound understanding of the needs of his age, a "central nature," close to the very heart of his people. By way of a practical expression of his devotion, he gave the critic's widow a pension and bought his library.* In the character of Pokorsky (in *Rudin*) the novelist blends the essences of his Stankevich and his Belinsky. "It seems as though a man has become a perfect wild beast," we are told in the novel, "but no sooner do you mention Pokorsky's name in his presence than all the remnants of nobility begin to stir within him, just as if you uncorked a forgotten bottle of perfume in a dark, dirty room."

The beginning of 1847 found Turgenev winding up his affairs preparatory to a trip abroad. Shortly before his departure he tried to persuade his mother to recognize Nikolay's marriage and offer him some financial help, as he was finding it hard to make both ends meet. These efforts were rewarded only with sobs and hysterics.

About the same time Bibi overheard him in a mild clash with his mother on the subject of serfdom. This was a rare occasion. Being of an unheroic temper, he preferred sulking in his tent to giving battle. She argued that her serfs were

---

* It is now in the Turgenev Museum at Oryol.

well fed and clothed, and what more did they need? He countered that they lived in constant fear of her, that they were treated not like human beings, capable of pleasure and pain, of love and hate, but like things, that at a whim she could do with them as she pleased, deport them, separate them from their families. All this seemed to her a matter of course. When he burst out, in a voice shrill with indignation, that the peasants would soon have to be freed, she declared that he was out of his mind.

Early in February he was in Berlin, a world away from serfs and serf owners.

Twenty years later he declared that his withdrawal from Russia had been a strategic retreat, executed so that he might the more effectively attack serfdom and thus carry out his Hannibal's oath against that enemy. "Almost everything I saw around me," he wrote, "confused, repelled, nay, outraged me." He could not breathe the air of oppression. Existence in the police state that Russia was under Nicholas I may indeed have been intolerable to a man who had had a taste of life in the relatively free air of the West. But Turgenev failed to mention perhaps the most cogent reason for his departure. He went to Berlin, as he was to go to so many places during the rest of his life, chiefly to be near Pauline Garcia Viardot.

10

NOVEMBER FIRST,

EIGHTEEN FORTY-THREE

Ivan was bumping his three-year-old shins against the clumsy heirlooms at Spasskoye when the youngest Garcia's first cry broke against the walls of her parents' Parisian flat. Pauline was a born cosmopolite: she had Spanish progenitors, an Italian godfather, a Russian godmother, and in good time a French husband. Further, she was a born musician, like her elder sister, la Malibran, inheriting the gifts of both parents and developing them to the point of genius. Her mother, who was a prima donna, came of good family, but her father was born in the Gipsy quarter of Seville and could not tell Pauline who her parental grandfather was. The handsome Don Manoel was characterized by his daughter as an ebullient mixture of passion, courage, folly, boundless kindness, childish naïveté and indomitable cockiness. He could do everything, from composing a sauce to composing an opera. The man was a fine tenor and an admirable actor. Eventually he became an impresario, taking his company, which included his wife and elder daughter, as well as himself, from one capital to another.

When Pauline was four years old she found herself in New York, where for nearly forty weeks running, generally on Tuesday and Saturday nights, her celebrated family deserted her to divert the fashionables with the first Italian opera ever produced in that city. The initial performance took place on the night of November 29, 1825, at the Park Theatre—on the site of what is now 21-25 Park Row, opposite the old General Post Office—the finer of the two theatres in New York at the time. The opera was Rossini's *Barber of Seville;* Don Manoel had created the role of Almaviva in the original production in Rome nine years previously. In the audience were such celebrities as Fenimore Cooper and Napoleon's brother Joseph, one-time King of Spain. *The New York Evening Post* reported the next day that "an assemblage so fashionable, so numerous, and so elegantly dressed, was probably never witnessed in our theater." This assemblage was "surprised, delighted, enchanted. . . .The repeated plaudits with which the theater rang were unequivocal, unaffected bursts of rapture." The opening night netted the company three thousand dollars. Box seats were two dollars, orchestra chairs one dollar, and the gallery seats sold for a quarter.

With the proceeds in his pocket Don Manoel, in September, 1826, extended his tour to Mexico City, where he remained two years. It was quite an undertaking at the time, but the Garcias were a hardy lot; the doctor who attended them in New York observed that they had "good constitutions and took little physic." Little Pauline, who made one of the party as a matter of course, was already speaking four of the languages in which she was to sing. Their adventure in the wild south ended disastrously. As they made their way to Vera Cruz on the return journey they were attacked by bandits, who disembarrassed Don Manoel of his fortune, which he carried with him in the attractive form of gold and silver coin. Pauline always remembered how her teeth chattered as she lay in her mother's arms, wrapped in the frightened woman's Scotch plaid, while the bandits were looting the caravan. One of them made off with Pauline's own little plaid, a possession which she thought to be exactly like her mother's and of which she was very proud. What she resented was not so much the loss of her cape as the indignity of seing it shrink to the proportions of a child's cloak across the huge shoulders of the Mexican.

When they again settled in Paris, in 1829, Pauline's musical education was taken in hand by members of her family, assisted by other professional teachers. She was to benefit from her father's instruction for only a short time, as he died three years later. She could not remember the time when she had been ignorant of music. It was an element of the air she breathed. Franz Liszt, under whom she studied composition, was very proud of her. He came to rank her with Pasta, Schroeder-Devrient and Rachel, and indeed assigned her a unique place in that dazzling sorority for her diversified gifts, her intellect, and her character. "The ant," as her family nicknamed her for her patient industry, had had a sound education and profited by it. Like Turgenev, she was devoted to the classics. She brought up her own daughters on Homer, so that Louise, the eldest, knew by heart every episode of the Iliad and the Odyssey, and Claudie called her rocking-horse "Balios" for Achilles' steed.

Pauline was sixteen years old when her voice was placed; it combined the registers of soprano and contralto; and it was then that she made her début on the concert stage in Brussels, although even previously she had assisted la Malibran at her recitals. Two years later, in London, she began her operatic career, as Desdemona. Louis Viardot, the director of the Italian opera in Paris, immediately engaged her for the next season.

When Pauline sang in the French capital for the first time, at l'Odéon, la Malibran had been dead for three years, and Alfred de Musset, who had adored the elder sister's voice, and whose stanzas had mourned her passing, was of course in the younger sister's audience. The first notes gave him the uncanny sensation that la Malibran had returned from the grave to sing for him. He recognized the same timbre, the same combination of roughness and sweetness, the same aftertaste as of the tang of a wild fruit. His admiration of the artist soon warmed to a more personal emotion, which was also to be aroused in him by her mother. He began paying court to both, at the same time bestowing his attentions upon Mlle. Rachel, who had made her début on the stage during the same period.

Whether due to Rachel's superior charm or to George Sand's maternal interference, or to the fact that Mlle. Garcia had rejected him, Musset drifted away from *"l'ingrate Pauline,"* as he called her thereafter, and in 1840, Pauline was married to Louis Viardot. Saint-Saens speaks of him as one of the handsomest men of his time, but he was also more than twice as old as his bride.

The match was largely engineered by George Sand, a friend

of Viardot's and an admirer of the prima donna, whom she called "the Lord's miracle." The pair visited her at Nohant, her estate, the year after the wedding. There the two women promenaded and played billiards while the men hunted, and in the evening young Mme. Viardot was at the piano with Chopin. Pauline was the model for George Sand's heroine, Consuelo, in the novel of that name, and the flattered—and flattering—original wrote to the novelist that to have assisted her in creating "this remarkable figure" was undoubtedly "the best" she had ever done in the world. During her frequent absences from France, on tour, Pauline continued to keep in touch with Mme. Sand, who remained a lifelong friend of the family.

Louis Viardot gave up his post to become Pauline's impresario. He accepted in his usual equable fashion the ungrateful role of the husband of a celebrity, and soon after the wedding Pauline resumed her triumphant career. She was by no means beautiful; she had no illusions on that score. She had, she believed, only a second-rate voice, yet she claimed, paradoxically enough, that this was the secret of her success: had her natural endowments been richer, she would have been less of a conscious craftsman and therefore less of an artist. As it was, she owed her achievements to a virtuosity depending on her infinite capacity for taking pains. She found her audiences in all the European capitals, and her reputation as a singer and dramatic actress rolled up like a snowball. According to Saint-Saens, her voice made of light pieces the badinage of giants and gave a superhuman grandeur to tragedy, her true medium.

During the 1842-43 season she was singing in Paris at the Théâtre Italien, where Heinrich Heine often came to hear her. About Easter she went to Vienna to sing for the Emperor of Austria on his birthday. In the summer she was heard by the King of Prussia, at a concert arranged in Berlin by Meyerbeer. Of her three distinguished auditors, only the prince of poets voiced his opinion of her. He wrote of her in 1844:

She is no nightingale, who has only the talent of her species and who sobs and trills exquisitely her spring routine; nor is she a rose, for she is ugly, but of a noble, I might almost say a beautiful type of ugliness, such as has sometimes fascinated and inspired the great painter of lions, Delacroix! Indeed, la Garcia suggests less the civilized beauty and tame grace of our European homeland than the terrible splendor of an exotic wilderness, and during some moments of her impassioned performance, especially when she opens wide her large mouth with its dazzling white teeth, and smiles with such ferocious and bewitching sweetness, you feel as though the monstrous plants and animals of Hindustan or Africa were about to appear; you fancy that giant palms, enlaced by thousand-blossomed lianas, must now shoot up, and you would not be surprised if suddenly a leopard or a giraffe or even a herd of young elephants were to rush across the stage.

Heine made these notes in a mood of reminiscence and regret, for during the season of 1843-44 la Garcia, as the opera-goers liked to call her, was a thousand miles away from Paris. She had accepted an engagement to sing in Petersburg, at a salary of fifty thousand francs, plus the proceeds of one special performance. That season saw the return of Italian opera to Petersburg for the first time since the half-witted martinet Paul I abolished it in a fit of parsimoniousness in 1798. The capital was all agog. The opera opened in October at the Bolshoy Theatre with the very piece which had initiated the New York performances: *The Barber of Seville*. The tall, bald German conductor lent an added note of color to the evening by waving his baton in a yellow-gloved hand. Mme. Viardot sang the role of Rosina for a packed house which she swept out of skepticism into a frenzied ecstasy.

That evening, marking another triumph for her, also assured the success of the new musical venture. Night after night, until Lent closed the season, the opera house was filled to capacity, impecunious music-lovers overflowing into the aisles, balancing themselves on every possible and impossible ridge, and even perching, at the risk of their lives, in the space between roof and ceiling around the aperture from which the central chandelier was suspended. It is on record that two students crossed the Neva before the ice was tested and the gangways laid, simply to hear the incomparable Viardot. The opera was the chief topic in all the drawing rooms, so that finally the wearied hostesses agreed to rule it out of the conversation entirely. There was no end of gossip, not all of it kindly, about the prima donna. It was repeated at Mme. Panayeva's as elsewhere, that the great artiste had Jewish blood in her veins. Else why should she be so grasping? Perhaps not without reason, the reputation for being greedy clung to her. She was certainly the sort of woman who insisted on receiving her due. Turgenev took up the cudgels in her defense.

He must have been in the first-night audience which burst into a fury of applause on the last note of Rosina's aria *"Una voce poco fà."* Not long thereafter, on the morning of November 1, 1843, he met the singer for the first time. For years he celebrated the return of this "sacred" day. He went to her apartment—it was in a corner house on the Nevsky opposite the Alexandrinsky Theatre—in the company of a notoriously ridiculous little major. Turgenev writes to Mme. Viardot on the ninth anniversary of this meeting that he always thinks with pleasure of the stupid fellow because chance had associated him with that morning.

The woman who stood before him that November day, seen by the sober eye was a thin, flat-chested, slightly stooped person, with a wide, full-lipped mouth, prominent features, and huge, hot, black Spanish eyes. A pencil drawing of the period which was found among Turgenev's papers confirms the universal testimony to the homeliness of the woman, but conveys no hint of the fascination of the artiste. Before her engagement to Viardot, Ary Scheffer, a Dutch-born painter settled in France, on being introduced to her, said to her future husband: "She is atrociously homely, but should I see her again I would fall madly in love with her." Which he did. It must have gone not very differently with Turgenev.

The young man, who was presented to her as a good hunter, an interesting talker, and a poor poet, found himself not the most distinguished among a group of the prima donna's admirers. It gradually narrowed itself down to what Turgenev called her "Old Guard," which consisted of himself, a count, a general, and his most serious rival: the son of the director of the Imperial Theatres. The latter, according to legend, had a private green-room built just off the stage for Mme. Viardot's comfort. After the performance the prima donna would rest there on the skin of a bear shot by one of the faithful. Four gentlemen were admitted to enjoy seats of honor on the four gilded paws, each of which had its number and its regular occupant who had to tell a story during the intermission. Mme. Viardot, in a white peignoir, was enthroned in the center. Rumor had it that on one of these golden corners—Number 3, to be exact—sat the rapt Turgenev.*

Mme. Panayeva expatiates in her memoirs on how he dinned his infatuation into everybody's ears. He annoyed her especially by his uninvited invasion of her box, where his huge frame would interfere with every one's view and his ear-splitting applause arouse the indignation of the neighboring boxes. On one occasion, she writes, he broke up a game of preference, in which Belinsky was taking a hand, to relate how his divinity had with her own fingers rubbed his aching temples with Eau de Cologne. Since his mother kept him short of money, he had sometimes to appear in a cheap seat. It is reported that, ashamed of being seen there, he explained to his fashionable acquaintances that he was looking after claqueurs he had hired.

The few letters from Turgenev to Mme. Viardot for the period up to his departure from Russia in 1847 show an interest too deep for a mere friendship, but are not importunate enough for passion. The singer was in Russia for three successive seasons. It was after the first of them that Turgenev was writing her, on March 9, 1844: "We, poor famished creatures, feed on our memories," the plural referring to the Old Guard. "I wanted to look into our dear

---

* In his recent biography of Turgenev (London, and New York, 1954) Mr. Magarshack states, without offering any evidence, that Pauline Viardot took "hardly any notice" of Turgenev and that to make up for her "disregard," he composed a dramatic piece, his first one, entitled "Carelessness." The characters in it, all Spanish, include a beautiful young married woman, her husband, twenty years her senior, and a handsome youth, three years older than she, who is desperately in love with but wholly neglected by her. Mr. Magarshack is at pains to make the point that the ages of the trio are exactly those of Pauline, Louis Viardot, and Turgenev, who has other traits in common with the young man in the play. The biographer adduces all this as proof that the playlet presents Turgenev's involvement with the prima donna. The fact is that "Carelessness" was composed not later than June, 1843 (see Belinsky, *Pisma* v. 2, p. 372), months before Turgenev laid eyes on Pauline.

little rooms," he added, "but someone is living in them now." The words seem to smile to themselves secretly, but the context does not allow one to interpret them as suggesting intimacy. After the prima donna's second Russian engagement his relationship with the Viardots was sufficiently friendly for them to invite him to their estate, the Château de Courtavenel. He stayed there long enough to become well acquainted with the whole household.

From the beginning, Turgenev's interest in the lady embraced her family as well. He is in correspondence with her mother, he receives letters written jointly by the Viardots, he sends their small daughter Louise "a fat kiss." He fills his letters with such impersonal matter as the theatrical gossip of the capital and intelligence concerning his griffon answering to the name of Paradise Lost, and his English bay mare, Queen Victoria. On the other hand, he not only begs Pauline to take care of her health, but speaks of following her engagements in the papers, discusses her repertoire, points out certain defects in her acting, advises her about her reading and on how to improve her German pronunciation, apologizing for his pedantry, due, he explains, to his keen interest in her "least movement and gesture."

Her letters appear to have been few and far between—none of them has been published. "It was very cruel of you," he writes to her on October 21, 1846, "not to have written me a word from Courtavenel. . . . Your silence has greatly saddened me, I assure you. Allow me, then, before I end this letter, to express my sincerest wishes for your happiness and believe me that, having known you, it is as difficult to forget you as it is not to become attached to you." She must have resumed the correspondence, for on November 8 he was writing her: "Now that the dam has been breached, I intend to flood you with letters." And further: "We are already old friends, three-year-old ones. I shall remain the same—I cannot and, indeed, I do not want to change."

When she was about to leave Petersburg after her third season there an acquaintance of Turgenev's, a certain prince, came to pay his respects to the departing prima donna. Standing in the twilit foyer as he waited to be announced, he noticed a tall, heavily built man panting over a trunk which would not close for him. At first the prince ignored him, thinking him a servant. But the man's obvious incompetence attracted the visitor's attention, and he and Turgenev recognized each other with mutual embarrassment. Talking rapidly, Turgenev explained that M. Viardot had left for Paris in advance and that Mme. Viardot was about to follow him. Half a century later the prince, recalling the incident, spoke of the curious fear for Turgenev that had seized him at that moment.

Mme. Viardot did not return to Petersburg for a fourth season, and on November 20, 1846, she being then in Berlin, Turgenev wrote to her that the coming year would bring her one more auditor at the *Opern-haus* there. "What a wonderful thing it is," he writes in a subsequent letter, "the mere possibility of telling you *'au revoir'*!"

11

THE DARK LADY

Three months later Turgenev was applauding Pauline Viardot in *Les Huguenots* at the opera house of the Prussian capital. Berlin revisited after half a dozen years appeared to him a changed city. Bettina no longer dyed her hair, Max Stirner looked tame and sad, Schelling was silent, and Werder, unserenaded, expounded Hegelian logic, as Turgenev wrote home, to an audience of three students, of whom only one was German, and he a Pomeranian. The Left Hegelians fared no better. Alone the influence of Feuerbach's iconoclasm sustained itself, Turgenev believed, amidst the general indifference to speculative thought. He sensed the end of what he called "the literary, theorizing, philosophic, fantastic epoch of German life." His acute perception of this change he owed to the fact that a parallel process was going on within himself. Another decade will pass, and he will be unable to understand his own notes on the lectures he had attended in Berlin. Indeed, his was a harder, more realistic mind, no longer dallying in the metaphysical playground, rather fitting itself to the harness of literature.

He followed Mme. Viardot to Dresden in the spring of the year. With him went the consumptive Belinsky, a veritable babe in the woods away from home, who threw himself upon his friend as upon a nurse. After twelve days there, which cannot have offered the young man many glimpses of his idol, although he stopped at the same hotel as the Viardots, Turgenev accompanied the invalid Belinsky to Salzbrunn, where the latter was sent to take the cure. There the two were joined by the plump and practical Annenkov, a wealthy landowner and born satellite, who was to become Turgenev's lifelong friend, factotum, and guide in the conduct of his literary affairs, "a rock amidst the agitated sea," as the novelist was to put it, and from late May to the close of June the air of the quiet Silesian watering place was stirred by many discussions in a strange tongue. It was here that the ailing critic wrote Gogol the letter of furious invective against the infamy of serfdom, the plague of bureaucracy, and the abomination of the official church, which, spread in innumerable handwritten copies, became the manifesto of Russian liberalism. This letter, which was instrumental in sending Dostoevsky to Siberia,* Turgenev accepted as his credo.

It was nearly midsummer when, after a brief visit to London, Turgenev came to port at last at the Château de Courtavenel. The estate of the Viardots lay about forty miles south-east of Paris, in the midst of the meadows and forests of Brie. The castle was a moss-grown structure, dating back to Henri IV, with all the feudal appurtenances of turrets, drawbridge, and moat, and a rear view which reminded the châtelaine of a jolly grocer. Summering here, the owners opened its gates to their relatives and friends. The household adopted the young Russian, and he in turn responded with an all-inclusive gesture of affection. The castle offered him the spaciousness, if not the abundance, to which Spasskoye had accustomed him, without its offending brutalities, and here too there were game in the brush and fish in the streams. In the drawing room, moreover, there was frequently music, which may have been to Turgenev, as it was to Orsino, "the food of love," but which also satisfied an impersonal and permanent appetite. And above all, whether or not the hostess was there in the flesh, Courtavenel provided the exquisite reassurance of her presence.

The château was, however, only a summer home, and when the singer left for her autumn and winter tour in Germany, Turgenev, like her mother, moved to Paris. This was the first of several separations during the three years he

---

* The reading aloud of Belinsky's letter at radical gatherings was one of the charges against Dostoevsky, when in 1849 he was tried and condemned to capital punishment, which was commuted to a term of hard labor in Siberia.

spent in France. Far from weakening the bond between them, the months of her absence seemed to deepen his feeling for Pauline.

It was impossible for him to follow her in her peregrinations because of lack of funds. He had left Russia with a very modest sum in his pockets and his tailor's bill of two hundred rubles still unpaid, not to mention other debts. Three lean years, financially speaking, were ahead of him. Remittances from home were few and far between, and he was virtually thrown upon his own resources. He had gone abroad against his mother's wishes and she did not let him forget it. She kept saying, "I must send Vanichka some money," but seldom did so. In acknowledging, on Christmas Day, 1849, the receipt of three hundred rubles from an editor, he wrote that the money had saved him from death by starvation.

Unweariedly he pored over the papers that recorded the prima donna's triumphs. When, during a later solitary stay at Courtavenel, an aunt of Pauline's, on leaving the château, lent the penniless Turgenev thirty francs, he used them on a trip to Paris simply to read in eight papers the English press notices of the singer's London successes. While she was preparing for her début in *Le Prophète,* he wrote: "In Heaven's name, let me know in advance the day of the first performance. . . . That night somebody at Courtavenel will not go to bed before midnight." He kept his promise and wrote to her as the clock struck the hours which, he presumed, called her before the curtain. The same somebody applauded her in effigy and threw flowers to her portrait, which, he said, "unfortunately does not resemble you." He was a critical admirer. He advised Mme. Viardot, he cautioned her, and there is ground for believing that she deferred to his opinions on music and acting.

He was solicitous about her health, repeatedly begging her to take care of it and warning her against overwork at rehearsals. On January 4, 1848 he wrote to her:

I know where you are staying; isn't it near the Brandenburger Thor? You will excuse me if I allow myself to speak about certain details of your apartment. Why are certain regions of it which are only referred to by their English name—perhaps because the English are most discreet in their vocabulary—why are these regions subjected to the inclemency of the elements and the rigors of cold? Please be careful, and do something about it. It's more serious than it appears at first blush, especially at this season of grippe and rheumatism. You will probably laugh at me and the subject which I mention in my letter. I see from here how you smile, raising your right shoulder and inclining your head in the same direction (that's your customary gesture and I advise you not to give it up, because it is very beautiful, especially when it is accompanied by a peculiar little grimace).

In Paris Turgenev found a room for himself near the Palais Royal and settled down to plain living and earnest writing. When the wolf howled at the door he threw his inkbottle at it. He spent long mornings at his desk. He gave hours to the study of Pauline's native tongue. He read widely in several other languages as well. He discovered compatriots, old friends like Bakunin and new ones like Herzen, the future memoirist and brilliant, if brittle, forensic writer, who, like himself, had left Russia the previous year. He saw much of Pavel Annenkov, whom he described to Mme. Viardot as "an excellent fellow whose mind is as fine as his body is fat." The incipient novelist spent much of his time getting the education that one could pick up in the streets, the cafés, the galleries, concert halls, theatres of the Paris of the late forties.

Through his pages he scattered, as had been his mother's habit, slight precise sketches of men and beasts. The storyteller peers out in such passages as this, from a letter of January 19, 1849:

I have made the acquaintance of two dogs: one communicative, gay, flighty, with little or no education, witty, fond of banter, something of a rogue, on the best terms with everyone and, to tell the truth, without true dignity; the other: gentle, wistful, lazy, gluttonous, steeped in Lamartine, ingratiating and disdainful at the same time. We frequent the same café. The first belongs, if a dog can be said to belong, to a little army surgeon, very lean and very crabbed; the other has for a mistress the cashier, a little old woman who has worn out her teeth chewing on kind thoughts.

A letter would lie on his desk for days, until, when finally mailed, it assumed the character of a diary. He kept his correspondent informed of what he did with his time, filled pages with accounts of his reading and writing, with comments on music and musicians, with domestic details. He recounted his dreams—dreams were of particular interest to him, and he attributed hidden meanings to them. And there were his opinions on life and literature. Often they carry a sting. Modern playwrights, he says, "have read a great deal and have not lived at all." In giving Belinsky the literary news of Paris at about the same time, he can mention only "eunuchs, pigmies and bluestockings." Current art, he tells Pauline, is marked by a mediocrity infected with exhibitionism, the writing "stinks of literature." And he quotes the Bible to her: "We are like dogs returning to their vomit," adding: "There is neither God nor Satan any more, and the advent of Man is far off." He attributes the lamentable state of arts and letters to the fact that life is atomized, there is no bond among people, no great general movements. Industry, he ventures, may be "the liberator and regenerator of mankind," concluding: "the greatest poets of our age are, in my opinion, the Americans, who are planning to pierce the isthmus of Panama and talk of laying a transoceanic cable." He looks forward to a new literature after the consummation of what he calls "the social revolution," without troubling to be any more explicit.

Such were his reflections as he watched *The Bench of Boobies,* a revue at the Palais Royal. He found it amusing, "but, my God," he exclaims, "how anemic, pale, flabby, pitiful all this is, compared to what, I don't say Aristophanes, but some pupil of his, could have done with the material. Ah, what wouldn't I give to see a fantastic, extravagant, jeering, touching comedy, pitiless toward everything that is weak and bad in society and even in man himself. . . . But no, we are forever delivered into Scribe's power!"

Whoever thirsts for pure, living waters must go back to the literature of the past. For the moment he is deep in Calderon. There is a giant, an extraordinary genius, "the greatest Catholic playwright, as Shakespeare is the greatest human, the greatest anti-Christian one." He finds strength and grandeur in the Spaniard's unshakable faith, but something repellent and cruel in his credo. True, this humbling of man before the divine will, Turgenev argues, this conception of *grace* as indifferent to virtue and vice—all this is a triumph of the human mind, since a being who so boldly acknowledges his utter insignificance thereby rises to the height of the strange Deity of whom he believes himself to be the plaything and who is, of course, his own creation. "Nevertheless," he continues, "I prefer Prometheus, Satan, their rebellion and individualism. Atom though I may be, I am my own master; I want truth, not salvation, and I expect it from my reason, not from grace."

He has conceived a strong distaste for both the rituals and the spirit of traditional religion. He finds Pascal's *Lettres Provinciales* admirable: "Everything is there: good sense, eloquence, comic verse. And yet it is the work of a slave, a slave of Catholicism." The reading of a book on Christianity moves him to write to Pauline: "You cannot imagine the painful effect produced by all these legends of martyrs, all these flagellations, processions, the worship of relics, these autos-da-fé, this ferocious contempt for life, this horror of women, all these wounds and all this blood!" He witnesses a funeral mass at Hyères, and his description of the spectacle —the coffin draped with a black pall, the yellow candles— winds up with the declaration that he prefers the wide sky of the ancients, the oakwood pyre and the games.

Mme. Viardot was not the woman to be shocked by these tirades, with their echoes of Aeschylus and, especially, Feuerbach (on December 7, 1847, Turgenev wrote her that of all the German philosophers Feuerbach was "the only *man,* the only character, the only talent.") Yet she could not have been fully in sympathy with her admirer's inconoclasm, accustomed though she was to the companionship of unbelievers. Writing to a friend a dozen years later, she said that her mother, combining much Catholic superstition with a total lack of religion, was not sure that God existed, but would not swear that there was no Devil, while her late father had believed in neither God nor Devil. As for herself, she could not formulate her faith, but was firmly convinced that the soul was immortal and that *"tous les amours se trouveront un jour."* She added: "All I know is that there is in us a divine spark which does not perish and which will end by forming part of the great light."

In the second year of his stay abroad Turgenev's peaceful

routine was broken by a political upheaval. At six o'clock in the morning of February 26, 1848, he was lying abed in a Brussels hotel when he heard a man shouting: "France has become a republic!" He hurried back to Paris, reaching the city as soon as torn-up tracks and a wrecked train allowed him, and arrived in time to see cockaded workmen taking the barricades apart. Bakunin had rushed from Brussels to Paris a day or two earlier; he went to participate where his friend went to watch. The first days in Paris Turgenev was "in a daze," as he put it later. He loitered in the streets for hours. He heard Rachel, draped in the tri-color, sing the Marseillaise in her "sepulchral voice." He followed, not very closely, the course of the revolution.

During those historic weeks he was an habitué at the apartment of a Russian general of liberal views by the name of Tuchkov who was staying in Paris with his wife and two daughters. Returning early in May from Rome, the Herzen household, which included several young women, settled in the same house, and it became a kind of Russian center. It was not a cheerful place; most of the company saw signs of the failure of the people's cause. It was Turgenev's role to clown it among the mourners. He played chess with the General and amused the ladies with mimicry and tomfoolery of sorts. He perched on the window sill and crowed like a cock; he draped himself in Mme. Herzen's black velvet cape and acted the madman till the women shivered and begged him to stop. When all diversions palled, he would avail himself of any unoccupied couch with a genius for curling up his big body in the smallest possible space. He brought his favorite gardenia scent to Natalie Tuchkova, who was eventually to become Herzen's mistress after having been the wife of his intimate friend, Ogaryov. Both she and Mme. Herzen, who had heart-to-heart talks with him, found him dumb on the subject of Pauline.

He was still in Paris during the sultry June days when the red flag was wagging from the new barricades like "a sharp, evil tongue," as he phrased it retrospectively. One of these barricades he was to choose as the place for the futile death of his Hamletic hero, Rudin. He saw something of the fighting and of the savage suppression of the insurrection. One day he narrowly escaped arrest by a national guardsman from the provinces on the suspicion of being a Russian agent fomenting trouble. By that time the meteoric Bakunin was no longer in Paris. He had gone to Germany on money borrowed from the provisional government (according to his friend, Herzen, he accepted money from strangers as children do from their parents), in order to rouse the Poles in the Duchy of Posen against the Czar.

Turgenev soon shook the bloodstained dust of the capital from his feet and went home, as it were, to Courtavenel, where he presumably stayed most of the summer. In October he traveled through southern France, and Pauline received letters from him dated Hyères, Toulon, Lyons. On the whole, he found France "decidedly unbeautiful." He seemed to dislike the country in which the woman he loved was to keep him so many years of his life. Hadn't Belinsky, a twelvemonth since, called it a land of shame and its face the cuspidor of all the nations of Europe? A fortnight before returning to the capital Turgenev wrote to tell Pauline that on the fifth of November she might expect one more guest at table in her little Chinese salon. "I demand," he added, "a charlotte russe that day." Having arrived at the appointed time, he was forthwith taken ill. Writing home early in December, Herzen informed their common friends that Turgenev was "suffering severely from his eternal illness." It was apparently bladder trouble, which was to attack him again some years later.

During that winter he was a daily visitor at the Herzens. What with the defeat of the revolution and with reaction triumphant, the house was enveloped in gloom. Among the crowd of radicals who frequented it the host made a distinction between those who, like himself, were engaged in an autopsy of the old world and the quacks who offered socialist nostrums for the cure of its ills. Turgenev belonged to neither group and could have contributed little to their acrimonious wrangling. In any event, he was a welcome guest. Early next summer, when Paris was being ravaged by cholera, Herzen himself nursed him through what he believed to be an attack of the dread disease. The patient maintained that he could smell it—a reek of dampness, toadstools, and of an old, abandoned, foul place. "A natural coward," Herzen wrote to a friend, "for three days he (Turgenev) lamented his end." In his relief at convalescing he made an attempt, which proved futile, to compose a song, both words and music.

Then came a third summer at Courtavenel. Part of the time his hosts were away, yet he lived, so he wrote Pauline, as in an enchanted castle, where the table spread itself and the linen laundered itself. He had his old room with its friendly willow-green wallpaper. It goes without saying that he was lonely. He wrote the singer that he had seen her in his dream, bending over the ship's screw and looking at the white foam on the green water. For a while he was alone with the cook Véronique, and he threw out the suggestion that he might marry her to reward her for her services, inasmuch as any other mode of payment was a chimera to him. He amused himself by hanging literary allusions on the trees about the place, naming a certain chestnut Hermann and seeking for a Dorothea, calling a particular elm Alarmed Virtue, and the like. The weather was glorious, and he noticed, among other things, that "in calm weather a poplar has the look of a schoolboy, and a very stupid look, except in the evening when the leaves seem almost black against the pink sky. But in that case there must be complete calm, alone the leaves on the treetops being permitted to stir slightly."

He chatters to his absent hostess "like a magpie who has remained an old maid." He gives her accounts of the rat that was caught in the kitchen after a long chase; the belligerent little white demon of a cock that has an aversion to him, the gnats that turn his body, like Hippolytus', into one wound, the leveret that drowned in the moat. "Is it suicide?" he asks. "Not likely; at his age one still believes in happiness." At Spasskoye he used to spend delicious hours lying on the grass and listening to what he called "the noises of the earth." Now he enumerates the sounds he heard one July evening as he was standing on the bridge over the moat. Among other noises he distinguished the chirping of four cicadas in the trees and "the faint splash made by the fish on the surface of the water, which resembled the sounds of a kiss."

The same letter, dated July 6, contains a list of the books he has read at Courtavenel, with comments: four works of history, including a manual by "a Catholic-democrat—such an unnatural union can only produce monsters"; two books on Napoleon, one of them "the work of a refined flunkey, if a flunkey can be refined"; Lady Montagu's *Letters,* "a charming book"; a historical novella in Spanish—"puerile"; Vergil's *Georgics* in Delille's translation—"I couldn't finish it; it is very colorless, and these Alexandrines flow with such disgusting facility, they are thin and insipid like water; the original, too, is nothing very marvelous; all this Latin literature is cold and artificial, a littérateur's literature"; Voltaire's *La Pucelle* —"generally speaking, very boring. . . But some wonderful phrases, daring and witty allusions, searing, blood-letting gibes show the great master"; the Koran—"I have only started reading it. There is grandeur and good sense in this book, but the oriental bombast and obscurity of the prophetic language will soon disgust me."

His position at Courtavenel was somewhat ambiguous. He stayed on in the ill-defined capacity of one who, without being a pensioner, was not exactly a guest. Whether because of friendly interest or a nagging sense of obligation, he tried to make himself useful, weeding the garden, clearing the moat of rushes, teaching little Louise German, arranging the library. Occasionally he reveals his uneasiness. "I feel as though I look like a braggart," he writes, "but at bottom I am just a little boy. I have my tail between my legs and I am seated very shabbily and miserably on my haunches, like a dog who feels that he is being made fun of and who looks vaguely out of the corner of his eye, blinking as if dazzled by the sun. . ."

In general, his letters to Pauline are marked by a cheerful equanimity and effortless humor, and their tone is one of profound solicitude and deferential friendship. Yet the springs of passion sometimes agitated their calm surface. Heine's *"Madame, ich liebe Sie"* seems to be the quintessence of these chatty bulletins. Whether or not her letters to Turgenev have been destroyed, they have not, unfortunately, been made public. Was the singer the passive recipient of his adoration? Did she reciprocate his feeling? Were they lovers? The tenderness and outspokenness of a phrase here and there in his letters, which were published, it should be noted, after her death, suggest the possibility, though by no means the certainty, of an affirmative answer to the last question. A missive dated Lyons, October 13, 1848 (they had spent part of the previous summer together at Courtavenel) opens thus: "Good day, dearest, best, most precious lady, good day, unique being!" In the course of it he confesses that he had tried to write a poem to her, but failed: "I could only look, dream, remember." He ends by calling down God's blessings on her, "the dearest angel," and he signs himself: "Your old dear friend." On July 11, 1849, he writes: "Dear, precious being! I think of you every moment, of pleasure (*Vergnügen*), of the future. Write me even on little scraps of paper—you know what . . . You are the best of all that exists on earth." And again, on July 23: "I cannot tell you how often I thought of you all day long. On my way back [from a country festival] I called your name so furiously (*entrüstet*), I stretched out my arms with such longing that you must have heard and seen me." After declaring that his vows and wishes for her success are strong enough to uproot oaks, he concludes: "Dear, precious one! May God be with you and bless you! (*Liebe, teuere! Gott sei mit dir und segne dich!*"). This employment of the intimate second person singular is unique in the correspondence, but not so the use of German in the warmest passages of the letters. The language may have had a sentimental aura for him, associated as it was with his youthful romanticism. It was a tongue of which Louis Viardot had no knowledge, as he admitted on a page of his *Souvenirs de chasse*.

The letter of July 23, 1849, quoted above, contains this remark, in German: "What is the matter with Viardot? Is he perhaps annoyed at my staying here [at Courtavenel]?" Yet the relations between Turgenev and Pauline's husband seem to have been uniformly cordial. They shared the pleasures of the chase and the younger man did not hesitate to borrow money from the older. On June 24, 1850, just before his departure for Russia, Turgenev wrote to Viardot: "I do not want to leave France, my dear good friend, without having told you how much I love and esteem you, and how I regret the necessity of this separation. I shall not feel truly happy until at your side, rifle in hand, I can once more beat the brush of dear Brie." It is difficult to believe that Turgenev was writing thus to a man whom he had cuckolded.

12

"I AM CHAINED TO

THE EARTH"

Undoubtedly Turgenev did not remain untouched by the fever of joyous excitement into which the news of the February revolution threw the liberal and radical circles everywhere. But his interest in the political drama that unfolded before his eyes was not profound. What in a letter to Pauline he called *"politisches Pathos"* was not, he felt, part of his make-up. The streets of revolutionary Paris had taught him the rudiments of the class struggle, but the lesson made no lasting impression. He had but a feeble grasp on the events that he had such ample opportunities to watch and such well-informed friends to interpret for him.

On May 15, 1848, the workers made an unsuccessful attempt to dissolve the Constituent Assembly and, in the words of Marx, "to regain their former revolutionary influence." That day Herzen tramped the streets from morning till night, caught between hope and dismay. Until then he had believed that with the establishment of the republic the power of the bourgeoisie had been broken. May 15 opened his eyes. With a heavy heart he admitted to himself that the revolution was defeated.

Turgenev was in the crowd that watched the demonstrators as they marched toward the Assembly, and, indeed, described his impressions in a letter to the singer. It is an account set down by an artist more concerned with the minutiæ of the spectacle than with the significance of the political event. He notes that the shouts of *Vive la Pologne!* (a slogan adopted by the demonstrators in protest against the refusal of the Provisional Government to help the Polish insurgents) were more sinister than the cries of *Vive la république!* because of the difference between the vowels "o" and "u." The peddlers of cigars and licorice water who circulated in the throng that packed the Place de la Concorde, he observes, were "avid, satisfied and indifferent" and looked like "fishermen bringing in a heavily laden net." He could not make out what the people crowding the square wanted, what they feared, with whom they sided—they appeared to wait apathetically for "the end of the storm." Irresolution and confusion prevailed. "What is history, then?" he asks, as he sees it in the making, "Providence, chance, irony, fatality?" He gives up his aloof objectivity when he remarks that, after the demonstrators have been dispersed, "order, the bourgeois, have triumphed, with reason."

Not that he had definitely ranged himself with the bourgeoisie. He watched the June insurrection and its bloody finale as "a flâneur," a neutral "fighting on neither side of the barricades," to use his own words. His *Recollections of Life and Letters* include a touching account of an episode in the history of those days: at the risk of being summarily shot a French workman makes his way into the enemy's camp in order to reassure a father, a bourgeois father, of his child's safety. These pages are a tribute to the moral nobility of the simple old laborer as well as of the comrades at whose bidding he had carried out the mission. The sketch concludes with the remark that twenty-two years later such people were burning Paris and shooting hostages. He set down the incident not to exalt the workingman but to illustrate the complexity of the human heart.

The June massacres affected Herzen and some of his friends like a personal tragedy. He regretted that he had not accepted the rifle a workman had offered him on the Place Maubert and died on a barricade: "I should then have taken with me to the grave two or three beliefs." His wife dared not wish that her children would live, lest history treat them to the horrors it had shown her. To Herzen the defeat of the revolution meant the bankruptcy of political democracy and indeed of Western civilization generally. He was still committed to a vague variety of ethical socialism as a way out of the impasse, but he decided that the European nations were powerless to achieve it. He did not remain disconsolate long.

In his disillusionment with the West he turned hopefully eastward, and, like the very Slavophils whom he had scorned a few years earlier, conceived the idea that salvation would come from the common folk of his native land: with what he believed to be their egalitarian and collectivist tradition, embodied in the village commune, their hostility toward centralized government, they would bring about the triumph of socialism and thus open the way to a better civilization.

Turgenev shared neither Herzen's despair nor his new faith. Looking east and west, he was inclined to cry a plague on both their houses. He wrote Pauline, on June 20, 1849: "The poor Hungarians! An honorable man will end by not knowing where to live. The young nations are still barbarous, like my dear compatriots, or else if they rise and want to march, they are crushed like the Hungarians, and the old nations, rotten and gangrenous as they are, are dying and spreading infection." He went on dismally: "And then, who said that man is born to be free? History proves the contrary. It was not in the spirit of the courtier that Goethe wrote his famous line: *'Der Mensch ist nicht geboren frei zu sein.'* It is simply a fact, a truth, which he announced as the exact observer of Nature that he was."

"Man is not born to be free." The events Turgenev witnessed supported other unpleasant opinions of his about human nature, especially as it functions in crowds. He remained nevertheless a libertarian, a believer in the power of enlightenment to prepare the individual for a life of freedom, an upholder of the democratic principles proclaimed by the great French Revolution. Russian military successes against the Hungarian rebels prompt this outburst on his part: "To the devil with national sentiment! For a man with a heart there is only one fatherland—democracy, and if the Russians are victorious, it will receive its death blow." He puts kings and armies on a par with hail and cholera as an indication that God may be a misanthrope, and in a letter to Mme. Viardot, dated July 6, 1849, he launches into a diatribe against Napoleon and incidentally against government: ". . . this hideous phantom, which, hollow, stupid, incapable of producing anything, with the word Order in its mouth, a sword in one hand and gold in the other, is crushing us all under its iron heel."

In thus voicing the animus against Leviathan, which Ba-kunin was to erect into an extremist ideology, and in speaking of the gangrenous old nations, Turgenev was probably echoing his friend Herzen, to whom he was close at the time. In more than one respect, however, their thinking was at variance. While Herzen, at least temporarily, welcomed "the chaos and destruction" that would annihilate the old world root and branch, making room for a new and just order, Turgenev instinctively shrank from the use of force for political ends, dreading its dangerous potential.

He was temperamentally opposed to violence, and he may have avoided political commitment because he recognized that his responsibility lay elsewhere. It was in these years that he began to find himself as a writer. His business was with men and women, their social setting, their ways of thinking and acting. Doctrines concerned him only in so far as they affected persons. The natural world had his closest attention, and he soon accepted the fact that it had no regard for human values. The soul, he writes to Pauline, is but "a feeble radi-ance that ancient night eternally seeks to swallow." Nature can be beautiful, but it is mindless and brutal. "The night-ingale may throw us into delicious ecstasies while an unhappy half-crushed insect is dying in its crop." He will eventually see even a garden, apparently all peace and loveliness, as actually a field of carnage where creatures ferociously devour each other. Feuerbach, who had helped to weaken the attrac-tion that the transcendental had held for him in his youth, may have confirmed him in his view of Nature as a force wholly indifferent to man's concerns and aspirations, indeed, in its blind ruthlessness, hostile to them. This will remain a firm intellectual premise for Turgenev. And yet in his fictions the natural world is not seldom humanized, and seems in harmony with man's feelings, responding to them as well as evoking them. Certain aspects of Nature speak to the heart from his pages in the accents of serenity and joy.

Knowing that life is frail and doomed, he cherishes it all the more. On the first of May, 1848, he was wandering alone for hours in the woods not far from Paris. At night he was writing to Pauline:

I cannot see without emotion a bough covered with young green leaves clearly outlined against the blue sky. Why? Yes, why? Is it because of the contrast between this little living sprig, which sways at the least breath, which I can break, which must die, but which a generous sap animates and colors—and this eternal and empty immensity, this sky, which is blue and radiant only owing to the earth? . . . Oh, I cannot bear the sky! But life, its reality, its caprices, its fortuitousness, its habits, its ephemeral beauty—all that I adore. I am chained to the earth. I should prefer to contemplate the precipitate movements of a duck on the edge of a marsh, as it scratches the back of its head with a wet foot, or the long glistening drops of water, slowly falling from the muzzle of a motionless cow, who has just drunk from a pond in which she stands knee-deep—I should prefer to contemplate these rather than all that the cherubim can behold in the heavens.

Turgenev shares Heine's willingness to leave heaven to the angels and the sparrows, but whereas the poet was speaking in obedience to his social conscience, the future novelist expresses the consciousness of the artist. In thus testifying to his growing self-knowledge he offers the earliest clue to his style. He was now composing most of his plays and the pieces that were to form his *Hunter's Notes,* better known as *A Sportsman's Sketches.* Both at the château and in Paris he worked hard and steadily. He was to tell a friend that Courtavenel was "the cradle" of his "fame." In 1847-50 he wrote at least twice as much as in any equivalent period during the forty years of his literary activity. His mind functioned with uncommon facility and his brain tired no sooner than his hand. "Never have ideas come to me in such abundance," he told Pauline in a letter. "They have presented themselves by the dozen. I have felt like a poor devil of an innkeeper in a small town who finds himself suddenly swamped by an avalanche of guests and ends by not knowing where to lodge his crowd."

In trying his hand at playwriting, Turgenev was at once responding to a native impulse and yielding to that interest in the theatre which was as much Pauline's as were her personal effects. After a rather unpromising start in the shape of a parody of the cloak-and-dagger Spanish drama in the manner of Prosper Mérimée, he went on to compose, in quick succession, plays of a different cast, drawing his materials mostly from the life of the petty provincial gentry in the native set-

ting. He was not the man to produce anything remotely resembling the Aristophanesque comedy for which he had expressed a longing, even if Russian censorship had permitted
it. He wrote a number of light pieces, not altogether dissimi-
lar from the offerings of Scribe and Musset, which he had
found amusing if worthless. But in Turgenev's playlets the
farcical element and the badinage do not muffle a note of
social criticism that was anything but soothing to his audience.
They show the gentry in a decidedly unattractive light. Then
there are the more substantial pieces, comedies not of situation
but of character, depending on "internal action," quite in the
vein of Chekhov. The most notable example is *A Month
in the Country,* one of his two full-length plays. It centers,
like Balzac's *La Marâtre* (the première of which, on May 25,
1848, Turgenev may have witnessed), on the struggle between
a young girl and a mature woman for a youth's affections. It
should be noted that in 1844 he started a one-acter, which
has remained unfinished, about two sisters in love with the
same man.

Watching his one-acter, *The Bachelor*—his first piece to
reach the boards—he came to the conclusion, as he wrote
Pauline on December 8, 1850, that he had "a theatrical voca-
tion." But, partly under the influence of unfavorable notices,
he soon gave up the idea of himself as a playwright. Indeed,
his gifts demanded a less confining medium than drama. He
grew to dislike his plays as he disliked his verse. But he included the former, ten of them all told, in his collected works
as closet pieces. "Unsatisfactory on the stage," he wrote in
his preface to them, "they may be of some interest as reading matter." Yet he had composed them for the theatre, with
particular actors in mind, and when, under Alexander II,
the rigors of censorship somewhat abated, most of them were
produced, and with considerable, if intermittent, success,
several surviving down to the Soviet period. Some were also
applauded by foreign audiences. *A Month in the Country,*
completed in 1850 in Paris, was not allowed to be printed
until five years later and then in a version mutilated by the
censor, a widow having been substituted for the wife in the
interests of propriety. The text was provided with a note by
the playwright to the effect that it was not a comedy but "a

tale in dramatic form, obviously unfit for the stage." First produced in 1872, it has achieved a permanent place in the Russian repertory, especially owing to its revival by the Moscow Art Theatre in 1909 for the generation that exalted Chekhov. In the mid-twentieth century an English version of it was staged in New York.

The origin of *A Sportsman's Sketches* was more casual than the subsequent career of the book might suggest. The first sketch appeared in the initial number of *Sovrennenik* (*The Contemporary*), a Petersburg monthly, which had been started by Pushkin and in 1847 taken over by Nekrasov, with Turgenev's and especially Belinsky's active assistance. The sketch was used as more or less of a filler, and was tucked away in the back pages among the miscellaneous items. Turgenev gave it to the editor just before leaving for the West and with no intention of picking up the thread again. He still considered himself primarily a poet. Yet so warmly was the first piece welcomed that he soon found himself writing a series, the title of which was supplied by the editor.

The result was a group of narratives, ranging from the sketch with a documentary slant to the formal short story, and concluding with a lyrical encomium to his favorite sport and its background of forest and steppe. The narrator, tacitly identified with the author, observes his neighbors at their dinner tables and the peasants in the enforced and withal relished comradeship of the hunt. These pages fill the lungs and clear the eyes. Agreeably, if a little too complacently, the story halts like a leisured traveler to abandon itself to the odors of woods and fields, the warm smell of hay and horses, to the colors of the hilly patchwork of plowed and fallow ground. Everywhere Turgenev shows that love of landscape which the painter Kuo Hsi ascribes only to the virtuous. The landscape evoked is that of central Russia, where the forest yields to the steppe.

The men and women who pass across this natural background hold to the distinct social planes on which they live and move and have their being. The book is an album of likenesses, each sharply visualized. There are the masters and the class that keeps them. Townspeople scarcely figure here. Among the serfs who catch Turgenev's eye are those who possess dignity and moral resources and, with some alloy of superstition, a certain spirituality. His sympathy for the underdog does not, however, blur his vision. A member of the kept class himself, he harbors a sense of guilt, and in consequence idealizes the peasants, but only to a slight degree. He draws them with full appreciation of their humanity, yet makes no attempt to gloss over the brutalizing effect of their position or conceal the fact that, given half a chance, they can turn into ruthless despoilers of their fellows. In "The Singers" he discovers a group of villagers in a moment of aesthetic enjoyment which mounts to a fine frenzy, but he concludes on a sordid note: the crowd, including the singer, drunk and turned abject; across the foggy field one boy calling another home to be whipped. Wisely enough, Turgenev limits his observation to house serfs or, generally speaking, peasants who have slipped out of the routine ways. The average tiller of the soil in normal circumstances—of whom he had, after all, very slight knowledge—is not in the picture.

The men gain by contrast with their masters. Not evil by nature, these are shown as hopelessly corrupted by limitless power over the human beings they own. Unobtrusively, sometimes by a casual remark, the author lays bare their sense of caste, their grossness, their cruelty toward their serfs, and stresses their managerial ineptitude. There is the cultivated gentleman who has his servant flogged for failing to warm his wine, the several landowners who sell their serfs to gratify a private whim, along with the impoverished gentry who see no way to get their dinners except as hangers-on. The fiery Chertopkhanov, with his exaggerated sense of honor, is the white crow of the flock.

One recognizes in the author the man who was revolted by his mother's behavior toward her serfs, but did not interfere with it. To a certain extent the creature of his caste, he cannot completely identify himself with the peasant. While sensitive to the moods of nature, he lacks the feeling for the soil that dominates him who tills it. The book poses the problem of serfdom from the viewpoint of one who abominates the institution, but there is nothing of the tract about it. The abolitionist never shouts down the story teller. The author's attitude is that of a bystander observing the scene before him.

Fully half of the tales ignore the sore subject altogether. They are socially neutral studies of people and situations. Such, for example, is "The Tryst," which defines what Henry James called the "great constringent relation between man and woman" in the terms of a dandified flunkey aping his betters and a simple-minded peasant girl whom he is casually dismissing from his affections. Such, again, is the tale of the country doctor and a death-bed passion told in a manner which anticipates Chekhov. "The Hamlet of the Shchigry District" is the history of a neurotic given to sterile self-analysis and self-flagellation, the type that Dostoevsky was to vivisect more acutely in "Notes from the Underground" some twelve years later. This sketch contains a jaundiced version of Turgenev's German period. The note of wistful retrospection which sounds throughout his work yields here to scorn and skepticism.

There is little overt drama in *A Sportsman's Sketches,* and the general effect is that of a portfolio of pastels and etchings. The author stands outside looking in, a position which allows him perspective but makes for a somewhat chilling detachment. At the same time he has an immense curiosity about people and is, further, able to set down what he sees with a sure, if delicate, touch. The book possesses that combination of parochialism and universality that is the mark of a classic.

13

"BONNE NUIT, MAMAN"

Paris and Courtavenel alike had roused in Turgenev a nostalgia, traces of which appear in *A Sportsman's Sketches*. His thoughts kept returning to the shapes, the odors, the colors, of his native scene: unkempt villages, the thatched roofs huddling together under a mild sky; caravans of slow carts creaking along dust-padded roads; white, humble churches rising out of the dun plain; an unhurried beggar etched against the green hemp patch; the moist smell of the forests; and the tilled fields, huge and monotonous, hunching themselves slightly on the horizon and rolling on beyond. On a summer day in 1849 he saw a gray crow in the fields around the château. "The sight of this compatriot moves me," he wrote to Mme. Viardot. "I take off my hat to him and ask him for news of my country." He turned the incident into a joke, making a quatrain on it à la Béranger.

During the winter of 1849-50 he had made up his mind to return to Russia in the spring. But to do so he needed much more than his fare, for he had run up a number of debts. He could not count on his mother for help. "My break with Maminka is now final," he informed an editor on Christmas Day, 1849, in a letter which has already been mentioned, "and *I have to earn my daily bread*." But Varvara Petrovna, taken seriously ill, relented and remitted the necessary rubles on condition that he return home without fail.

On June 29, 1850, Turgenev embarked at Stettin for Petersburg. The previous month he had revisited Courtavenel to bid adieu to the place, and on the nineteenth he was writing to his hostess, who was filling an engagement in Germany: "Frankly, I am as happy as a child to be here . . . Russia will wait—that immense and somber figure, immobile and veiled like Oedipus' sphinx. It will swallow me later. I seem to see it fixing its heavy, inert gaze upon me with gloomy attention, as befits eyes of stone. Don't fret, sphinx; I shall come back to you and you will be able to devour me at your ease if I don't guess your riddle! Leave me in peace a little while longer! I shall come back to your steppes!" His last meeting with Pauline was on June 17. This was probably in Paris. On the day he left the city, a week later, he addressed a farewell letter to her husband. "No doubt, one's country has its rights," he wrote, "but the true fatherland—is it not where one has found the most affection, where the heart and the spirit feel at ease? There is no place on earth which I love as much as Courtavenel."

He was returning to Russia with a heavy heart. To the ache of separation from Pauline was added the disagreeable foretaste of what he might expect at home. The February Revolution is France had started a severe reaction in the empire of the czars. Never before had censorship been so umbrageous and implacable. Two months after the Paris events Turgenev's former professor at the University of Petersburg, a man of most conservative views, and himself a censor, made this entry in his diary: "Terror has seized all thinking and writing people." Turgenev knew that his aloofness from politics would afford him small protection. His friends, Bakunin and Herzen, had decided to expatriate themselves. The thought had crossed his mind, too, but only to be rejected.

The prospect of facing the mistress of Spasskoye was equally depressing. He suspected that her temper had scarcely been improved by illness. Varvara Petrovna was exasperated with hope deferred. In the summer of 1848 she had been preparing for the reception of her "Benjamin," as she called her absent son. But he did not come. The next winter she again pressed him to return and sent him six hundred rubles. In the summer Spasskoye resumed preparations against his coming. His wing was being renovated and the flower garden put in order. The poplar-circled pond where as a boy he had gone sailing with his brother Nikolay, and which had dried up, was being cleaned; and on the bank facing the highroad Varvara Petrovna erected a signpost with the inscription *"Ils reviendront."* But no son of hers came along that road.

When, a year later, Ivan finally arrived, his mother received him in her town house with every sign of rejoicing. By that time her elder son, with his impossible spouse—their children had died in the meantime—was also living in Moscow. Varvara Petrovna had summoned him from Petersburg, and after a delay of four years, recognized his marriage, though refusing to receive his wife. She had done this, stipulating that he retire from the service and manage her estates for her. She had dismissed the man who had succeeded Uncle Nikolay as her steward. She bought a house for her elder son and provided him with servants, horses and carriages, but failed to supply him with money with which to run the establishment. This intolerable situation was aggravated by the fact that he and his wife were injured in an accident and needed expensive medical care.

Ivan did not fare much better. His mother gave him generously of her time, but was niggardly with his pocket money, so that he had to borrow a few coins from the servants to pay his cabmen. At the same time she made mock of her sons by showering expensive gifts on her sixteen-year-old foster daughter, Bibi, and providing her with every comfort and luxury, including a *dame de compagnie*. She tried to hold her children by the short-sighted expedient of keeping them financially dependent on her.

When Ivan remonstrated with her about his brother's plight, forbearing to mention his own, she consented to deed each of them a piece of property. The papers were actually made out, but in such a form as to be invalid—a fact which she knew, which they knew, and which apparently she knew they knew. Upon receiving the farcical documents the two sons did not thank her, but on leaving they said, *"Bonne nuit, Maman,"* and kissed her hand as usual. She made the sign of the cross over them as she had done for thirty years, yet as she dealt out the cards for her game of patience, Bibi, sitting in the next room, saw her fine white hands, reflected in the mirror, tremble. There was no method in her madness. Although she actually retained the properties, she secretly ordered the crops thereon sold at any price, so that there was not even seed grain left. The morning after the comedy the brothers held a council of war and decided to take possession of Turgenevo and another small estate that they had inherited from their father, and to remove thither.

When Ivan paid his usual visit to his mother that forenoon she kept up the pretense of having made her sons independent. This broke the camel's back. Losing control of his tongue, he asked his mother the purpose of the farce she had enacted, declared that she was making a vain parade of her power over them, and that no one could be happy near her. He concluded by saying that neither he nor Nikolay wanted anything from her, and would try to make out on what their father had left them. Her retort was to cry out in her irritatingly nasal voice that she no longer had children, and to fly into a passion. Ivan moved to his brother's house and never saw his mother again. The next morning she received a letter from Nikolay advising her of their plan to remove to Turgenevo. When Ivan called she refused to see him, and dashed to the floor the portrait of him that had stood on her desk since his student years in Berlin. Later in the day, finding that her sons had carried out their threat, she had another fit of hysterics. The unhappy woman then left for Spasskoye.

Ivan, at Turgenevo, was hardly well-off. Separation from Pauline gave an edge to his passion. While centering on her, it embraced, as heretofore, her entire household. There was a lively exchange of missives between them. She is "an angel of kindness," he writes; "a great and noble soul" peers out of every line of hers; her letters have made him "the happiest of men." He keeps rereading them, he learns them by heart. Having sufficient reason to feel forlorn, he reaches out for comfort to his recollections of Courtavenel and its mistress. "I see you walking on the grass at Courtavenel," he writes her on September 9, "a guitar in your hand . . . And my memory for places immediately brings back to me the sky, the trees, your dress with the brown pattern, your gray bonnet. It seems to me I feel on my face the light autumnal breeze that whispered in the apple trees above us." Or else in his mind's eye he sees them all at table, enjoying themselves, chatting loudly, perhaps speaking of him. Autumn is bleak at Turgenevo. He watches the cranes winging their way across the sky and listens to their cries, until it seems that they taunt him because they can travel southward while he must remain alone in the snows.

In his letters he discusses, books, music, her work (her role in Gounod's new opera, *Sappho,* must be more than a triumph —"a revelation"), he mentions his literary successes, but with great modesty, describing himself as a twopenny writer. On one occasion, in response to a query from her, he calls beauty "the only thing that is immortal," going on to say that "it is everywhere, showing even in death, but nowhere does it shine as strongly as in the human being; here it speaks most forcefully to the mind." Above all, his letters are protestations of deathless devotion. "I shall cease to love you tenderly and deeply," he writes to her on September 9, "when I cease to exist." He leaves the country for the capital and he assures her: "Know that no matter where I may be, you do not have a heart more devoted to you than mine." Petersburg does not distract him, though he is very busy there. "Not a day passes but the beloved memory of you comes to me a hundred times. Not a night passes without my dreaming of you." (One of his dreams is recorded in the letter of December 5, 1850: "It seemed to me that I returned to Courtavenel during a flood. In the court, above the inundated grass, huge fishes were swimming. I enter the foyer, I see you, I stretch out my hand to you, you begin to laugh. The laughter hurts me . . . I don't know why I am telling you this dream.") The letter continues: "Now, separated from you as I am, I feel more than ever the strength of the ties that unite me with you and," he adds, "your family. I beg Heaven to send me patience and not delay the moment of my seeing you, which I bless in advance a thousand times." She has an earache, and he is deeply distressed: he cannot bear the thought of being well while she suffers.

On the seventh anniversary of his meeting with Louis Viardot, which happens to coincide with his own thirty-second birthday, he writes to Pauline: "I rejoice to say that in these seven years I have found no one better than you; that to have met you on my way has been the greatest happiness of my life; that my devotion and gratitude to you are limitless and will die only with me." Present, she enchanted him;

Turgenev as a student,
from a watercolor made in Berlin in 1838 or 1839

Title page of the manuscript of
A Sportsman's Sketches, Part 1 with the
censor's imprimatur, and the folder containing
the papers about the dismissal of the
censor who passed *A Sportsman's Sketches*

The head of the Petersburg School District burns *A Sportsman's
Sketches* (a caricature, 1852)

absent, she brought him literally to her feet: "My God," he writes to her in German on October 31, "I would like to lay my whole life as a carpet under your beloved feet, which I kiss a thousand times. A thousand greetings to all, and as for you, you know that I belong to you wholly and forever." The seventh anniversary of his meeting with Pauline herself occasions this declaration: "In my whole life there are no memories more dear to me than the ones that relate to you. I am happy to feel after seven years the same profound, sincere, unalterable sentiment dedicated to you. The consciousness of it acts upon me benignly and penetratingly, like a bright ray of sunlight. Happiness seems to be my lot, since I have deserved that the reflection of your life should mingle with mine! As long as I live I shall try to be worthy of such happiness. I have respected myself since I began to bear that treasure within me."

Aside from the usual gifts of letters and pressed flowers, Turgenev received from his lady a unique token. A letter, dated November 12, in which he asks permission to dedicate *A Sportsman's Sketches* to her, concludes: "A thousand greetings to all," and in German: "And as for you, I kiss your feet for hours on end. A thousand thanks for the darling fingernails." A letter to her written a fortnight later ends as follows: "I want to live and die at your dear feet. I kiss them for hours, and I remain your friend forever."

When Turgenev had returned from France he discovered that little Pelageya, his daughter by his mother's seamstress, had suffered from more than her father's neglect. He found her at Spasskoye in pitiable circumstances. Her mother was in Moscow and she was being cared for by one of the laundresses, and was the butt of the servants. He decided that something was to be done for the child and laid the problem before Pauline. "I want that there should be nothing in the world about me that you don't know," he wrote to her on September 18. "Nine years ago I was staying in the country, and I was bored. A rather pretty seamstress in my mother's employ attracted my attention. I whispered two words to her, and she came to me. I gave her some money and then I left. That is all, as in the tale about the wolf. In due time this woman became what might be expected; the rest you know." He went on to say that all he could do for the mother was to protect her from want. As for the child, he declared: "It is necessary that she should forget her mother completely." And he concluded: "My God! how kind you are! And how good it is to confess to you!"

Mme. Viardot offered to take the little girl who was then eight years old, and bring her up with her own child. Accordingly, Pelageya, who was to be known thereafter as Pauline or Paulinette, was shipped to Paris. On November 8 the father writes: "Little Pauline must be in Paris by this time, if nothing happened to her on the way. I thank you in advance for the caresses which you will give her and the kindness with which you will surround her. I repeat, the only thing I told her in parting was that she must adore you as her God. In this she will not be alone. She, of all people, must not think of you except with hands folded and knees bent." Falling into German, he begs her to permit the child to kiss her hands often: "Remember that if they are not my lips, they are lips which are near to me." And on November 26 he writes:

Little Pauline has arrived. You are pleased with her and you have already become fond of her. Dear, dear friend, you are an angel! Every word in your letter breathes inexpressible tenderness, kindness, gentleness. How can I help falling madly in love with the little girl? . . . I am very happy that you have found in her a resemblance to me and that the resemblance gave you pleasure. Please make a little pencil sketch of her. I repeat, I shall become deeply attached to her the moment I learn that you love her . . . I feel that Pauline is becoming dear to me because she is with you.

He thanks the other members of the household for their kindness to the little girl and concludes: "You are all angels, and I love all of you madly."

Five days later he writes: "She [little Pauline] has reason to call you *Maman*—it is you who will make her my real daughter . . . I like to imagine her heart in your hands," adding in German: "You know why. My life and my heart, too, are there, as before. You have not let it drop, have you?" With the humorless egotism tolerable in a lover but rather graceless in a parent, he writes: "I implore you, when you receive this letter call Pauline and allow her to kiss your hands, both hands, you hear? And think of me while she enjoys that happiness. Then write me that you did so." Three days later:

I have just received, dearest, most precious, worshiped friend, the letter in which you give so many details about Pauline . . . Well, if *our* daughter is a good and affectionate little girl, all the better. You see, I told you that she worshiped you. Yes, she does worship you. I feel it in my heart. What else could you expect? Is she not my daughter? Please send me the portrait of her which you have made, and let her write underneath: "Pauline, drawn by Mamma."

Several days later he informs Mme. Viardot that he can afford to spend as much as twelve hundred francs a year on the little girl's maintenance, and he adds: "You must not forget to let her kiss your hands for a whole minute . . . Oh, how lucky she is, that little snotnose!" He was able to make this generous provision for his daughter because he was no longer dependent on his pen for a meager living. He was about to realize his expectations as the heir to a large estate.

After his quarrel with his mother he had written her several times, but received no reply. His secret visits to Spasskoye in order to inquire after her health had afforded him no glimpse of her. In the autumn the dropsical old lady had moved to her gloomy Moscow house. She continued to make daily entries in her diary, which lay on a shelf attached to her big mahogany bed. It is said that one entry ran: "My mother, my children, forgive me! And you, too, Lord, forgive me, for pride, that deadly sin, has always been my sin." Nevertheless, the insolence of her spirit persisted to the last. She received the viaticum, but she did not make a Christian end. The day before her death, which occurred on November 16, she finally asked for her sons. Nikolay came, and she took leave of him, but when Ivan, who was in the capital, reached Moscow, she was already in her grave.

On November 24 he was writing to Pauline about the deceased:

Her last days were very sad. May the Lord preserve us all from such a death! She only tried to stupefy herself. On the eve of her death, when the death rattle had already begun, an orchestra was

playing polonaises in the next room, by her orders. It is proper to
regard the dead with respect and pity, and so I will say nothing more.
Yet as I cannot but share with you all I know and feel, I shall add
one more word: in her final moments, shameful to say, my mother
thought of nothing else but of ruining us—me and my brother. In
her last letter to her steward she gave him clear and explicit instructions to sell everything for a song, to burn everything if necessary. . . .
Anyhow, all this must be forgotten. . . . But I feel it would have
been so easy for her to make us love her and grieve for her!

Varvara Petrovna had burned all her papers before her
death, but the diary that she kept during her last months
accidentally escaped the flames, though apparently it has
since been lost. It fell into the hands of her sons and gave
Ivan a sleepless night. For days he could not take his mind
off those pages. "But I mustn't think of it any more," he
wrote to Pauline. "I am alone in the room. It is very late;
the moon shines gloriously; the brilliance of the snow is
softened, it almost caresses the eye. Diane [the flesh-colored
piebald English setter he had brought from France] is with
me; she is *enceinte,* and if God grants her life, within less
than a month she will bring into the world puppies resembling
her, because I discovered a hound here who is the spit and
image of her and is possessed of talents. I want to lay the
foundation for a new race of magnificent dogs; in time I want
people to say: 'Do you see this dog? It is a grandchild of
the famous Diane.' I just asked Diane if she still remembers
Sultan. She pricked up her ears and winked very meaning-
fully."

Varvara Petrovna left no formal will, but the heirs were
persuaded that she had settled the sum of 50,000 rubles on
Bibi. According to Turgenev, the girl had turned out to be
"a little viper," a sly, vicious, heartless, vulgar creature who
gave the brothers endless trouble. He blamed the abominable
education that she had received under his mother's tutelage.
Used as he was to living with decent people, he couldn't bear
the situation, as he wrote to Pauline, and for two weeks was
unable to work. The heirs finally met Bibi's claims by giving
her an IOU for 15,000 rubles—there was little money in the
cash-box—in addition to Varvara Petrovna's wardrobe and
certain valuables. Her own family refused to take her in, but
a friend of her father's agreed to give her a home. As for the

little Asya, their uncle's by-blow, Nikolay's wife undertook to bring her up.

The heirs divided the land between them, Nikolay and his wife, an acquisitive pair, taking advantage of Ivan. Spasskoye, with other estates, totaling 15,000 acres (some 12,000 and nearly 27,000 respectively, according to other reports), went to him. The new master made generous provision for his mother's personal attendants and liberated the household serfs, alloting them some land. He allowed the rest of his serfs—the male "souls" alone numbered about 2,000—to substitute quitrent for the customary corvée, but he did not free them. He may have decided that liberation, to achieve its purpose, must be the result of a general reform. At any rate, for the decade that was to elapse before the Emancipation Act he remained in possession of what his friend Herzen called "baptised property." But he was a conscience-stricken slaveowner, ashamed of his privileges and half-hearted in his enjoyment of them.

His meekness in dealing with his serfs was due in part to his wretched inability to assert himself. Naturally, they took advantage of their "blind" master (his pince-nez had won him the nickname). He had granted some of his freedmen land close to the manor, and it is said that the grateful recipients cut off the path to a certain well whose water was particularly prized by their benefactor. An anecdote, attributed to Turgenev himself, illustrates his abject helplessness. He is driving to a neighbor's in his own carriage, drawn by his own horses, both the driver and the footman being his own serfs. He is in a great hurry. Suddenly the carriage comes to a halt. After many patient minutes he looks out and sees his two men on the box playing cards! He withdraws his impertinent head and the game proceeds. When his men are quite finished, the journey is resumed.

14

THE CROWN OF MARTYRDOM

The lean years had now come to an end. Turgenev's annual income, as he wrote to Mme. Viardot, amounted to the handsome sum of twenty-five thousand francs. True, that carelessness about money matters which had exasperated his mother, even now left him sometimes short of ready cash. But his properties were so large that even though they were woefully mismanaged he was fairly well-off. For a while he stayed with his brother in Moscow. His presence made the old house on Ostozhenka a magnet for some members of the former Belinsky circle, such as Timofey Granovsky, the historian, Dr. Nikolay Ketcher, the patient if uninspired translator of Shakespeare, Vasily Botkin (Don Basilio), a sybarite and a dilettante, the son of a rich tea merchant.

But the place was uncongenial. Most of his time and money he spent in Petersburg, making occasional visits to Moscow, and going on long hunting trips. The years had worn off his youthful angles, and even if his friend Annenkov found in him the "puerile vices" of earlier days, he also discovered those "amiable qualities of the soul and mind" which impressed so many others. Fresh luster had been added to the gloss of European culture which he had early acquired, his mind had been fed and his talk mellowed.

He was naturally welcomed in the drawing rooms, and, as the celebrated author of *A Sportsman's Sketches* and of several successful plays, he was deferred to in the meeting places of the *literati*. Already budding writers were inviting his opinion on their efforts. Turgenev responded generously. One of these young men, in describing a first interview, drew a portrait of him as a broad-shouldered giant, with a sharp aristocratic profile, and large, well-kept hands, cutting more of a figure than his heroes ever could. He was as careful of his person as his mother had been of hers, and imitated her in taking special pains with his hair. He was always to keep his thick silky mop, but like Shelley, grew gray early, and in his thirties he was quite grizzled. In 1854 a cabby, seeing him stride downhill, observed to him sententiously: "Yes, that's what a hill is; it makes even an old man run." Turgenev's gray head on his young shoulders made him an interesting figure to the ladies. But an acquaintance not affected either by his literary halo or his sex, saw merely a large man with a weak mouth and a skull padded with fat, who gave the impression of being as soft as butter.

Turgenev was the most distinguished figure in the group which hung about *The Contemporary*. This was a close confraternity, in a sense, a closed corporation, whose shrewd and not always scrupulous business head was Nekrasov, a poet as well as a publisher. The intimates who made up the group were bound to one another by friendships of long standing, by the fact that they were nearly all of the gentry, by a common interest in a literature which placed Russia beside the Western nations, by a fund of sharp wit which found vent in elaborate hoaxes and occasionally in mere ribaldry. Turgenev defended the latter on the grounds that, being perpetrated in the reign of Nicholas I, it was, like the Decameron, the effort of revelers in time of plague.

On February 21, 1852, Gogol died in Moscow. Turgenev's admiration for the author of *Dead Souls* was perhaps exceeded only by his worship of Pushkin. He had met the great humorist but once, a few months before the latter's death, although he had sat under him years previously during Gogol's brief professorship. Turgenev carried away from the visit the memory of a keen, healthless man, with a schoolmaster's manner, and measured, emphatic speech coming through bad teeth. Slight as was Turgenev's knowledge of the man, he wore mourning for the writer. "I may say without exaggeration," he wrote to a friend, "that never within my memory did anything make a greater impression on me than Gogol's death. . . . The tragic fate of Russia is reflected in the fate of those of us who are nearest to its heart."

Indeed, coming as it did at the very height of the reaction, Gogol's death shook the more sensitive as the sound of a slamming door makes a nervous man quake. "Truly, it seems to me," Turgenev said in another letter, "that dark, silent waters have closed over my head and I am sinking to the bottom, growing cold and numb." He wrote an obituary notice for a Petersburg paper, sobbing aloud over it. The article was prohibited by the censorship committee. Its chairman opined that it was unbecoming to eulogize Gogol in such "exuberant terms" and to declare his death "an irreplaceable loss." In spite of his professed conservatism, Gogol, being a writer, was a suspect character. Turgenev sent the rejected manuscript to his friends in Moscow with the request to get it published there, which they did, the local censor being ignorant of the fact that the article had been forbidden in the capital. When this was reported to the Emperor he ordered Turgenev jailed for one month and then confined to his estate for an indefinite period under police surveillance. Accordingly, on April 16 he was arrested and incarcerated in a station house.

In writing to the Viardots, on May 1, 1852, of his unhappy situation, he did not blame the Emperor, saying that the matter had been presented to him in such a light that he could not help acting as he had. Turgenev was in error. Count Orlov, Chief of the Gendarmerie, in his report to the Czar recommended only secret surveillance for the culprit; it was Nicholas who imposed the stricter sentence. Turgenev was right, however, in pointing out that his transgression was merely a pretext for punishing him as the author of *A Sportsman's Sketches*.

The month in jail was not without pleasant distractions. In the beginning the prisoner could not complain of solitude. The narrow street on which the station house looked out was jammed with the carriages of his visitors. Indeed, these calls became so numerous that they assumed the character of a political demonstration and as a result they were prohibited. For a whole fortnight his name was tirelessly declined in the drawing rooms of the capital. A middle-aged female admirer sent him some soda powders and an icon. Young girls with husbands in their pretty heads were at pains to walk past his window and favored him with pressed flowers sewn on pale-blue note paper. Nor did he subsist on the coarse prison fare.

His dinners came regularly from Mme. Panayeva's kitchen. He did not go dry either, and after twenty years he was to regale his Parisian friends with the story of how the police captain, drunk on his prisoner's excellent champagne, nudged his elbow and lifted his own glass with a husky "To Robespierre!"

Another of his prison anecdotes was that his cell, which was next to the room where convicted serfs received their floggings, contained the records of the station house and that he amused himself by examining the secret files. The cell was small and extremely stuffy. The prisoner invented an ingenious way of getting his constitutional in these cramped quarters. Twice a day he carried every card of two packs from one corner of the room to the other and back again,—making altogether four hundred and sixteen trips, a walk of about a mile and a half. All these various diversions afforded him sufficient leisure to write "Moomoo" and to study Polish. This last occupation was a source of worry to one of his friends, since it was folly, she wrote him, for a prisoner to be learning the tongue of Russia's hereditary enemy under the very eyes of the police.

When, in May, he went to Spasskoye at his Emperor's instance, he probably traveled over the new railway between Petersburg and Moscow, virtually the first railroad to be built in Russia, its sole predecessor being a suburban line connecting the capital with Tsarskoe Selo (now Pushkin). The emotions of the native returning home is a subject upon which the novelist wrote many profoundly evocative pages. Once more the triumph of time over faces and furniture thrust itself upon him. Once more he was in the midst of the placid, drowsy country life which appeared to Lavretzky, the hero of *A Nest of Gentlefolk,* to move as inaudibly as water among marsh grasses. Once more he was surrendering himself to the rural ennui which both liberated and depressed him. The contrast between the clipped, civilized landscape of western Europe and the rude immensity of the home scene was in itself dispiriting. There the very soil spoke of man, his mastering will, his cumulative labors, his solid heritage; here the human creature was nearly obliterated by a vast plain, the surface of which he just scratched, and which barely suffered his flimsy habitations. The empty solitude of these fields, the shapelessness and sameness of the land had a hypnotizing, enervating effect.

Two years had passed since the walls of the Spasskoye manor had watched Varvara Petrovna's matchless rages, and her son must sometimes have wanted just a moment of her querulous presence, and often have missed, in the unkempt house, her careful eye and stern hand. He was free to roam the countryside in pursuit of game, to call on his neighbors and receive friends, but he was not permitted to visit those of his estates which were not situated in the same province as Spasskoye, let alone go to Moscow to consult a physician. The police officer who had him under surveillance always doffed his cap on approaching him, but the man's appearances were an annoyance. He noted in his memorandum book that his charge eyed him as though he were the devil.

Turgenev was exaggerating when he wrote to a friend: "I am not dead yet, but the deep solitude in which I live gives me an idea of the silence which awaits us beyond the grave." As a matter of fact, his neighbor, the poet Fet, calling on Turgenev in defiance of his family, who feared association with a reprobate, found the latter "surrounded by ladies as honey pot by flies." He had continual companionship in the manager of the estate, one Nikolay Tyutchev, and that gentleman's relatives. Indeed, they succeeded in interfering with him almost as much as his mother had done. Turgenev was not one to insist on his rights, and so Tyutchev (whom he had chosen in preference to his tight-fisted brother Nikolay, fearing that the latter would be too hard on the peasants) genially usurped the place of the master of the manor. The deportee found himself relegated to a wing. There is an obscure tale that the Tyutchevs even made an attempt upon his bachelorhood, and certainly he would have made a very good match for his manager's sister-in-law, a sentimental, self-complacent maiden who, as Turgenev said in a letter, played the piano with fingers of cotton batting.

He hungered for music as men hunger for meat, and he prevailed upon Mme. Tyutcheva and her sister to give him what makeshift for it they could. They played, four-handed, Mozart, Beethoven, Mendelssohn, Weber. He describes these musicales to Mme. Viardot: "I stand behind the ladies' chairs, I turn the leaves, and I pretend to conduct. In moments of enthusiasm I cannot prevent myself, under the pretext of singing, from emitting something in the nature of horribly false notes which cause nervous spasms in all present." He preferred singing to any other form of music, "but in my throat," he wrote many years later, "instead of a voice sits a scrofulous sucking pig."

He had another diversion at Spasskoye in the shape of a singularly attractive brunette with an exquisite figure, small hands and feet, and a proud bearing most unusual in a serf girl employed as a chambermaid. The story goes that he bought her from a cousin of his for seven hundred rubles—an ordinary maid then costing fifty rubles at most—but a kinder view would suggest that he purchased her freedom with that sum. He dressed her as a lady and seems to have tried to teach her to read and write, but the lovely Feoktista was no Liza Doolittle, and he soon desisted. Although he assured Mme. Viardot that he wanted her to know everything about him, the available correspondence does not show that he mentioned this affair to her. Indeed, it was only in 1915 that anything definite became known about it. That year there came to light a letter of his written in 1865, in which he says:

> In 1851, '52, and '53 a girl by the name of Feoktista with whom I had a liaison lived with me here [at Spasskoye] and in Petersburg. . . . Eventually I helped her to get married to a clerk in the Naval Ministry and she is now flourishing in Petersburg. When she left me in 1853 she was with child, and in Moscow she gave birth to a son, Ivan, whom she placed in an orphanage. I have sufficient grounds to believe that he is not my child. I cannot, however, be absolutely certain of it. He may be, after all, of my own making.

We gather from the rest of the letter that Feoktista lost sight of her child, who had been transferred from the institution to the care of a peasant in a village the name of which escaped the mother's memory. It appears that he fared ill there and passed into the hands of a lady who was subsequently taken sick and went to a hospital, abandoning her charge. Feoktista was on her way to Moscow to find her son, and stopped at Spasskoye en route, "to get a look at me," as

Turgenev put it in the letter. This was to serve her as an introduction to a friend of his, who was requested to help Feoktista in her search. "If this Ivan is alive, and should be found," the letter concludes, "I am ready to place him in a trade school and support him. . . . The husband knows nothing; or rather, he is a very meek and decent sort." The fate of the woman and her child is unknown.

The first summer of his exile, a cold and rainy one, Turgenev spent in relative idleness, frequently ailing. In the autumn he exchanged the pen for the fowling piece. A harsh winter set in early that year, and as Turgenev's passion for sport shrank with the cold, he returned "to human feelings and ideas," as he wrote, "like a drunkard after his drinking spell." This was the first winter that he had spent in the country since his boyhood, and it was also to be the last. He evoked the white season, as it must then have presented itself to him, in *Fathers and Children*: "the cruel silence of the cloudless frosts, firm creaking snow, pink hoarfrost on the trees, a sky of pale emerald, caps of smoke on the chimneys, puffs of steam from doors opened for a moment, faces looking fresh as though bitten, and the bustling trot of chilled horses." It was a season of leisure and literature for him. He had a substantial library consisting mostly of eighteenth-century books, and there were occasional games of chess. But in spite of these distractions, the hibernal scene afflicted him with melancholy. He had always been afraid of the sky, and now the earth itself had the sky's blank insubstantial immensity. If Turgenev occasionally plumed himself on the role of another Ovid, he did not fail to perceive that the uses of adversity were sweet. There were moments when he was glad he was not in Petersburg. He had formed plans of using his enforced leisure to enlarge his education. He intended, he told the Viardots, to go on with his studies of the Russian people, "the strangest and most astonishing people in the world." At Spasskoye he could control his diversions better than he could in the capital, what with the continual demands that society there made upon him. Further, the contacts which the country afforded were such as to gratify the artist if not exactly to entertain the man. He could regard his provincial neighbors with an objectivity difficult to apply to his familiars, and certainly not to be relished by the latter. Here was, after all, a side of Russian life that he had been away from for so long that it was virtually new to him. Here, with greater assurance than in a more sophisticated scene, he could participate, without ever ceasing to play his own little game, without ever blinking his acutely observant eye.

He was like the narrator in his story "Asya": "I enjoyed going where others went, shouting when others shouted, and at the same time I liked to look at the others shouting." In the country people were less likely to notice that while he shouted he was looking at them. That his friends noticed it and were discomfited by it has been given as the probable explanation of the disagreeable impression which he sometimes made. Thus, Herzen's wife, a discerning and sensitive woman, felt in Turgenev's presence as though she were in an uninhabited room: "There is dampness on the walls and it gets into your bones, and you are afraid to sit anywhere or to touch anything, and the only thing you want is to get out into the open as soon as possible."

In the same breath she speaks of how she was chilled and repelled by what she calls his "microscopic view," that is, his habit of minutely examining the nose or the leg or some feature of the dress instead of the whole person under his eye. She found Turgenev a "good man," and declared him easy to get on with, "but after he is gone," she said, "there is nothing left; perhaps because he is too unconcerned about me, our relationship is as light as a soap bubble." One suspects that not a few people with whom he had to do found him similarly unconcerned, unconsciously preserving the distance which would give him the correct perspective.

15

THE TURNING

OF THE ROAD

On July 18, 1852, while Turgenev was confined to Spass-koye, *A Sportsman's Sketches* came out in book form under a Petersburg imprint. Circumstances had prepared a peculiarly favorable atmosphere for its reception. It took on the guise of a political act. The aristocratic salons labelled it "an incendiary book" and the Minister of Education, in a secret report to the Emperor, treated it as a dangerous piece of writing, likely to cause disrespect on the part of the lower classes toward their rightful superiors. Liberal-minded people applauded it because it allowed them to feel that their own sentiments on the vexing subject of serfdom were shared by a cultivated person of distinguished literary gifts. The Westernists prized the work because it implicitly recommended a free rural economy on the German model. The Slavophils, disregarding the author's disapproval of the *obshchina,* were pleased to find in it testimony to the moral and spiritual excellence that the masses, under brutalizing conditions, had preserved. Both factions saw the book as an effective attack on serfdom.

Of course, Belinsky's friend and disciple heartily disliked this national institution. His protest would have been sharper, had it not been for the muffling effect of censorship. Of the eight stories that he planned for the volume but never wrote, one, which would certainly have been banned by the censor, had for its theme the murder of a *barin* by his serfs. The man was known among them as "the land-eater": he had been steadily reducing the acreage they were permitted to cultivate for themselves. They took revenge by cramming several pounds of excellent black earth down his throat, the cook standing by and pressing it upon his master's palate. When Turgenev, at a riper age and in an expansive mood, considered his own epitaph, he expressed the wish that it might mention the services of *A Sportsman's Sketches* to the cause of emancipation. "Emperor Alexander," he said, "had me informed that, among other things, the reading of my book led him to free the serfs." This epitaph was never written, nor was Edmond About's* suggestion carried out, that Turgenev's sole monument should be a pedestal bearing a slave's broken chain.

As a matter of fact, although the book unquestionably helped to create an atmosphere favorable to abolition, its author did not have the temper of a reformer. At heart he was a noncombatant. He sympathized with Montaigne, that skeptic in an age of faith, that observer in an age of action. "If I had been Cicero," Turgenev is credited with saying, "I confess that after the battle of Pharsalia I should have cringed before Caesar even more than he did. He was a man of letters, and to a man of letters politics is poison." It was a poison which had a certain attraction for this disciple of Belinsky.

With the appearance of *A Sportsman's Sketches* between covers Turgenev felt that he had come to a turning of the road. A gate had closed upon his youth, leaving him, he believed, on the sober plateau of middle age, where he was to remain until, with equal precocity, he adopted the attitudes of an elderly gentleman. Simultaneously he endured one of those fits of despondency that were to assault him periodically. In writing from the jail he announced to the Viardots that his life was over: he had eaten all his white bread and must hereafter chew what remained of the black. In the years to come such an attack would usually be accompanied by the resolution to give up writing forever. This time he decided that as a writer he must strike out in a new direction. The *Sketches* had been out for only a few months when he was saying to friends that the book struck him as the work of a total stranger. On his thirty-fourth birthday he wrote to Annenkov:

---

* Edmond About pronounced the funeral oration at the memorial service for Turgenev, held at the Gare du Nord in Paris before his coffin left on board a train for Russia.

I must take another road. I must find it and bid farewell to my old manner forever. I have had enough of trying to extract the triple essence from human characters and pouring it into small bottles: "Sniff it, please, gentle reader, uncork it and sniff it. It has the Russian bouquet, hasn't it?" Enough, enough. But the question is, am I capable of something big and calm? Am I going to succeed with clear, simple outlines? That I don't know, and I shan't know until I try. But believe me, you will hear something new from me, or you will hear nothing. For that reason I am almost glad of my winter seclusion. I shall have the time to collect myself; and, above all, in solitude one is away from things, literary and journalistic especially. I shall become somebody only when the littérateur in me is destroyed, but I am thirty-four, and at this age it is difficult to be reborn. Well, we shall see.

He wanted to deal with the great commonplaces of existence in an objective way, without displaying his own views and sentiments, without flippancy, facile irony, or the tendency to caricature and sermonize, natural in a disciple of Gogol (he told Botkin that he knew where Gogol's shoe pinched). To see life steadily, indeed, to see it whole, as Pushkin saw it, was his desire. "The striving after impartiality and integral truth," he wrote, "is one of the few good qualities for which I am grateful to Nature." He insisted that he had no illusions about the calibre of his own talent. He lost no opportunity to belittle it. In every century, he told Annenkov, there are at most two or three men whose words have the strength and firmness that only the life of the people can give. "Such men are in the wholesale business; you and I are retailers who provide for daily, transient needs." Yet he felt that he was doing less than his best in his stories and sketches, those fragments and snippets. It was incumbent upon him, he declared, to put his mind to a carefully studied work of major proportions, attempting both to record and interpret the problems of a broad social group at a particular moment in its history. His friends, too, were urging him in the direction of a large work.

Turgenev never ceased to cultivate the minor genre and was to produce thirty more short pieces. They differ from the earlier stories in that on the rare occasions when men and women of the people are presented, they are usually in the background. For his short pieces, as for his novellas and his novels, he drew his material from the experiences of the gentry, to which he himself belonged, and of the educated commoners who were beginning to swell the ranks of the Russian middle class. It was to this cultivated segment of the Russian people that his writings addressed themselves.

For the present, "simplicity, calm, clarity of line, conscientious craftsmanship, that conscientiousness which derives from certainty"—all this, he told Konstantin Aksakov, was merely an ideal that beckoned him. In consequence, he put off the writing of the novel, the elements of which had been fermenting in his mind for years. But he was teased and prodded by the uneasy knowledge that time was running out. Finally, during his enforced stay at Spasskoye, he prevailed upon himself to begin a novel. It was provisionally called *Two Generations*. In February, 1853, he was "tunneling through it like a mole." He wrote the first part of it, amounting to twelve chapters, and sent the manuscript around to his friends for an opinion. He was never to outgrow the habit, which began with his literary career, of seeking criticism and deferring to it, particularly if it was adverse. The consensus in this instance was unfavorable, and so this first experiment was never concluded. The fragment of the work, which was published some years later under the title, "A Private Manorial Office," presents what is substantially a portrait of the flighty generalissimo who was Turgenev's mother.

He anticipated with some dread a second winter in the country, but was spared that cup. On the anniversary of his arrest he sent the Heir Apparent an appeal which began thus: "I heartily repent my wrongdoing, however involuntary, and, desiring not to be reckoned a wilful rebel, I make bold to lay before your Imperial Highness my very humble petition." Like his first petition, which had been addressed to the future Alexander II from the jail, it remained without effect. But owing to the friendly intercession of Count Alexey Tolstoy, the poet, who held a position at Court, Count Orlov, in making a report to the Emperor, recommended that Turgenev's residential disability be terminated. Nicholas consented, but ordered that the writer should continue to be kept under strict surveillance during his stay in the capital.

The Spasskoye captivity was over. In December, 1853, Turgenev was again in Petersburg, installed in a flat on

Povarskoy Lane, under the care of his cook Stepan, whom he had brought with him from Spasskoye. His rooms showed more than the usual disorder to be found in bachelors' apartments. He was the sort of man who is at the mercy of his servants. The domestic chaos that he suffered was enough to make his mother turn in her grave—she who had governed her household with such harsh pedantry, so that even the pigeons were regimented, receiving their oats when a bell sounded precisely at noon; she who had kept an inventory of the family wardrobe, even to Ivan's wadded green silk dressing-gown, with a note of the date on which it had been presented to him; she who had written down opposite each day's menu each day's faultfindings. Thus she had been at pains to note that her sausages were not so good as Mme. Krylov's, that she must find out where the best pickled cucumbers were to be bought, that it was now unfashionable to shoot champagne corks at the ceiling, and that if you don't warn your maids about bedbugs, you are likely, as she was, to be bitten out of a night's sleep.

Her son, while equally fastidious in the matter of sausages and bedbugs, was generally too lazy to admonish his servants to secure the one or to destroy the other. As a result, his valet was apt to be indifferent as to whether the master dressed in a cold room or a warm one. A friend coming in to see him one chilly morning found him arguing with his man on the subject, and finally crying out with a kind of peevish humor: "All right, you're clever and I'm a fool, but for pity's sake, I have enough sense to know when I'm cold!" He had not outgrown the habits of the young student who wrote love letters for his valet in Berlin. Where to be born to one's caste is more a matter of course than to be born with five wits, familiarity is likely to reach good-naturedly across the impregnable wall.

Before returning to the capital Turgenev had written to Annenkov that he intended to live there very modestly, devoting himself solely to "literary work, a circle of friends, music, and chess. . . . It's time for me to settle down. It's not for nothing that I have turned as gray as a rat." But he could not keep this resolution. Life in the country had sharpened his taste for social commerce. His literary friends of the *Contemporary* circle gave him a dinner to celebrate his liberation, following it up with several less formal symposia. He was renewing acquaintance not merely with men of his own way of thinking, but also with such extreme nationalists as the brothers Aksakov, Konstantin and Ivan, the Peter and Paul of Slavophilism. For a while they thought that here was a chance of making a proselyte. But they mistook Turgenev's interest in Russia's past for agreement with their views of the country's history and their proud prognostications of its messianic destiny. Their hopes were shattered in the course of his stay at Abramtzevo, their family estate, in January 1855. On this occasion the place swarmed with guests, so that Vera, the daughter of the house, noted in her diary that after dinner the drawing room looked like a Moscow rout. There were sleigh rides over the immaculate snow, naps to fortify the company against the long meals and longer talks, philological discussions between Konstantin Aksakov and the young linguist Hilferding, which made Turgenev wring his hands and furnished a target for his best jokes. Khomyakov, that vehement lay theologian, had brought along his latest paper on the nature of Orthodoxy, written in French, for which there was only a small audience, but there was a large circle ready to listen to Konstantin read aloud a fresh page from his father's genial memoirs.

Turgenev found this pastime more to his taste than the debates with Khomyakov and Konstantin about the virtues of the village commune and of the way of life in old Muscovy. Aksakov was as fanatical on these subjects as when, in the first flush of nationalist enthusiasm, he had adopted a native costume so quaintly authentic that, according to a Moscow wit quoted by Herzen, peasants in the street took him for a Persian. And how could you argue with a man who looked with such disdain on the nations of the West? Nor had Khomyakov changed since the time, ten years earlier, when the ladies who had assisted at the nocturnal bouts in the salons of Moscow had admired the toss of his blue-black mane and the force of his dialectics. He was more certain than ever that the Orthodox Church was the only true embodiment of Christianity, while to Turgenev the whole question of the respective merits of the Eastern and Western Churches was like the controversy over the eating of non-existent gryphon in Voltaire's *Zadig*. He outraged both men by declaring that his own entire religion was comprised in Belinsky's famous letter to Gogol, which advocated not faith but reason, not nationalism but humanism, not Eastern Orthodoxy but Western civilization.

Konstantin's revenge was to dub Turgenev's attitude toward life gastronomic. The guest had the grace to say to his friend's mother: "I promise you that at least next Sunday I will go to church. You, for one, don't despair of me as your son does." But if his remark was calculated to please the old lady, it did not ingratiate him with the younger members of the family. Hot upon his visit, Vera made this entry in her diary:

> I decidedly disliked Turgenev. . . . He has no notion of faith. He has lived immorally, and so his ideas are sullied by his life. Besides, he is only capable of experiencing physical sensations. All his impressions pass through his nerves, he is not capable of either understanding or feeling the spiritual side of things. . . . He lacks even pagan force and loftiness of soul. All he has is spiritual and physical flabbiness, in spite of his huge stature.

Vera did not know that a year or so earlier he had written to a young friend: "Without faith, deep and strong, life isn't worth living." He could not have meant religious faith, but certainly he was anything but closed to "the spiritual side of things."

His commerce with the Slavophils merely served to intensify his distaste for doctrinaire thinking, for ideological systems without roots in experience.

The contacts that he made at this time were seldom with such exacting people as the Aksakovs. He now counted among his acquaintances virtually all the writers of note. His house was, in his own words, neutral ground. Thither Count Sollogub brought "his dragging legs, a finger stuck in his vest, and his tongue stuck in his cheek"; the double-chinned Goncharov came with his deceptive phlegm; Botkin, the perfect connoisseur of Spanish bullfights, English literature, and French cooking; Ostrovsky, looking more like a comfortable Moscow merchant than the playwright he was; the aesthete and critic, Druzhinin; the giddy Grigorovich. Here also came a young aristocrat, Count Leo Tolstoy, the only member of the *Contemporary* circle in uniform, having lately seen service in the

Crimea, a man who in addition to his successes with cards and women had already scored a literary triumph.

Turgenev had never looked the dandy more than now, and his towering figure with the large gray head was conspicuous in the drawing rooms. He was as good as ever at making the ladies laugh, mimicking, punning, and at reciting the verses of his friend Fet. But if he wore his buffoonery like a flower in the buttonhole of his dark-green velvet jacket, there were times when he chewed on his melancholy as on the stem of an old pipe. The half dozen stories that he had written since the completing of *A Sportsman's Sketches* betray, in passing, a sad resignation to the dreary business of living and aging, and suggest a theme he was later to amplify concerning love as an irrational force which enslaves whom it does not destroy.

Some of the writing was done in the country, where he spent the summers and the early autumn months, busy with his pen when his fowling piece did not claim him. He now shared the Spasskoye mansion with Uncle Nikolay and his family, consisting of a young wife and two small daughters. Since Tyutchev had proved incompetent, and the old man had been employed for years by Varvara Petrovna as manager of the estates, Turgenev, who was fond of him, was glad to install him again in that capacity.

Whether or not his failure to achieve a new manner was the cause, he became despondent about his literary career. His pet word "enough" was beginning to be often on his lips. In vain his friends protested, Nekrasov telling him in a letter dated June 30, 1855: "Of all the writers and readers in Russia only one person thinks that your career is over—you." Always readier to believe those who censured rather than those who praised his work, he took pleasure in commending the critics who flayed him. He felt that the time had come for him to "alight" from Pegasus; at least he said so. It was in these low days that he wrote to one of his young literary protégés, whose works have been blessed with oblivion: "My activity, it seems to me, is already finished. But I shall consider myself happy if I succeed in being midwife to your writings." In the summer of 1855 he wrote *Rudin*.

The novel was composed in six or seven weeks, at Spass- koye. Having set "Finis" to the manuscript on July 24, Turgenev, at the instance of his critical friends, spent the rest of the year revising it. He took the piece more seriously than anything he had done up to that time. In the course of revision the story underwent noteworthy mutations. The author apparently vacillated between stressing the positive and the negative traits of his protagonist and ended by endowing him with grave failings as well as elements of greatness, without, however, making the combination wholly plausible. Dmitry Rudin, the central figure, is a rootless man, incapable of action as of feeling, a man of words not deeds, aptly described by another person in the novel as having genius but no character —*A Man of Genius* was the book's first title, presumably an ironic one. The main plot follows Turgenev's by now familiar pattern of a strong, loyal, high-spirited girl who is left brokenhearted by a man too spineless to sustain their common ideal. But before the book comes to an end Turgenev makes a valiant effort to rehabilitate Rudin by showing that, after all, he is capable of moral fervor, is faithful to generous ideas and that his golden eloquence, however rhetorical, does infect the young with a fine eagerness for the good, the true, and the beautiful.

The novel appeared in the first two issues of *Sovremennik* for 1856 and in the same year was printed separately. That the author was not satisfied with the final text may be seen from his having thought it well to add a postscript to the epilogue in the second edition, which came out in 1860. Therein he has his hero die quixotically on a barricade in an alley of the Faubourg St. Antoine on the last day of the Paris revolution of 1848. It is as though the novelist who started out to stone his German period in the end softened toward the vaporizing ghost he had evoked. His tolerance was apt to weaken his sword arm.

His contemporaries thought that he had modeled Rudin on Bakunin, not the firebrand who at the writing of the novel was languishing in the Schlüsselburg (now Petrokrepost) Fortress prison, but the impetuous friend of his youth who swore volubly by Hegel's dialectics. Herzen observed that Turgenev created Rudin in his own image. Without denying either allegation, he wanted to believe that in his first novel he had projected a *typical* figure, epitomizing a significant aspect of the generation to which he belonged. It was that of "the idealists of the thirties": scions of the gentry who had acquired nothing but a vocabulary from their contacts with German romanticism and metaphysics, misfits unable to find a place for themselves in the Russian scheme of things, indeed strangers in their own country, victims of an excessive cerebration that dries up the springs of spontaneity and issues in sterile self-analysis. In more than one short piece, notably in "The Diary of a Superfluous Man," Turgenev had dealt with this phenomenon. These stories were preliminary studies for the larger canvas that is *Rudin.*

Turgenev had been writing his novel to the steady tolling of funeral bells and the wailing of peasant women over their dead. Cholera was ravaging the countryside in and about Spasskoye, as it was also depleting the ranks of the troops in the Crimea. Ever since, six years previously in Paris, he had suffered an attack of what he believed to be this disease, he had had a morbid fear of it. He fretted about his stomach, complaining about gastritis, stomach fever, and even cancer of the pylorus,—he named one of Diana's pups for this euphonious part of his anatomy. Whenever he had indigestion he took to his bed and declared himself lost. In this respect, as in so many others, he did not favor his mother. When, in 1848, cholera hit Spasskoye, she showed no fear and took no precautions, assuming that the disease would not dare touch her or her household; nor did it. It was perhaps natural that Turgenev did not allow his work to be disturbed by the agitating news from the front, for, after all, Sebastopol was hundreds of miles away. But that he went on covering the paper with his comely sloping script while the danger of cholera was at his very door testifies to genuine self-possession and a rare capacity for working under difficult circumstances.

To judge by his writings, the war did not engage his interest deeply. He must have savored his friend Tyutchev's pun: *"C'est la guerre des crétins contre les gredins."* The news of the fall of Sebastopol elicited the comment: "If only we could profit by this terrible lesson, as the Prussians did by the Jena defeat! But no; we aren't even allowed to write about it." Like most thinking Russians, he probably felt that the war showed up the rottenness of the bureaucratic system. It is less probable that he realized the far-reaching consequences of the Crimean disaster. It was to usher in the period of reforms which gave the final blow to the tottering structure of patriarchal Russia and to the serf-owning gentry whose exodus was long overdue. Turgenev, setting down in the pages of *Rudin* his recollections of a vanished period of his own youth, was ensconcing and illumining certain aspects of Russian life which were even then disappearing forever.

16

"THE ONLY WOMAN"

"It is a pity that you are absorbed in a feeling for a single person." Thus Turgenev said to a young literary protégé who was about to marry for love. There was something to be said in favor of an unhappy marriage, but the cramping emotional routine of a successful union was fatal to the artist. One should approach every woman as a potential mistress: variety, not satisfaction, is what talent feeds upon. For himself, he found he could work best when the page was warmed by the glow of a casual affair, more especially with a married woman, "who can manage both herself and her passion." He could not understand this young man's curious predilection for a mere girl. As the years went by he was to regret that he had not married, but he seems to have retained the belief that any permanent relation with a woman was harmful to an artist.

That Turgenev was not always ready to pursue the game that sniffed at his traps is plain from such an incident as his affair with Yekaterina Ladyzhenskaya. The lady belonged to the eligible category of married women—indeed, was the mother of four children. Moved by a more than ordinary interest in literature, she started a correspondence with the author of *A Sportsman's Sketches*. The fact that she kept secret her epistolary adventure proved, even before she confessed the intention, that she had vaguely hoped to *"faire un peu de roman."* At first Turgenev was complaisant, and spoke with absent-minded gallantry of her "beautiful hands" —the feature he was most sensitive to in women he admired —forgetting that he had never seen them. She managed to arrange a meeting at the house of a common friend, but to her further advances he turned a cold shoulder. He told Botkin that she was one of those women who keep chasing their own tails—an occupation fit only for kittens. The lady herself attributed his lack of enterprise to laziness.

There may have been another reason for his backwardness. Just then his interest was centered elsewhere. He had a distant cousin named Olga, a girl exactly half his age, with whom he was preoccupied, the gossips said, to the point of an actual proposal. She was a demure creature, and a diligent if not an accomplished musician. In May, 1854, when upon his first visit to the Aksakovs he was scandalizing them with his worldliness, he delighted his host by a filial confession of his matrimonial hopes. The genial old huntsman consulted the cards as to the outcome. Three months later Turgenev wrote him that his plans had fallen into the water "as the cards predicted."

The facts of the case are uncertain. It is believed that his suit was accepted, but that in the end he refused his happiness, leaving Olga in a wretched state. At all events, in July, 1855, having received a letter from her, he was writing to Annenkov: "Lately I've again been thinking a good deal of O. A. [Olga Alexandrovna]. Say what you may, she's a charming creature." Shortly afterward he sought diversion in the company of a pretty little Pole, whose favors he rewarded with such gifts as a silver service. But he remained solicitous about Olga Alexandrovna, remarking to a friend that "it would be a pity if this beautiful soul were doomed to suffer the oxidation of spinsterhood." Two years after the unfortunate event Olga had recovered her balance and her good habits, so that Leo Tolstoy held her up to his then fiancée, a frivolous fair, as a model. Olga's aunt had told him that the young woman rose at seven in the morning, played the piano until two in the afternoon, and spent her evenings over some book. The following year she consoled Turgenev, and presumably herself, by taking a husband.

In retreating from an entangling alliance, Turgenev was behaving like so many of his own heroes, young men unable to be the same in their own act and valor as they were in desire, and so failing at the critical moment to accept the responsibilities of action. For himself he could find at least two ways of rationalizing his evasiveness. There was in the first place the artist's fear of domestic interference with his main business in life: the fear he had expressed as a warning to his young confrère some years earlier. There was, besides, the excuse of an anterior passion whose tenacity even he had not fully measured. To the maternal if astigmatic eye of a middle-aged lady who was fond of him, this attachment appeared to be no more than a ghost, a memory, which must dissolve at the touch of a real affection. Turgenev's life was to prove the strange vitality of this ghost, to prove also "the pity" and the frail comfort of his absorption in a feeling for a single person—Pauline Viardot.

It has been seen that during the first months after his return to Russia his relationship with the prima donna was as intimate as the miles between them permitted. Exactly half a year after they parted he asks in a letter: "How much time will pass before I shall have the happiness of seeing you again?" If at least he could glimpse her in a dream, as he had done several days previously! Having come into his inheritance, he could presumably have gone back to France. He did not. At the end of 1850 he writes to Pauline: "What if we could see each other in the coming year?" And he adds, in German: "Even if I could do it, I would come only if you called me." Did she fail to call him, or did he stay on in Russia to savor his newly won fame, what with the great acclaim of *A Sportsman's Sketches* and the success of several of his plays? In any event, his letters continue to attest his devotion to Pauline. At the moment when the curtain rises in Moscow on the première of his one-acter, *The Provincial Lady,* he whispers her name to bring him luck, and that, he writes her on January 18, 1851, was what made the play a hit. He is happy to know that everything in his life is linked with memories of her and with her "influence."

After a hiatus in the correspondence of more than a year there is a letter from him to the Viardots apprising them of his arrest. "The saddest thing about it," he writes, "is that I must definitely bid adieu to any hope of going abroad. For the matter of that, I never deceived myself on that score: leaving you, I knew that it was for a long time, perhaps forever." It may be that he had in mind the political situation in Russia, which made the possibility of foreign travel doubtful.

Winter came early in 1852. In October he writes to Pauline from Spasskoye that work and reminiscence alone are left to him. "But that work may be easy and memories less distressing, I need your letters, with the echoes of a happy, active life, with the fragrance of sun and poetry, which they bring me. By the way, always put some grass or flowers in the envelope." With a blizzard hammering at his windows and a phrase from Gounod's "Autumn" running through his head, he recalls to his friend their siestas under the poplars, with the leaves dropping about them from a fretwork of boughs against an incredible blue. He has but to shut his eyes to see it, a beauty that he fears he may never know again. "Let us sit down side by side," he says to Diana, "and recall Courtavenel." On the ninth anniversary of meeting Pauline he writes to her: "Today, just as nine years ago, I am all yours, heart and soul, and so it will be nine years hence. You know it."

Early in January, 1853, Pauline, accompanied by her husband, arrived in Petersburg for an engagement. The involuntary recluse laments the fact that he is chained to Spasskoye. On the 29th of the month he writes to her: "Oh, it seems to me, should I ever see you again, I could only cry with joy." Louis Viardot is taken ill and returns to France, leaving Pauline alone, and in March and April she gives three concerts in Moscow. His letters do not reach her on time, and, not hearing from him, she is worried. Two of her notes to him are "extremely laconic," giving the impression that every word in them "strives to be the last," as he puts it, but others are "dear." She did not visit him at Spasskoye, perhaps reluctant to defy the conventions, but it appears that he managed to see her by secretly traveling to Moscow with a borrowed passport—a venture that might have had serious consequences for him. In May he writes to urge her to come to Russia the following year. "If you come to Moscow with Viardot," he adds, "I hope very much that you will visit me here." And he speaks of his happiness, were she to walk with him in the Spasskoye garden, so dazzlingly bright with spring foliage and loud with nightingales, thrushes, orioles, cuckoos. The letter ends thus: "Adieu, *theuerste Freundin*. Be happy. A thousand greetings to Louis Viardot. I tenderly kiss your dear hands and remain yours forever." His next letter to her that has been published is dated July, 1857.

As has been stated, Turgenev's Spasskoye exile terminated in November, 1853. The Crimean War was then in progress, and so, of the countries on the singer's usual itinerary, Germany was the only one open to a Russian subject. Besides, even if peace had prevailed, it is highly unlikely that a person under police surveillance could have obtained a passport for foreign travel. The fact is that he remained in Russia. It has been noted that there is a gap of four years in his correspondence with Mme. Viardot. The letters must have been lost or withheld from publication. He hears from Mme. Viardot frequently, he tells his daughter in a note to her written during the summer or autumn of 1855, and it is unlikely that he failed to respond. As a matter of fact, the note to Paulinette was apparently enclosed with an unpublished letter to Pauline or to the Viardots collectively. In the communication to his daughter he says that, if the war is over, he will come to see her the following spring. It was not before the mid-summer of 1856 that he was again on his way abroad.

He did not go for his health: he was enjoying a temporary respite from illness, both real and imagined. He did not go, like Dostoevsky, to escape his creditors: he had none. He did not go, like Tolstoy, to break with his fiancée: he appears to have done that two years previously. He did not go for the sake of his work, since his material and the leisure in which to shape it were to be had in abundance at home. He had promised to visit his daughter, who was installed in a Paris *pension*. But he went abroad chiefly for the same reason that he had gone nine years previously—to be close to Pauline.

He left home against the advice of his friends and his own good judgment. The steamer which carried this aging creature out of Russia, he believed, was cutting him off from his last chance of a normal family life. But this was apparently his "fate," he had told Countess Lambert, a newly-acquired confidante, adding shrewdly: "People lacking character like to invent their 'fate,' which frees them from the responsibility of a will of their own." It may be assumed that he set out with a heavy heart. How would Pauline receive him? What had the six years of separation done to their relationship? Yet tucked away in his luggage there must have been a vague hope that it would be possible to cement the bond between them again.

On July 21, 1856, he embarked for Stettin and from there presumably went straight to Paris. He found that Paulinette had actually grown into a *jeune fille* as tall as Mme. Viardot, and—thank Heaven!—forgotten every word of Russian. It is not known if the reunion with Pauline too occurred in Paris. At all events, by the middle of August he greeted once more the familiar scenes of Courtavenel. Nothing had altered very much. Nothing was quite the same. There was his former little pupil Louise, now a girl of fifteen and no longer an only child, but with two sisters: Didie (Claudie) and Marianne. There was Louis Viardot, at fifty-six no more middle-aged than Turgenev felt himself to be at thirty-eight. There was Pauline herself, the idol of the opera house and the concert stage, with her one-shouldered shrug, her lovely hands, her enormous eyes. Her features had scarcely changed. Perhaps she closed her wide lips a little more firmly, her eyes lighted less with her ironic smile. Her voice was at its peak.

One day in September Fet called on Turgenev and stayed at the château overnight. After dinner the two Russians retired to Turgenev's room, and in the course of the talk that ensued he is said to have opened his heart to his visitor on the subject of his relations with the hostess. The tale goes that, striding hugely across the floor, with his hands clasped above his head, and squeaking with excitement, he cried: "I am under this woman's thumb! She shut out everything else from me long ago and forever. It serves me right. The only time that I am blissfully happy is when a woman stamps her heel on my neck and presses my nose into the dirt." And he concluded with the far more baffling remark: "My God, what good luck it is for a woman to be ugly!"

Fet set down this reminiscence many years after the event in a frame of mind dominated by the conviction that Pauline Viardot was a Circe who had kept the novelist captive. He must have distorted what he had heard. It is doubtful if Turgenev was as much of a masochist as Fet's report makes him out to have been. The poet may have caught him in a momentary mood of rebellion against the power that the prima donna exercised over him. That there were such moments is scarcely to be doubted. Turgenev is one of the great celebrators of the tender passion. He exalts the enchantment of love, its ability to array the world in glory, to fill the heart with "the gay terror" of imminent happiness, to ennoble and to liberate. But he recognized that it can have another character. It can be a disease, an obsession, an irrational force destroying the finer instincts, oppressing and subjugating. The bondage of love is a recurrent motif in his pages. "In love one person is a slave, the other—a tyrant, and not for nothing do poets speak of the chains of love." Thus a protagonist in the story, "A Correspondence," written in 1854 and printed two years later. One is tempted to suppose that such tirades reflect the author's personal experience.

However that may have been, it is difficult to credit the accuracy of Fet's report, the more so since by Turgenev's own admission, those summer weeks gave him a taste of genuine happiness. It was all the keener because, as he put it, quoting a line of verse, "The last flowers are dearer than the luxurious firstlings of the fields." He was with people whom he loved and, he told Tolstoy, who loved him. "Each day seemed a present," he wrote to Botkin in November. "In a word, we were as happy as trout in a clear stream when the sun strikes it and penetrates the water. Have you ever seen them on such a day? They are very happy then—I'm sure of that." Life had zest and a natural variety. Of course, there was music. After the years of starvation he could not have enough of it. They went through all the symphonies and sonatas of Beethoven and a good deal else, but no Wagner, who was the *bête noire* of the company. When, a few years later, all Paris hissed the premiere of *Tannhäuser,* Turgenev, so he said, took a key out of his pocket and contributed to the general hooting. In time, Mme. Viardot accepted an invitation to sing excerpts from this very opera and gradually became reconciled to the new music. Turgenev granted that there might be beauty in it, but it was so different from everything he loved that it was too hard a wrench for him to bring himself to like it. He found *Rheingold* intolerable and *Meistersinger* atrocious, and dubbed their author a "eunuch-

Priapus." Not that he was more receptive to other innovators in his favorite art. He had a low opinion of Russian music, Tchaikovsky and Rimsky-Korsakov excepted. Liberal in all other respects, he remained a complete conservative in music, reserving his devotion for such masters as Mozart, Gluck, Beethoven, Schumann.

Naturally, there were other entertainments. The Potato Theatre rang to the lines of Molière and Racine. This remodeled lodge owed its name to the fact that the admission fee was a potato, which every member of the audience had to dig up in the kitchen garden and deposit in a crate that stood beside the door. Louise, playing Athalie, was privileged to wear a scarlet robe cut by her grandfather Garcia, decorated with fringe and spangles by her grandmother Garcia, and originally worn by her aunt, la Malibran. Paulinette, who was spending her vacation at Courtavenel, was charming in *Iphigénie*—Turgenev was very much pleased with his daughter, finding her frank, kind, and appealing. He himself was sometimes impressed into the cast. There were also books to be read aloud and, of course, walks and boat rides. In her memoirs Louise (Mme. Héritte-Viardot) retails at length the practical jokes the children played on Turgenev, in which her mother sometimes took part. As for his own *métier,* he kept in practice even with parlor games. When they played *jeux de têtes,* and he drew the profiles to which the company attached characteristics—Pauline's, he noted, were the subtlest and most intelligent—he retained the sketches and some of the commentaries to use in his stories.

Were these days radiant for him with a particular happiness? Was Pauline his mistress, as she may have been during his earlier prolonged stay in France? These queries were answered in the affirmative, categorically if incidentally, in a collection of Turgenev's letters to his daughter first published, with biographical commentary, in 1931 by Eugène K. Séménoff. On June 20, 1857, the prima donna was delivered of her fourth, and last, child, a boy christened Paul Louis Joachim. A footnote in Mr. Séménoff's work reads: "The boy whom Pauline brought into the world in July (*sic!*), 1857, was and is considered to be the son of Turgenev. Paul himself is convinced of it; his daughter, Alice Viardot, has

Vissarion Belinsky

Pauline Viardot
painted by N. Ploszczynski, engraved by Lallemand.
Mme. Viardot believed this to be her best portrait

confirmed it to me personally." While Mr. Séménoff's allegation does not inspire confidence, it is nevertheless true that, as far as is known, it has not been denied by the persons directly concerned, above all by Paul himself, who was alive at the time. It finds some slight support in a passage from the reminiscences of a certain S. Romm, who as a young girl studied singing under Mme. Viardot in the early 80's. Having observed the family at a concert, she noted: "Paul's tall stature and large expressive features involuntarily attracted attention; his entire appearance contrasted in a striking manner with that of the other members of the family."

On the other hand there is indirect evidence that militates against Mr. Séménoff's statement. After dining with his brother at the Viardot villa in Baden one autumn day in 1862, Nikolay Turgenev wrote to his wife: "The Viardot children treat him [Ivan] as a father (although they don't resemble him in the slightest degree—don't let's gossip); in other words, I think that there were relations between them [Ivan and Pauline], but many years ago, and that now he simply lives with them and has become a friend of the family." Five years later Turgenev wrote, congratulating Annenkov on the birth of a child: "So now you are the father of a child given you by the woman you love. Such happiness," he volunteered to this intimate, "I have never experienced, and I am glad that it has fallen to the lot of a man of whom I am fond."

Certainly there was nothing to suggest Turgenev's paternity in the way in which he greeted the arrival of the baby. In July, 1857, he was at a German spa taking the cure. On receiving news of the happy event, he responded with a letter to the Viardots. He begins by kissing and congratulating his "dear friend Viardot" from the bottom of his heart and goes on to say: "It is pleasant to have a son, isn't it? And when you have three daughters, it is even pleasanter." The rest of the letter, which is addressed to the mother, and is written in a humorous vein, opens with hurrah in six languages and continues: "Long live little Paul! Long live his mother, long live his father, long live the whole family! Bravo! I told you that all would be well and that you would have a son! I congratulate and kiss you all." He asks for a detailed description of the young man's features and the color of his eyes, for information regarding his first witticisms and a brief account of the revolutionary day [June 20, 1789, was the date of the Oath of *Jeu de Paume*] which the little *sans-culotte* had chosen for his entrance into the world. He predicts that the *Conversations-Lexicon* for 1950 will contain an entry for the famous Paul Viardot, son of the celebrated Pauline Garcia and the gifted author and translator of *Don Quixote,* Louis Viardot. "And your awakening on the 21st was pleasant, wasn't it? And the little one's cries—is there any music," he asks the prima donna, "that can compare with it?" And he ends: "I kiss you all again, beginning with Monsieur Paul, and I remain your old friend." If the baby were indeed his bastard, it is scarcely conceivable that Turgenev would have written in this fashion about the newborn to its mother and her husband, his "dear friend."

The paternity of Pauline's second daughter, Claudie, Turgenev's special favorite, of whom he spoke as though she were his daughter, has also been attributed to him. But it is plain from a letter of his to I. P. Borisov, dated March 24, 1869, that she was born on May 22, 1852, and for the two previous years he had been separated from her mother by a thousand miles. It was also rumored that Turgenev was the father of Marianne, the youngest of the Viardot daughters. A letter, written by a Russian expatriate shortly after the novelist's death, which came to light in 1925, has this bit of gossip: "It is suspected that Mme. Duvernoy (Marianne) is Turgenev's daughter. She is a beauty of the Spanish type, like her mother, who in my opinion is still a perfect Juno—but there is something suspicious, something smacking of Oryol, about the nose." This rumor has no more foundation than the other. As for the paternity of Paul Viardot, under the circumstances it remains a moot point.

In the late autumn Turgenev left Courtavenel, following the Viardots to Paris. No sooner was he established in the apartment he had rented for himself and his daughter than he was beset by his old illness that, as he wrote to Botkin, had last attacked six years earlier: bladder trouble. It meant persistent pain which interfered with both work and pleasure. The letters that his friends began to receive from him were heavy with lamentation. He felt all the time like rubbish that people had forgotten to sweep out. He was poisoned. He was rotting like frozen fish in a thaw. He was squashed like one of those white mushrooms with green filling that you always tread upon in Russian woods. He was a wretched shed ready to collapse. He was as brittle as glass.

His physical sufferings alone do not account for his acute depression. He may have been going through a critical period in his relations with Pauline and having a bad time of it. According to Mr. Séménoff, the novelist's wretchedness has a simple explanation: he had discovered that he had "rivals" for the lady's affection luckier than himself, among them the painter, Ary Scheffer. "For my part," Mr. Séménoff writes, "I am certain of it though I have no written proofs." He does not trouble to give the reasons for his certitude, except to state that the man was designated as such a rival "by public rumor and people in the Viardots' very entourage." It is true that on first meeting Pauline in 1840, just before her marriage, Ary Scheffer, then forty-five years old, fell in love with her, as has been indicated. We have it on her own authority that he continued to love her until he died, in 1858. Several months after his death she wrote to her friend, the German conductor, Julius Rietz:

Never did he speak to me about his love, except lately, when, as he said, it was no longer dangerous for me to know it. He managed to adopt the role of father toward me and keep it to the end. He won my entire confidence, he was my refuge. I had moments of great pain in my life, he gave me the strength to overcome them by showing me art in its most solacing, most divine aspect. I had the discouragements of an artist, a kind of annihilation of all my faculties, and by his severe and tender words he, as it were, resuscitated me. I nearly lost my mind—his lofty reason restored my mental balance. When my suffering was too great for words, he knew how to guess what was going on in my poor heart, all the recesses of which were familiar to him, and he was able to heal the wound by his tender friendship and by his inalterable and intelligent kindness. And that is how these eighteen years have gone by, I adoring him like a daughter, he showing me a father's fortifying and always beneficent love.

A month later she confides in the same correspondent, saying that she had once had a moment of weakness when she had been on the verge of committing "a grave fault," but

Scheffer, who watched over her "like a father," had prevented
her from this misstep and helped her regain self-control. "I
didn't commit the fault, for which I thank God and my poor,
well-beloved Scheffer . . ." In a letter dated March 3, 1859,
she spoke of her husband and Ary Scheffer as "always her
dearest friends." In the light of these confidences one must
dismiss as a baseless invention the picture of the sexagenarian
Ary Scheffer suddenly leaping into the role of Turgenev's
lucky rival. It should be added that although the novelist
detested Scheffer's paintings, the two men were on friendly
terms.*

---

* Following Eugène K. Séménoff, even to relegating the remark to a
footnote, Mr. Magarshack states in his biography that Paul Viardot
"always regarded Turgenev as his father," adding, as his own contribution, "and Paulinette as his half-sister." Furthermore, he writes: "He
[Turgenev] had good reason to believe that he was the father of the
baby [Paul Viardot]." Presumably leaning on the same authority, Mr.
Magarshack introduces Ary Scheffer into the picture. He declares, without supporting his statement by any evidence: "When Turgenev left
Courtavenel for Paris at the end of October [1856], he already suspected
that she [Pauline] was having an affair with Ary Scheffer, who was painting her portrait at the time." For this last detail Mr. Magarshack is alone
responsible. It happens that Scheffer's well known portrait of Pauline
Viardot was painted not in 1856 but, as is clear from a letter of hers to
Julius Rietz, almost immediately after they became acquainted, that is in
1840. (The date is confirmed in a communication to me from L. J. Bol,
Director of the Museums at Dordrecht, Holland, Ary Scheffer's birthplace).
Mr. Magarshack makes the situation more piquant by asserting that Turgenev and Scheffer were Pauline's lovers simultaneously and that the
discovery of this had "a shattering effect" on the novelist, bringing on
an attack of his illness. (What the patient described as "neuralgia of
the bladder" the biographer diagnoses as "entirely a nervous affliction,"
which had first attacked him in 1850 before he left France, "when
Pauline jilted him for another lover." The man remains anonymous and
otherwise unidentified. Mr. Magarshack provides the lady with one
more, equally insubstantial, lover. We are told that, at the age of fifty,
she took him "openly," and that Turgenev, to show his resentment,
"during that year wrote no letters to her from Russia." Pauline was
fifty in 1871. Between February 11 and March 13 of that year the
novelist addressed ten long, affectionate letters to her from Russia. They
are printed in *Sovremennyi mir,* 1912, 3.) Noting that Turgenev returned to Courtavenel in the summer of 1857 and stayed there for
two months, Mr. Magarshack asks why he did so. "Was it because
he wanted to see his son? Would anything else have induced him to
go there, knowing as he did that Pauline Viardot was still Ary Scheffer's
mistress?" How Turgenev came to know that the man whom Pauline
regarded as a father was "still" her lover is one of Mr. Magarshack's
secrets. The novelist's suspicion of Pauline's unfaithfulness to him mentioned earlier has now hardened into certainty, for Mr. Magarshack

There is nothing to indicate that the novelist's distress was prompted by jealousy or by a sudden cooling toward him on Pauline's part. Before he left Russia he had written to Countess Lambert that, his heart being no longer young, he had given up counting on personal happiness in the "troubling" sense that youth gives the word. Perhaps he had misjudged himself. Once more in the company of Pauline, he may have discovered that he wanted more by way of troubling happiness than this woman was able to offer. Possibly he gained a clearer insight into her nature.

All that Pauline claimed to have inherited from her Gipsy father, along with a hatred of hypocrisy, was the vagabond spirit. An air of transiency hung about her Paris home, so that to Dickens, who dined with the Viardots in January, 1856, their house looked "exactly as if they had moved into it last week and were going away next. Notwithstanding which, they have lived in it eight years." Her household, then, resembled her father's. But though she worshiped at the same altars, music and love were not, as they had been for Don Manoel, her sole religion. The Spaniard is characterized by a former colleague who figures in Turgenev's *Spring Freshets* as *"un Vesuvio."* His daughter did not answer to this description. Indeed, she confessed herself puzzled about how so "calm" a human being as she could have been the offspring of two such people as her parents. Turgenev himself was not unaware of this trait of the woman he loved. "There is a great deal of calm in your character," he wrote to her in arguing that the role of Iphigenia in Goethe's tragedy of that title, a work of classical simplicity and chastity, ought to suit her to perfection.

Her calmness was, however, not a matter of feeble emotions but of strong self-control. "What happiness," she wrote, "to see your will carry off a victory over passion, over instinct!"

---

goes on to say: "But, of course, the irony of the situation was that he could never be sure that he *was* Paul's father." Of course not: Paul's father may have been Louis Viardot. In any case he could not have been, as Mr. Magarshack thinks Turgenev may have thought, Ary Scheffer. According to the *Memoir of the Life of Ary Scheffer*, by Mrs. Grote (London, 1860), his wife, to whom he was devoted, died in the summer of 1856, and for the rest of the year he was in a state of mental distress and physical prostration.

Such triumphs did not come easily. "Love kills when it cannot burst into flame," she told Julius Rietz in a letter. "To put it out, ah, that is a fearful torment, excruciating, terrible, deadly." She may have been remembering the temptation she had withstood with Scheffer's help. On that occasion, she wrote, she had nearly died, she had wanted to commit suicide, but when that friend stopped her and brought her home, "half demented," she had gradually regained her will power, "crushed her heart" and done what she felt to be her duty.

In his *History of the French Revolution* (vol. 6), after describing the *Fête de la Raison* at which the actress, Mlle. Maillard, had impersonated Reason, Michelet writes: "The day when the world, grown wise, will restore to women the priestly office they held in antiquity, who will be surprised to see, marching at the head of the national procession, the good, the charitable, the saintly Garcia-Viardot?" The prima donna was no saint, but she did have an unusually high regard for the ethical code. The fact that most women singers were "courtesans" depressed her, and she disliked living in the Babylon that was Paris. "Ah, most assuredly it is fine to be a great artist," she wrote, "but on condition of being first and foremost a human being in the moral sense of the word." She was a devoted mother and, apparently, a faithful wife, though she did not love her husband, a man twenty-one years her senior, in whom she found every virtue except "the childlike element, freshness of spirit." She confessed to Julius Rietz in a letter dated March 26, 1859: "I could never give Louis any other feeling [than friendship] in return for his strong and deep love, much as I wished to. I sometimes felt that it was wicked of me, that it was an injustice of Fate, that it was cruel, what you please. But human will has only a negative effect on the heart—it can silence it but cannot force it to speak. I shall confess to you very quietly, in your ear, that these little trips which I made alone this winter were a refreshing holiday for me. On the one hand, they were a rest for my heart, somewhat weary of the expression of a love which it cannot share. On the other hand, absence only strengthened my friendship, esteem and great respect for this man, so high-minded and so devoted."

She gives the impression that, for reasons which remain

obscure, she fought shy of physical passion. Fleeing from love, she took refuge in a friendship compact of tenderness and maternal solicitude. She made a cult of this relationship, exalting it, lavishing upon it in her polyglot vocabulary an extravagant ardor. She wrote to Rietz: "My friendship is passionate yet tranquil—that is why it is so beneficent to me. . . . Without sacred friendship I would have died long ago. Through it I was resurrected like Lazarus; without it I couldn't live. It is my salvation, the warming ray of my existence. . . . I can give as much friendship, constant, self-denying, firm, tireless, as any human being." Ailing hearts seem to have had a special appeal to her. It was apparently her fate, she observed on one occasion, to act as a sister of charity, but she loved the *métier*.

It was, then, a safe, discarnate, inclusive sort of affection that she offered, one surmises, to her devotees: to Berlioz, who, at the age of fifty-six, surprised and somewhat dismayed her by a passion that flared up suddenly (*"blitzplötzlich"*), to Ary Scheffer, to Turgenev. There is no doubt that what he felt for her was passion. Writing to Tolstoy on January 7, 1857, Turgenev said that he loved Pauline "more than ever, and more than anybody in the world." Two months later he mentioned in a letter to Annenkov a bronze bear he had received from Mme. Viardot which he prized because it was the spit and image of his correspondent and also because "it was given to me by the only woman I love and always shall love."

17

FOLLY'S DUE

It was cold comfort to be sitting on the edge of another man's nest, even if the edge was broad and well cushioned. And yet it must have been clear to Turgenev that this was the prospect he was facing. "By the way," he wrote to Tolstoy early in the new year 1857, "what are the absurd rumors that are spreading among you? Her [Pauline Viardot's] husband is well, has never been better, and I am as far from a wedding as you, for example." He was tormented by the thought that he had wasted his life, let it slip between his fingers. His youth was far behind him, and there was no use stirring the ashes: not a spark remained under them. He was too old not to have a real home of his own. Where was he to live? What should he do with the rest of his days? If only he could work! But his ailment unfitted him for any effort that demanded concentration. His bladder trouble had worsened, and he blamed the climate of Paris for it. He thought his pain was a symptom of gallstones, the disease that had killed his father, and this added to his distress. Tolstoy, after staying with him for a while, wrote home that he was "pitiful to see."

To make matters worse, his collected stories in three volumes, issued toward the close of 1856, met with a cool reception. At least so he believed. Obviously, he was bankrupt, his talent had run dry. In a letter dated March 1, 1857, he told Botkin that his prose was as bad as his verse had been and that all he could in decency do was retire. The young Tolstoy, who was in Paris, holding his tongue and taking in everything about him, was the only hope of Russian literature. "As for me," Turgenev wrote, "let me whisper in your ear, with the request not to repeat it to anyone: except for the piece ("The Trip to the Woodlands") promised to Druzhinin [editor of the review, *Biblioteka dlya Chteniya*], I will not publish or, for that matter, write a single line to the end of time." He had then written only the first of his six novels and none of his better known shorter narratives. "The other day," he continued, "I didn't burn all my rough drafts, plans, etc., for fear of imitating Gogol, but tore them up and threw them into the water closet. They're all trash. . . . This is not an outburst of pique, but the fruit of slowly ripened convictions. . . . As I have a fairly good command of Russian, I intend, if I am well, to occupy myself with a translation of *Don Quixote* [Louis Viardot turned the book into French]. You will probably think that all this is exaggeration," he concluded, "and you won't believe me. You will see, I trust, that I have never spoken more earnestly and sincerely."

Unable to write, he pored over the books of others. He told Herzen that he had swallowed Suetonius, Sallust, whom he did not like at all, as well as Tacitus and part of Livy, and had read De Quincey's *Confessions of an Opium Eater*— twice. He said that he led the life of a hermit, yet he made many new acquaintances—though no friendships—in spite of his ailing state. On one occasion the author of *A Sportsman's Sketches* was introduced to the author of *Uncle Tom's Cabin,* "a kindly, plain and—imagine—bashful lady," he wrote to Druzhinin, "with two carrot-headed daughters in red burnouses and fierce crinolines—very odd figures." He also frequented the houses of one or two Russian aristocrats who had settled in France, and spoke admiringly of their pretty daughters. Prince Nikolay Trubetzkoy's estate near Fontainebleau gave him an opportunity to go hunting with Louis Viardot.

He was spending this wretched winter—he called it "terrible"—in the Paris of Little Napoleon and saw it with a jaundiced eye. The city was booming with a spectacular prosperity. All din and dazzle, he wrote to the old Aksakov, Paris could turn the head only of a callow youth or a doting ancient. The French *literati* of the younger generation were noisy, petty and empty, with provincial notions, mannerisms instead of talent, given to log-rolling rather than criticism, and there was a total absence of faith and conviction, even aesthetic conviction, among the lot of them. Added to the hubbub these men were making was the sickly whine of Lamartine, the tremolo of Hugo, the chatter of George Sand. As for

Balzac, his followers were "kowtowing to Chance, calling it Reality and Truth" (on a later occasion he characterized Balzac as "an ethnographer, not an artist." The novelist was so repugnant to him, he wrote at the end of his life, that he could never read more than ten consecutive pages of him). Further, "the level of morality is sinking daily, and all and sundry thirst for gold—that's France for you!" If he was staying on in Paris it was owing to certain peculiar circumstances beyond his control. "But when spring comes," he assured his correspondent, "I will fly home, where life is still young and rich in hope." For a while the Westernist came under the spell of the Slavophil thesis contrasting the vigor of virginal Russia with the senility of the effete West. To another friend he wrote that everything Russian had become "nearer and dearer" to him.

Over and over again he repeated that in the spring he would return to Spasskoye without fail, even though, as he told Tolstoy, with his departure he would have to say farewell to his last dream of happiness. In the spring, instead of going to Russia, he traveled to England to see Herzen, who had been established in London since 1852. As Turgenev arrived there early in May, at the height of the season, he was able to use to good advantage his letters of introduction. He made many "pleasant acquaintances." He met Disraeli, perhaps in his capacity of novelist rather than in that of statesman. He found Carlyle interesting, in spite of his undemocratic views. He also encountered Macaulay and Thackeray, who, upon being regaled with a Russian folk-song, laughed till his large paunch quivered. He just missed a meeting with Palmerston, and if he had not been in such haste to return to the continent, he might have spoken with the Prince Consort himself. Before crossing the Channel again he went to Manchester, where he saw "many marvelous things." Altogether, the English were an agreeable surprise to him: "truly a great nation."

He had intended to proceed from England to Russia. Instead, he made for Sinzig, a German spa. As the waters, far from doing him good, only aggravated his condition, he went to Boulogne, apparently for the sea bathing. Here, somewhat skeptically, he agreed to undergo "electrical" treatment—he was ready to try anything in his misery—but the relief was only temporary. He was simply *"la merde,"* he assured Botkin. "A man who gnashes his teeth with pain and vexation from morning till evening and at night knocks his head against the wall is not a human being and is not worthy of human society; I reek of the corpse and I have become heartily sick of myself . . ." In writing to the same friend two days later he returned to the sore subject of his neuralgia, which had chosen a "nasty spot" to lodge in. "What distresses me particularly," he said, "is that formerly the pain vanished or became markedly weaker as soon as I left Paris; but now the change of place brings no relief—and I am in the same agony in Boulogne as I was at Sinzig." He informed Countess Lambert that he had decided to return home for a lengthy stay. "I have been roaming about and leading the life of a Gipsy long enough." Notwithstanding this decision, he went back to Paris. His wanderings ended at Courtavenel.

He arrived there on August 23, and the following day he was writing to Nekrasov: "As you see, I am here, that is, I have committed the very folly against which you warned me. . . . But I couldn't help myself." He had intended to spend three weeks there; he stayed nearly two months. The need to be near Pauline was tyrannical. Having recuperated from her confinement, the prima donna was again filling concert engagements, and it is possible that Turgenev felt rather neglected during those weeks. In September he invited Nekrasov to his Petersburg apartment a month hence to help eat a turkey with rice, which he undertook to carve. The fowl escaped the knife, for late in October he was with Botkin in Rome.

It was "Don Basilio" (Vasily Botkin) who had originated the idea of a trip to Italy, and Turgenev, after some hesitation, fell in with the suggestion. He managed to justify to himself and others this drastic change of plan. The prospect of a winter in Russia did not smile to him. Besides, he did not want to return home empty-handed. If there was any stuff left in him, he said to himself, Rome, out of its accumulated humanity, would grant him the mood and the energy for work. He did not fear the distractions of Italy, whose cities, as Henry James found, draw the artist "away from his small questions to their own greater ones." And then, a change of scene might, after all, mitigate his wretchedness. The Eternal City, he hoped, would renew for him, if for the last time, "the sense of youth and beauty"; would stimulate him with "great traces of a great life"; would give him solitude without loneliness, and assure him of "that peculiar tranquillity, full of inner attention and quite movement" which, as he had written to Countess Lambert, is essential to a writer, to the artist generally. There was also the thought that in the spring, before returning to Russia, he would be able to see once more, as he wrote to Tolstoy, "the people close to me," chiefly, of course, Pauline.

She seems to have been on tour at the time of his departure and he must have taken leave of her by letter, as he did of Louis Viardot with whom he was on the best of terms. At all events, he kept writing to Pauline from Rome, but received no answer. On November 2 he begged his daughter to reply by return mail, giving him news of Mme. Viardot and of the whole family. After a lapse of two months he was reproaching Paulinette for having failed to send him word about Mme. Viardot. "So far," he explained ruefully, "I haven't received a single letter from her." Three weeks later he commissioned his daughter to kiss Pauline's hands *"bien fort."*

Whether because he did not hear from Pauline or for other reasons as well, his miseries were not to be exorcised by Rome's magic. He warned Tolstoy against the fate that had befallen him: he felt that his life was over and, at the same time, that it hadn't begun, that what he had in prospect was "the vagaries of youth combined with the sterile emptiness of old age." He was ruined, he told Fet, like an ant hill poked by ruthless children. To Annenkov he wrote that a black pall enveloped him and was not to be shaken off. Or, melancholy rather than bitter, he would remark that the beauty he perceived on every hand an ailing, aging man could watch but not partake of. Nevertheless, he was able to work. He managed to complete a narrative he had started at Sinzig, and the sense of accomplishment made him feel, as he put it, like another Arion safe ashore. The tale was "Asya," a story of great charm. He concluded an epistolary plaint to Annenkov by saying: "Still, I try not to let the soot pass into what I do." This applies to

"Asya," though scarcely to the somewhat earlier piece, written under the same stress: "A Trip to the Woodlands," which bears the personal note of *A Sportsman's Sketches*. Here the author's black mood is unmistakable. Alone in the thick of the forest and a prey to the panic induced by nature's inhumanity, he sees his whole past life as "a poor handful of dusty ashes." Again, watching a sun-drenched dragonfly poised on the tip of a twig, he seizes on it as a symbol of that equilibrium of vitality which is the core of life and which man with his passions and struggles disturbs at his peril.

In "Asya" the dominant note is that of wistful sadness. The story opens with the observation that youth mistakes gilded honey cakes for its daily bread and ends with a reflection that the faint breath of a withered flower can outlast the joys and sorrows of the man who had pressed it and indeed the man himself. The background here is a small Rhineland town, like Sinzig, or those that the author had known in his young days. In the foreground move two men and a girl who share youth's limitless and objectless expectancy. The tale is a nostalgic evocation of a love that flames up only to be snuffed out. An honorable, well intentioned young man misses happiness by failing to respond at the decisive moment to the ardor of a moody yet whole-souled girl of exquisite sensibilities. The situation is a favorite one with Turgenev, contrasting as it does male inadequacy and female strength of character. Typical, too, is the chaste blossoming of passion and its pathetic frustration. Here, as in much of his work, the indefatigable hunter is tracking down no less a quarry than youth itself. A man confirmed by illness in his sense of middle age, he invests the earlier period of life with an enchantment as impalpable and compelling as a remembered fragrance.

It was fitting that "Asya" should have been written in Rome. This city, which, to a man nourished on the classics, was full of togaed ghosts quarreling in the Forum, bargaining at the baths, at once saddened and soothed him with its vast, historic pageantry. Whatever else the Roman ruins did to him, they didn't add to his depression. The place, he found, affected him like music, something in minor, perhaps, but none the less cordial and benign. It could, he wrote later, replace, in a measure, everything—society, happiness, even love. It was not the Rome he had seen in his student years, nor was he any longer the young blood who had evoked the shade of Caesar with a saucy shout. And his companion was not the heavenly Stankevich, but the old glutton who, as Turgenev put it, had several mouths in addition to the carnal one: an aesthetical, a philosophical, etc., and ate noisily with all of them: Vasily Botkin. Botkin, who knew his Cellini as Stankevich had known his Hegel; who used to teach his friends to find as much transcendental pleasure in sniffing the aroma of turkey stuffed with truffles as in listening to Schubert's songs; who could be outraged almost to the point of violence by an unfashionable waistcoat; who could deeply admire the way Turgenev painted his radicals, and thank God for the government that suppressed them.

It was not on Botkin alone that Turgenev relied for company. There was also a small and select colony of his compatriots, most of them belonging to the nobility, with whom he occasionally teaed and dined. They were pleasant enough people, but the inquisitive Grand Duchess Yelena Pavlovna was somewhat tiresome; at the end of every one of her sentences he found, he said, a corkscrew. And here, as in Petersburg, his orbit crossed at once the *haut monde* and the confraternity of artists. At the Café Greco, on via Condotti near Piazza di Spagna, which had been offering entertainment for two hundred years, he passed the time of day with some of the Russian painters and sculptors who had come to Rome to study and to work. In his opinion they were, every one of them, ignoramuses devoid of talent, good draughtsmen and nothing more. What particularly distressed him was that they swore by their compatriot, the now forgotten academician, Bryullov, and despised all other painters, beginning with Raphael. "Art in Russia," he told Annenkov, "is still in a bad way."

The one man in this group who attracted Turgenev was Alexander Ivanov. After more than a quarter of a century of work here, this painter had become quite a Roman, and something of a local celebrity. He was known for having spent more than twenty years over a single canvas, which, although not yet completed, he was exhibiting to a select public. He worked steadily at the same theme: Christ appearing to the people. He was harried by the baffled desire to paint, with the utmost historical accuracy in details, his changing conception of the Saviour. His chief difficulty was that he had lost his faith and embraced the unorthodox views of David Strauss. He went so far as to visit Strauss, with whom he held unique converse, himself speaking Italian, which Strauss did not understand, while the theologian spoke Latin, of which the painter was quite innocent. No one will ever know what the German thought of this squat, middle-aged Russian, with the broad white forehead and soft cheeks of a child, the awed eyes of a hermit, and plump stubby-fingered hands.

What Turgenev relished in this earnest soul was the combination of a boundless naïveté with flashes of searching intelligence. Then too, he admired the man's work for the intellectual quality which informed it, and which compensated him for its technical short-comings. Already he felt that a work of art at its best involved the artist's rational powers to the full, and that without understanding there is no aesthetic appreciation. Besides, he sympathized with Ivanov's passion for observation, which is evidenced in all of the two hundred and fifty-eight sketches for his main canvas. He saw a great deal of the painter, and, together with Botkin, took him on a short trip to Albano. Turgenev's account of the excursion affords a glimpse of the trio as they halted, in the golden light of the fine autumn day, at Rocca di Papa: he, melted by the felicity of the hour, and all attentive; Botkin, feeding his senses on the weather and the ancient stones; Ivanov, squatting on the brink of a well, and biting at a piece of dry bread which he had taken out of his pocket and was dipping now and again into the water. The idyl had its flaw: this companion showed signs of being unbalanced—the result, Turgenev supposed, of his having been a solitary for twenty-five years.

Turgenev had hoped that the southern climate would benefit his health. He was disappointed. His neuralgia got much worse. Looking back at his winter in Rome, he wrote to Tolstoy: "The disease poisoned my best days." Nevertheless, all through his stay there he neglected the doctors. In

March he left Rome with voluble regret, but in all his subsequent peregrinations he never returned to it. He stopped off in Florence, where he spent ten memorable days. He also visited other cities, including Venice, and several pages of *On the Eve* pay tribute to its fascination. In the same novel he admitted that "It is useless for a man whose life is over, who has been broken by fate, to visit Venice: it will be bitter to him, like the memory of the unfulfilled dreams of his young days." He must have tasted something of that bitterness.

Early in April he was in Vienna for the purpose of consulting a celebrated physician. After a session with Dr. Sigmund the patient concluded that he was to spend the rest of his life in that pathetic effort to postpone the inevitable end which is the whole occupation of old age.

He declared that he was going home to stay there to the end of his days. Indeed, he decided that it would have been better for him to have remained at home. He had acted like a man bent on smashing his head against a wall, he wrote to Countess Lambert, while knowing very well that the wall was made of stone and was harder than his head. At least he hoped that the lesson would not be lost on him. He announced to Nekrasov that he would be in Petersburg by the end of May and that no power on earth would keep him abroad any longer, winding up with a quotation:

> "Enough! Away with you!
> You've given Folly all that is her due."

Leaving Vienna, he proceeded to Dresden for a rendezvous with Annenkov. The latter was astonished to find, instead of a moribund creature, a man in flourishing health. To account for this, Turgenev advanced the theory that a person seriously ill shows every sign of health during the periods of respite: the disease allows nature to fatten its victim, so that, returning, it may find food for a feast. From Dresden he traveled to Leipzig for the sole purpose of hearing Pauline sing, and then on to Paris, from which he made a trip to London to see Herzen. He was a guest at the annual banquet of the Royal Literary Fund for needy authors, presided over by Lord Palmerston, and wrote an article about it for a Petersburg magazine in order to stimulate interest in a projected Russian institution of the same kind. At the end of his acute and entertaining account he spoke of the feeling awakened in him whenever he was confronted with public life in England. "Yes, I said to myself, here, as in all other matters on which this nation, great in spite of its many defects, has set its lion's claw—here, too, it shows strength, soundness, competence."

He wrote Nekrasov that he was returning to Paris, but intended to give himself only a fortnight there. "Having read the word 'Paris'," he continued. "you will think: 'He's a liar; he'll stay on there.' To which I reply: a certain person will not be in Paris then, and I shall go merely to see my daughter." His presence in the French capital allowed him to be best man to Prince Orlov, the Russian ambassador; he had acted in the same capacity for Fet the previous year. It was his fate, he reflected, always to be groomsman and never have one of his own. Not until June did our weary Ulysses smell the smoke of home fires.

18

A NEST OF GENTLEFOLK

A dinner at Donon's celebrated Turgenev's home-coming. The air of the June evening resounded with the noise of droshkies clattering through the courtyard to the door of the old, aristocratic restaurant. Champagne flowed. The mercurial Nekrasov was there. And Goncharov, screening his jealousy behind a retiring manner. And Ivanov, freshly come to this confusing, unfamiliar, hard-headed Petersburg, and more dazed than ever. It was good to be back again in this genial atmosphere.

Turgenev had digested no more than half a dozen less elaborate dinners before he found himself back at Spasskoye. He spent four diligent months there, and when the winter season revived the life of the capital he went back to it, carrying with him the manuscript of *A Nest of Gentlefolk*. This novel, the main action of which is laid in the year 1842, is remote from the issues that agitated the public at the time it was written. It is the pathetic story of Lavretzky's disappointed love for Liza. For a few incomparable hours he believes that with her help he can mend the life broken by a worthless woman. He has scarcely realized the freedom granted him by the supposed death of his wife, when she turns up like a bad penny to destroy the incredible happiness that he had briefly accepted as possible.

All the minor characters and subsidiary situations are skilfully made to assist in indicating the secret inception and delicate progress of the love of Lavretzky and Liza. Their meeting in the garden is a piece of writing which gives out fragrance like a wind-shaken bush. Such a passage makes up for the gossamery quality of the heroine. For Liza, the Russian Gretchen, is less a flesh-and-blood woman than a symbol of unattainable happiness and irrecoverable youth. In the end she takes the veil that she may atone by prayer, presumably for her own sin, that of loving a married man, and also for the sins of others. She therefore has a place in the company of Turgenev's heroines who lead lives of sacrifice and dedication, though she does so on the religious plane and her successors will be secular-minded. Liza begs Lavretzky to reconcile himself with his wife, thus performing his duty as she does hers.

Lavretzky's mother was a peasant woman, his father a landed gentleman thoroughly alienated from his people by long residence abroad. Lavretzky himself is pictured as a prodigal son turning his face from the West and coming home to cultivate his ancestral acres. There is an unmistakable flavor of Slavophilism about the arguments he uses to confound Liza's unsuccessful suitor, the odious young bureaucrat, Panshin, in a discussion which is the sole political passage in the book. Lavretzky speaks of Russia's youth and cultural independence, rejects "arrogant changes, unjustified either by knowledge of native conditions or faith in an ideal," demands that the inherent worth of the common folk be recognized and humbly revered. Panshin, on the other hand, is the Westernist. The trouble with Russia, he declares, is that it is only half Europeanized. All nations are exactly alike, he glibly announces, give them good institutions and these will transform the life of the people. In a chapter of his reminiscences, written a decade later, Turgenev pointed out that, "an arrant and incorrigible Westernist" himself, he had been delighted to show (in *A Nest of Gentlefolk*) the vulgar side of Westernism and have the Slavophil Lavretzky triumph over his opponent. He had obeyed the logic of his characters, not his private preconceptions, thus giving evidence of the objectivity that he held essential to the novelist's equipment.

The final glimpse we catch of Lavretzky is when he returns, after an absence of eight years, to the garden "where for the last time he had vainly stretched out his hands toward the forbidden cup in which the golden wine of delight bubbles and sparkles." And yet, Turgenev insists, the "lonely, hearthless wanderer" was content; he had undergone that saving change which alone enables men to remain decent to the end: "he had really ceased to think of his own happiness, of selfish aims." He had become an admirable gentleman farmer, who labored not for himself alone; "as far as lay within his powers, he had provided well for his peasants." Having anchored in the harbor of middle age, he regarded the new craft that was taking the wave with sadness but no bitterness or envy. It is as though Turgenev had cast Lavretzky in the part for which he was himself the understudy. For some time he had held the conviction that a man past his youth could live honorably only if he gave up all thought of personal ambition and felicity, heeding nothing but the dictates of duty. Goethe's line, *"Entbehren sollst du, sollst entbehren!"* is the epigraph of Turgenev's story, "Faust," published in 1856. The moral of it is formulated thus: "Life is hard work. Renunciation, constant renunciation—that is its secret meaning, the clue to its riddle; not the fulfillment of cherished thoughts and dreams, no matter how exalted they may be, but the performance of one's duty—that is what one must care about." Such is also the lesson of *A Nest of Gentlefolk.*

In the character of the old musician, Lemm, the novelist indirectly pays homage to the romantic Germany of his youth, to its idealism, its earnest sentimentality, its genius for that art toward which all the others move. France, on the other hand, or more properly, Paris, is treated with implied disparagement as a depraved, pleasure-loving, coldhearted belle. It is in the malicious portrait of Lavretzky's wife and the faint sketch of her French maid that all Turgenev's distaste for the country which he was eventually to make his home is most vividly felt.

A Nest of Gentlefolk, published in the issue of *The Contemporary* for January, 1859, established its author as a novelist of the first rank. It was the most universally acclaimed of his major works. According to Annenkov, it inaugurated a literary Truce of God. The reviewers devoted long pages to it in the bulky magazines, and it was a grateful topic at dinner tables and in drawing rooms. What contributed to the immense success of the melancholy tale was the poetic charm enveloping it: the aura that rests upon a passing era like the light of a setting sun. More than any other of Turgenev's novels, *A Nest of Gentlefolk* supports Botkin's thesis that his friend was, properly speaking, a lyricist.

The winter was one of busy if not especially zestful living: dinners at Donon's and Dusseau's; the establishment of a fund for needy men of letters; some slight semi-political controversy; an affair, rather too arduous for a man turned forty, with a person of the demi-monde. A second postscript to his letter to Botkin of February 10, 1859 reads: "Alexandra Petrovna has exhausted me to the marrow of my bones. No, brother, at our age it should be no more than once in three months." He spent a good many more quiet evenings on Furstadtskaya Street in the delightful drawing room of Countess Lambert. It was connections of this rank that won him the reputation of a snob. During this season the malicious Goncharov wrote Botkin that their friend was perpetually calling on countesses and princesses: "If he doesn't pay three visits in an evening, he is downcast." But even if Turgenev had originally sought the Countess Lambert because he hoped that a lady who was the daughter of a Minister of Finance and who had been presented at Court might be of service to a writer under police surveillance, certainly their acquaintance ripened into a friendship to whose genuineness his letters richly attest. She was neither young nor beautiful, but cultivated, charming, and intelligent, and she maintained one of the leading salons in Petersburg. He was grateful to her for offering him one of those serene and secure relations which suited the autumn of his days. Here was a sympathetic ear for his little monologues on life, and his recitations of Pushkin's incomparable verse, a lap into which to pour his troubles, another pair of critical eyes to review his manuscripts.

There were moments, indeed, when this comfortable companionship was threatened by the invasion of a disturbing element. "If I were your husband," Turgenev wrote to his friend in October, 1859, "and my wife were in the habit of writing such letters [as I am receiving from you] I would be rather worried." He wrote to her fondly too—she said he had the soul of a siren—and probably talked to her in the same vein as he bent over her hand; but in his letters at least, he was never unfaithful to Pauline. "I consider it my duty to tell you that there are only two creatures on earth whom I love more than you: one, because she is my daughter, the other, because . . . you know why." The friendship begun so tardily for both of them endured for a dozen years, and then lapsed painlessly.

He must have exaggerated the depth of his feeling for Paulinette. His letters to her are warm, solicitous, full of sage paternal counsel. He lists her mistakes in spelling and grammar, harps on the importance of her music lessons, urges the necessity for forethought, diligence, kindness, particularly kindness, everywhere and always; he warns her against running into debt, notes with alarm her tendency toward slyness and vanity, upbraids her for twittering like a bird when she speaks. He would scold her less, he says, if he did not love her so much. In any event he was glad to do what he could to make an attractive *jeune fille* of the plain-featured girl, but it would appear that he was prompted less by affection than by a sense of duty.

The letters that he was now addressing to Pauline Viardot breathe friendly devotion, but the ardor of former days is somewhat subdued. Having received word from her of Ary Scheffer's demise, he writes, on June 26, 1858: "When death strikes down someone among us, the remaining friends must close ranks. I do not offer you consolation, I merely reach out a friendly hand to you; a heart deeply devoted to you says that you can depend upon it as fully as you depended on the one that is no longer beating." He keeps her *au courant* of his works and days. Her own contribution to the correspondence seems to have been scanty. Along toward the end of the year she became involved in a violent *amitié amoureuse* of the kind she reveled in. "The adopted child of my heart," as she called him, was the forty-seven year old German composer and conductor, Julius Rietz, who has already been mentioned in these pages. She went out of her way to add him to her circle of friends, subjecting him to an avalanche of mammoth epistles, filled with confidences and protestations of ardent, deep, pure, sacred friendship. After two or three years Rietz seems to have tired of it all and let the relationship fade out. In one of her last letters to him, dated January

8, 1860, the prima donna asked: "The beautiful, delightful, warm friendship—could it have been nothing but a short-lived blaze? Have I deluded myself to the point of mistaking a butterfly for a bear?" When her amical passion was at its height, such an old faithful as Turgenev was apt to be neglected.

At the end of March, 1859, he came to Spasskoye, presumably to attend to affairs in connection with the estate. He was marooned there, the roads having been obliterated by rain and thaw, and the rivers being in flood. The snipe had not yet arrived and he was impatiently awaiting them. So also was his dog, Diane's daughter, Boubou, so christened by Pauline, who had known her in her puppy days at Courtavenel. Diane herself died on September 6, 1858, at Spasskoye. "We buried her this morning," he had written to Paulinette two days later. "On this occasion I cried, and I don't blush to confess it; a friend was leaving me, and friends are rare, two-legged as well as four-legged ones." Boubou came about midway in the canine dynasty that began with Napol, a dappled coffee-colored animal of French parentage, and ended with Pegasus, in whose veins were mingled the blood of an English setter and a German sheep dog. Boubou was particularly favored with a mattress in Turgenev's own room, where she slept under a quilt; if the quilt fell off during the night, she would nudge him with her paw and he would rise to cover her up again. It was for her that he took the *Journal des Débats*. She liked the paper. After a day's hunting she found it soothing and soporific. It was the only sheet large enough to cover her completely and protect her from the flies when she wanted to doze. There was now a meditative gravity in her eye, which led him to suspect that she had studied German philosophy all winter. He himself had long since lost interest in that sort of thing.

"Here I am in my old nest again, my dear, good friend!" he writes Pauline. "But I am here only for three weeks. The thought consoles me when I look out of the window: snow and mud on the ground, rain in the air, a big, wet, dirty sheet instead of sky, wind moaning like a sick person—dreadful!" But already there are hints of spring. Having noted

them, he asks his correspondent how she is getting on with
the role of Lady Macbeth. "It is a beautiful part, great,
simple in spite of the lady's shrewdness, profound and yet
difficult, almost dangerous. But as King Lear says in Shakespeare's tragedy (do you remember how we read it at Courtavenel under a flowering acacia and then in a diligence . . . do
you remember?) 'Danger and I—we are two lions littered
in one day and in one lair, but I am the elder and the stronger
one.'" Tricked by memory, Turgenev here has telescoped
four lines from *Julius Caesar*:

> ". . . danger knows full well
> That Caesar is more dangerous than he:
> We are two lions littered in one day,
> And I the elder and more terrible."

He goes on to ask: "What if we were to put on *Macbeth* at
Courtavenel? I would take the part of Banquo's ghost—it
is a silent one." Alluding to his plans for *On the Eve,* he
writes: "At the moment I am in labor. I have a subject for
a novel, which I keep turning over in my mind, but the
baby refuses to appear," and he bids her look up in a medical handbook the worst position for an infant about to be
born. He concludes: "Au revoir in no more than six weeks,
I hope. A thousand greetings to Viardot and all friends. I kiss
your hands."

He was still in the country for Passion Week, and at Easter
he attended the midnight Mass at the little village church,
which smelled heavily of sheepskins and candle snuff. His
shoulders ached with the weight of his fur coat and his heart
with the savored melancholy of remembering a boy's Easter
nights. "Life is poured out to the last drop," he wrote to
Botkin of that hour, "but the fragrance of the just-emptied
vessel is stronger than when it was full."

With the advent of spring he was again leaving Russia.
In Paris he rejoined his daughter and may have seen the
Viardots. When Paulinette had first become part of their
household he had written to Pauline that "our" daughter,
as he called her, must be brought up in "our" religion. Whatever the agnostic may have meant by that, it was certainly

not any variety of institutionalized Christianity. And now he found himself engaging a Russian priest to give the girl religious instruction, for she had expressed the desire to become a regular communicant of the Greek Orthodox Church into which she was born. If this disconcerted him, he was certainly dismayed to find that his daughter was at odds with Pauline. It is reported (by Eugène Séménoff) that Paulinette was shocked to discover that there was an illicit intimacy between her father and Mme. Viardot. According to this informant, during the winter of 1856-57, when Paulinette was fourteen and "understood everything," she saw Mme. Viardot behaving in their apartment as though she were at home, and years later spoke of this to her own daughter, Jeanne. Whatever the sources of her enmity, the fact is that the girl was hostile to the woman her father bade her call *"Maman"* and whose hands she was insistently enjoined, by this strangely obtuse parent, to kiss.

After a brief visit with Herzen in London he went to Vichy for a water cure. He took his ailing body around to doctors as he submitted his manuscripts to his friends for criticism. At the resort he received a distressing letter from Paulinette. She tried to set him against Mme. Viardot and actually advised him to stop going to Courtavenel. He replied that he could not accept, nor indeed permit, the tone she allowed herself in speaking of Mme. Viardot, to whom she owed gratitude and "complete obedience." He also scolded her for being egoistic, touchy, and liking only those who liked or spoiled her. This did not mend matters, and Paulinette continued to harbor a growing dislike of her foster mother.

After a successful water cure at Vichy, Turgenev found himself by midsummer at Courtavenel. The wild pigeons cooed in the garden. The children were always hurrying out of doors or calling one another in the corridors. The wheels of the household ran smoothly in their accustomed grooves. The whole scene was almost as a year ago he had left it basking in the serenity of Indian summer. But the waters of the moat had dried up. Were the springs of his passion drying up as well? He was certainly under no further illusions as to what Pauline desired their relation to be. She had her own interests, her own family, her own life, to which he could contribute only as a friend. She wrote to Rietz on July 20:

> Turgenev, the friend I have recently told you about, is still with us; he belongs to the few whom I call friends. . . . We read a great deal together—that is, habitually. We began Homer only yesterday. . . . I know nothing pleasanter than to read aloud a good and beautiful book with a sympathetic spirit, with a dear friend.

About the same time this friend was confiding in Countess Lambert that his soul was sad. "What am I here for," he asked, "and why look back when I am already taking leave of everything dear to me? . . . They say that man dies several times before his death . . . I know what has died in me; why then stand and look at the closed coffin?" What had died, he explained, was not his feeling but the possibility of its fulfillment. The bond remained.

19

ON THE EVE

While taking the waters at Vichy, in the summer of 1859, Turgenev began the actual writing of *On the Eve*. The Italians were then engaged in fighting the war of liberation in which Garibaldi was to play a leading role. On the day of the battle of Solferino (June 24, 1859) Turgenev was penning one of his frequent letters to Countess Lambert:

> If I were younger, I would give up all work, and go to Italy, to breathe this now doubly blessed air. So there is still enthusiasm on earth! So people can still sacrifice themselves, can rejoice, can be beside themselves with ecstasy! If I could at least see how they do it! But I have already grown too sluggish, and I'm too lazy to leave my accustomed rut. . . . All the fire that's left in me has passed into my literary faculty. Everything else is cold and quiescent.

He said the same thing in a letter to Annenkov, adding that it was just as well for a "born spectator" like himself to keep away, because if he were in Italy he might do something foolish.

He had done the preliminary work on his new novel in the spring. A notebook had been filled with brief biographies of his characters. He went so far as to keep a diary for one of them (Shubin), as he told an American visitor many years later. Unfortunately, the manuscript of this diary, no part of which he included in his tale and which exceeded in bulk the novel itself, was destroyed about a dozen years after the book came out. The germ of the story had been planted in his mind in 1855. A friend living on an estate near Spasskoye, about to set off for the Crimean front, had handed him a manuscript containing the history of his love affair with a girl who at first reciprocated his affection, but later preferred a Bulgarian with whom she left Russia for his own country, where he soon died.

Turgenev's absorption in his work was complete. He dreamt of his characters. Their lives were his life so utterly that he could not give his interest to anything in which they had no part. The creatures of his imagination at once stimulated and sucked his energies. He was too deep in his work to speak of it freely to his friends, and yet he could think of nothing else. In midsummer, 1859, he was sitting in his room at Courtavenel, congratulating himself upon the freedom he had found there to go on with his novel. He had fled thither from Paris, after a month at Vichy, from where he had written to Annenkov, "Everything French stinks in my nostrils." The capital had been doubly abominable with hundreds of trains bringing crowds to witness the spectacle of Napoleon III reviewing his Italian troops in the borrowed style of imperial Rome. Turgenev wound up his letter from Courtavenel:

> Every military festival is a horror to me, and this one especially. There will be bayonets, uniforms, shouts, arrogant *sergents de ville,* adjutants dripping sweat. It will be hot, close, and smelly—*connu, connu!* It's better to sit before the open window and look at the motionless garden, slowly mixing figments of the imagination with memories of distant friends and distant Russia. It is fresh and quiet in the room. The children's voices ring through the hall. The sounds of Gluck float down from upstairs. What more would you have?

These moods of serenity which recurred at Courtavenel were a foil for the dejection that seized him as soon as he left the place.

That autumn his melancholy weighed on him with particular heaviness. There was, he felt, an element of tragedy— perhaps he meant pathos—in the fate of nearly every human being. He longed passionately for a family, a home of his own, and he knew the impossibility of realizing his dream. He had abandoned the notion that an artist needs freedom from the trammels of domesticity. Besides, he was haunted by a sense of "the futility of all things earthly," as he put it, and the nearness of a "something" for which he found death too small a name. With this went "a turning to God," he wrote, surprisingly, to Countess Lambert. It was, however, a passing mood. His subsequent letters to this devout friend evince an appreciation of the blessings of religious faith, but he does not fail to admit, humbly and unhappily, that he is no believer, at best an agnostic. "Why do you think that Polinka [his daughter] doesn't go to church?" he asks. "Not only did I not 'rob her of her God,' but I go to church with her myself. I wouldn't commit such an attempt on her freedom, and if I'm not a Christian, that's my personal affair, perhaps my personal misfortune."

In September he found himself at Spasskoye. There was a shortage of game because of drought, so he was bent over his desk again. As usual, he was uncertain about the quality of his work. He felt like a quarrier, striking away for all he was worth, yet seeing nothing but dust. It was October 25 when he finished *On the Eve* and he copied it in a notebook, the first page of which bore the line: "May I bring you luck!" written in French by Pauline Viardot. Then more than ordinary misgivings assailed him. For one thing, he decided that the plot was faulty. Perhaps his friends would encourage him with a favorable verdict. Having promised to dedicate the novel to Countess Lambert, he loaned her the manuscript, but she declared it false from beginning to end, and was seconded by her husband. He looked from his contemned pages to the fire snapping in the stove of his Petersburg apartment. Then he sat down and wrote a note. Annenkov, as so often, was to be his court of final appeal. The good man hastened to Turgenev's rooms, where, as he had been forewarned, he found the fire going. But he also found that Turgenev had summoned him in the secret hope that he would restrain the vandal hand. He had little difficulty in pointing out to the author the merits of his work and saving it from the flames.

While the atmosphere of *Rudin* is one of futility and frustration, and nostalgia pervades *A Nest of Gentlefolk,* a buoyant spirit of expectancy and promise informs *On the Eve.* The action takes place in 1853, one of the last years of the reign of that iron autocrat, Nicholas I. It was a time of darkness, but the title is not alone in intimating that the darkness is soon to lift.

"My tale," said Turgenev, "is based on the idea that we must have *consciously* heroic natures in order to move forward." He was calling for tough-minded, dedicated inviduals, devoted body and soul to a public cause. As he watched the social scene, sitting, not quite at ease, in his fauteuil, he looked in vain for such a man among his compatriots; the type had not yet emerged. Accordingly, he took for his protagonist a Bulgarian. This Insarov, a merchant's son, is an ardent patriot, preparing to take part in an insurrectionist movement against Turkey. The purpose to which he is vowed has the backing of the entire nation, which is ripe for revolt against the foreign tyranny. This gives him unfaltering firmness and strength. Turgenev, characteristically, has him carried off by consumption before he can strike a blow for the liberation of his people. Moreover, the author fails to interest the reader in this excellent and wooden creature. He is obviously contrived, a lay figure draped in the then fairly fashionable garments of militant nationalism.

Projected against a familiar Russian background, the story revolves less about Insarov's plotting than about his love affair with Yelena, the daughter of a family of Russian gentlefolk. It is she who is the central figure of the novel; to her it owes its force and meaning. Endowed with an intense, passionate nature and moved, in Turgenev's words, by "a vague, yet strong aspiration toward freedom," she is capable of making a brave choice and holding to it. She joins her lot to Insarov's without flinching from the hardships and dangers it involves. When, shortly after their marriage, he dies, she remains faithful to his memory by going on with the work to which he had been pledged. "Why return to Russia?" she asks in a farewell note to her mother. "What is there to do in Russia?" She deserts her country, this torpid land that can produce only self-centered dilettantes, well-meaning idealists incapable of action, conscientious, cold-hearted officials.

The book is in a sense an impeachment of an age and a generation that have failed to breed a fit mate for such a woman. "There is no one as yet among us, there are no men, look where you will," soliloquizes Shubin, one of the heroine's unsuccessful suitors. He goes on to say that the country has brought forth only dark, grubbing souls, phrasemongers, self-consuming little Hamlets who keep feeling the pulse of their thoughts and sensations. "When will our time come? When will men be born among us?" he asks Uvar Ivanovich, another secondary figure, and that vast, gluttonous sphinx of a man replies: "Give us time. They will come." At the very end of the postscript to the novel, which deals with events separated from the main action by five years, Uvar Ivanovich, asked the same question in a letter, twiddles his fingers vaguely and fixes his enigmatic gaze on the distance. Was this intended to suggest that the author wondered whether in Russia, where the situation was a complex one and the foe not a foreign oppressor but an internal enemy, men of Insarov's kind would arise? In any event, the skeptical note is too faint to mar the hopeful tone of the book.

On the Eve failed to receive the unanimous applause accorded its predecessor. The conservatives condemned it as dangerous and immoral. They were particularly shocked by the way in which the author flaunted his sympathy with his willful heroine. In moderately liberal circles the novel was received with reserve. Young Russia, the inchoate group that dreamed of a radical change, welcomed the tale with enthusiasm. They read it as a work of heartening political import. The very fact that a person like Yelena could have been so convincingly projected pointed to a fermentation, a rising sap, the stir of young life, impatient with old evils and schooling itself to fight them. Indeed, the heroine of *On the Eve* was to become a pattern for the selfless young women who in later years joined the cohorts of the revolution.

Simultaneously with *On the Eve* Turgenev published an essay of broad sweep, "Hamlet and Don Quixote," which formulates a suggestive view of the patterns of personality. Mankind, he contends can be divided into Hamlets and Don Quixotes, though in the fewest individuals is the type pure. The prince of Denmark is the skeptic, spoiled for action by too much thought, and wryly cherishing his own ego, for he finds nothing in the world he can cling to whole-heartedly. The knight of la Mancha embodies boundless faith in and selfless devotion to an ideal. He values life only as a means of assuring the triumph of truth and justice. A man of action, possessed of an indomitable will, his blind single-mindedness may make him ludicrous and is sure to make him great. The one is the complete ironist, the other the complete enthusiast. Don Quixote discovers, Hamlet elaborates. The former is belabored by the shepherds; the latter flagellates himself. The hidalgo is truly humble; Hamlet's self-abasement is mixed with a sense of superiority to others. Despising himself, he thrives on that contempt. The masses cannot look to him for leadership; they will see Don Quixote's failings as clearly as Sancho does, yet follow him through fire and water. The knight refuses to believe his eyes when Dulcinea appears to him in the guise of a slattern; Hamlet is cynical or rhetorical in his attitude toward Ophelia, being himself incapable of love. Don Quixote may fight windmills and mistakes a barber's tin basin for a magical golden helmet, but who knows exactly, asks the author, where reality ceases and fantasy begins? "It seems to me, therefore, that the principal thing is the sincerity and strength of our convictions; the result lies in the hands of the Fates . . . Our business is to arm ourselves and fight." If there are to be no more Don Quixotes, he concludes, "let the book of history be closed: there will be nothing in it worth reading." The death of either hero is moving, but Don Quixote's "unutterably" so. In his last moments the knight lays aside all his pride, declaring that, as in the old days, he is simply "Alonzo the Good." The essayist comments that "everything shall crumble to dust, but good deeds shall not vanish like smoke"; and he paraphrases the Apostle: "All things shall pass, love alone shall endure."

Turgenev, himself much the Hamlet, does not fail to sympathize with the Dane's predicament. He finds eternal values in the prince's nay-saying. The latter's skepticism is not to be mistaken for chilly indifference; he is as much an enemy of sham and other evils as his counterpart. Yet this essay, as, less explicitly, *On the Eve,* attests Turgenev's admiration for the knight errant, a type foreign to his own nature.

The novel, as has been pointed out, alienated the illiberal segment of his public. On quite another score it also lost him a friend, one whom he had met through Belinsky years back: Ivan Goncharov. The two had been rather intimate, reading their manuscripts and confiding their literary plans to one another. At Goncharov's instance, Turgenev omitted from *A Nest of Gentlefolk* a conversation between Liza and her old aunt which resembled a scene in a projected work of the elder novelist's. Turgenev was lacking in the professional jealousy by which Goncharov's entire career was poisoned. With more than his usual solicitude, he urged his friend on, wishing that he himself were a pretty woman, so that he might more effectively prod his laggard confrère.

When *A Nest of Gentlefolk* appeared simultaneously with Goncharov's *Oblomov,* and scored a far greater success, Goncharov was miserable. He had always considered this Turgenev a literary trifler, capable of turning out agreeable sketches, but certainly not one to sustain the herculean effort entailed by a novel. He was particularly envious of his rival's facility. The world of his own fancy, Goncharov explained on one occasion, would unroll before him like a broad expanse of land—field and forest, town and village—glimpsed from a mountaintop, and it was a slow, laborious process to come down from the height, to note the details of scenes and characters, to enter into each separate life, and to recombine all into a chosen pattern. Turgenev's imagination worked rapidly with simpler elements. It seized upon an individual, or a group of individuals, and invited them to act in a self-revealing manner.

When the irritated Goncharov tried to put Turgenev in his place by writing him that, whatever his talents, he was incapable of truly plumbing character, or of constructing a sound fable, the latter replied:

I can't go on scribbling *A Sportsman's Sketches* ad infinitum, and I do not want to give up writing. So all that's left for me to do is to compose narratives in which, without laying claim to unity or strength of characterization or deep penetration into life, I can express what pops into my head. Who looks for a novel in the epic sense of the word needn't come to me. . . . No matter what I write, it will always be a series of sketches. *È sempre bene.* . . . However, enough of this. All this fuss leads nowhere. We shall all die and stink after we are dead. All things earthly are dust and ashes. So long, you unjust man, I shake your hand.

In his reply Goncharov reiterated that while his friend was only scratching life's surface, he himself, serving art like "a yoked ox," was plowing a deep furrow. Turgenev accepted the remarks of his critic with what seemed like the silence of consent. He was not surprised to find Goncharov at the dinner given him before he left for western Europe in April, 1859, and to receive his Godspeed. At the same time the author of *Oblomov* was telling himself that the "universal traitor" and spoiled darling would no sooner cross the frontier than he would dismiss from his mind all his friends at home, to greet, with the same faithlessly jovial countenance, his friends abroad. At least, so Goncharov wrote to Annenkov.

When, nine months later, *On the Eve* appeared, Goncharov was plunged into fresh torments. Again he wrote a letter of sullen insinuation to Turgenev, making the covert suggestion that this prolific rival had plagiarized his own novel, *The Precipice,* fragments of which he had read to Turgenev, after their friendly custom, from the manuscript. Again Turgenev was too kind or too lazy to engage in controversy. But one day Goncharov, meeting a common acquaintance, and hearing that the man was dining with the author of *On the Eve,* said with the vehemence of intense hatred: "You tell Turgenev that he's giving dinners on my money." The reference was to the four thousand rubles which the novelist had received for his book. Turgenev was indeed told, and shortly demanded satisfaction, with the alternative of having the case arbitrated by a committee of literary men.

The arbitrators—there were three of them, including Annenkov—met on March 20, 1860, in Goncharov's apartment, and handed down the unanimous decision that since the works of the two authors grew out of the same milieu, it was natural that they should chance to contain some similar situations, ideas, and expressions, "a circumstance which exonerates and excuses both parties." Turgenev left the room greatly agitated, after saying to Goncharov: "I remain an admirer of your talent and, together with others, I shall probably have further opportunities to delight in it, but from this day on there can be no friendly relations between us."

He buried the hatchet four years later when they met at the grave of a friend, who happened to have been one of the arbitrators. Yet while his resentment was fading—he was too temperate for sustained enmity—Goncharov's morbid jealousy was growing steadily stronger, until it took the unmistakable form of paranoia, with Turgenev in the role of his archenemy. One day many years later Turgenev encountered him walking in the Summer Garden, a Petersburg park. Goncharov drew back, shouting "Thief! Thief!" and brandishing his walking-stick. In 1875 he composed a circumstantial memoir, setting down for posterity the history of their relations. These pages, which were only published in 1924 by the Leningrad Public Library, make Turgenev the villain of a piece staged in a madman's mind.

In 1855, we learn, Goncharov confided to Turgenev in great detail the plan of his novel, *The Precipice,* at which he had been working for six years and which did not appear until thirteen years later. "He listened without stirring," writes Goncharov, "holding his breath, with his ears nearly glued to my lips, as he sat near me on small divan in the corner of the study." Out of the information then imparted to him, Turgenev had carved *A Nest of Gentlefolk, On the Eve, Fathers and Children,* and *Smoke.* What he couldn't use himself he turned over to foreigners, and that was how *Germinie Lacerteux, Das Landhaus am Rhein, Madame Bovary* and *L'Education Sentimentale* came to be written. Having thus robbed his friend, the conscienceless wretch organized an immense conspiracy designed to keep him informed of whatever Goncharov wrote or planned or uttered, with a view to interfering with the latter's work at every turn. The unhappy victim could never be sure that during his absence from home, his manuscripts were not being copied by one of Turgenev's thousand agents; moreover, his conversations were reported verbatim and his letters regularly opened. Indeed, it was to these very letters that Turgenev's minor works owed their existence. Turgenev was living abroad, first, in order to conceal his literary impotence from his compatriots, and, second, in order to be able to dispose of the stolen goods, as well as to see that nothing by Goncharov should be translated into a Western language.

The document is one to interest psychiatrists, and the literary critic may well give thought to the paradox of Goncharov's diseased mind having been the matrix of fiction untouched by morbidity.

20

THE NIHILISTS

On The Eve marked for its author the lapse of an old association. Unlike most of his previous work, it did not make its first appearance in *The Contemporary,* to which he had obligated himself in 1856 to contribute all his future writings. It was printed in a rival monthly, published and edited by Mikhail Katkov, a fellow student of Turgenev's at the University of Berlin and a former member of the Belinsky circle. This was *Russky vestnik* (*The Russian Herald*), which presented the novel in the issue for January, 1860.

The office of *The Contemporary* was in the house which Nekrasov shared with the Panayevs, as he shared the ownership and editorship of the magazine. Here friends and contributors came to see Nekrasov at odd hours, often to discuss tea and literature with him as he lay late of a morning. Turgenev had felt very much at home in this house, which was something of a literary club. But when he returned from abroad in 1858, he found the place distinctly uncongenial. He discovered that a young man by the name of Nikolay Chernyshevsky, who for several years had been a prolific contributor to the review on a variety of subjects, had become Nekrasov's right hand, while the important department of criticism was practically run by a twenty-two-year-old obscure reviewer, Nikolay Dobrolubov, who lodged in a wing of the house.

Chernyshevsky had first attracted Turgenev's attention when in 1855 he had published a treatise on aesthetics. His thesis was that the proper function of literature and the arts generally was essentially pedagogical: to reproduce, interpret, appraise reality, to be "a textbook of life." Works of art, he argued, were mere copies, substitutes, having little intrinsic value. He particularly disparaged poetry and music. Underlying this crudely materialistic, utilitarian doctrine was the desire to put the Muses to work as handmaidens of social betterment. Turgenev was outraged. To him art was an absolute, transcendent good, one of the palliatives for the disease that life is. He needed music as he needed air for his lungs, and poetry acted upon him as a physical stimulant. The man, he fumed in private, should be publicly branded; the dissertation was "both false and harmful," it was "more than a bad book—a bad act," it was "disgusting carrion." This opinion was shared by a number of other contributors to *The Contemporary,* including Tolstoy. Chernyshevsky's subsequent literary essays mollified Turgenev somewhat. The man championed Gogol, while Turgenev favored a return to Pushkin, resulting in a synthesis of the trends represented by the two masters. Nevertheless he allowed that the critic was "useful"; that his acute understanding of the times compensated for his lack of taste. Chernyshevsky for his part went out of his way to pay generous homage to Turgenev. Yet their fundamental antagonism persisted.

Chernyshevsky had a faithful and brilliant disciple in the person of Dobrolubov. This earnest, hardworking young puritan shared his master's implacable hatred of upper-class culture and the social order on which it rested. He, too, regarded literature as a means toward an end: the civic education of an intellectual leadership emerging from the oppressed masses, men and women "with strong nerves and a healthy imagination," capable of directing the fight for a new society. In his writings he acknowledged the humanitarian sentiments Turgenev had expressed in *A Sportsman's Sketches.* Some of the novelist's pages enchanted him, others moved him to tears. Above all, he prized Turgenev as a sensitive and reliable recorder of Russian life who did not distort the facts to suit his private views and prejudices. But, within the limits set by the censorship, he did not mince words in inveighing against what repelled him in Turgenev's disposition and outlook: commitment to moderation, reliance on gradual changes, an attitude of passivity and pessimism, advocacy of the morality of renunciation and self-sacrifice, an inclination to see man as the slave of his environment.

The two "seminarists" (both Chernyshevsky and Dobrolu-

bov, born into priestly families, had attended divinity school)
were intellectual proletarians, arrogant, intransigent, with
democratic instincts and extremist convictions. All the barriers
of age, social class, temperament, education, ideology separated them from most of their fellow contributors: comfortably
situated men of good breeding, liberal opinions, established
reputation. There were moments when the latter succumbed
to the notion that the newcomers were cultural Vandals
threatening to destroy the arts by subjecting them to political
ends, while they themselves were guardians of the nation's
menaced light. Turgenev seems to have shared this view.
Mme. Panayeva credits him with repeating that the insolent
seminarists, having been raised on lenten fare, were intent on
sweeping from the face of the earth poetry, the fine arts, all
aesthetic pleasure; that they were literary Robespierres. It is
doubtful, however, if his hostility was as complete as that of
the other *literati* grouped around *The Contemporary,* notably
Tolstoy. While not politically-minded, Turgenev was not a
champion of art for art's sake, certainly no dweller in an
ivory tower. He had spoken in earnest when he observed,
back in 1855, that "there are epochs when literature cannot
be an art alone." Early in 1858 Tolstoy (the moralist not as
yet having pecked open his shell) was writing to Botkin:

"What would you say if now, when the filthy stream of
politics is trying to swallow everything and to soil, if not do
away with, art—what would you say if the people who
believe in the independence and immortality of art were to
come together and demonstrate this truth both by deed (the
practice of art) and word (criticism), and try to save what
is eternal and independent from the accidental, one-sided
and all-pervasive political influence? Why shouldn't we be
those people? That is, Turgenev, you, Fet, I, and all those
who share our opinions. Our tool could be a review, a mis-
cellany, what you will."

Turgenev's response to this suggestion was far from warm.
"Political affairs are repugnant to you," he wrote to Tolstoy
on April 8; "true, they are a dirty, dusty, vulgar business;
but there is dust and dirt in the streets, yet we cannot do
without cities." The projected publication did not materialize.
It would have been dedicated to a lost cause.

Before long Nekrasov was leaving things pretty much in the hands of the newcomers and the old guard was allowed to drop out. Turgenev could have achieved a *modus vivendi* with the radical pair. Chernyshevsky's manner turned his stomach like zedoary, the remedy for worms, he wrote, but he recognized that certainly the man's work, as a whole, had its merits. He could have accepted the substance of what Dobrolubov was saying to the fiction writer. It amounted to this: study the times in which you live; give us recognizable types of men and women; don't treat us to phantasies that take us away from the harsh realities with which we must cope; if you cannot help us deal with them, you had best hold your peace. Belinsky's stand toward the end of his life had not been very different, except that he had what Dobrolubov sadly lacked: "the sacred fire of aesthetic perception" in Turgenev's phrase. He was repelled by this youth, finding him cocksure, inquisitorial, cynical, coldhearted. Dobrolubov's eyes, he jested, turned the soup cold and frosted the window panes. But he was also attracted by this stiff-necked, tough-minded, self-disciplined individual, so enviably different from himself. Was this the Russian counterpart of Insarov, presaged in *On the Eve*? The novelist studied him as a model and, when he came to cast a character with the temperament of a revolutionary, found good use for the metal that was in him.

Turgenev would have stayed with the review to which Belinsky had given the last years of his life, had he been less often provoked. The "seminarists" constantly rubbed him the wrong way. Chernyshevsky was civil enough—he was aware of the novelist's value to the magazine and he may have hoped to win him over to the radical cause. But Dobrolubov demonstrated his contempt for the proprieties by being extremely rude to Turgenev. Moreover, the two subjected the novelist to attacks, some of them underhand, in critical notices, both in the pages of *The Contemporary* and elsewhere. In reviewing "Asya" Chernyshevsky took advantage of the occasion to deny that Russian progress owed anything to the upper-class liberal, thus indirectly assailing the author of the story. Dobrolubov discussed *On the Eve* at great length in his wonted manner, using comment on the novel to convey a political message in Aesopian language. The article was not without praise for the book, but its main point was that Insarov was not real to the reader, and that in any case the author should have chosen as his hero a Russian, a man of the people eager to fight not the foreign foe but the internal enemy, in other words—a revolutionary. As for Turgenev's first two novels, Dobrolubov observed that they had lost their actuality. "It is clear," he wrote, "that the kind of people we need now are not men who would raise us above our environment, but rather men who would raise our environment to the level of the rational demands of which we have become conscious." This was another covert call for drastic social action. The critic also found fault with the novelist's essay on Hamlet and Don Quixote.

It happened that Turgenev saw Dobrolubov's essay in proof. He urgently requested Nekrasov not to print it, arguing that it was "harsh and unjust" and would only get him into trouble. The request went unheeded. The last straw was an anonymous review (from Chernyshevsky's pen) of a Russian translation of Hawthorne's *A Wonder Book for Girls and Boys* in the June 1860 issue of *The Contemporary*. Turgenev discovered in it what he believed to be an insinuation that in *Rudin* he had deliberately caricatured Bakunin in order to please his wealthy literary friends, "in whose eyes every poor man is a scoundrel," as he wrote to Annenkov. "That is too much," he added, "a decent person cannot be a contributor to such a publication." And he enclosed a note to Panayev, saying that he would have nothing further to do with the review. Annenkov omitted to deliver the letter, in the hope that a peace would be patched up. But for once Turgenev was adamant. "Hamlet and Don Quixote" was the last work of his to be printed in *The Contemporary* (January, 1860). Its issue for June, 1861, carried a statement to the effect that the novelist's connection with the periodical had been severed because of ideological differences. Turgenev was outraged by the implicit suggestion that he had been dropped, when the truth was that he had been the one to withdraw, in spite of Nekrasov's repeated efforts to induce him to remain with the magazine. When his name appeared in the review again it was only as an object of attack.

"The tempest in a glass of water," as he called his quarrel

with *The Contemporary,* injured his standing with the radical youth, for whom the great review (in 1861 it had all of 6,800 subscribers) was a beacon and a banner. And then there was his personal loss: the defection of his old friend, the editor. The man's verse, with its didacticism and obtrusive civic note, was not to Turgenev's taste, but that in no wise affected his attachment to Nekrasov. He was aware of the ugly stories that had been circulating about the poet's involvement in a certain lawsuit, which had prompted Herzen to call him a thief. But Turgenev had a large tolerance for the moral failings of his intimates. Yet now when he himself was a victim of the man's double-dealing, his forbearance gave out. They exchanged letters for the last time in the spring of 1861. Thereafter all contact ceased.

Turgenev made peace with Nekrasov only when the latter was ready to descend into his grave, in May, 1877. A glimpse of the meeting is offered in one of the brief sketches included in his *Poems in Prose.* One sees the dying man, with his yellow skin and scant gray beard, his bare chest heaving, difficult tears in his inflamed eyes, at the moment when he places his hand, lean as a picked bone, in the large hand of his horrified visitor. It seemed to Turgenev that there was a third presence in the room, a tall, quiet woman, clothed in white from head to foot, with deep, pale, absent eyes and stern, pale, silent lips: Death. "That woman joined our hands. . . . She reconciled us forever." In that presence Turgenev was always ready to forgive: how could you bear ill will towards any man about to suffer the unanswerable insult of extinction?

Turgenev's break with *The Contemporary* naturally put an end to his traffic with Chernyshevsky and Dobrolubov. It would have terminated shortly in any event, as the former was soon to pay for his radicalism with imprisonment and exile to Siberia, while the latter died in November, 1861 of the same disease that had carried off Stankevich and Belinsky. On hearing the news, the novelist wrote to Annenkov: "Dobrolubov's death has distressed me, although he was getting ready to eat me alive."

The change that had come over *The Contemporary* was symptomatic of the ideological schism that occurred in the wholly unorganized and partly inarticulate forces of the opposition during the early years of the reign of Alexander II. The issues that came to the fore as preparation for the abolition of serfdom got under way helped to produce the split. Since the beginning of the new reign the intelligentsia had been growing and losing its predominantly genteel character, what with an increasing number of commoners in moderate circumstances joining its ranks. By the end of the fifties an extremist faction, however small, was in existence. Its hostility was directed not only against supporters of the regime but also, emphatically, against the upper-class liberals who favored patchwork reforms and peaceful evolution from a quasifeudal order to one based on free enterprise.

A tiny contingent of intellectuals, followers of Chernyshevsky, wanted to see the landlords expropriated, the centralized monarchic state destroyed, and the country eventually transformed into a federation of communities, each engaged in agriculture and industry on a cooperative and equalitarian basis. These hotheads looked eagerly toward a popular explosion. The March 1, 1860 issue of *Kolokol* (*The Bell*), the journal edited by Herzen in London, carried a letter to the editor which emanated from this group and was probably written by Chernyshevsky or Dobrolubov. The letter pointed out that nothing good would come of the impending agrarian reform and that the peasantry was ready to rise against the masters. It concluded: "Our situation is terrible, only the axe can save us, and nothing but the axe." The advocates of revolution had uncertain allies in the handful of expatriates grouped around Herzen and the Free Russian Press he had established. In their publications these émigrés exposed administrative abuses at home, and their chief preached "communism in bast shoes," an allegedly indigenous variety of agrarian socialism.

A far larger segment of the radically-minded youth had no political axe to grind. They also resolutely repudiated the past. Their aim was not, however, to liberate society and break the chains that weighed upon the downtrodden masses, but to free the individual from time-hallowed modes of thinking and acting. Dobrolubov appealed to these idol-breakers when he hailed men animated by "ruthless negation." They responded even more warmly to the intellectual leadership of Dmitry Pisarev, who in 1861 at the age of twenty-one burst upon the scene with an essay against scholasticism. "Here is the ultimatum of our camp," he wrote: "what can be smashed should be smashed; what will stand the blow is good, what will fly to smithereens is rubbish; at any rate, hit out right and left—no harm will or can come of it." Himself of gentle birth, he raised his hand against all the conventions and values of the ancestral order.

Chernyshevsky summoned "new men and women" to turn the socialist dream into reality. Pisarev called those who shared his ideas "critical realists," but also accepted the word "Nihilists" as a designation of them. The term was raised from obscurity to a byword by Turgenev. It denoted the frame of mind characteristic of a rootless, refractory generation, living in an age that, in the words of the Preacher, was "a time to break down." Brash and irreverent, the Nihilists sneered at authority and called in question accepted beliefs and opinions. In reaction against the canting and shamming of their elders, they professed to be cynical, unfeeling, practical. They claimed to be egoists on principle, though enlightened ones. They were suspicious of beauty and regarded truth with the eyes of Pilate. Their manners and their appearance set them apart. Spurning the proprieties of social intercourse as hypocritical, they affected rudeness. Instead of addressing their parents respectfully, they were apt to "thou" them in familiarity. The men wore sack coats rather than frock coats, spectacles instead of eyeglasses, and spurned gloves. The "emancipated" women bobbed their hair, put on plain dresses and, giving fathers or husbands "the twelve-pound look," went off to study stenography or midwifery.

With special zest the Nihilists denied the fine arts. Chernyshevsky and Dobrolubov granted that literature had its uses in an imperfect world: the writer can create nothing to equal reality, but if his fictions make society conscious of its deformities and lead to their correction, he has justified his existence. Pisarev went further. He undertook an assault upon aesthetics as the Bolsheviks were to undertake an assault upon Heaven. There was some virtue, he allowed, in a painter: he might sketch a grasshopper to illustrate a manual on insect pests. As a means of education, novels could, he conceded, serve a worthy purpose, but not music or poetry. "No man of our generation," he wrote, "is likely to waste his life in piercing sensitive hearts with deadly iambs and anapests." Writers, he suggested, could make themselves genuinely useful by employing their talents in popularizing the ideas of positivist thinkers and the scientists' contributions to knowledge. The Nihilists worshiped science, particularly the natural sciences, as a force certain to free the mind of the chains of superstitions and the fog of transcendentalism, as, indeed, a panacea. Like the French Encyclopedists before them and the Bolsheviks after them, they used the brooms of a crude materialism and a cocksure rationalism to sweep the Augean stables of tradition and authority.

Properly speaking, Nihilism, as has been indicated, was an intellectual trend, which, in aiming at individual freedom and self-fulfilment, affected chiefly manners and morals. In the public mind, however, it was associated not only with atheism and free love, but also with political insurgency. Pisarev himself held no brief for a popular uprising, but he recognized that the lot of "the naked and the hungry" was the problem of the age, and he had vague socialist leanings. Eventually some of his followers found themselves in the underground cells that began to form in the sixties.

Many aspects of nihilism, either in its narrow or its broader sense, could not but be distasteful or even revolting to a man of Turgenev's background, temperament, associations and convictions. His falling-out with *The Contemporary* illustrates this. And yet these young rebels and rowdies exercised a certain fascination over him. With all their obtuseness and their puerile wrong-headedness went an enviable vitality and single-mindedness which he missed in himself. Somehow they seemed to be close to the heart of the age whose chronicler he felt it incumbent on him to be. The still distant revolution was to cast its shadow over all the major works of his that followed *On the Eve*.

21

FREEDOM

During the summer of 1860 Turgenev was constantly on the move, traveling in Germany, France, England, drinking the waters at Soden, taking sea baths at Ventnor. In the little museum there he came upon an object that he never forgot: the broken prow of a galley, covered with the rust of centuries, beneath which was decipherable the ship's name: *Giovane Speranza,* Young Hope.

It happened that vacationing at the English seaside resort in August was a group of Russians so large that he suggested they seize the Isle of Wight. They included several liberal-minded friends of his. A great topic of conversation among them was the plan of founding a nation-wide society for the spread of elementary education in Russia. Its purpose was to supplement and bolster up the impending abolition of serfdom with emancipation from the bondage of illiteracy. The initiative had come from Turgenev. Had he not been one of those who had sworn to Stankevich to work for the cause of popular enlightenment? He actually drafted a tentative program of the society, and together with a circular letter it was submitted to a number of people for criticism. There the matter rested, since the project ran into resolute official opposition.

Turgenev's days at Ventnor were lightened by some philandering with a pretty German girl, "a little flirtatious, a little pensive." She and her mother were staying in the house where he roomed. At the time he also had a far less ephemeral interest in a young woman whom he described as a sphinx flashing riddles in the shape of telegrams. A native of the Oryol province, like himself, Maria Markovich had married a Ukrainian and for some years had lived in the south. According to Turgenev, she looked as though she did not know in which hand you hold a pen. Yet, under the pseudonym of

Marko Vovchok, she wrote stories, in the Ukrainian vernacular, about the horrors of serfdom in the Ukraine. He liked
them well enough to translate them into Russian. When he
went abroad in the spring of 1859, she and her little boy were
his traveling companions, and the next year he made a trip
to the little town of Schwalbach to visit her. In his letters to
her he mentioned a "strange" desire to have her near him.
He referred vaguely to certain things that had taken place in
his "small Paris room" where they had had long talks, adding
that he did not quite know what to make of it all, but had
worked out an explanation not flattering to himself. Their
correspondence ceased in 1862.

In July he came to Courtavenel at the instance of its
mistress. Little Paul had been seriously ill, and she wanted to
take a rest "in peaceful, friendly company," he wrote to
Annenkov, adding: "for me her will is law." To Maria Markovich he was writing: "In the old days how my heart beat,
how breathless I was when I approached it [the château],
and now it has all quieted down—and high time, too. I intend
to spend ten days here, no more (these two words speak of
new times)." He ended by wishing his correspondent freedom
from herself—"the most necessary freedom." Was he free
from himself? He confessed to Fet that he was going through
"the difficult twilight period of . . . quiet without rest, of hopes
that resemble regrets and regrets that resemble hopes." He
liked this last phrase so well that he put it into his next novel.
"A little more patience," he went on, "and we shall at last
enter the haven of old age, and there we shall find old men's
activities and even old men's joys."

When October found him again at Courtavenel it was borne
in upon him that "a sad mist" had enveloped his relations
with Pauline. Perhaps for that reason he did not stay there
long. He made Paris his winter quarters, sharing the apartment on rue de Rivoli, 210, with his daughter and her
English governess, a good woman with distinguished manners,
though apt to be impatient, he feared, with "youth's natural
gaiety." Paulinette had turned out to be a practical, strong-
minded, church-going person, with the makings of a good
housekeeper, and not a trace of "the artistic"—the very opposite of her father. The relations between the two were smooth

enough, but he was sensible of the fact that he had little in common with his daughter. "She doesn't love music, or poetry, or nature, or dogs," he wrote to Countess Lambert, "and I love nothing else." As the months went by, he noticed what he believed to be signs of improvement in her character, but there was the same distance between them. If only he could marry her off to some decent fellow! Then he would be free, for, as he told this confidante, "all other ties have, not so much broken, as melted away."

He felt as though he had been a contemporary of Sesostris, the Pharaoh, who by some miracle had continued to move among the quick and had preserved a love for the good and the beautiful, a living yet wholly impersonal emotion. He may have been alluding to what he took for a turning point in his relations with Pauline, when he wrote to the Countess the previous month from his wintry Paris: "The other day my heart died. . . . The past dropped away from me completely, but being separated from it I realized that nothing was left me, that my whole life had dropped away with it. It was painful, but I soon turned to stone. And now I feel that I can still go on living. But should the least hope of a return come to life again, I would be shaken to the roots of my being. This is not the first time that I have known this ice of numbness under which silent grief is hidden. . . . Let the crust thicken, and grief must die."

About one thing he was mistaken: the tie that bound him to Pauline was not broken; it had not melted away. He remained attached to her and to all that was hers until he died in the rural retreat he shared with her and her family. For better or worse he came to accept, like her other devotees, the role of a friend. The strength of his feeling for her must have led him to exalt her ideas, so that he came to find a charm in the notion of a platonic friendship, for all his periodic excursions into more carnal and less permanent liaisons. On the other hand, the very vehemence with which she was wont to protest her amity must have stirred at odd moments the hope, that had seemed altogether quenched, of a closer bond.

That winter his dislike of France was exacerbated. He loathed Paris particularly. The city air, he claimed, weakened his imagination; he was working steadily but slowly. It was hard for him to live in a country where "poetry is trifling and wretched, nature positively unbeautiful, the music makes you think of puns and vaudeville, and the hunting is abominable." The very sound of its "finical" language made him wince. "French, like an obsequious flunkey, forestalls you," he tells Countess Lambert, "and sometimes makes you say *not quite* what you think, which is much worse than if it made you say something *completely* different from what you think." On another occasion, begging her to write in Russian, even though her mastery of it left something to be desired, he pleads thus for their native tongue:

> You will see that although it does not have the boneless pliability of French, for the expression of many thoughts, and indeed the best thoughts, Russian is wonderfully fine, because of its honest simplicity, freedom, and strength. Strange—these qualities: honesty, simplicity, freedom, and strength, are not to be found in the people, but they are present in the language. . . . Consequently, some day they must appear in the people, too.

As was so usual with him, his distaste for the foreign scene served to sharpen his nostalgia for Russia, and vice versa. In November, 1860, he thanks Fet for his letters, which carry with them the sounds and scents of autumn at home: the smell of plowed ground when the air is touched with chill, the whirr of woodcocks in the nearly bare aspen grove, the smoke that hangs about the grain-kiln, "the honest odor" of the steward's sheepskin and the pleasant creaking of his boots in the hall. As the months of 1861 draw on, and Turgenev is still in Paris, he thinks wistfully of spring in the Spasskoye park, with the nightingales fluting amorously among the new leaves. The next year, in which he was to have only two months at home, he again complained to Fet about his homesickness. He felt as though his soul had left him, to haunt his native ravines. By this time some of his friends had begun to suspect that he cared less for his soul than for his aging, ailing body, which relished the creature comforts afforded by western Europe. The novelist protested that the charge was groundless. Certainly a viveur would have avoided a place as hateful to him as Paris was to Turgenev.

What especially rankled was that he found himself staying

on in the French capital while Russia shook from stem to stern with the great news of the emancipation of the serfs. By an irony of fate, even when the first definite step toward abolition had been taken by the Government, Turgenev had not been on deck. "You cannot live in a foreign land while the fate of your country is being decided," old Aksakov had written him. Yet he continued to idle wistfully in Rome. If he had been at home during that winter of 1857–8, he, like the rest of the gentry, would have been invited by his Emperor to help organize one of the committees on ways and means of effecting the great reform.

Here was something to rouse the most sluggish blood. Here was a topic to set agog the small colony of Russians gathered in the city of the Cæsars. Turgenev attended their meetings, and listened to the speeches with interest. He had things to say on his own account. He knew the gentry—a stupid, greedy, chicken-hearted lot. They were certain to put spokes in the wheels of progress. If only the landowners could be made to understand that the Government would do nothing to hurt them! If only the Emperor could realize that there were gentlefolk who understood his intentions, and were ready to lend a hand! Perhaps if there were a new review devoted to just these questions, an organ which would speak to the gentry on behalf of abolition—a periodical that could be a clearing house of information on all the problems connected with the reforms! Turgenev went as far as to draw up the plans for such a review, but the authorities found the idea "premature," and that was the end of the matter. In those days he could not take his mind from the enigma of Russia. "Is this Leviathan," he was writing to Countess Lambert, "going to stir and take the waves? Or is it going to get stuck midway?"

Shortly before leaving for Russia in June, 1858 he reported to Herzen that, to judge by the information that was reaching him, reaction at home had "at last reared its head." But he was not discouraged: "do what they may, the stone has started rolling down hill, and it cannot be stopped." Some fear, however, regarding the consequences of the reform for the gentry seems to have been lurking in his mind at this time. Prosper Mérimée who, among other things, was a senator with high connections, wrote to Empress Eugénie of a long talk he had had with Monsieur Turgenev, "a very sharp-witted man," who had told him that emancipation might lead to "a terrible catastrophe": revolution, and the hanging of all the landowners.

While the terms of emancipation were being debated in the provincial committees, Turgenev attempted to prepare against its coming by abolishing *barshchina* (corvée) on his estates. In the summer of 1858 he went home with the firm intention of making an arrangement with his peasants whereby he would till his land with hired labor, his serfs paying him an annual quitrent in money for the use of the acres portioned off to them and being free to dispose of their time as they chose. It is the regime on which the liberal landowner Kirsanov in *Fathers and Children* prides himself. Turgenev expected to lose about a quarter of his income as a result, but he hoped that eventually hired labor would prove so advantageous as to make up for the loss. Besides, he liked to feel that he would in fact be a landowner, not an owner of "souls!" To his chagrin he discovered that many of these unaccountably preferred corvée.

It was generally believed that emancipation would be proclaimed in February, 1861. In the middle of the month a rumor spread in Paris that an uprising had broken out in Warsaw. "God preserve us from such a misfortune!" Turgenev wrote to Countess Lambert. "Insurrection in Poland, like any insurrection and conspiracy, can only cruelly harm both Poland and Russia. Not by such roads must we advance." As expected, the manifesto was signed on February 19 and made public in Petersburg and Moscow a fortnight later. The news was telegraphed to him by Annenkov.

"God bless the Czar!" Turgenev wrote back. Even the most stiff-necked and suspicious of Alexander's subjects shared this emotion at that moment. Here was something to have lived for. If only he could have been at home! When Herzen reproached him for living abroad at this time, he replied: "Why turn the knife in the wound? What can I do if I have a daughter whom I must marry off and on whose account I must willy-nilly stay in Paris? All my thoughts, my whole being, is in Russia." He didn't care much about seeing how Moscow and Petersburg received the news; but if he could have stood in some village church, unobserved and observing, while the peasants listened to their priest read the words that gave them freedom! There were phrases in the manifesto, however, that would, he was sure, make the serfs scratch their poor silly heads: the document, which, as a matter of fact, was composed by the Metropolitan of Moscow, looked to him as though it had been originally written in French, and translated into Russian by some German. At any rate, there it was, and when he attended a thanksgiving service in the Russian church in Paris, his lashes were wet.

But one couldn't just be emotional about it. One had to go home and settle things. It wasn't a business to look forward to with pleasure. He knew what it meant to deal with the peasants. You might come to terms with them about a quitrent arrangement, but then you could whistle for your money. The work they did for you was sure to be botched. A landowner had best sell his timberland before the peasants, what with vandalism and thievery, had left it bare. No decree could give them overnight the sense of responsibility, legality, fair play, which centuries of slavery had crushed in them.

The law declared the person of the serf free, without compensation to his owner, but the peasant holdings remained the property of the *pomeshchik* (landowning noble). He was obliged, however, to provide the freedmen with acreage, and the peasants, on their part, were required to accept it and either pay the landowner a rental for it, in money or labor, or buy it and make annual redemption payments to the Government. When the full meaning of this dawned on them they had a cheated feeling. They struggled darkly with the notion that the gentry, having lost their serfs, had no further right to the land. In temporizing and delaying they were moved by the hope that a new and complete "freedom" was bound to come, and it was some time before they accepted the situation as inalterable.

When early in May Turgenev was back at Spasskoye, he had trouble enough in carrying out the provisions of the reform. To his former serfs he was the helpless, kindly son of their stern old *barynya*, Varvara Petrovna—the Kingdom of Heaven be hers!—an absentee landlord of whom they could easily take advantage. They kept on hemming and hawing, refusing to obligate themselves definitely. It was not until the spring of 1862 that the peasants at Spasskoye finally put their marks on the papers which brought the settlement to a conclusion. In these transactions, he told Annenkov, he had been so generous that it was disgraceful. He had no illusions about the spirit in which his largess would be accepted. The muzhiks behaved as might be expected of freedmen, more conscious of their rights than of their obligations. What was needed in dealing with them, he felt, was patience and pedagogy.

Just before February 19, the historic day, Turgenev was visited by doubts as to whether the new order would be better than the old, which was crumbling before his eyes. His skepticism lingered, and there were moments when he was disgusted by the way the situation was developing. Yet his faith in the promise held out by the reform, though severely tried, was not defeated. He summed up his feeling on the subject when he wrote in his novel, *Smoke*: "The new was slow in taking root; the old had lost all strength. The incompetent jostled against the unscrupulous; life, shaken up, quivered like a quagmire, and only one great word*—freedom—moved, like the spirit of God, on the face of the waters."

Not seldom he found his former serfs troublesome neighbors. They remained obsequious enough, so that he wrote to his steward begging that when he came to Spasskoye they would not poison his existence by constant kowtowing. But at the same time he had to watch their horses browsing freely over his flower beds. In spite of their attitude, he continued to treat them in a more or less paternal way, from time to time presenting the Spasskoye villagers with pieces of land. It is a matter of record that on one occasion he gave them a strip of woodland which they promptly sold, only to get drunk on the proceeds. His welfare work included the erection of a hospital, a home for the aged and a school. He had a chapel built near a village pot house to get rid of the latter, the law providing that a public house could not stand within a given distance from a house of worship.

In the early autumn he found himself at Courtavenel.

---

* When the novel first appeared in *The Russian Herald,* the phrase read: "only the Czar's great word. . . ."

After some weeks there he was back in his Paris apartment for the winter. Toward the end of it he told Countess Lambert that he existed in "a vacuum, misty and heavy." He may have been alluding to his feeling for Pauline Viardot when earlier in the season he had written to the same correspondent: "My former relations have coarsened somewhat, but also grown stronger, like bark on an aging tree; apparently nothing will change them now." He went on to say that he himself was growing a bark: his inner tissues were still fairly soft, but the fibres which were in contact with the outer world were hardening. "Little by little," he concluded, "I am getting ready for the inevitable end." Just then he was putting the finishing touches to the manuscript of *Fathers and Children,* the novel that more than his other work shows him to have been conscious of and sensitive to the life around him.

22

FATHERS AND CHILDREN

Always ill at ease when it came to traffic with abstract ideas, principles, opinions, Turgenev felt sure of himself only when he was dealing with what is visible, audible, tangible. "When I don't have to do with concrete figures," he wrote, "I am entirely lost and I don't know where to turn. It always seems to me that exactly the opposite of what I say could be asserted with equal justice. But if I am speaking of a red nose and blonde hair, then the hair is blonde and the nose red; no amount of reflection will change that."

Belinsky had said at the outset of Turgenev's career that while he was extremely observant, he had no imagination. The young author had agreed with this judgment wholeheartedly. To the end he was possessed by a self-distrust which led him to lean heavily upon what the world offered to his observation. George Moore went to the root of the matter when he said that Turgenev had the illuminative rather than the creative imagination and that he "borrowed" his stories, leaving them, as far as structure went, much as he found them.

Turgenev confessed that he envied the English their secret of making a successful plot, an ability which he found lacking in himself as in so many Russian writers. He had a prodigious memory, which served him well. He liked to insist that his characters were not invented, but discovered. He stalked them with the patience, the eagerness, and the skill with which he pursued his woodcock and his partridge. Indeed, it appears that he almost invariably drew from living models and that his fictions were fathered by experience rather than by fancy. He told a friend that it was his custom, after meeting a stranger, to set down in his notebook any peculiarities he had observed. He studied Lavater's work on physiognomy from cover to cover. Drawing rooms, railway carriages, reading rooms were his favorite observatories. He did not hesitate to incorporate verbatim in his story, "The Brigadier," a private letter which he found among his mother's papers. If he had had his choice, he once remarked, he would have been a writer like Gibbon. The novelist had the historian's need for documentation.

A writer of fiction, he held, dare not be a dilettante. He must maintain close contact with life. To represent it truthfully and fairly, without philosophizing about it or trying to improve it—that was the greatest happiness for the artist. But since reality "teemed" with adventitious matter, the novelist's gift, he insisted, lay in the ability to eliminate all superfluities, so as to render only that which, in the light of his knowledge and understanding, appeared significant, characteristic, what Turgenev liked to call *typical*. He believed that the writer, while aiming at the universal, must deal with the particular, and he quoted Johann Merck enthusiastically: "With the ancients everything was local, of the moment, and thus it became eternal." Annenkov said that he represented "the personified flair of contemporaneity" in Russian literature. Looking back at his novels toward the close of his life, Turgenev wrote: "I strove, within the limits of my power and ability, conscientiously and impartially to represent and incarnate in appropriate types both what Shakespeare called 'the body and pressure of the time' and the rapidly changing countenance of the educated Russians, who have been the predominant object of my observations."

In the case of *Fathers and Children,* as in most of his writings, the germ came to Turgenev not in the form of a situation or an idea, but in that of a person. Chancing to meet in a railway train a provincial doctor who, talking shop, had something to say on the subject of anthrax, the novelist was struck by the man's rough, matter-of-fact, candid manner. (He was to end his days in Siberia). It flashed upon the novelist that here was a representative of a type, one which was to become known as the Nihilist. An individual of a similar cast, also a physician, was among the Russians he encountered on the Isle of Wight. As he looked about him, he seemed to see everywhere signs pointing to the emergence of that type. But finding no trace of it in the fiction of the day, he wondered if he were not chasing a ghost.

The notion of building a novel around this figure occurred to him during his stay at Ventnor in August, 1860. In the fall, when he was back in Paris, the idea returned with renewed force, and he found himself increasingly absorbed in it. By October the stuff for his new novel was all in his head, but, he wrote, "the spark which must kindle everything has not yet blazed up."

It was presumably about this time that he began to get up for his characters the "dossiers" without which he could not begin work on a novel. He was in the habit, as he told Henry James among others, of setting down "a sort of biography of each of his characters, and everything that they had done and that had happened to them up to the opening of the story." As in the case of *On the Eve,* he kept a diary for one of the characters, but this time it was not the journal of a minor figure, but of the protagonist, Bazarov.

When that delightful period was over during which the figures for his novel floated like nebulæ through his mind, and once he had a good grasp of his characters, Turgenev's final move, according to James, was the arduous business of devising the action which would lead them to reveal their inner natures. In *Fathers and Children* the novelist put Bazarov through his paces by taking this brusque commoner on a visit to a house of gentlefolk; by leading him into arguments with his two middle-aged, cultivated hosts; by making him fall hopelessly in love with a beautiful lady, indolent and undersexed; by involving him in a stupid, almost comical duel with one of his hosts; by engaging him in talk with his earnest, apish, pliant disciple; by sending him home to see his pathetic old parents; by bringing upon him an untimely death, the result of an infection contracted at a rural post-mortem.

The method he followed here is his habitual one—realization of the characters not by analysis of their consciousness, but by exhibition of their behavior. Like so many of his fellow craftsmen, he exalted into a dogma his way of working. When he was brooding over the plan for *Fathers and Children* he set down for a literary protégé this precept: "The writer must be a psychologist, but a secret one: he must sense and know the roots of phenomena, but offer only the phenomena themselves,—as they blossom or wither." Ten years earlier he had said, in the course of a critique, much the same thing in other words: "The psychologist must disappear in the artist, as the skeleton is concealed within the warm and living body, for which it serves as a firm but invisible support."

From the moment when we first see Bazarov taking his time about offering his bare red hand to his host, and turning down the collar of his nondescript coat to show his long, thin face, with its sandy side-whiskers and cool green eyes, to the moment, a few months later, when the dying atheist raises one eyelid in horror as the priest administers the last sacrament, we are in the presence of a figure that dwarfs all around him and carries the whole weight of the story. It is also a figure that shows the fullest measure of Turgenev's powers of characterization. He believed that a novelist must be "objective," concerned to represent the world about him rather than his response to it, that his art required an interest in and a cumulative knowledge of other people's lives, as well as an understanding of the forces that shaped them. Bazarov, the tough-minded, hard-fisted medic, with his brutal honesty, his faith in a crudely empirical science that he uses as a cudgel wherewith to hit out at the genteel culture he abominates, this professed "Nihilist," is an example of what the objective method can achieve. In some respects, he is perhaps fashioned after an image at the back of Turgenev's mind, the image of the man he admired and could not be.

During the winter he was at work on the first chapters, and on July 19, 1861, he was writing to Countess Lambert from Spasskoye that in about two weeks he expected to taste "the only joy in a writer's life," to wit, "penning the last line." He finished the novel on July 30. In later years he asserted that he had written it seemingly without volition, almost surprised at what came from his pen.

The agony of revision followed, the most troublesome he had known, or so he claimed. At first buoyed up with confidence in his tale, he became more and more doubtful of it as he received his friends' comments. Countess Lambert had nothing good to say for it. "People in whom I have great faith," he wrote, "advised me to throw my work into the fire." As with *On the Eve,* he had the impulse, which he did not obey, to take this advice. Katkov, the editor of *The Russian Herald,* in which *Fathers and Children* was to appear, was displeased to see that the author adulated "the younger generation" (a euphemism for the radicals) and placed Bazarov on a pedestal. Turgenev wrote back to say that it was not his intention to present an apotheosis of his protagonist and that he would try to remove that impression. He added that in his opinion Bazarov, though "empty and sterile," was nevertheless "the hero of our time." He went over and over the text, cutting, adding, altering.

What increased his uncertainty was the news of student riots in Petersburg and Moscow. Under these circumstances was it proper, he wondered, to bring out a novel that had a bearing, however remote, on the political situation? He pleaded with Katkov for a postponement of publication until spring, arguing that he found it necessary to revise the work thoroughly and unhurriedly—"to replow it," as he phrased it. The author's hemmings and hawings went on until the exasperated Annenkov, who had undertaken to see the manuscript through the press, was ready to wash his hands of it. Turgenev declared that the novel was published only because "the merchant demanded delivery of the goods he had bought" and because he himself needed money.

Fathers and Children made its appearance in the issue of *The Russian Herald* for February, 1862, and shortly afterward was published separately with a dedication to the memory of Belinsky. When in the spring of the year Turgenev returned to Petersburg from Paris, he found the capital excited by a number of conflagrations which razed a section of the city and which rumor put at the door of revolutionary incendiaries. An acquaintance, meeting him on the Nevsky, exclaimed: "See what *your* Nihilists are doing! They're setting Petersburg on fire!" Turgenev had not invented the term—it was first used by St. Augustine to denote unbelievers—any more than he had invented the type, but his employment of the word and his projection of the character made for the vogue of both. Eventually he came to regret having provided what he called "our reactionary rabble" with a convenient term for their *bête noire*. The word was also used loosely by the general public. A girl wanting a new frock was likely to face her parents with the threat of turning Nihilist if they didn't come round. Where, as in Russia, literature has great prestige, the novelist is peculiarly able to become the arbiter of fashion in personality. The novel was read by everyone, from the Empress down to people who had not opened a book since their school days, and before long one discovered at least a dash of Bazarov in every young man of independent spirit.

Turgenev's conscious attitude toward his protagonist was ambiguous. He noted in his diary an hour and a half after finishing the novel that while writing it he had felt "an involuntary attraction" toward his hero. He said the same thing in a letter to Herzen a few weeks after publication. "If the reader doesn't love Bazarov, with all his coarseness, heartlessness, pitiless dryness and brusqueness," he had written a fortnight earlier to the young versifier, Sluchevsky, "it's my fault—I haven't achieved my purpose." About the same time, however, he wrote to Fet that he did not know if he loved or hated Bazarov, and defending himself again the accusation of having produced a tendentious work, he claimed that he had drawn his character as he might have sketched "mushrooms, leaves, trees," things he had seen until, in the Russian phrase, they had "calloused his eyes." In 1869 he asserted publicly that he shared Bazarov's convictions, except for his view of the arts. Privately he admitted that in saying this he had gone too far. Unquestionably the admiration the author felt for his hero went hand in hand with a desire to preserve the values that this iconoclast rejected. We have Turgenev's word for it that Nikolay Kirsanov, one of the two landed proprietors who represent the older generation, is a self-portrait.

One of Bazarov's sentiments was undoubtedly shared by his creator—dislike of the nobility. Turgenev's treatment of it in this novel afforded him the satisfaction of the flagellant. "My entire tale," reads the letter to Sluchevsky quoted above, "is directed against the gentry as a leading class." Look at these Kirsanovs, both young and old, and what do you find? "Weakness, flabbiness, inadequacy." And these are gentlefolk of the better sort. "If the cream is bad, what can the milk be like?" How well he knew these people—their good intentions, their feeble achievements, their tender sensibilities, so readily touched by a line of verse, a point of honor, enchanted memories of a dead love, the glow of a setting sun which makes the aspens look like pines! But the knowledge that made for contempt fed his sympathy, too, and Nikolay Kirsanov, at least, is a lovable fellow.

Throughout, his craftsmanship is at its best. Even the minor characters are deftly sketched in. The description of Bazarov's illness gave Chekhov, himself a physician, the sensation of having "caught the infection from him." Bathed in an atmosphere of tenderness and pathos, the passages about Bazarov's parents are among the most moving in literature. As he wrote the last lines, in which the old couple are shown visiting the grave of their only son, Turgenev had to turn away his head, so that his tears would not blot the manuscript, and even in such a dry-eyed age as ours, there must be readers who do not finish the paragraph without blinking.

True, the comings and goings crowded into the few weeks during which the action unfolds seem somewhat contrived. The structure of the novel lacks the formal beauty of *A Nest of Gentlefolk* and *On the Eve*. The touching passage at the close is flawed by the last few lines, with their suggestion of a half-hearted piety. These blemishes are negligible, however, in a work of such wide validity. *Fathers and Children* is a novel to which Turgenev gave his full powers: his intuitions, his insights, the fruit of his contacts with a variety of men and women, his reflections on experience, his sense of the pathos of the human condition. Rudin and Lavretzky can each be fully understood only in the context of his age and his country. Bazarov, while unmistakably Russian, is a universal and a profoundly attractive figure.

Immediately after publication the novel became a storm center. The critics and the public alike differed sharply in their interpretation of its meaning. The conservatives either applauded the author for having shown up those dreadful Nihilists or indignantly charged him with kowtowing to them, with "crawling at Bazarov's feet," as a correspondent put it. Pisarev was one of the few articulate leftists to acknowledge the novel as a reliable and not unsympathetic study of the "children" by a fair-minded representative of the older generation who was a great artist. In the pages of *The Contemporary* the tale was dismissed as a worthless piece of literature which eulogized the "fathers" and viciously lampooned the younger generation, and specifically Dobrolubov, for reasons of personal spite. For the most part, the radical youth agreed with this reviewer. The followers of Dobrolubov and Chernyshevsky found something exaggerated, something distorted in Bazarov's views and behavior. What above all must have kept these youths from accepting him as one of them was his lack of interest in bettering the lot of the masses. In their eyes such an attitude was simply abominable. On a hot afternoon Bazarov and the young Kirsanov are lying in the shadow of a haystack and philosophizing. The Nihilist is in a mood for metaphysical speculation. Talk turns upon Russia, and he observes to his companion in a deliberate tone:

> "Here, for instance, you said today, as we passed the cottage of your steward, Philip—it's such a fine, white one—you said that Russia would attain perfection when the last peasant would have such a house, and everyone of us ought to help to bring this about. . . . But as you spoke I hated this last peasant, Philip or Sidor, for whom I am to wear myself out and who won't even say thanks to me. . . . And what do I want with his thanks, anyway? He'll live in a white cottage, and burdocks will be growing out of me. Well, and what next?"

We have Turgenev's word for it that there were those who burned him in effigy. Some of his young compatriots who studied at Heidelberg wrote to him threatening to descend on him in Baden to settle accounts. In short, coming at a moment when political passions were smoldering, the novel "poured oil upon the fire," as Turgenev put it.

He could find only three men who grasped what he had tried to do, one of them the poet Maikov, to whom he wrote: "Now I can say to myself that I couldn't have written complete nonsense, if people like you and Dostoevsky pat me on the head and say: 'Very good, my boy, we give you 80% on that.' " He went as far as to tell Annenkov that "for the first time" he was "seriously satisfied" with his work. Yet he could not conceal either from himself or from others that its reception disconcerted him deeply: "I was struck by hands

I wanted to clasp and caressed by hands from whose touch I wanted to fly to the ends of the earth." Fortunately for his peace of mind he never knew the worst. A secret police report, which came to light decades after his death, stated that the novel had "a beneficent influence on the public mind," and that "to the surprise of the younger generation, which had recently been applauding him, with this work Turgenev branded our underage revolutionaries with the biting name of 'Nihilist' and shook the doctrine of materialism and its representatives."

Some half a dozen years after the appearance of *Fathers and Children* Turgenev urged Ludwig Pietsch, who planned to write an article about the book, to express astonishment at the attitude of the Russians towards it. "Because of Bazarov," he wrote, "I was (and, for that matter, still am) bespattered with muck and filth; so much abuse and opprobrium, so many curses have been heaped upon my head (Vidocq, Judas, lout, ass, poisonous toad, spittoon—this was the least that was said of me) that it would be a satisfaction to me to prove that other nations see the matter in a different light."

The idea that Bazarov was a caricature, a lampoon, Turgenev insisted, was utterly preposterous. The novel's total effect, he told Herzen, was meant to be the triumph of democracy over aristocracy. "I envisaged a somber figure," he wrote Sluchevsky of his hero, "savage, huge, ugly, only half-emerged from the soil, strong, and yet doomed to perish, because he stands only on the threshold of the future." In the same letter the novelist said of Bazarov: "I called him 'Nihilist'; read: 'revolutionary'." As he has no program of political action except to smash "other people," the appropriateness of that term may be questioned, but there is certainly the stuff in him out of which rebels are made: aggressiveness, intolerance, withering contempt for upper-class liberal softies ("a real man," he says to Arkady is "one who . . . must be either obeyed or hated."), scorn of fine sentiments and moral scruples, readiness to spare neither himself nor others. Indeed, the core of the novel is not so much the conflict of generations as the theme touched upon obliquely in *On the Eve*: revolution. The promise held out in the latter novel is to some degree fulfilled in *Fathers and Children*. When Turgenev was in the midst of it he found himself one day in the company of his compatriots and the conversation turned on the sporadic riots that followed the liberation of the serfs. He is said to have drawn himself up to his full height and quoted Pushkin's famous dictum: "Heaven save us from seeing a Russian rebellion, senseless and ruthless." Yet he was instinctively attracted to the rebel.

"We mean to fight," Bazarov declares. But he has no more of a chance to carry out his intention than Insarov does. The author metes out a premature death to both. The Bulgarian's demise is wholly unmotivated; Bazarov, we are told, perishes because he was born too soon. One suspects, however, that this protagonist was killed off in obedience not solely to the logic of his situation but also to the law of the author's nature. Somehow he could not quite bring himself to grant his characters a sense of accomplishment which he himself seems never to have tasted fully.

23

DIFFERENT CLAY

Eighteen hundred and sixty-one should rightly have been a red-letter year for Turgenev. There was the Act of Emancipation. There was, on the personal plane, his work on *Fathers and Children.* But whatever satisfaction both may have offered him was tainted by a number of unpleasantnesses. A publisher who had undertaken to get out a collected edition of his writings, in four volumes, went bankrupt, and left him out of pocket. Early in the year he quarreled with Nekrasov. Before the year was over he was twice on the verge of a duel with Tolstoy.

The history of the relation of these two is a record of the conflict between a man whose conscience was active chiefly where his writing was concerned, and who did not cling to any rigid standard in his personal life, and a great novelist whose deepest, if at first unconscious, interest was not good writing but the good life. They had been hearing of each other through common friends and admiring one another's work for some time previous to their first meeting. Tolstoy, months in advance of their actual encounter, commissioned a young relative who knew Turgenev to embrace the novelist for him, and a few weeks before they came together Turgenev wrote to Tolstoy, then on the Crimean front, expressing the hope that he would be spared by the bullets for the Muse. *A Sportsman's Sketches,* Tolstoy placed with Rousseau, Dickens, the Gospels, Prescott's *Conquest of Mexico,* as a book which deeply influenced him in his teens. When his own sons were growing up, he recommended it to them as better than any of Turgenev's novels. As for Turgenev, he cried hurrah over Tolstoy's "Sebastopol Tales" and drank a glass of champagne to the author. Three years earlier, while confined at Spasskoye, he had discovered in *The Contemporary* an anony-

Turgenev in his forties (?).
Photograph by G. Denyer

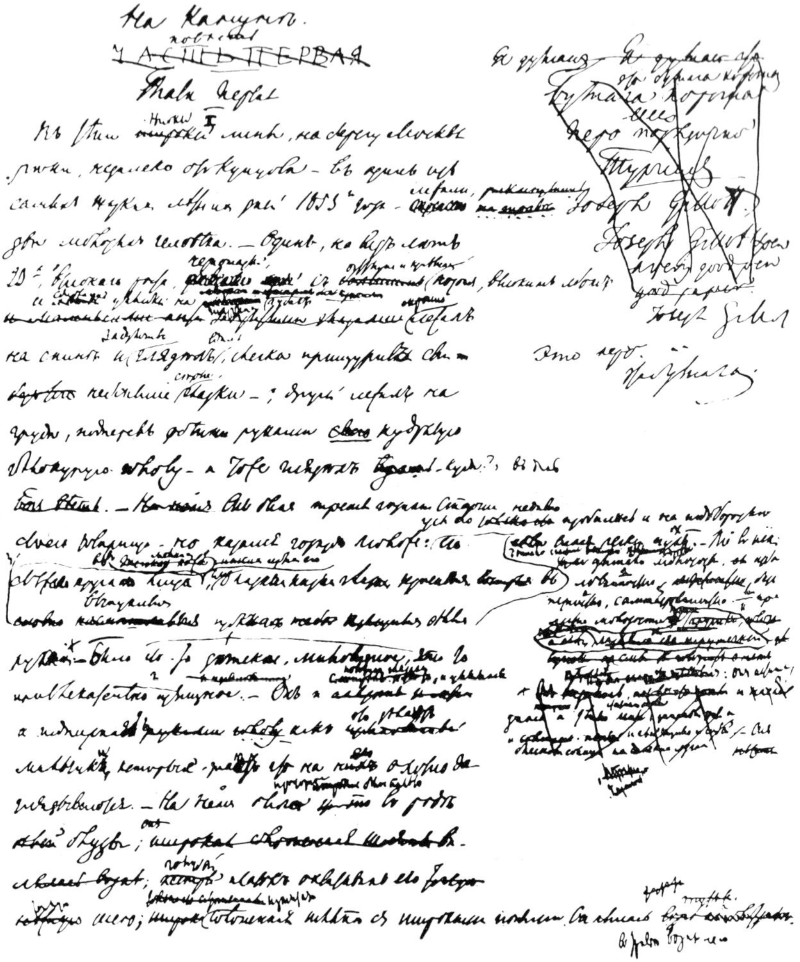

First page of draft for *On The Eve*

mous piece called "Childhood" which he was moved to read aloud to a group including Tolstoy's sister, who recognized the life portrayed, but did not suspect that her brother Leo was capable of such writing.

By the time the two men were finally brought together, Turgenev was already the leading literary figure in Petersburg. Tolstoy, ten years his junior, was an army officer with more than one published narrative to his credit and a strong taste for wine, cards, and Gipsies. They had no sooner met, on November 21, 1855, than Tolstoy became Turgenev's guest, or what Varvara Petrovna, who allowed a "guest" only three days, would have called a "resident." A friend of Turgenev's, coming into his Petersburg apartment one winter morning, saw a saber on the hatrack and was asked by the servant to be quiet, as its owner, the young Count Tolstoy, was asleep in the drawing room. The young man was sowing his wild oats with an abandon impossible to his elder, who took both his vices and his virtues more easily. On December 9, 1855, Turgenev was writing to Annenkov: "Just think of it! Tolstoy has been staying with me over two weeks. . . . You can't imagine what a fine and remarkable fellow he is, although, because of his savage ardor and buffalo-like stubbornness, I've nicknamed him the Troglodyte. I've conceived a strange affection for him, which has something paternal about it."

This affection was soon tried, and sorely. The count had as many spines as a hedgehog, and Turgenev never knew where to have the baffling creature, who was alternatively proud and humble, reserved and effusive, earnest and frivolous, simple and full of snobbish affectations. Tolstoy's behavior in the *Contemporary* circle was a constant source of irritation. He seemed to take pleasure in stepping on every one's toes. He came uninvited to a dinner meeting of the group, held in memory of Belinsky, and inquired of the company how they knew that Belinsky wasn't "a son of a bitch." They revered George Sand. Tolstoy sneered at her. In the hearing of Mme. Panayeva, who practiced what the lady novelist preached, he would remark that George Sand's women should be tied to the wheels of a chariot and dragged through the streets of Petersburg. When they spoke warmly of Herzen, he made disparaging comments. And he loathed their Shakespeare. In his diary he noted: "The editors of *The Contemporary* repel me. A gathering of littérateurs and learned men is repulsive." He thought that these luminaries were incapable of the generous self-surrender which he demanded in human intercourse— demanded, but himself refrained from, except for sudden embarrassing outbursts of affection. And he doubted the sincerity of Turgenev's opinions and feelings.

Turgenev found himself involved in futile arguments with his young friend, which only ended in sullen tiffs. Fet's memoirs offer a glimpse of two such squabbles that tooks place at Nekrasov's. Thus we hear Tolstoy shouting, with a flash of his maddening steel-gray eyes:

"I stand in the doorway, with a dagger or a saber, and I say, 'As long as I live, no one shall enter here.' That I call conviction! And you —you're trying to hide your real thoughts from each other and you call that conviction!"

Turgenev, in the thin falsetto of rage, (he retained the shrill voice of adolescence late in life) gasps irrelevantly:

"Why do you come here? This isn't where you belong. Go to Princess So-and-So."

"I don't have to ask you where to go, do I? Anyway, idle talk won't turn into conviction because of my coming."

And then there is the scene in which Turgenev, his hand at his throat, and "with the eyes of a dying gazelle," squeaks: "I can no more; I have bronchitis," whereat Tolstoy grumbles: "Bronchitis is an imaginary disease; bronchitis is a metal," and forthwith retires to the next room, where he curls up in glum silence on the divan. Turgenev strides up and down in despair.

"Darling Tolstoy," says a friendly witness, trying to make peace, "do calm yourself. You don't know how he esteems and loves you."

But Tolstoy, with dilating nostrils, growls:

"I won't stand for it! He does it to tease me. It's on purpose that he's pacing up and down and wagging his democratic haunches."

In the beginning, at any rate, separation acted as a counter-irritant. In a letter to Tolstoy written soon after Turgenev left Russia in 1856 he blamed himself for their failure to get along. He had not wanted a superficial relationship, he explained, and in trying for something more, had been awkward, and given offence; noticing his mistake, he had retreated, perhaps too abruptly—hence the "ravine" between them. He predicted, however, that eventually they would come to love one another and each would rejoice at the other's success. Two months later he is assuring Tolstoy that though there is much about him that is jarring, he loves him, and, indeed, feels tender towards him—at a distance. Before the year is out he is able to say that the "ravine" has long since shrunk to a "scarcely noticeable crack."

In February, 1857, Tolstoy, fleeing from a sentimental entanglement, joined Turgenev in Paris. The two saw a good deal of each other. Turgenev carried the newcomer off with him when he went to Dijon for a change of air, and they sat inside the hearth to warm their bones, each of them working on a story. Returning to Paris, they went together to cafés, churches, concerts. They spent pleasant evenings before the fire over a bottle of wine. They were bored with each other. They quarreled. They made up. Turgenev was hardly a jovial companion, what with his black melancholy and his illness aggravated by a hypochondriac disposition. He found his comrade more reasonable than heretofore, although still at odds with himself and so unable to put others at ease.

Tolstoy's diary for these weeks reflects his shifting attitude toward his friend. Turgenev is a bad man, Turgenev is not really bad; Turgenev is lively, Turgenev is dull; Turgenev is a child (this on the occasion of a visit to a shooting gallery); Turgenev is going to pieces; Turgenev is vain, Turgenev is cold, Turgenev is wallowing in his unhappiness; Turgenev is intelligent, Turgenev has no faith in intelligence, Turgenev does not believe in anything. Tolstoy admires Turgenev, Tolstoy avoids him, Tolstoy loves him. But "Turgenev does not love, he only loves to love." When the younger man left for Geneva in the spring he made this entry in his journal: "Went to see Turgenev. On leaving him, I cried. I don't know just why. I love him very much. He has made—he will make a new man of me."

When, in the summer, Turgenev went to Sinzig, Tolstoy prepared to follow him, but *en route* stopped off at Baden. On July 29, Turgenev received word from him to the effect that he had been cleaned out at roulette. Next day Turgenev arrived in Baden and found his friend penniless and suffering from what the Russian editor of his letters considered an unmentionable ailment. He lent him some money which was promptly gambled away. He then persuaded the profligate to accompany him to a seaside resort. Before they could entrain, however, Tolstoy received a letter informing him that his sister Maria with her children had left her husband, who had made her life miserable in more ways than by having four mistresses, and Turgenev supplied the fare so that Tolstoy might return home. Being short of funds, Turgenev had to borrow the money. "Vanichka is a dear. And I am ashamed of myself before him," Tolstoy wrote in his diary the day of Turgenev's arrival in Baden. "Vanichka has left. He certainly raked me over the coals," he wrote the day of Turgenev's departure.

Intimate contact only served to bring out their essential incompatibility. Tolstoy noted in his diary that neither of them had any real sympathy with the other. During their stay in Paris, Turgenev was writing to Annenkov: "In spite of all my efforts, I can't get close to Tolstoy. He's built too differently from me. Whatever I love, he doesn't, and vice versa. In his presence I feel embarrassed, and it is probably the same with him. . . . He will develop into a remarkable person, and I shall be the first to admire and applaud him, at a distance." He had long since given up the notion of playing the mentor to this extraordinary man. He had realized with complete humility that when it came to writing, Tolstoy had nothing to learn from him. Already the previous year he was telling the young author: "We have little in common except literary interests, I'm convinced. Your life is moving toward the future, mine is built upon the past. I cannot follow you. You cannot follow me, either. You stand too firmly on your own feet to become any one's follower. . . . You are too astute not to know that if either of us it to envy the other, it will have to be I." As a matter of fact, envy was utterly foreign to Turgenev's nature. From the very beginning to the very end of their relations, he never ceased to appreciate and extol the genius of the artist, however much he was vexed by the vagaries of the man. "When this new wine ripens," he wrote of Tolstoy in 1856, "it will be a drink fit for the gods," and not long afterward, as has been said, he made bold to declare the young man "the only hope" of Russian literature.

Although Turgenev knew that it was impossible to put leading strings on such a skittish fellow, he could not refrain from advice and remonstrance. He harped upon the danger of dilettanteism. "I'd like to see you at the bench," he wrote to Tolstoy on January 29, 1858, "with your sleeves rolled up and in your work clothes." He urged Tolstoy to stick to literature, for which he was obviously cut out, and not try to be anything else but a writer. The idea did not appeal to Tolstoy, who said it wasn't in his nature. At the time he was planning to go in for forestry. Hearing of this, Turgenev wrote to Annenkov: "What a man! Though he has excellent legs, he insists on walking on his head." With more insight than efficacy he warned his confrère against locking himself into a "system," a rigid set of ideas, thus limiting his field of vision. "A system," he ventured, "is the tail of Truth, as it were, but Truth, like a lizard, will leave its tail in your hand and escape: it knows that it will soon grow another." And he urged Tolstoy to read Shakespeare. Not that Tolstoy had by that time achieved a coherent "system." In his own words, his mind was then a cage in which a cat and a dog kept unwilling company. The cat was a jungle creature, at home in the wild, innocent alike of reason and conscience, beautiful and happy in its natural brutality. The dog was a Christian, teachable, reflective, thirsting for moral sanctions, dedicated to the human habitation and treading with a somewhat sad obedience the path of brotherly love. The wranglings of these two tenants of Tolstoy's spirit filled his inner life. They were at the root of the unpredictability and contrariness of his temper which, added to a proud, intolerant, independent manner, rendered intercourse with him so trying.

It was impossible to get on with this difficult genius who so often acted like a wrong-headed prig, this self-righteous Puritan who behaved like a rake, and, with little originality, called Paris "Sodom and Gomorrah," only to leave it for the gaming-tables and cocottes of Baden! If Turgenev bent to pat the dog, he was likely to be scratched by the cat; if he stroked the cat, the dog would show his teeth. How could one not be vexed with a man who so closely identified the good life with the natural life that he would have the race throw culture to the winds? To exalt Nature, who knows neither justice nor reason, neither good nor evil; to dismiss culture, which is man's sole refuge from the horror of the natural universe! How could one bear with a man who looked down on the intellect, condemned consciousness (in 1851 Tolstoy wrote in his diary: "Consciousness is the greatest moral evil that can befall a man."), and, contemptuous of humanity's experience, was inclined to erect his own findings into a universal law?

And yet Turgenev could not but admire one who did not, like so many educated Russians, content himself with the intellectual spoils of Europe, but was trying to earn his ideas in the sweat of his face. At the same time it was easier for Turgenev to deal with a plebeian Dobrolubov, who would make art the handmaiden of social reform, than with this young count who, while saying that art was supremely worth while and indeed the chief hope of a perfectible world, actually distrusted the power of art and was always on the verge of interrupting the artist that was in him—to do a little open preaching. Turgenev found Tolstoy writing stuff like the story "Lucerne" (1857), "a compound of Rousseau, Thackeray, and the Shorter Orthodox Catechism."

The fact that they had the same social background, training and traditions only served to emphasize their differences. Turgenev refused to understand a man who was "a mixture of a poet, a Calvinist, a fanatic, and aristocrat; a kind of Rousseau, but more honest than Rousseau, a highly moral and at the same time far from likable creature." Tolstoy, for his part, could not stomach a man who was a mixture of a poet, a skeptic, a jester, a well-born democrat; a highly reasonable and at the same time womanish creature. A person of Tolstoy's make-up was bound to see in Turgenev's urbanity mere insincerity; in his moderation, the despicable temper of a Laodicean; in his partiality for the intellect, a chilling aloofness from what is vital; and in his whole outlook and attitude what another friend condemned as "meek, cheerful indifference."

As an old man, looking back across the years, Tolstoy complained that Turgenev had never understood him, but had valued in him only what he did not prize in himself, whereas he had been disgusted by his senior's overweening aestheticism and lack of convictions on every subject but literature. In the conflict between these two personalities there is not a little that recalls the relations between the humanist, Erasmus, the first man of letters in modern times, and the zealot who began by admiring and ended by berating him—Martin Luther.

The discovery of their incompatibility did not put an end to their intercourse. Attracted to each other in spite of themselves, they repeatedly tried to fraternize, only to rediscover, as Turgenev wrote to Fet in 1859, that they were "made of different clay." The same year he announced in a letter to Botkin: "I am through with Tolstoy: as a man he no longer exists for me. I wish him and his talent everything good, but as for me, no sooner have I said how d'you do? to him than I want to say good-by. We are poles apart. If I like the soup, I am certain Tolstoy will hate it—and vice versa." And yet their antipathy was not of the kind that makes for mutual avoidance. They were drawn to each other as though what they really felt was that ambivalent emotion which excruciated Catullus. If we are to believe Turgenev, it was Tolstoy who sought him out, to plague and madden him. Tolstoy probably took a contrary view of the matter. Be that as it may, a great deal of irritation must have accumulated on both sides when, one May morning in 1861, a furious quarrel flamed up between them at the house of their friend, Fet.

Their host's account of the clash, combined with the reported remarks of Turgenev himself, admits us to the scene. The conversation turning on the upbringing of Turgenev's daughter, he said that her English governess had asked him, with British punctiliousness, to name the sum the girl should spend on charity.

"She insists," he went on, "that my daughter should visit the poor and take their worn clothes home to mend them with her own hands."

"You think that's a good thing?" asked Tolstoy.

"Yes," said Turgenev. "The girl gets in close touch with actual want."

"And I think," Tolstoy shouted, "that a starched miss stepping squeamishly into a poor man's lodgings is an abomination. A dressed-up girl holding dirty stinking rags in her lap takes part in an insincere theatrical scene."

Turgenev's nostrils dilated: "I beg you not to say that."

"Why shouldn't I say what I think?" from Tolstoy.

"So you think I'm bringing up my daughter badly?"

"I meant what I said and without being personal I simply expressed my thoughts." At this point, to go by Turgenev's reported story, Tolstoy blurted out: "If she were your legitimate daughter, you would educate her differently."

Fet discreetly passing over this remark, omits also Turgenev's retort: "If you keep on talking like that, I'll slap your face!"

Turgenev dashed from the room, returning shortly to apologize in no uncertain terms to his hostess, but only vaguely to Tolstoy. The two of them left the house forthwith, to go their separate ways. The subsequent history of the affair is a tangled one. From a way station Tolstoy wrote a letter to Turgenev, asking for a written apology which he could show the Fets. A reply failing to come at once, and his rage mounting, he wrote again, challenging the offender to a duel, and proceeded to send for his pistols. Turgenev had answered the first letter promptly, but a mistake of his messenger had delayed Tolstoy's receipt of this reply. It contained a straightforward apology, which he said Tolstoy could show the Fets. Tolstoy wrote an acceptance of this apology, and Turgenev replied:

> I say in all sincerity that I would gladly stand under your fire in order to wipe out my truly insane words. That I spoke as I did is so foreign to my habits that I cannot ascribe it to any other cause than irritation, due to the extreme and constant antagonism of our views. That is why, in parting from you forever . . . I consider it my duty to repeat that in this matter you were right and I was wrong.

For several days a duel had seemed inevitable to him. Now he felt that everything was over for good and all.

Some six weeks after the quarrel Tolstoy made this entry in his diary: "Final break with Turgenev; he is a perfect scoundrel. But I think in due time I will surrender, and forgive him." Three more months go by, and in an access of virtue such as now and then made the "troglodyte" brim over with loving-kindness and gave him the desire to start life afresh with the day, he writes to Turgenev that he is sorry their relations are hostile, and begs his forgiveness. This humble letter fails to reach its destination; meanwhile the addressee hears that his own apology is being shown around by Tolstoy as the self-abasement of a coward. And now it is Turgenev's turn to call out Tolstoy. Just at this time, by an ironical chance, Turgenev was revising *Fathers and Children,* in which the gentry's dueling mania is held up to ridicule. Tolstoy's reply was conceived in a spirit of Christian humility:

> Gracious Sir: In your letter you call my conduct dishonorable; besides, you personally said that you would slap me in the face, but I ask your forgiveness, acknowledge myself guilty, and refuse the challenge.

This letter too was delayed, so that in January, 1862, Turgenev, writing to Fet about this sequel to the story, declared that Fate in the person of the post office was obviously against them, and continued:

> I conclude that our constellations move in the ether with decided hostility, and it is best, as he [Tolstoy] himself suggests, that we avoid meeting. But you can write to him or tell him when you see him that . . . . from a distance I love him very much, respect him, and follow his career with sympathy, but that at close range everything assumes a different aspect. What's to be done? The two of us must live as though we existed on different planets or in different centuries.

This solution was scarcely practicable. "I take the keenest interest in this remarkable man," Turgenev wrote to Botkin on September 30, 1864, "though I cannot be in the same room with him." They continued to be anything but indifferent to each other's work, and the gossip of their mutual friends made vicarious contact unavoidable. Thus, in 1865 Turgenev learned that his sudden departure from Spasskoye had been ascribed by Tolstoy to a desire to avoid an encounter. He wrote to his informant that Tolstoy played too small a part with him to influence his movements and that there would probably have been no danger of a meeting in any case. He disclaimed any ill feelings but expressed the fear that Tolstoy was the same disagreeable person as before: what sort of man was it who made friendly inquiries about you of one acquaintance, and told another that he hated you more than ever? In 1871, hearing that Tolstoy was ill, he was deeply troubled: he remembered that two of the man's brothers had died of tuberculosis. "The sole hope of our orphaned literature," he wrote to Fet, "cannot and must not disappear from the face of the earth as promptly as his predecessors: Pushkin, Lermontov, Gogol."

For seventeen years this indirect give-and-take was their nearest approach to a personal relation.

24

"I AM A EUROPEAN"

When Turgenev fell into the habit of taking an annual trip abroad, as he did from 1856 on, he scarcely ever omitted to cross the English Channel. Doubtless one great reason for his visits to London was the fact that his expatriate friend, Herzen, had been settled there since 1852. For his compatriots this man was as much a London attraction as, for other tourists, the Tower or the Cheshire Cheese. Turgenev was a not unfamiliar figure at Park House, beyond Putney Bridge, and at the more spacious five-story Orsett House, occupied by Herzen, his children, and Mme. Ogaryova who was his mistress, and Ogaryov himself, her nominal husband and his own lifelong friend. A stream of visitors came to pay their respects to the redoubtable editor of *The Bell* (*Kolokol*), smuggled copies of which came even to the studies of officials in Petersburg and to the Emperor's desk.

Turgenev had disliked the notion of Herzen's launching a political journal when he was capable of such magnificent writing as was to be found in his memoirs, *My Past and Thoughts*. However, when, on July 1, 1857, the paper, dedicated to "the liberation of Russia," became a fact, he heartily applauded it. "Where should conservatism come from in Russia?" he had asked in a letter to Herzen written several months before *The Bell's* first peal sounded from the banks of the Thames. "You can't go up to a rotten fence and say: 'You are not a fence but a stone wall that I will use in building.'" He could not but sympathize with a journal which was to be the voice of those rendered tongueless by the censorship, and which stood for freedom, reason, science, as against oppression, fanaticism, superstition.

He did not write for *The Bell*, but offered the editor aid and comfort in his brilliant campaign against administrative abuses at home. He helped Herzen keep abreast of what was going on in Russia, supplied him with matter that could not be published there, forwarded correspondence from liberals who preferred not to communicate directly with the notorious émigré. Furthermore, he sought to influence the policy of the journal. He was apt to plead for leniency and counsel restraint in attacking the authorities, particularly the Czar. "Please, do not scold Alexander Nikolayevich," he wrote to Herzen. "As it is, all the die-hards in Petersburg abuse him cruelly. He may become disheartened, if he is lambasted from both sides." On one occasion he was indirectly approached by a grand duke whom Herzen had threatened to expose, and who hoped that Turgenev would allay the storm. Herzen acknowledged Turgenev's assistance, and such lesser favors as half pound packages of the best French snuff, with a stream of affectionate letters. When the exile gave Turgenev a note of introduction to his friend Garibaldi, it was so complimentary that he sealed it, to spare the novelist's modesty.

During the years before the Emancipation *The Bell* vacillated between moderation and extremism, between confidence in the good intentions of the Emperor and a segment of the upper classes on the one hand, and trust in the democratic forces on the other. After the serfs were freed the journal took a more consistently radical stand. In its pages Ogaryov characterized the Emancipation as "a new serfdom." News of peasant dissatisfaction with "the freedom" led Herzen to believe in the possibility of a popular rising. The course of events compelled him to swing leftward. An occurance that marked the end of 1861 contributed to this. On a December evening he was embracing Bakunin, who had escaped from his Siberian prison and reached London via Yokohama, San Francisco, and New York. He had learned nothing and forgotten nothing during the blank decade of his confinement. He had, he said, the instincts of a stormy petrel and was now impatient to make up for the years of silence and inactivity by getting to work on the destruction of Austria-Hungary and the establishment of a federation of free Slav peoples.

Between the urgings of this unquenchable rebel and the proddings of Ogaryov, a staunch if fuzzy-headed radical committed to the principle of collectivism, Herzen found himself turning the paper, somewhat half-heartedly, into an organ of revolutionary agitation. At the same time he continued to preach the gospel of what was to become known as Populism: the doctrine that the native institutions of the Russian folk were the germ of the social upheaval which would renew civilization.

When in May, 1862, Turgenev was in London, he made a point of seeing Bakunin. So warm was their encounter that a few months later Bakunin could write to him: "You alone in the enemy camp remain a friend, and with you alone we can speak, turning our hearts inside out." Out of regard for their old comradeship, Turgenev was willing, indeed glad, to contribute annually for an indefinite period the sum of fifteen hundred francs toward his support. He was sorry for the friend of his youth, but he saw in the grizzled, shaggy giant who ate and worked and idled hugely, who argued, borrowed, and sweated perpetually, nothing but a flighty, irresponsible demagogue, a ruin, a played-out agitator, a Rudin not lucky enough to have met death on a barricade. As for Ogaryov's views, he found them equally objectionable, a product of unreason and ignorance of the life of the people. Nor had Herzen's theories become more acceptable to him.

The two aired their differences in a series of exchanges, heated yet amicable enough. Herzen conducted his side of the debate chiefly in eight missives entitled "Ends and Beginnings" and printed in *The Bell*, July 15, 1862 to January 15, 1863—it being an open secret to whom these undirected communications were addressed. Turgenev prudently confined his replies to private letters.

The burden of Herzen's song echoed the conclusions he had reached a dozen years earlier. The "Romano-Germanic" civilization, he argued, had become a silver sty for a conservative, mean-spirited, property-worshiping bourgeoisie, to whose vulgar standards both the lower and upper classes were rapidly conforming. But while the West was reaching a dead end, the Slavic East held out the hope of opening a highway to the good society. There, on the Russian plains, lived a race of barbarians untouched by the capitalist blight. They need not commit all the old blunders and land in the same morass with the rest. In America on a new soil there had arisen a people apart (true, Herzen characterized it as the product of the off-scourings of the old nations; at the time he was out of humor with "the Disunited States": the Civil War was playing ducks and drakes with his six per cent United States bonds). There was nothing in the nature of things to prevent Russia, too, from developing in its own way. Its very backwardness offered it a chance to bypass the the capitalist phase with its middle class degeneracy, and to be the first to achieve the socialist order. The short-cut to socialism was, indeed, a distinct possibility in Russia, for there the new society could grow from native roots. Herzen had in mind the *artel* (artisans' cooperative) and the *obshchina* with its immemorial practice of equality, collective land tenure and communal self-government.

Turgenev rejected this amalgam of socialist aspirations and Slavophil sentiment in its entirety. The antithesis of West and East, flattering to the latter, had never appealed to him. No, he argued, Russia was "a wench like her elder sisters, only that her bottom is broader . . . She will be a slut like the others. Of course, she is not as pretty." His opponent's diagnosis of what ailed modern society was correct, but it applied to all mankind. "You are like a doctor," he wrote to Herzen, "who, having described the symptoms of a chronic disease, declares that all the trouble is due to the fact that the patient is French." The Russians, he went on, belonged to the *genus Europaeum,* and so must travel the road traversed by the nations of Europe. (Six years later he will reiterate this conviction in the introduction to his *Recollections of Life and Letters.*) As for looking to the *muzhik's* innate socialism for salvation, that was preposterous. "The masses whom you worship," he wrote, "are conservative *par excellence* and carry within themselves an embryonic middle class, wearing a tanned sheepskin, living in a stuffy, dirty hut, filling its belly to the point of heartburn, and loathing all civic responsibility and activity—such a middle class as will beat hollow the Western bourgeoisie which you characterized so aptly in your letters." Returning, in another letter, to the subject of Herzen's cult of the Russian peasant, Turgenev declared: "Your god loves what you hate and hates what you love." The idea of revolution existed only in the heads of the intellectuals; it was wholly alien to the masses, he asserted. Not that the prospect of an abrupt and violent overturn was anything but abhorrent to him.

If to Herzen the *obshchina* was the precious dowry of that Cinderella among the nations, Russia, to Turgenev it was a stumbling block on the path of progress. Twenty years earlier in a memorandum on Russian economy he had advocated its abolition. "Say what you may," he wrote the elder Aksakov on May 25, 1856, "the rights of the individual are destroyed by the peasant commune, and for those rights I am fighting and will fight to the end." Over a decade later he was telling Herzen that Russia was anxious to get rid of the *obshchina*. As for the virtues of the *artel*, he quoted the remark of a man who knew it from experience: "If you haven't worked in an *artel*, you don't know what a noose is." On November 29, 1869, he wrote to Fet that the *obshchina* was ruining the peasantry and so was unprofitable for the rest of the population as well.

One instalment of "Ends and Beginnings" hinted that, in retreating from the leaky tents that housed his compatriots and from the shrieking of their lusty young to the grandfather's corner by the European hearthstone, Turgenev was obeying the impulse of a middle-aged, tired, cold-hearted epicurean. He denied the impeachment. Even if he were twenty-five, he would be committed to Western ideas and institutions. And when Herzen accused him of being a Nihilist, not a rebellious one, like Chernyshevsky and Dobrolubov, but a weary, hopeless one, like Schopenhauer, he repudiated the charge. He was nothing of the sort, he protested, declaring that he saw something tragic in the destinies of all the European nations, Russia among them. "For all that," he went on, "I am a European, I love the banner under which I have marched since my youth, I believe in this banner." He left no doubt that he gave his allegiance to civilization, justice, the principles of the French Revolution.

At one point in the debate Herzen observed with irritation that his opponent was not politically-minded. The novelist readily agreed, but added that it was better to be a nonpolitical like himself than a political after the fashion of

Bakunin or Ogaryov. The former's notion, to which Herzen, too, was partial, that the educated classes were worthless was particularly offensive to Turgenev. For him the country's sole hope lay in the enlightened minority. It was the all-important task of the intellectuals to transmit Western civilization to the people. What the novelist objected to in the writings of that addle-headed pedant, Ogaryov, was the advocacy of socialism. "The public that reads *The Bell* is in no mood for socialism," he wrote to Herzen; "it needs purely political agitation, which you have given up, thus breaking your sword." The "agitation" that Turgenev had in mind amounted to propaganda for an address to the Czar, hailing the Emancipation Act, but suggesting certain amendments, and petitioning him to convoke a National Assembly for the purpose of elaborating additional reforms. He put an end to the debate by declaring: "Our opinions are too divergent; why go on teasing each other fruitlessly?"

It was one of life's little ironies that just after the two men had agreed to disagree, the Government should step in and prefer charges against Turgenev, as well as dozens of others, for traffic with "the London propagandists," as Herzen, Bakunin, Ogaryov, and their associates were officially styled. The affair is known as "the trial of thirty-two," this being the number to which the accused were finally reduced. The solicitous and well-posted Annenkov warned his friend, who was in Paris, that the authorities might request him to return home. Turgenev was nonplussed. Neither the new Russian ambassador, to whom he had recently been introduced, nor his predecessor, with whom he had lately dined, had breathed a word about such an eventuality. But Annenkov was right. It appears that in the summer of 1862 a number of letters from Herzen and Bakunin to their friends in Russia, together with other compromising documents, came into the hands of the Russian secret service. These papers revealed Turgenev's services to the London group, notably his part in collecting funds for the support of Bakunin. It was discovered that he had carried certain communications from the expatriates to a leader of an underground organization in Russia. Early in 1863 he received an official request to appear before a senatorial committee to answer the charge of dealing with the London émigrés.

There is no doubt that Turgenev grew panicky. He appealed for help to a reactionary journalist with Court connections. He held counsel with his friends. Should he write an open letter to a Paris daily in order to forestall the possible accusations? He could say that Herzen and Bakunin were the companions of his youth, that he was not in sympathy with their ideas, and that politics was not his concern. The letter was not written. Instead, he petitioned the Emperor to excuse him, on the grounds of ill health and important business, from appearing in person, and to have a questionnaire sent to him in Paris. He pointed out that he was a writer, who must be judged by his works, and that these clearly reflected the moderation of his views. Referring to the Act of Emancipation, he wrote: "When you, Sire, have immortalized your name by accomplishing the great deed of justice and humanity, it is difficult to understand how a writer can be held suspect who, in his modest sphere, as far as in his power lay, sought to promote the same high ends." He begged the Emperor to believe the sincerity of his words, and concluded: "Personal gratitude is added to the loyal sentiment which I am in duty bound to entertain for the person of your Majesty."

Having written thus to the Czar, he sent off a letter to Herzen, saying that he had asked the Emperor for a questionnaire, that he had already taken precautions against the possible confiscation of his properties, and that in any case he had no intention of appearing before the Committee: let the Government do its worst—it would only cover itself with shame. And he asked for the return of the letter in which he had criticized the address to Alexander II drafted by Ogaryov and had sketched out a substitute for it. To Annenkov he had previously written that he had asked for a questionnaire, which he would fill out with complete candor as he had nothing to hide. Perhaps counting on his letter being read by the police, he reminded this correspondent that the latter was in the habit of calling him the Government's "secret adherent."

The plea for a questionnaire was granted, and on March 22, 1863, he dispatched his replies to the Senate. He stated that he had never shared Bakunin's views or taken part either directly or indirectly in his schemes. As for Herzen, he had become increasingly estranged from the man, not because of any change in his own convictions but because "Herzen turned republican and socialist, Herzen fallen under the influence of Ogaryov, certainly had nothing in common with any right-minded Russian, who does not separate the people from the Czar or the sincere love of reasonable freedom from belief in the necessity of the monarchical principle." Their personal relations, he pointed out, had terminated with his visit to London in May 1862. And he reminded his judges that in "Ends and Beginnings" Herzen had set down an unflattering opinion of him as "a chilly epicurean, a laggard who has seen his day," and that his own retorts had been candid and unsparing. He admitted that, for old times' sake, he had contributed a thousand francs toward Bakunin's maintenance and helped to arrange his wife's trip from Siberia to Premuk-hino, and wound up with a dignified protestation to the effect that he abhorred all manner of darkness, including the darkness of conspiracy. In support of his declaration he attached four letters to him from Herzen and Bakunin. One of the latter's messages contained a passage highly damaging to its author regarding "a military operation" against the Russian Government, planned by himself and others.

The written replies did not satisfy the senators. Discrepancies were discovered between these depositions and the testimony of other defendants. He was again requested to appear before the commission in person. But as time went on, he was sufficiently reassured to joke about the whole matter. He imagined how he would be cast into jail; how Botkin would "whine," and his "ladies"—Mme. Viardot and her daughters —shed tears; how *The Contemporary* would hint that the editors had always been on excellent terms with the martyr; how, like Dostoevsky or Silvio Pellico, he would write his prison memoirs; how Viardot would translate the book, and Europe would read it, but refrain from interceding for him through diplomatic channels; how his ladies would then send him a steel saw in a knitted scarf and he would escape; how the Government would meanwhile discover that he was innocent and appoint him Governor General of Bokhara.

After three postponements due to illness he appeared before the Senate Committee in January, 1864, to testify in person. Several times he confronted his judges, six old men wearing uniforms and decorations, and he was brought face to face with two other defendants. The senators were polite, indeed gracious, and he was completely at ease regarding the outcome of the affair. At a concert he had had a cordial exchange with Prince Dolgoruky, chief of the Empire's police. Prince Suvorov, too, the Governor General, had been extremely amiable to him. "All this proves that they do not see a conspirator in me," he wrote to Pauline on January 28. "Besides, fat Venevitinov, whom you know, one of my judges, told me that my case is a trifling one." Before the end of the month Turgenev was officially exonerated and permitted to leave the country. This was long before the end of the trial of his fellow defendants, some of whom were sentenced to years of hard labor.

Turgenev's relief at the happy conclusion of the affair was crossed with vexation. Back in Baden, he discovered this shaft in the issue of *The Bell* dated January 15, 1864: "A correspondent mentions a gray-haired Magdalene (of the male sex) who wrote the Emperor that she was losing sleep and appetite, white hair and teeth, because she was tormented by the fear that he did not know of her repentance, as a result of which 'she has broken off all relations with the friends of her youth.'" He responded with an indignant letter to the editor, dated April 2. He could believe Bakunin capable of such mudslinging, he wrote, but not Herzen, and he enclosed the text of his appeal to the Czar. Of his replies to the questionnaire he declared: "If I could show them to you, you would be convinced that without concealing anything, I did not insult any of my friends. The thought of repudiating them did not occur to me. I would have considered that unworthy of me. I confess that I recall those replies not without some pride. In spite of their tone, they aroused in my judges esteem for and confidence in me." Fortunately for his reputation as a liberal and as a loyal friend, those replies were securely buried in the files of the Russian secret service, and became known only many years after his death. Herzen wrote back shrewdly to say that he was not deceived into believing that his correspondent had kept his nerve, and advised him to stop meddling with politics.

One of the things that he remembered against Turgenev was the latter's attitude toward the Polish insurrection of 1863. Herzen himself had espoused the cause of the rebels—with disastrous results for *The Bell*—though he strongly suspected that it was a lost one. Turgenev did not deny the Poles the right to independence, but he preferred to see the two peoples live in peace and amity under the wing of the Russian eagle. He hated violence, whether the Poles or his own compatriots were guilty of it. *The Bell's* appeal to the Russian army officers to show special consideration toward the new Polish conscripts (it was the irregular recruiting of Poles that had caused the rebellion) brought tears to his eyes. At the same time he wrote to Annenkov that he hoped "this insane insurrection" would be put down for the sake of both countries. He was no jingo, like his publisher, Katkov, or his friend Botkin, but he allowed that Russia's national security was to be considered in a situation which was far from simple. Seeing some right on both sides in this tragic conflict, he found himself uncomfortably on the fence. Herzen could have put up with his unpolitical friend's failure to protest against the atrocities committed by the imperial government in suppressing the rebellion. He could even sympathize with a man's contributing money for the relief of the Russian soldiers wounded in action against the rebels. But when the famous novelist attached his name to his donation, Herzen recoiled in unforgiving disgust.

One after another they withdrew from Turgenev, the old familiar companions: first Goncharov, then Nekrasov, then Tolstoy, now Herzen and Bakunin.

25

"DEAREST, DEAREST . . ."

Returning from Paris in 1862, Turgenev arrived at Spasskoye early in June. Whenever he found himself in what he called his "empty nest" he succumbed to melancholy. Not for nothing did Pauline call him *"le plus triste des hommes."* But now his dejection was diluted by indifference. He knew that this mood would wear away, and the days would run on smoothly: "beads clicked off on an abacus." Like his house, his desk, his armchair, he was old.

By August he was again abroad. He had left Russia in a pet. Because of *Fathers and Children,* he felt, he was facing a blank wall of misunderstanding when he was not assailed by abuse. He was in no hurry to appear again before the tribunal of the critics and the public. Besides, he may have sniffed the first breath of that gust of reaction which was soon to chill the lukewarm liberalism of the bureaucracy. At the same time he seemed to see the bubbles of a revolutionary ferment that would have pleased Bazarov, but from which his creator shrank. It looked to him like the evil product of the long years of repression suffered by a brutalized nation. (Signs of smoldering fires of radicalism would continue to alarm him.) He had done his bit to set the wheel of Russian progress rolling. "I'd rather not watch it jolt and sink into the mud," he wrote. This was the sentiment of an elderly man who felt out of place in a country that appeared to be entering awkwardly upon a new and troubled era. And wasn't age actually upon him? He was forty-four! Writing to Countess Lambert on his birthday, he declared that practically his whole life was behind him. A few days earlier he had described to her his state of mind in what he called his "old age": "If the sun shines and I have no pain, I have no desires." (As a matter of fact, he spoke of his old age on turning thirty-six.)

Yet was he such an apathetic ancient? Certainly he was as responsive as ever to the pull of one sentimental leash. Fifteen years previously he had been beckoned abroad by the lovely hands of Pauline Viardot. Now, in peevishly withdrawing from his native land, he again sought the comfort of her presence. She was settled with her family in Baden, where they were to make their home for eight years until the downfall of the Second Empire was to reconcile Louis Viardot, an ardent republican, to the French regime. It was in this town, not unfamiliar to Turgenev, that he spent the rest of the summer and most of the autumn, going to Paris for the winter, which proved to be a rather unproductive one. He assured his friends that he was a Russian more than ever and deeply interested in what was going on at home, but he stayed abroad. He was to remain a voluntary exile from his country. Though he went back more or less regularly—on an average, once in every eighteen months—it was Russia that he visited and Western Europe that he lived in. Previously, for all his long stays abroad, it had been Europe that he visited and Russia that he lived in. Of the two decades left him, the months that he spent in the country of his birth added up to only two years. Not that he had deliberately chosen expatriation. It just happened.

In the spring he was back in Baden. His daughter was with him—a rather unhappy arrangement, it turned out, as she did not get along with her former foster mother. In fact, during the summer there seem to have been clashes between the two, which Turgenev found very painful and for which he blamed Paulinette. Early in the fall she returned to Paris, while he remained in Baden. The business of marrying her off weighed on his mind. There was no lack of suitors, but she kept turning them down. In the spring of 1863 the situation looked hopeful. Writing about it to his brother, he refrained from naming the prospective bridegroom for fear of the evil eye: there had been disappointments in the past. In spite of this precaution, the match came to nothing. Another fell through a year later. When he decided to winter in Baden, he installed Paulinette with her governess in a small apartment at Passy, near the home of a Mme. Delessert, who knew half of Paris and kindly promised to find a fiancé for the twenty-two-year-old girl. "God grant it! I am beginning to lose hope," he confessed to Countess Lambert.

Mme. Delessert kept her promise. In December, 1864, Paulinette informed her father that "the right one"—she used the English phrase—had appeared, and the customary *pourparlers* commenced forthwith. "Mme. Viardot has told me that she hopes some day you will realize how gratuitously cruel you have been to her," he wrote to his daughter, "and she rejoices in the happiness that is in store for you." On February 25, 1865, Pauline Tourguéneff was married to Gaston Bruère, a thirty-year-old Parisian who looked like Prince Albert and who owned what seemed to be a profitable glass factory in the town of Rougemont. There was a good deal of legal red tape involved because Turgenev had had to go through many formalities, so that when the marriage contract was finally signed, he felt like a general who had fought a hard battle. He thought his daughter looked radiant on the day of the wedding, and he rather enjoyed the elaborate Church ceremony (the bride had embraced Roman Catholicism—at his instance, secretly, for publicity would have resulted in "grave unpleasantnesses" for him). He believed that the man was created to make her happy and that the two were eminently suited to each other. "I have the greatest confidence in and sympathy with your good Gaston," he was writing to his daughter three days after the wedding; "tell him that I embrace him as a son and that he must always and on all occasions count on me as on a father."

The previous autumn he had announced to Countess Lambert that he saw no reason why he should not settle in Baden permanently and build himself a "nest in which to await the inevitable end." When he was writing these lines excavations on the site of the villa which he was having built for himself next to that of the Viardots had already been completed. A twelvemonth later, having ordered five hundred trees and shrubs for the grounds, he was looking forward to the shade they would cast over the constitutionals of his declining years. He hoped that the house would be ready for occupancy in 1866. Meanwhile he was staying in a furnished flat on Schillerstrasse.

His home came to be where his heart was. His relationship

with the woman whom he had not ceased to address as "Mme. Viardot" was at last seen by both of them as inalterable and secure. A kind of emotional equilibrium was apparently established. His attachment had survived the cold spells that had seemed to him all but fatal. It was a hardy plant, and now it bloomed like a sunflower. "I assure you," he wrote to Pauline on February 27, 1867, "that my feeling for you is something entirely new in the world, something that has never before existed and will never repeat itself!" Allowing that this protestation belongs to the undisciplined language of the heart, it is nevertheless true that there is something unique—as well as baffling—about the quality and intensity of his involvement. Ludwig Pietsch, who saw a good deal of both Turgenev and the Viardots in Baden, spoke of his love for Pauline as *"reiner Minnedienst,"* chivalric devotion of a Platonic kind. According to another German friend, it was *"ein Seelenbund,"* a union of souls involving no "erotic relations." Turgenev seems to have resembled the woman in the case in being essentially given to sentiment, certainly not a sensualist. Further, one imagines that this incomplete, ambiguous liaison offered him the satisfaction of self-pity and allowed him to nurse a sense of frustration and unfulfillment. To some degree it must also have nourished his work.

There were, of course, separations. When the singer was on tour Turgenev followed her triumphs as he had when he and his passion had been twenty years younger. Occasionally he, too, left Baden, to consult a physician or read Russian newspapers in Heidelberg, to go to an art exhibit in Munich, to attend the première of *Meistersinger* in Karlsruhe, to see his brother in Dresden, to call on the newly wedded couple at Rougement, to visit Paris, and there were trips to Russia, partly foraging expeditions. On such occasions the two exchanged letters, of which only his—and not all—are available. As we know, early in 1864 he traveled to Petersburg in answer to a summons from the Czar's bureaucrats. *En route* he writes to Pauline from Berlin twice on the same day. It is bitterly cold and he tells her, with apologies for mentioning it, that he will buy a second set of flannel underwear. The windows of her little salon must be padded with felt, and she should not walk on the pond in this kind of weather. He cannot get used to the idea that he is so far from Baden; people and objects pass before his eyes, as in a dream, without seeming to affect him. He arrives at his destination, and his next letter is dated: "Baden—alas, no: Petersburg!" Not until he is back in "the blessed land" where he has left the better part of himself will he be happy. The Russian sphinx might have been made of air, a phantom, a vision, a ghost.

Frequent letters follow. He writes with the assiduity of earlier years, filling his pages, as he did then, with circumstantial reports of his doings. He describes a dinner in memory of a lately deceased friend at which he overate; a costume ball, giving details of the latest fashions; an evening at a play so dull that he wanted to creep under his seat. Above all, he is busy with the topic of chief interest to his correspondent: music. There are accounts of operas, concerts, song recitals, comments on singers and conductors, discussions of new compositions, snatches of musical gossip. There must have been kind words in the mail that he received from Baden, for he confesses, on January 16, that he is "ashamed to be loved so much."

Oh, for the joy of reunion! He counts the days. After a month's absence he writes: "I must be granted the happiness of seing you at the station—you will, I hope, meet me? I will telegraph to you from Berlin. My heart leaps in my side. I cannot think about it much: it is such an enormous happiness that I know I shall be tormented by forebodings and fears that it will not be . . . But, no! God is good, and He will be pleased to look at a man mad with joy." The note of deathless adoration, struck in his early letters, is repeated with fresh force. On January 24 he writes: "My heart literally melts as soon as your beloved image—I shall not say: appears before my mental eye, for it never leaves me—comes closer, as it were." Then follows a passage in German—as of old, he falls into this language at moments of abandon, though he continues to use the formal pronoun: "I constantly feel on my head the dear weight of your beloved hand, and I am so happy to feel that I belong to you that I could swoon in continual worship. When will the blessed minute come that will give my eyes a chance to see yours?" A Russian lady who met Pauline that year on the promenade in Baden found her large black eyes the only beautiful feature in her long, sallow, equine face.

In February, 1867, Pauline is giving concerts in Berlin. Turgenev writes to her in German: "Oh, my friend, I am so happy at the thought that everything in me is so intimately bound up with and dependent upon your being. If I am a tree, then you are both my root and my crown." In his next letter he tells her that his whole being is sloping toward her "like a funnel." The comparison is one he had heard her make, and it fits him so well that he cannot forbear using it. Again, falling into German and the language of the smitten adolescent, he writes: "Oh, my ardently loved friend, I am constantly thinking of you, day and night, and with what boundless love! Whenever you think of me you may say to yourself: 'My picture stands before his eyes and he worships me!' This is literally so." (He always carried her picture with him, and his study in Baden, a few blocks away from the Viardot villa, held a photograph, a portrait, and a bust of Pauline.) Six days later he writes, again in German: "I cannot tell you how passionately I long every night for your dear presence. And all night long I dream of you." Did his words echo in his ears? He had written in virtually the same vein nearly twenty years previously. "And now I can't work any longer," he continues, "as all my thoughts constantly revolve about you, and everything else melts before your dear image like snow."

He plans to follow her to the Prussian capital on his way to Petersburg, but an attack of gout lays him low. If he could only be taken to her in a perambulator! The invalid recovers in time to meet her in Berlin and spend all too brief a time with her before proceeding to Petersburg, in order to arrange for the publication of his new novel. "Pity your poor friend," he writes to her on board the train. "Never has separation been so painful. At night I shed bitter tears . . ." Having reached the shores of the Neva, he sends her word to reassure her about his health and promises to write every day. Then he goes on, in German:

Dearest friend, sole adored being! I cannot tell you how immeasurably sad I was. Those days in Berlin, that sudden marvelous meeting —all that, and then this bitter parting—it was really too much for me. And under the weight of the unforgettable impressions I simply broke down, as I have never done before. Ach, my feeling for you is too great and powerful! I can no more, I cannot live far from you. . . . The day when your eyes have not shone on me is a lost day. But enough, or else I shall lose control of myself. . . .

In a letter marked the next day, still to Pauline's Berlin address, he writes: "The Prussians would love me if they knew with what tenderness I write and pronounce the name of their capital." And he continues, in German, still addressing her formally: "Dearest, dearest, never has a human breast cherished a feeling like mine for you. Adoration is the least name to call it by." He tells her that he has remitted to her the ten *Friedrichsdor* he had borrowed from her in Berlin and without which he would have been in serious straits— as it is, he arrived in Petersburg with four rubles in his pocket. Furthermore, as in the previous letter, he advises her to lock her doors carefully. When he goes to see his publisher in Moscow, the city seems a prison to him and his longing for Baden makes every day "endless and heavy." The sigh of relief that he will heave when he finds himself home again "will make all the mountains and the Black Forest tremble." The dull skies and snowy streets of Moscow are a foil for the green and golden world spread out below his window on Schillerstrasse: sunshine, the smell of lilac, the song of black-birds on leafy boughs!

"God, how eager I am to return to Baden!" he writes to Pauline after some weeks in Paris in 1868. And from Petersburg in the summer of that year comes the same cry: "Oh, Baden, oh, valley of the Tiergarten! Where are you?" The vaunted white nights of the North fret his nerves, and he is dogged by a vague, sweetish odor of dampness that nauseates him. A dreadful place to live in—this city, but it holds a spot that he cannot pass without an access of tender-ness: the house in which Pauline had stayed a quarter of a century earlier and to which so many memories cling. In Moscow he has a severe attack of gout and, forced to postpone his return to Baden, he feels like a mouse in a trap. "When we are reunited," he writes to Pauline, "we must stay together as long as possible and by joining forces defend ourselves from the ugly things that the envious gods visit upon us."

As was pointed out earlier, from the first Turgenev's affection was generously extended to Pauline's entire household, including her husband, and there were even crumbs for the cats. He must have the happiness of seeing them *all* at the station when he returns to Baden. His embrace is wide enough to include *"toute la maisonnée."* Having given Pauline the news of the decease of his friend, Druzhinin, he adds: "Death is great and terrible, and if she could hear what you say to her, I would implore her to leave me on earth a while longer. I still want to see you, and for a long time yet, if that is possible. Oh, my dear friend, live long, and let me live beside you *all*."

Even before the close association of the Baden period, Turgenev had become virtually a member of the Viardot family. To Louise, the eldest and least lovable of the children, to Claudie, his darling, to the thin little Marianne, to Paul, the baby, he was as familiar as their father. As for the excellent Viardot himself, Turgenev collaborated with him on translations from the Russian and was his faithful companion on hunting trips. To Mme. Viardot he offered himself as a staff and a shield whenever it was a question of getting her villa ready for the winter, of marrying off her daughters, or of running to the chemist's to have a prescription filled in a hurry. And all this was over and above his affection for her person and his interest in her art. He was always there, ready with advice, eager with assistance, solicitous, equable, and somewhat impractical. Frequently he dined with the Viardots. The large, lolling bulk of the old bachelor belonged to the evening scene in the drawing room as much as Viardot dozing by the fire, the girls bent over their sketchbooks, the lady of the house at her piano or at her desk copying music. As at Courtavenel, there were parlor games, including *Jeux de têtes*. He still excelled in drawing profiles, and his and Pauline's characterizations ranked highest as heretofore.

He was sufficiently in the confidence of the "iron-faced" Louise to carry her a proposal from a hopeful suitor. When she came to Baden in 1864 for her confinement, Turgenev, little as he liked her, surrendered his flat to the young woman who was making Mme. Viardot a grandmother, and moved into two rooms in the same house. He was fond of little

Marianne, and devoted to Claudie. Her he singled out for special evidences of his affection. To force himself to get down to the tedious job of writing a foreword to the new edition of his works, he makes a vow that when he returns to Baden (from a visit to Russia) he will deny himself Didie's kiss unless he has worked at the confounded thing that day. The girl has a talent for painting, and for his birthday she draws a Descent from the Cross, " really," he exclaims, "a wonder!" When, later on, they all move to Bougival, a suburb of Paris, he will reserve a well lighted corner of his study for the young artist. He sends a picture of her to his poet friend Fet with the injunction: "Here's the person to write verses to!" She has thick hair over a fine brow, and a mouth like a bow, her large blue eyes contrasting oddly with her Southern features. At the German Court she was compared to Sakuntala. In a turban she has fashioned for herself out of an antimacassar she makes him think of "a young goddess, still untamed, out of some mythology of the future."

One of his fondest wishes was to have the Viardots visit his estate, and he had daydreams of seeing Didie trip down the alley in the Spasskoye park. "I positively adore this fascinating creature, so pure-hearted and graceful," he wrote to her mother on June 17, 1868. "I am deeply moved when her image rises before my mind's eye, and I trust that Heaven has reserved for her the happiest of lots. But her health," he continued, with transparent guile, "does not satisfy me. A month at Spasskoye, a milk diet and black rye bread—that's what she needs." It was during this visit to Russia that he sold a piece of woodland, getting a "pretty round sum" for it, which enabled him, he said with satisfaction, to start laying by money for Didie's dowry. In the summer of 1870 he informed a friend, who was holding some shares of stock for him, that he had bought them for his "dear Claudie Viardot" and that, should he "suddenly croak," they were to be delivered to Mme. Viardot in Baden.

As was noted above, Turgenev was undoubtedly not the father of either of the girls. Yet if he could not rejoice to recognize himself in either of them, he loved them for their mother's part in them. He kisses Didie's hand because it reminds him of Mme. Viardot's. He notes, affectionately, the girl's "dry smile," as, twenty years before, he had remarked the crooked smile of the prima donna. He writes Mme. Viardot that, beside the great altar in the temple of his heart, he has erected another, smaller one, dedicated to Claudie. He once told the girls that he was happy to know that he would never live to see their young faces lose their bloom; "we must regenerate ourselves," he reflected in that connection, "through the youth of those we love." They were to him the miraculously renewed image of Pauline Viardot.

26

THE BADEN NEST

"Little Mother Wednesday, be like Tuesday, just as little Father Tuesday was like Monday"—there were periods when the Baden days flowed so placidly that Turgenev could ask no more of the gods than that no breath of change should threaten his serenity. Having alighted in so friendly a valley, and in the most congenial company, he knew moments when he wished to arrest the wheel of time. The velvet lawns, set with nicely spaced trees, under which shawled and bonneted ladies promenaded, the quiet waters, the roll of gentle hills, dark and bright with plowland and fallow, was a setting that he loved both for its own mild charm, and, chiefly, because he saw it, like a landscape behind the head of one of Perugino's Madonnas, as the background for the rarest of women.

True, on the human side, the town itself had its drawbacks. It had changed little since the summer of 1857, when he had first visited it. At that time he had been depressed by the place. His friend, Yakov Polonsky, the poet, had described it as "a diminutive Babylon," a town of hotels, summer cottages and bawdy houses, where luxury and vice rubbed elbows. During the season Baden was infested with gamblers, who came from the four corners of the earth to swarm about one of the few roulette boards allowed in Europe, and with pompous Russian generals gulping waters from springs once resorted to by gouty Romans. It was a meeting-place for the dandies and diplomats of Paris, Vienna, and Petersburg; a hunting-ground for expensive French lorettes, Rumanian adventurers, indigent Italian counts, opulent American occultists.

Yet before the classic portico of the *Konversationshaus* and on the shaded paths beside the Oos one could also meet people of real distinction who cared as little as Turgenev for the continuous carnival that the watering place offered. Artists, especially musicians, were attracted to Baden both because its air and its natural scenery were grateful to fatigued nerves, and because it afforded them a brilliant and appreciative audience. Some, like Pauline Viardot and Clara Schumann, came to settle; others came to summer or on a flying visit. Turgenev had seldom found a circle more to his taste than the company that centered around the Viardot house. His craving for music had never been so exquisitely and generously satisfied. The Viardots' exodus to Baden in 1863 coincided with Pauline's retirement from the operatic stage. With that tact which was one of her graces, she withdrew without waiting for any sign of the decay of her powers, concluding her career with a superb triumph in Gluck's *Orpheus and Eurydice*. Charles Dickens was among those who heard her in this opera shortly before she left the operatic stage. "Last night," he wrote on November 30, 1862, "I saw Mme. Viardot do Gluck's *Orphée*. It is worth a journey to Paris to see, for there is no such art to be otherwise looked upon. Her husband stumbled over me by mere chance and took me to her dressing room. Nothing could have happened better as a genuine homage to the performance, for I was disfigured with crying." It is said that Louis Viardot brought Dickens up to her with the words: "Permit me to present a fountain."

After her retirement from the opera Mme. Viardot devoted herself to the concert stage and to teaching. At forty-four, when she was celebrating her silver wedding anniversary—if her marriage was admittedly without love, it was not without honor—she moved Turgenev with wonder at her ability to be very well, very active and very cheerful. He was fairly well himself, but far from active and, for all his moods of serenity, he could hardly be called cheerful. Musical celebrities and local society people were frequent guests at the Viardot villa. The visitors included the daughter and little granddaughter of one of the first women to stir Turgenev's imagination as well as his pulses—Bettina von Arnim, now dead, like the Berlin days of his in which she had figured.

For their friends and acquaintances the Viardots arranged Sunday musicales. They were held in the afternoon in a concert hall that served as the workshop for the hostess' pupils. It stood in the garden on which the villa fronted. A proud

Turgenev.
A pencil sketch made by Pauline Viardot
September 22, 1879

A caricature of Turgenev
drawn by himself in pencil,
Paris, 1878-9

successor of the Potato Theatre, it was an imposing basilica-shaped wooden structure provided with two grand pianos and an organ, the bellows of which Turgenev worked on occasion. The matinées were often attended by Queen Augusta of Prussia who usually vacationed at the spa. She would be one of the first to arrive and would sit in a front row. Sometimes the King, who was not musical, would slip in quietly, taking a seat near the door so that he could escape easily. He might be accompanied by such a guest as Bismarck, and once the royal couple brought their grandson, then about ten years old, who was to be the last German Emperor.

At these informal concerts Pauline was as brilliant as ever, whether she regaled her public with one of Schumann's *Lieder,* an old Italian aria or a Spanish canzone. It was not only so prejudiced a listener as Turgenev who held that while other artists were mere singing birds, her voice carried the rush of eagles' wings. There was one song in her repertoire which brought tears to his eyes and sent a chill down his spine: "Der Doppelgänger." Heine's weird lyric and Schubert's grave melody, borne upon the dark current of this voice, shook him to the core. Hadn't he, more than once, watched an anguished stranger aping the gestures of his lovesick youth, only to have that stranger confront him with his own ghastly face?

Turgenev was not content to be Mme. Viardot's most eager auditor. When the retired prima donna tried her hand at composition he did everything possible to encourage her. He found a publisher in Petersburg for three albums of Russian songs which she had set to music, and when there seemed to be no market for a fourth, he quietly paid the cost of publication. Having no qualms about committing a pious fraud, he gave Pauline one hundred and twenty five rubles from his own pocket, submitting spurious evidence that the money came from the publisher. He even stooped to request Annenkov to insert a favorable notice of these volumes in some journal, adding: "I've never troubled about publicity for myself, but there is one person for whom I am willing not only to write advertisements but to do almost anything. . . ." To make her go on composing, he promised to set to work again himself. " 'Pass me the cassia, and I will pass you the senna.' A story for a sonata—is it a deal?"

That he should end by sticking his finger into the Viardot musical pie was only natural. During 1867-68 he collaborated with Pauline on four operettas, writing the librettos for them in French. Although they were performed repeatedly before choice audiences, the music has never been printed, and of the books alone the second, *Craquemiche or The Last Sorcerer* has been published, and that but partially, in a German translation. Turgenev may have been responsible for this. He was extremely sensitive on the subject of his writing for publication in a foreign language—a matter about which he knew his compatriots liked to gossip—and could not mention it without irritation. "Never in my life," he wrote in answer to a formal inquiry in 1875, "have I published a line not written in Russian; otherwise I would have been not an artist, but simply a good-for-nothing." He told Pietsch that a fellow who wrote in anything but his own mother tongue was, in his opinion, "a scoundrel and a wretched swine without talent."

Craquemiche has to do with the struggle of the Queen of the elves against a once powerful sorcerer and her triumph in freeing her enchanted forest from his wicked spell. The première took place in the large drawing room of Turgenev's villa, which was still unfinished. The cast was made up of the children and pupils of Pauline Viardot, who accompanied them at the piano. Turgenev's histrionic talent stood him in good stead and allowed him to play the leading role. The only other male member of the company was little Paul Viardot. The second performance, on September 23, 1867, was attended by the King and Queen, as well as the Crown Prince and Princess of Prussia, the Grand Duke and Grand Duchess of Baden, and other highly stationed personages. It went off splendidly. The male star, writing to Annenkov, noted that Craquemiche's throne speech, which parodied the orations of Napoleon III, the pet abomination of the Viardots and of Turgenev, called forth "thick laughter" from the King of Prussia. Three years later the Emperor of the French was to surrender his sabre to a general of this king who was to become the first ruler of the German Empire.

Clara Schumann, writing to Brahms from Baden on October 3, 1867, says that she had heard *Craquemiche,* as well as the first operetta, *Trop de Femmes,* three times, and always "with equal pleasure." They were "so cleverly written, so dainty, so light, so finished, and, with all that, so full of humor." The great pianist found in them fresh confirmation of her opinion that Pauline Viardot was "the most gifted woman" she had ever known. "When I saw her sitting at the piano and managing everything with perfect ease," she continued, "my heart melted within me, and I could have clasped her in my arms." Turgenev could not have been moved less.

The third operetta, *"L'Ogre,"* was first staged on May 24, 1868. The dress rehearsals took place in his drawing room. He found the villa swarming with girls, laughing, singing, trying on costumes, making a huge racket to the accompaniment of hammers, the shuffle of sceneshifters, and the curses of the ballet master from Karlsruhe, who, as Paul Viardot was to recall in his memoirs, scolded the Swiss girls for their heaviness, the Swedish girls for their awkwardness, the Germans for their slowness, the French for their chatter. Turgenev himself swaggered jovially in a false beard, a ruff and a plumed crown surmounting a red wig that he had bought in Paris, and exhibited the proportions if not the ferociousness of a proper ogre. Queen Augusta kept sending messengers to find out when the affair, for which these immense preparations were being made, would finally come off.

Usually the operettas were put on in the concert hall. After a performance a supper of cold cuts and potato salad was served the actors. If the spectacle took place in Turgenev's house, they would form a torchlight procession and march across the park that separated the two villas. The fourth operetta had the distinction of being performed at the Baden theater.

Turgenev had not lost the taste for acting that he had had since his youth. It must have been somewhat of a relief for him to shed his own unsatisfactory self and for a while lease the tenement of another existence. "The saddest of men" entered whole-heartedly into the comic parts of the operettas. Rarely did he feel misgivings as to the appropriateness of this silly mummery on the part of a Turgenev, an eminent novelist, and an aging man. Once when he lay on the floor in a scarcely dignified pose, impersonating the Pasha in *Trop de Femmes,* he caught a contemptuous smile slowly twisting the lips of the Crown Princess Victoria, the mother of the future Emperor William II. "Although, generally speaking, I haven't much respect for myself," he commented in a letter, "this was a little too much for me. Still," he went on, "these spectacles have been something altogether charming and worth-while."

In March, 1869, the Grand Duke of Weimar staged *Craquemiche,* in a German translation, at his own theatre.* About this performance Turgenev wrote an article for a Petersburg newspaper, which, he conceded, was *réclame.* The production was an affair of importance for Pauline Viardot, since it was to decide the question of whether she should enter upon a new career as a composer. Her friends, incuding Liszt, put themselves out to insure a triumph, but she, realizing that her success was due chiefly to their efforts, determined to confine herself to concerts and teaching. Turgenev could console himself with the thought that for his part he had done all he could.

Besides the pleasures that were the dearer for being bound up with Pauline, Baden offered him the active joys of the hunt, for which he was as keen as ever. When autumn approached, he could think of nothing else, even if his gouty foot could not stand the pressure of a boot. During the season he went off to the woods as often as three times a week, and foxes, hares, pheasants, partridges and boars figure in the hunting statistics with which he furnished his friends. His faithful companions on these trips were Louis Viardot and Pegasus. Since his early years he had had a strong affection and, as it were, a fellow feeling for dogs. At least one of them—Pegasus—seemed to reciprocate it. He would surprise his master with a deep sigh in his moments of melancholy. One evening when Turgenev was seized with a mysterious terror on the edge of a pond the dog threw himself at his feet, as though sharing his fright.

"L'illustre Pégase" was more famous in the duchy than the novelist. A touching eulogy to him forms the last section of Turgenev's *Recollections of Life and Letters.* He was, like his master, generously proportioned, and like him wore his

---

* The operetta has recently been staged in Jena.

wavy hair long; it was black, dappled with yellow. A cross between an English setter and a German sheep dog, he inherited from gifted forebears a nose that became the hero of a thousand legends. In addition to being an incomparable retriever, he was a shrewd strategist. His family had been known for the severity of its morals. He never lied. Nor did he betray his having noted a compliment—by so much as an overmodest look. He had only one fault: not having received a strict English education, he did not wait for the word of command before dashing to pick up the game. Another failing of his was that he frankly disliked Mme. Viardot, he who was generally so gracious with the sex, although, as his master once observed, he had suffered much at their hands. Could it be that he was jealous? Otherwise he was impeccable. But alas! The gods are envious of the great. Age came fast upon this magnificent creature and turned him into a slobbering moron. His master, who had refused fabulous sums for Pegasus in his heyday, now had on his hands a pensioner. The poor fellow was like an artist grown old, a singer who had lost her voice.

Gout was a serious obstacle to these hunting excursions. It made its first appearance in January, 1867, and remained the greatest of Turgenev's afflictions until the coming of the illness that was to end them all. In the winter of 1866 he suffered from muscular rheumatism, and recalling that three or four years earlier, when he had a node on his foot, a commissionaire of the Hotel St. Petersburg in Berlin had given him a salve which helped him with wonderful rapidity, he asked Pietsch to find the man, get the magic salve, and send it on. Pietsch was obliging, so was the commissionaire, and all was well.

Just before he settled in Baden, he had had real cause for alarm on the score of his health. A Paris celebrity had discovered in him the seeds of a fatal ailment, of whose exact nature we are ignorant, and on New Year's Day, 1863, Turgenev was writing to Annenkov: "I cannot take my mind off this incurable disease, which deprives me of strength, has aged me, and has in store for me the saddest future." The diagnosis proved false. What continued to worry him every now and then was his old complaint, and when those pains attacked him he fell back into his familiar despairs. He assured his friends that he could quite understand the feelings of a suicide whom he once saw dragged from under the wheels of an omnibus, and who, before expiring, explained that he had been driven to this act by neuralgia, and though all his bones were broken, kept on murmuring: "Ah, what a relief!" As a matter of fact, Turgenev's disease, if sometimes acutely painful, was not at all serious, and was soon to disappear except for an occasional twinge.

The air of Baden positively agreed with him. He suffered less than usual from the colds and attacks of grippe, laryngitis, and bronchitis which so easily secured lodgment in this leonine head and chest. Certainly he did not again wear the "muzzle," as he called the respiratory mask which he had been forced to don whenever he went out into the frosts of 1860; his sputum was free from the blood that had frightened him then, and he no longer dosed himself with cod-liver oil. He persisted, however, in the habit of bundling himself up with mufflers, comforters, knitted vests, flannel shirts, and the like. This giant from the land of snow was as sensitive to cold as any southerner. He must often have longed for the Dutch stoves of home, the hermetically sealed double windows, the padded doors. His mother's large wooden house in Moscow had been extremely warm. However remiss the Russians might be in other matters affecting creature comfort, they certainly knew how to secure heat and how to keep it. He was particularly distressed when he had to leave Baden in winter for some neighboring town.

The end of 1869 found him in Weimar. He went to arrange accommodations there for the family, and of course for himself, since they had decided to give Didie two months at the town's excellent art school. Weimar struck him as unpleasantly chilly. He complained that the houses were made of old cardboard, pasted togetherd with stale spittle, that the cold was intensified by the metallicity of the two bronze figures in front of the theatre, that when he woke up at night he discovered icicles in his beard, and that everybody wore everything to keep warm. In such circumstances no one was to be found on his Olympus but Jupiter the Cougher, Juno of the Quinsy, Apollo the Sneezer, and Venus de Bronchitis.

One thing which showed no signs of improvement was his

hypochondriac temper. He was subject to fits of irrational, uncontrollable fear: he imagined that he had been bitten by a mad dog or had himself taken a bite out of a poisonous piece of fish. He laughed at himself when the fit was over, but that did not prevent its recurrence. Cholera remained his chief phobia. He couldn't see a pharmacy in Moscow, Petersburg, Paris, London, without going in to ask for stomach drops. "I am like a madman," he said once. "I go as far as personifying cholera; I see it as a decrepit, yellowish-green, malodorous old hag." A sign of indisposition on the part of a fellow-traveler in a railway train was apt to throw him into a panic. "Perhaps it's cholera," he would whisper, and producing a bottle of Eau de Cologne would proceed to douse himself, his companion, and the seats, and even sprinkle a few drops in the direction of the puzzled stranger.

Not too far from the Viardots, and under the wing of Frau Anstett, who kept his furnished rooms at 277 Schiller-strasse, Turgenev felt as secure as was possible for him. Frau Anstett had for her boarder a maternal affection, which changed to adoration when he got her husband, a master potter, to make his will in her favor. The good soul, Turgenev sighed, was the only woman who had ever conceived a true passion for him, and in consequence she was continually press-ing upon him indigestible dishes, so that it was only by dint of the most subtle diplomacy that he kept himself alive. It was not until the spring of 1868 that he occupied the house which had been so long in the building and which was more fit to be the home of a man who grew up in a Russian manor. A spacious garden was attached to the villa, which was built in the style of Louis XIII, and it would seem as if Turgenev aimed at making the place a smaller version of the estate at Spasskoye, even to the fish ponds. When he moved into the villa he had the sensations of "a bride who had just gotten her trousseau," and at first the house made him feel "a little too grandiose and Sundayfied," but he had never been more comfortable. On returning to Baden from his excursions into France and Russia, he felt that he was coming back to his "nest," over the edge of which he could peer into the world.

27

SMOKE

Even at its best, the contentment which Turgenev knew as he looked upon the world from his Baden window was a poor thing. It was a shallow serenity, easily ruffled by the thought of decline and death, and permanently tainted by a sense of frustration. What depressed him was the feeling, by no means new, that he was finished as a writer. His letters of the years just before and after he became a Baden burgher are eloquent of this. The ink is no sooner dry on the manuscript of *Fathers and Children* than he announces that, to judge by his apathy, this is probably the last work from his pen: "It is time to pull the covers over my head and sleep." He reads nothing, does nothing, even thinks little. His literary vein is giving out. He is inaccessible to new feelings. Alone the vague and traceless play of fancy is left to one in whom all desires are dead and whose activity is failing. He lives tamely, having acquired the bodily and mental habits of senility. He vegetates, busied only with warding off small ailments. He has hung up his rusty pen as a veteran does his sword.

He made this last remark in a letter to Countess Lambert, dated March 10, 1865. That very year he said the same thing to his public, more elaborately in "Enough: a Fragment from the Notes of a Dead Artist." A rather nondescript composition, it opens with the aging artist's lyrical evocation of an early love, and ends with a meditation that can be interpreted as a rationale of Turgenev's withdrawal as a writer. The burden of these reflections is that nothing is worth while. One who has unlearned self-deception can have no hope. The terrible thing about life is just that it is not terrible, but petty, boring, flat. The only dignity in which man can clothe himself is the stoic acknowledgment of his own nullity. Nature cares nothing for human values. There are men who live by the great principles—liberty, justice, humanity; but stupidity and cruelty, "the tricks of authority and the habits of slavery," that Shakespeare saw about him still govern the world. Art is as futile as everything else. What is the use of the perishable images which we shape as we crouch on the edge of the empty dark? What heart can the artist have for producing his wares to be displayed in "the ghosts' flea fair, that market place where buyer and seller are equally cheated?" Enough . . . enough!

Turgenev's friends were used to these periodic gestures of abdication. So often he had been done with writing for good and all. But this time the situation looked serious. In the four years that followed the appearance of *Fathers and Children* he gave his public only three rather trifling pieces.

Besides, a new and alarming note had crept into the laments that issued from his Baden haven. He made the disquieting discovery that he was cut off from his own country. Russia, he told Countess Lambert in the letter referred to above, had become alien to him, and he did not know what to say about it. "In such cases, as the proverb goes, silence is golden." A year before he made this disastrous confession he had already been sufficiently troubled about the effect of his absenteeism on his writing to try to justify his living abroad. "There is absolutely no necessity for a writer to remain in his own country and try to seize upon its changing life," he had protested to his confidante, "at least there is no need to do it continuously." He had been at that sort of thing long enough, and how did she know that he wasn't about to attempt a work on a subject not specifically Russian, something of a wider significance?

As a matter of fact, the rabbit at which he hinted never hopped out of his hat. Indeed, it would have been sheer magic for him to produce a living piece of work unrelated to what was native to him. Six months previously he had, it is true, published a tale, "Phantoms," which had but scant bearing on the Russian scene. It is concerned with a ghostly vampire who, in exchange for a man's life-blood, carries him in nocturnal flights through time and space. Such passages as those which convey overpowering disgust with the pettiness and futility of life on this despicable planet, and which evoke the horrible image of death, are impressive, but the piece as a whole is heavy-footed and mechanical fantasy. When, seventeen years later, he again attempted themes unrelated to any element of his native background, as in "A Dream" and "The Song of Triumphant Love," the results were distinctly unhappy.

No, the idea of divorcing his writings from Russia was a snare and a delusion, and indeed he never seriously entertained it. For better or for worse, his art was wedded to his country. He must find his material in the lives of the men and women with whom he had grown up; he must explore the landscape that depressed him with its familiarity, and the mentality that had the fewest secrets from him; he must interpret, as he could not interpret the utterance of more voluble creatures, the silence of the Russian sphinx. Turgenev the lover could feel at home at Courtavenel, in Baden, London, Paris; Turgenev the novelist could be at ease only in his native atmosphere. Is it that the exercise of the artistic faculty demands a greater measure of intimacy than love?

That he exaggerated the degree of his alienation from his own country may be inferred from his novel *Smoke*. The scene is laid in Baden, but the foreign background is merely a foil for the Russian characters and the Russian interests which, here as always, are the novelist's main concern. He seemed to have conceived the idea for it early in 1863, when his debate with Herzen was under way. The actual writing was started only in November, 1865, and soon dropped. He had been idle so long, he told Annenkov, that he could say with Hugo that laziness had restored his virginity, and he felt as awkward as a novice. Less than six months after the letter containing this admission went off, the novel appeared in the issue of *The Russian Herald* for March, 1867. Turgenev had had considerable trouble with the editor, Katkov, who wanted the heroine portrayed as a virtuous matron and the generals as exemplary citizens.

Smoke is primarily a love story, in which the hero, Litvinov, is involved with two women. One, his fiancée, is a wholesome, whole-hearted girl of the sort Turgenev could appropriately place against the background of an old garden, with the shingle roof of the wooden manor house peeping through the silver poplars; the other, a general's wife, is an old flame of Litvinov's, more seductive, more passionate, more wilful than when she had first dizzied his senses, and now of easier morals. This lady goes out of her way to recapture Litvinov, and succeeds, but he has the strength to refuse the part of a secret lover, which is all she is willing to offer him, and after some water has flowed under the bridges, he returns to his patient fiancée, and the novel is served up with what Henry James calls "the time-honored bread-sauce of a happy ending." As usual, Turgenev shows us the brief consummation of a violent love. Amorousness he presents either in its shy beginnings or at its moment of climax; of love as a durable relation, as an everyday give-and-take, he has no more to say here than in any other of his novels.

Litvinov's private difficulty has for its context a larger predicament, that in which Russia found itself in the years immediately following the emancipation of the peasants. In *Smoke* Turgenev resumes the record of his times at the point where he dropped it in *Fathers and Children*. To do this he introduces two distinct groups from among the Russians who swell the crowd of Baden's transients. One is aristocratic and reactionary, the other, composed of the lesser gentry, is radical. Both are caricatured with the skill and biting malice of a Daumier. Both equally disgust Turgenev. What a flow of gall from so temperate a man!

His pen drips with venom when he touches off the titled set: these well-fed, perfumed, arrogant generals, who look back longingly to the blessed days of serfdom; these half-witted princes with their insipid jokes and vulgar snobbishness; these mummied beauties and dully malicious gossips, these condescending nonentities who play at art and love and politics with equal dilettanteism, and whose interest in spiritual matters is exemplified by an abortive effort to hypnotize a lobster. Nothing but boundless egotism animates these men and women.

If the indignation of a Juvenal fashions Turgenev's lines when he has to do with blue-blooded reaction, it is with grieved contempt that he describes the radical bedlam let loose in a Baden hotel room. The *obshchina,* the *artel,* the natural sciences, socialism, feminism, revolution, the People, Russia's mission—all these topics are bandied about by a smoky, beery,

noisy, furiously gossiping crowd of enthusiastic parrots, pre-
sumptuous sheep, and well-intentioned donkeys. The novelist's
animus is directed against the whole complex of inchoate
Russian radicalism: Chernyshevsky's utopianism, Pisarev's
"nihilism," particularly the militant Populism, with its Slavophil element, that Herzen had fathered. Indeed, Gubaryov, the
great revolutionary leader who is the idol of the doctrinaire
tribe, seems to have been modeled in part on Herzen's right
hand and Turgenev's bête noire, Nikolay Ogaryov. Futhermore, the extremism of this lunatic fringe turns out to be
quite ephemeral. At the end of the three years that the book
covers, it has evaporated. Gubaryov himself, on returning
home, reverts to his natural state, which is that of a bully and
a "dentist," the name given to such gentry as knocked out
the peasants' teeth with their own fists. The polished reactionaries and the unkempt fire-eaters are brother barbarians
under their skins. Russia has nothing to hope for from them.

The star to which the author would hitch that great, creaking, antediluvian wagon, his country, is *civilization*. The word,
"clean and holy," the reader is told, is constantly on the
tongue of Potugin, a character dragged in by the hair as
far as the plot is concerned, but effective as the author's
mouthpiece. He makes the thesis of the novel unmistakable.
To look down upon the West from the mystic height of an
ignorant and pompous nationalism, as the Slavophils do, is
folly as outrageous as to worship, like the radical set, the
peasant's *armyak* (coat) and to expect sweetness and light
to stream from his cockroach-infested hut. Culturally speaking,
there is nothing either in Russia's past or present to be proud
of. Its future depends on the people's ability to choose those
elements of Western civilization that are most suited to Russia's needs and make them their own. Turgenev's Westernism
implied no contempt for Russia, no denial of national identity.
His advice to his compatriots—the educated public turned
naturally to the novelists for counsel—amounted to this: give
up your vaporizing, your grandiose schemes, give up visions
of vast upheavals, and acquire the habits of hard, assiduous
work belonging to the discipline that has created European
culture, with its gifts of intellectual independence and inner
freedom. The times demand inconspicuous, modest, pedago-

gical efforts. The task devolves upon well-meaning, enlightened individuals, trained in useful skills, country gentlemen and commoners working hand in hand. Returning from abroad, where he had studied agronomy, the protagonist of the novel, the son of a small official who regarded himself as a plebeian and was proud of it, is seen as a representative of this group, which is the hope of Russia. In hammering on these ideas, Potugin was repeating publicly and with emphasis what Turgenev had privately been contributing to similar discussions for years. Indeed, Potugin's diatribes contain passages lifted almost bodily from the novelist's correspondence with Herzen.

The years have obscured the topical allusions in *Smoke* and made its reticences quaint. Then, too, the novel is not without structural defects, since the social motif dovetails only roughly into the passional theme. Yet the characters have vitality, the atmosphere is palpable, the satire spirited. There is nothing here of the feeling that permeates the jeremiad in "Enough." *Smoke* is not a tale of futility and frustration. It offers the spectacle of a man's will mastering his blind passion in the name of moral decency; it asserts the absolute value of all that was summed up for Turgenev in the word "civilization."

Nevertheless, the author's pessimism, fortified as it was by a reading of Schopenhauer, does creep into the pages. Litvinov, sitting in the train that is carrying him homeward from Baden, and watching the smoke curl backward from the engine, is suddenly assailed by the sense of the insubstantiality and transience of all things and the aimlessness of the interplay of events.

"Smoke, smoke," he repeated to himself several times; and suddenly everything seemed to him to be smoke—everything, his own life, Russian life, all things human, especially all things Russian. Everything is smoke and vapor, he thought; everything seems to change constantly; new images are everywhere, appearances scurry after appearances, but in reality it is all the same, the same; everything hurrying, hastening somewhere—and everything vanishes without leaving a trace, without reaching anywhere; the wind changes its direction and everything shifts to the opposite side, and there again is the same incessant, agitated and useless play.

Litvinov's musings are out of key with the import of the novel. But as they provide its title, the passage took on undue prominence and irritated Turgenev's readers, most of whom were apt to feel that life is real, life is earnest.

He had no illusions about the probable reception of the book, with its galling caricatures and antipatriotic recital of Russia's failings. And as a matter of fact it widened the breach between him and his public, caused by *Fathers and Children.* "It seems to me that no one has ever been so vilified as I for *Smoke,*" he wrote to Annenkov several weeks after its appearance. "Stones from every direction." He was bloodied but unbowed. It happened that the novel came out just when an ethnographical congress, attended by representatives of the several Slav nations, was meeting in Moscow. This gathering was less a scholarly convention than what Turgenev called "a pan-Slav squatting dance," and he was glad to think that his Potugin, though confined between covers, was on the spot to speak up against Slavophilism. The latter affected him "like a bad smell or a bad taste," to use his own words.

Whatever Turgenev may have said, he was far from indifferent to the opinion of his public, particularly its junior sector. He sent a copy of *Smoke* to Pisarev, whom he had met some months earlier, and asked the young man's opinion, probably expecting to find in him a sympathetic reader. Pisarev shared neither Chernyshevsky's hope for a popular revolution nor Herzen's faith in the *muzhik* as a born communist. "The problem of the hungry and the naked" was uppermost in his mind, but he was inclined to believe that the solution lay in the rational organization of private enterprise by men of good will forming a trained élite. His response to Turgenev's letter was characteristically blunt. He was not at all annoyed by the way the "radicals" were presented in the novel, he wrote, and he quoted the saying: "Fools should be thrashed even in church." He was sure, however, that the scenes at Gubaryov's had been introduced because the author, having hit out hard at the reactionaries, was afraid of losing his balance and finding himself in the camp of the Reds. Altogether the book impressed him as a strange and dismal sequel to *Fathers and Children.* What had the author done with his Bazarov? Why should he survey the Russian scene from such a little hillock as Litvinov, when he had erected, in the hero of *Fathers and Children,* a tall tower from which to view it? Did he think that the first and last Bazarov had died of a cut in his finger in 1859? To write a novel and leave out this powerful figure was like ignoring the elephant in the zoo. And *Smoke* represented Turgenev's second visit to the animal house, where *Fathers and Children* had been the first. Either the novelist had not seen the elephant at all, which was blindness, or, having seen him, had failed to put him into the picture, which rendered his account worthless.

Turgenev's response was that since his correspondent, like the rest of his readers, disliked *Smoke,* he himself could not but question the merits of this child of his. He conceded that there were Bazarovs about, but held that it would be arbitrary and false to represent the type in fiction at this time, for such a man had not yet shown himself in action. Furthermore, in *Smoke* Russian life was viewed not through the eyes of Litvinov, a decent if ordinary person, but those of Potugin, the complete Westernist. The author's work was a failure if he hadn't made people feel that there was in this man a smoldering but inextinguishable fire. And speaking as if the creature of his pen existed in the flesh, he added: "Perhaps he is dear to me alone, but I am glad that he has appeared."

Pisarev had remarked in his letter that he held aloof from factions. It is not good for a writer to be alone, Turgenev ventured, paraphrasing Scripture. Of course, he added, this isolation is often involuntary. He must have been thinking of his own isolation in the pleasant purlieus of Baden. He faced a grave predicament. He might everlastingly hold up Europe to his countrymen as a model for them to imitate, but it was they, not their model, that he must continue to explore. He needed the constant stimulus of fresh Russian impressions. It was an essential article of his literary credo that talent alone is powerless unless assisted by a steady contact with, and a careful study of, the *milieu* which happens to be the novelist's province. He held as strongly as ever Van Gogh did that "to grow, you must plant yourself in the soil." And yet, there he was a thousand miles from where his art required him to be, in a place which the presence of Pauline Viardot made his home. The fear that Russia was fading from his view was growing on him, and his expatriation loomed increasingly as a threat to his work.

28

THE EXPATRIATE

"I understand very well that my remaining abroad hurts my literary work, hurts it so much that it may put an end to it; but this cannot be changed." Thus Turgenev, writing from Karlsruhe in 1869. And again, from Baden the same year: "Every day I see more clearly that torn away from one's native soil one cannot keep on writing. It is time for me to retire." And ten years later, from Paris: ". . . You can write well only if you live in a *Russian* village. There the air is thick with ideas. . . . Here you remember the past, and nothing alive and vital can come of it." He would sometimes take refuge from remorse or reproach behind his flaunted senility: it didn't matter in what part of the world a superannuated man chose his ingle-nook; of what importance was it if his silence began a little while before death sealed his lips forever? And then he would submit that if he had remained at home, it would have been another story. "I am ready to allow," he wrote in 1871, "that the talent Nature gave me has not lessened, but I have nothing to apply it to. The voice is there, but there aren't any songs to sing." Living abroad as he did, he had nothing, he complained, to write about. In the meantime, he went on writing.

After the publication of *Smoke,* his name appeared mostly under shorter pieces, either stories or sketches much in his early manner. He adjusted himself to what he felt to be expatriation not by turning to account the immediate experiences with which life abroad furnished him, but rather by drawing upon his recollection of experiences at home. A reminiscential strain is the hallmark of the greater part of the work of his last fifteen years. "The Brigadier" (1868) deals with matters of "thirty years ago"; the occurrences narrated in "Lieutenant Yergunov" (1868) "took place forty years ago"; "An Unhappy Girl" (1869) suffered her fate in "the winter of 1835"; the events in "A Strange Story" (1870) happened "fifteen years ago"; "A King Lear of the Steppes" (1870) is told as a reminiscence of the author's youth; "Knock-Knock-Knock" (1871) elaborates an incident "of forty years ago"; "Spring Freshets" (1872) is a recollection of "things that had taken place long ago," notably in 1840. And there are a number of later tales and sketches which are even more clearly of a memorial nature. Every road led him back to the still waters of remembrance: aside from his feeling that he had lost contact with contemporary Russia, there was his romantic and somewhat pathological fixation upon the days of his youth; the very decadence of the social class into which he had been born; his gift for creating atmosphere, which the past seems to exude so much more richly than the present.

At the very beginning of his stay abroad, Turgenev confessed to Annenkov that he was now capable only of writing "fairy-tales" like "First Love." What he meant was stories with as little bearing on a particular time and place as "Cinderella" or "Ivanushka the Fool." The best of them, notably "King Lear of the Steppes," exhibit a wholesomeness, a vigor, a knowledge of men that fairly insure their durability. Fully a third of his stories are concerned with the incursion of the supersensuous into everyday life. For the most part they employ only the machinery of the occult: apparitions, prophetic dreams, mesmerism. In "Phantoms" the ghostly element is introduced as a device of an awkwardly mechanical kind, and in "Knock-Knock-Knock" it enters only to be shown up as spurious. Turgenev is at pains to leave a loophole for a natural explanation of the seemingly supernatural. Yet his spectral tales do suggest a desire on the author's part to convey the impression that there are more things in heaven and earth than are dreamed of in positivist philosophy. An avowed champion of reason, he was not unaware of its limitations and of the part the irrational plays in human affairs. He knew that art was the creature of both heart and head. He never quite freed himself from a vague attachment to the transcendental. Man may have to live in and for the moment, we read in "Enough," but he feels that he is "akin to something higher, eternal." The reader of "Faust" is told that life is governed by "secret forces," which occasionally thrust themselves into view, and that the bond between a man's fate and that of his children is a "mysterious" one. But if Turgenev found positivist fare somewhat deficient, he insisted that he adhered to it. His reaching out beyond the world of the senses was only the half-hearted effort of a fundamentally mundane mind. He repeatedly protested that anything resembling mysticism was alien to him: "To everything supernatural I am indifferent."—this from a statement of his views written in 1875 at the request of a lady whose son had to prepare a school theme on the subject "Turgenev's Philosophy."

There was a definite decline in Turgenev's productivity as the years went on. During the last two decades of his life his output was only a little more than half of what it had been the previous twenty years. Yet there was no grave interruption of his literary activity. He had one unfailing source of encouragement in Pauline Viardot. There was something stimulating in the very fact of being close to a woman who lived so energetically and abundantly for her art. Besides, if she didn't, like another Egeria, instruct him, she undoubtedly urged him on to write. With her aptitude for languages, she had picked up some Russian, and Turgenev fell into the habit of reading his work to her as he completed it. At the time when he was finishing *Smoke,* he wrote to her, she being then in Berlin on a concert tour: "Lord, how happy I was when I read you fragments of my novel! Now I will write much, solely to give myself that pleasure again. In Berlin, I shall read you everything to the last line, without sparing you, and I shall expect the imprimatur from you. I will change or omit whatever you dislike." And five days later: "You know you are my supreme judge and ruler. I am not sure if my work will be successful in Russia, but I have already scored the only success I am proud of: your approval." Years later Mme. Viardot was telling a Russian guest of hers that it was a long time since a line of Turgenev's had gotten into print without her having seen it beforehand. "You Russians," she added, "don't know how much you owe me for the fact that he goes on writing."

What effect her opinions and arbitraments had upon his

work can only be guessed at. Unquestionably she possessed good taste in literature. At the same time she had a sentimental and conservative streak, and as she grew older she was inclined to be squeamish. When he finished his "King Lear of the Steppes," upon which he had spent, in his own words, "all the strength of his muscles," he feared that Mme. Viardot would be shocked by its brutality. This story, he wrote, made the impression upon him of "a large rump, not the Rubens kind with flushed cheeks, but the ordinary fat-pale Russian sort." Today a reader would not know what to wonder at more, Turgenev's description of this excellent tale, which contains no word to offend the most chaste mind, or the peculiar sensitiveness of the great artiste. Yet there is no particular evidence in his work of her emasculating influence. In his writings, he avoided, like a gentleman, the raw and uncivilized, and it is hardly likely that if he had stayed at home and associated with virile intelligences, his novels would have had a lustier and harsher quality.

Beside Mme. Viardot's influence, there was another more adventitious circumstance which kept Turgenev at his desk: he needed money. Financially speaking, his base of supplies was a thousand miles away from where he lived, and that in itself constituted a serious inconvenience. With an Oriental distrust of the regular channels of communication, odd enough in such a good European, he preferred to depend upon the kind offices of devoted but dilatory friends. The temporary embarrassments from which he suffered in consequence recurred with annoying frequency. When in the winter of 1863 he wanted to go to Paris, this owner of thousands of fertile acres had to borrow money from Frau Anstett. He left his belongings with her as security, and when he got to the French capital he had to stay longer than he had expected, for want of cash to pay his fare back to Baden. When the remittances from his manager did arrive, they were apt to be distressingly small. In the spring of 1867 he figured out that for the past eleven years the annual income from his estates averaged fifty-five hundred rubles. What he called "the Athens of hired labor," meaning Spasskoye, was run at a deficit. Like most Russian landlords, he was hit by the readjustments incident to the Emancipation and, like so many others, he had to resort to the sale of portions of his acreage. In the half a dozen years after the abolition of serfdom he disposed of sixty thousand rubles' worth of land.

Money worries accumulated when he settled in Baden. The purchase of the land and the building of the villa meant a considerable outlay. Then there was his daughter's dowry, which came to one hundred and fifty thousand francs, two thirds to be paid outright, the rest in instalments, with a five per cent interest on the sum outstanding. To get together the initial amount, he had to borrow ten thousand francs from a usurer at ten per cent interest, and the Viardots made him an additional loan. It dawned upon him that the bad times alone could not account for the paucity of his income. Seeing that his brother, from properties of about the same size, was receiving four times as much, he decided that the fault lay with the manager of his estates, who since the middle of the fifties had been his uncle Nikolay. This jolly old satyr had never been particularly noted for his business capacities even in the days when the widowed Varvara Petrovna had leaned uncertainly upon him, and now age was getting the better of him. The master of Spasskoye, however regretfully, decided to dismiss his uncle, and engaged in his stead a younger and presumably more efficient person.

In January, 1867, the new appointee, a certain Kiszinski, appeared at Spasskoye, with orders to take over the management. Uncle Nikolay turned a deaf ear. He had taken care of his absentee nephew's estates for so long that they seemed more like his own, and the idea of handing them over to an utter stranger was preposterous. He invoked the spirit of Ivan's mother, complained that he was being ruined by his heartless nephew, and called Kiszinski a Nihilist. He sulked, he stormed, he wept, he locked himself up in his room, he refused to budge. Turgenev came to see that letters were useless, and that he would have to go home to put an end to the impossible situation: a hateful business, this standing up for your rights! In March he set out from Moscow over murderous country roads, firmly decided "to pull the sick tooth." *En route,* he succumbed to a combined attack of grippe and gout, and had to return to the city, where he took to his bed. Upon his recovery he returned to Baden, without having come near enough to the enemy to give battle, and in May he was forced to ask his uncle again, in no uncertain terms, to leave the premises.

Some years previously Turgenev had given his uncle a promissory note for a generous sum, with the understanding that it was not to be presented for payment until after the donor's death. The septuagenarian's wife was much younger than he, and it was supposed that she would profit by this informal arrangement, which amounted to a bequest. (As a matter of fact, she predeceased her aged husband.) When Turgenev discharged his uncle, he provided him with a pension. Shortly after the old man departed from Spasskoye with his family, the novelist discovered that the previous year the wily patriarch had presented the note. He had also imposed a lien on the properties of which he had recently been the manager and had even attempted to attach his nephew's possessions in Baden. There was a brief renewal of hostilities and a final settlement which cost Turgenev twenty thousand rubles in cash and nearly as much in cattle, horses, carriages, furniture, which his quondam manager had appropriated. Turgenev consoled himself with the thought that the affair had given him insight into the character of a Tartuffe of the steppes; he hoped eventually to share his costly knowledge with his readers. He had come off on top, but with every bone broken, he wrote to Annenkov in March, 1868. The condition in which the old man had left his nephew's affairs was lamentable. Kiszinski warned his employer that he could expect no income from his estates for some time. Turgenev was not, however, one to bear a grudge, and when, five years later, his uncle fell ill, he wrote to his brother begging him to go and comfort the invalid. Later on he himself went to see the old man, who had gone blind. They made peace, and on that occasion the host had too much champagne and indulged in "language of unbridled cynicism," as a Russian biographer puts it.

To meet the demands of the covetous old villain and to save Spasskoye from going under the hammer, its owner was forced to sell his Baden villa before it was completed. The buyer was his next door neighbor, Louis Viardot, who, Turgenev felt, was thus doing him a great service. It was as a mere tenant that he moved into the house upon which he had lavished much care. The sale was concluded on January 27, 1868— an inauspicious beginning for a year which he considered his climacteric. He had been born on a Monday, and in 1868 October 28 again fell on a Monday. Besides, New Year's Day was a Monday. Furthermore, he was to be fifty this year. And, in addition, the year was to bring the twenty-fifth anniversary of his meeting with Pauline Viardot, as well as the twenty-fifth anniversary of the beginning of his career as a writer. Surely all these signs and portents boded no good. Like his mother, he was given to superstitions in which numbers played a part; and like her, he smiled at his folly. As a matter of fact, the climacteric year was no worse than its immediate predecessors, except for the fact that it left him with the knowledge that he had half a century behind him. And soon to his little stock of cheerful aphorisms he will add a new one: "After fifty, a man lives in a fortress that is besieged by death, and that sooner or later must surrender to the enemy."

In June he went home, on one of his usual foraging expeditions intended to fill his purse with the proceeds from the sale of a manuscript or a tract of land, and also to satisfy himself about his new manager, and to renew lapsed contacts. He found the country in a sad state. "What an appearance Russia presents now," he wrote to his brother, "this land which everybody tells you is so rich! The roofs are torn up, the fences are down, not a single new building to be seen anywhere, except dramshops. The horses, the cows are dead, the people haggard. Three drivers could scarcely lift my trunk. Around Petersburg everything is burning: forests, houses, the earth itself. . . . All you see is men stretched out sleeping on their bellies; everywhere debility, flabbiness, dirt, poverty." Spasskoye afforded no refuge from the distressful sights he saw elsewhere. He felt like Marius sitting on the ruins of Carthage, he wrote. His departed manager had pillaged the place, cheated the hands, incurred debts, and left everything in a state of chaos. And as for his former serfs, emancipation seemed to have aggravated their condition. Through the entire fortnight that he spent on his estate he was like a hunted hare.

I couldn't stick my nose into the garden, without being assailed and attacked by former serfs, peasants, burghers, retired soldiers, peasant girls, peasant women, priests, deacons, the blind, the halt, impoverished neighboring gentry. Shaggy, hungry, they sprang at me from behind trees, from under bushes, from the very ground, threw themselves at my feet, and with mouths gaping like fledgeling jackdaws, they shouted hoarsely: *"Barin,* Ivan Sergeitch, save us, save us; we're dying!" In the end I had to flee, so as not to part with my all.

It was hard for him to believe that it was only a matter of three years since he had seen Spasskoye. Was it that the place had so altered, or was the change in him? His old hunting companion, Afanasy, who on their first trip, when Turgenev was a boy of seventeen, had pulled out of his tarry boot nearly a whole sucking pig and eaten it without bread, Afanasy who could once digest bullets, Afanasy who, never able to carry his liquor, had of old swaggered after a single glass, and now was reduced to tears by the same amount—Afanasy was a wreck. And Porphyry, under whose tutelage he had—it seemed only yesterday—made his first trip abroad, was now an old man.

The first night Turgenev spent under the ancestral roof he went to bed with a queer feeling: the old walls seemed to stare at him as at a stranger. And after all, he told himself with a pang, that is what he was. In the morning he took a turn in the park. It looked as immense to him as when he was a child —in fact, large enough to hold the entire Tiergarten valley. The trees, especially the old lindens, had, like Kiszinski's new beard, grown magnificently. But neither decay nor growth had obliterated the familiar landmarks. He walked past the place from which he had once stolen strawberries; past the tree on whose branches had perched the crow that was his first hunting trophy; to the spot where he had found an uncommonly large mushroom; to that diminutive battleground where he had watched an adder and a toad engage in a struggle that had forever injured his faith in a benevolent Creator. Every corner laid upon him the troubling hands of memory. And always, with the leap of recognition went the recoil of estrangement.

It was just a quarter of a century since his mother had placed the slim volume, his first—*Parasha*—on her drawing room table for all her visitors to admire. And now who was left in this unhappy country to admire his mature work?

True, in Germany and in France they were translating and apparently reading him. But *Smoke* had been a failure, and no new novel was taking shape in his mind. Obviously, he was played out, and he might as well close his literary career, appropriately enough, on the silver anniversary of his marriage to literature—as also of his quasi marriage to Pauline Viardot —now that his years had reached a round fifty. And so when he came to write what he planned as the final chapter in his reminiscences for his collected works, to be published the subsequent year, he turned it into a farewell to his readers. His service to letters, he wrote, had come to an end "amidst the gradual cooling of the public." He was laying down his pen in the belief that the new age demanded new men, and with some satisfaction in the thought that he, for one, had added his mite to the treasury. Before withdrawing, however, he begged leave to offer his young confrères a word of advice and to set before them a last request. His plea was that the young writers should do everything to preserve the strength and beauty of the language that was their great heritage. The substance of his counsel was: be truthful, especially about your own sensations; deepen and extend your experience through study; be free to doubt everything, even the worth of your own nation; above all, do not let yourself be caught in the trap of any dogma.

Some of the ideas which he expressed thus publicly crop up again and again in the course of his correspondence with Fet during the sixties. The point to which he keeps reverting is that freedom is the artist's natural prerogative. "You are buoyed up by joyous childlike faith, you feel like giving forth lyrical effusions; go to it!" he urged the poet. "You'd like to undermine every emotion, you'd like to poke your inquisitive nose everywhere, you'd like to crack things open like nuts; go to it!" Above all else, the artist must avoid the blinders of a "system." He was repeating to Fet what he had once told Tolstoy. "An artist who is incapable of seeing the white *and* the black, of looking both to the right and to the left, already stands on the brink of disaster." The writer owed allegiance only to his personal vision of the truth, and to the logic of his art. Not that Turgenev always held to this principle. Writing to a radical friend in 1876, he admitted that he should have toned down Bazarov so as not to play into the hands of the reactionaries. The artist, he said then, should have been sacrificed to the citizen: "The issue involved more important things than mere artistic truth, and I should have understood that." Yet in writing thus, Turgenev was more probably trying to see things from his correspondent's point of view, as he was apt to do, than expressing his own opinion.

The main bone of contention between him and Fet was the role of reason in art. Contemptuous of cerebration, Fet put his trust in the innate impulse that swells the bird's throat, and the fine frenzy that moves to utterance the Pythian priestess on her tripod. Though not unaware of the role played by the instinctual and the unconscious in the creative process, Turgenev exalted the rational member: "Art, I say, is such a great thing that the whole man, with all his faculties, including his intellect, is hardly enough for it." He could understand Fet's maligning the intellect, he observed, if he were a fanatic or a Slavophil, but he was a poet and should know better than to substitute for Pan's pipes "the cheap Rousseauesque penny whistle that has been soiled by the spittle of so many." And again, writing from his Baden home: "We here in the West send to school people who attack reason and recommend instinct and naïve unsophistication." Referring to Tolstoy's notion that only unconscious activity is fruitful, he asked: "How then did the Americans build the railroad between New York and San Francisco? In their sleep, unconsciously? Or isn't that a fruitful activity?" In *Smoke* Potugin declares: "Instinct, however closely it approaches genius, is unworthy of man; reason—simple, sound, commonplace reason—that is our true heritage, our pride."

29

MEEK PAGAN AND

VICIOUS CHRISTIAN

Passing through the gambling casino in Baden on Saturday, July 6, 1867, Turgenev noticed in the crowd a familiar face bent eagerly over the table. It was the healthless, big-browed, thin-bearded face of the author of *Crime and Punishment*. Knowing that gamblers dislike being accosted in the midst of play, Turgenev went by without speaking. He had last heard from Dostoevsky two years previously, when the latter, stranded in Wiesbaden, had appealed for a loan of a hundred thalers. The man had lost everything, including his watch, at roulette, and in the pension the sneering waiters would serve him nothing but tea. "You are much more understanding than the others," he wrote, "and morally it's easier for me to turn to you." Turgenev responded by sending him fifty thalers.

They had seen each other before that in the early autumn of 1863, when they met in Baden. Dostoevsky was then on his way to Italy with a lady who had been his mistress and whom he was now comforting almost fraternally for the defection of another lover. He concealed his companion from Turgenev, but not his weakness for gaming. Having had a stroke of luck in Wiesbaden several weeks earlier, he had conceived the notion that he could make himself the master of Chance, and had developed a passion for the wheel which was to torment him for a decade. At the time of this first encounter in Baden, Turgenev had felt rather friendly toward the unhappy gambler, and handed him the manuscript of "Phantoms" for the magazine *Time* (*Vremya*), which Dostoevsky was publishing with his brother. But the man was so engrossed by his mania that in the end he returned the piece unread.

Turgenev shipped the manuscript off to Annenkov, with a request to decide if "the nonsense" was worth printing. The supreme arbiter gave it his blessing, but the author was so long making up his mind about it that even this imperturbable adviser lost patience.

Just before Christmas Turgenev received a letter from Dostoevsky begging the piece for a new review, *The Epoch* (*Epokha*), which he planned to start in January, 1864, the old one having recently died a violent death. The editor, who had read the manuscript during its peregrinations, argued that a dose of fantasy and poetry was just what the public needed at a moment when a factual, utilitarian, Quakerish manner had driven literature into an impasse. Even from a utilitarian point of view, he went on, the piece held its own, for "Phantoms" was veritable music, and surely music is "useful, since it is a kind of language expressing what consciousness has not yet grasped." Indeed, the only fault he found with the piece was that it was not fantastic enough. Here spoke not only an enemy of literal realism, but also an editor trying to lasso a valuable contributor. Whether because of Dostoevsky's plea, or because of an energetic letter from Annenkov, Turgenev yielded, and "Phantoms" appeared in the first issue of *The Epoch*. After reading it in print, Dostoevsky wrote about it to his brother in a very different vein: "There is much rubbish in it, something nasty, sickly, senile, impotent, and so without faith—in a word, the whole Turgenev, with all his convictions—but the poetry will make up for a lot."

He might continue to solicit contributions from the elder novelist, and praise him to his face, but scarcely a shred was left of the excited admiration he had felt for the man in the distant days of their youth. An obscure, poverty-stricken fellow, Dostoevsky had suddenly been hailed as a genius by the great Belinsky himself and welcomed into the literary circle of which the author of *Parasha* had for some time been a member. The spring of 1845 was then unfolding its white night over Petersburg. In the intoxication of the season and his new fame, the shy, proud young man had, by his own account, nearly fallen in love with Turgenev: "A poet," was his comment to his brother, "a gifted man, an aristocrat, handsome, rich, intelligent, educated, twenty-five years old—

I don't know that nature has refused him anything. Finally, a character of profound integrity, beautiful, formed in a good school." Dostoevsky's story, "White Nights," written in 1848, bears an epigraph from a lyric by this poet.

As for Turgenev, he shouted Dostoevsky's name from the housetops, scolded him paternally—being three years his senior —for wasting his substance on women, and together with Nekrasov wrote a cruel epigram on him when success turned the head of this queer, talented youth. It was hard for him to resist the temptation of feathering his wit with malice, even if the shaft must strike a friend.

Turgenev was in his full stride as a novelist—indeed, the foremost writer in Russia—when in 1859 Dostoevsky, returning to life and letters after the ten years' hiatus caused by his Siberian exile, found himself at the very starting point of the race. The Russian republic of letters being small, it was natural for the two men to come into contact again. The following year both of them took part in a benefit performance of Gogol's *Inspector General*. Thereafter they corresponded now and again and regularly read each other's books. Dostoevsky, coming out of prison, swallowed *A Sportsman's Sketches* at a gulp and smacked his lips over it, and Turgenev found a Dantesque touch in *The House of the Dead*. He considered its author to be one of the two or three people who had grasped his intention in *Fathers and Children*. Yet their personal relations remained without depth and body.

The years that established each on his separate height showed how divergent were the orbits in which their lives moved. A wider gulf of temperament and mentality divided Turgenev from Dostoevsky than from his other great contemporary, Tolstoy. As early as the middle sixties Turgenev must have begun to see what the complexion of Dostoevsky's thinking was like. The man was obviously headed for the Slavophil camp—indeed, for everything that went against Turgenev's grain. His literary work, too, although attesting a talent of a high order, was full of things intolerable to the elder novelist. "Neuropathic nonsense" was Belinsky's term for the experiments with which Dostoevsky followed up his first novel, and the phrase must frequently have recurred to Turgenev as he read the later works. He found the first part of *Crime and Punishment* admirable, but the remainder struck him as "sounding like a prolonged colic." These novels flaunted the psychology which he would have hidden out of sight; they reeked of the clinic; they lacked all reticence and measure; they were empty of lyrical overtones.

For all that, being a tolerant, skeptical, self-distrustful man of the world, Turgenev was less likely to involve himself in a quarrel with this old acquaintance than to allow their relation to lapse painlessly. But the meddling arm of circumstance thrust itself between them. Hearing from Goncharov that Turgenev had seen him at the roulette table that Saturday in July, 1867, Dostoevsky felt that it was incumbent on him to go to see the man. Not that he looked forward to the visit with any pleasure, but inasmuch as he owed Turgenev money, he felt that his failure to call would be construed as evasion. Accordingly, the next Wednesday at noon, Dostoevsky made his way to the quiet house on Schillerstrasse where Turgenev lived, and found him at home—in fact, just sitting down to lunch.

Dostoevsky had come to Baden with his stenographer, who, a few months earlier, had become his second wife. That very day at tea he told his Anya about the visit, and on the same evening using her little hooks and dashes she set down his words in the diary in which, with the meticulousness of her calling and a woman's interest in trifles, she regularly recorded the happenings and talks of each day, the harassing ups and downs of a gambler's fortunes, the sum spent for every spool of thread and piece of soap, the sums received for articles pawned, and the sums laid out for the rare sprees when her husband was at once in pocket and in good humor.

The visit, we learn from Mme. Dostoevsky's journal, lasted an hour and a half. The entry tells us that Turgenev seemed to be galled by the reception accorded *Smoke,* and kept peevishly returning to the subject. He spoke of the rumor that he was to be expelled from the ranks of the gentry on account of the novel, and said that this would give him the greatest pleasure. "As usual," writes the diarist, "Fedya [Dostoevsky] spoke to him somewhat sharply, advising him, for instance, to buy himself a telescope in Paris, and, since he was living so far from Russia, to train it on that country; otherwise he would not understand what was going on there." The visitor also told Turgenev that he was deceived in thinking himself a realist. The talk turning away from literary matters, Dosto-evsky vented his irritation against the Germans, saying that they were generally stupid and often crooked. The host took this as a personal affront; in fact, he said plainly that he was now a German himself. They managed, however, to part without an open break. How wicked it is, the entry concludes sententiously, for a Russian to speak with contempt of his native country. "Well, God forgive him! I know, though, that Fedya was frightfully enraged by this talk with Turgenev, and that this abominable habit people have of repudiating their own badly upset him."

Some weeks after the encounter Dostoevsky, writing to his friend Maikov, poured out his heart on the subject of that renegade, Turgenev. This epistolary account of the interview is an elaboration of Mme. Dostoevsky's report. He begins by pointing out that he went to the house in a frame of mind likely to make the visit a very awkward one. He had lost all liking for the man, he wrote, long before this; he couldn't stand his Pharisaical manner of setting out to embrace you and then offering his cheek to be kissed; he, Dostoevsky, had been owing him fifty thalers since the Wiesbaden days (a debt, which he was not to make good until 1876); above all, he had just been reading that revolting novel, *Smoke*. And in this mood he had to listen to his host repeating all the blas-phemies against Russia uttered in that book. "He told me himself that the leading idea, the main point of *Smoke* was this: 'If Russia sank through the ground, that would be no loss to mankind. . . .'" The traitor thought that the Russians "must crawl in the dust before the Germans," spoke of civili-zation as "the one universal and inevitable road," and called the Slavophil will to be different "piggishness and folly." Of course, a man of this temper did not believe in God: "He announced to me that he was definitely an atheist." Dosto-evsky retaliated with the remark about the telescope, and when Turgenev showed irritation, said "with really very well feigned *naïveté*: 'I didn't expect the failure of *Smoke* would upset you so much; the thing isn't worth it; spit on it.' 'I'm not at all upset. What are you talking about?'" It was then that

Dostoevsky took up his hat, but first he had to hit out at the Germans: they were more dishonest than the Russian people and certainly stupider. At that Parthian shot Turgenev grew pale and said: "You are insulting me personally. I have settled here definitely. I consider myself a German and not a Russian, and am proud of it." "Though I read *Smoke* and have spoken to you for a whole hour," Dostoevsky replied, "still, I didn't expect this from you. Forgive me if I have insulted you."

Before the year was over, Turgenev learned from Annenkov that what seems to be a copy of this letter to Maikov had been sent to Bartenev, the editor of the historical review *Russian Archives* (*Russky Arkhiv*), with a request not to publish it before the year 1890. In the letter of protest which the indignant novelist addressed to the editor on January 3, 1868, he pointed out that he could not possibly have discussed his intimate convictions with his visitor, since the man, owing to his morbid attacks and for other unmentioned reasons was "not wholly in possession of his mental faculties." He continued:

I saw Mr. Dostoevsky only once. He sat with me no more than an hour, and retired after having relieved his heart by ferociously abusing the Germans, myself, and my latest book. I had neither time nor desire to argue with him. I repeat, I treated him as I would a sick man. The arguments which he expected from me must have presented themselves to his deranged imagination and he lodged information against me with . . . posterity. Doubtless, in 1890, neither Mr. Dostoevsky nor I will engage the attention of our compatriots any longer, and if we are not wholly forgotten, we shall be judged not by one-sided denunciation, but by the results of our whole lives and work. . . .

Recalling the unfortunate affair some three years later, in a letter to Polonsky, Turgenev spoke more freely:

He [Dostoevsky] came to me . . . not to pay the money he had borrowed of me, but to give me hell for *Smoke,* which he thought, should be burned by the hand of the executioner. I listened to this philippic in silence, and what do I learn? That I expressed within his hearing criminal opinions, which he hastened to communicate to Bartenev. . . . It would have been simple slander, if Dostoevsky weren't crazy—which I don't doubt in the least. Perhaps he hallucinated.

As the meeting was tête-à-tête, we shall never know how it would have appeared to a third person. It is hard to believe that Turgenev held his peace all the time that Dostoevsky was with him. Even if he doubted the appropriateness of expressing himself freely before his visitor, it is quite plausible that he did talk about the things which were nearest his heart. That Dostoevsky twisted whatever he may have heard from Turgenev's lips is even more credible. He was naturally inclined to exaggerate and intensify. His mental state at the time showed a lack of balance extraordinary even for him. His gambling fever was at once an indication of, and a contributing cause to, his nervous disorder. If he did not actually hallucinate, he must have given his imagination free rein.

Not that he imputed these opinions to Turgenev without ground. Turgenev did have harsh things to say about Russia. His attitude may have been due in part to an unconscious desire to excuse his expatriation. But if he contemned his country, it was because he loved it. He did on one occasion declare publicly that he owed Germany too much not to love and respect it as his "second fatherland." But he admired it less for its own sake than because it embodied the principles of "civilization" which he wanted to see take root at home. He did lack religious faith. The universe was to him a concern run without any reference to human values and showing no evidence of the overlordship of even an absentee God. But he was apt to regard his unbelief as an affliction. He was a rationalist, not a materialist. Dostoevsky's hatred—and he had a genius for hating—utterly blinded him, and led him to see the gentle Turgenev as an arrogant Judas, a man without a country and without a God.

Among the things that fed Dostoevsky's animosity was his envy of his confrère's financial security. That he, having come back to his work from the Siberian inferno without any resources and with a number of financial burdens, should be forced to take one hundred rubles per sheet, while the other, with his vast estates, should get four hundred rubles, was a crying shame. The difference in their fortunes was to rankle in him for many years. It was galling to know that this *flâneur* was insured against want. If he himself were to have no cause to worry about bread and butter for a couple of years, he knew he could write a book that would be talked of a century hence. Yet the gulf between them was not so much a matter of outward circumstances as of utter incompatibility. While Dostoevsky saw man as a free agent, climbing spiritual peaks by an athletic act of will, to Turgenev man was a galley slave, chained to the hard seat of necessity, at best a stoic at the oar.

When Dostoevsky left Turgenev's apartment that uncomfortable Wednesday, he promised himself never to cross its threshold again. The next morning at ten o'clock Turgenev called upon him—a visit which he took as a hint that Turgenev wished to terminate their relations—he had been told that the couple slept until eleven and received no visitors before twelve. The Dostoevskys remained in Baden seven weeks, but the two men met only once more, at the railroad station, and by Dostoevsky's account they looked at each other without bowing. Their personal association was not again resumed. Turgenev, while recognizing the significance of his fellow novelist's work, felt it a thing utterly alien to himself. He described Dostoevsky as "the Russian Marquis de Sade" and called him "the most vicious Christian" he had ever known. The vicious Christian, for his part, bore Turgenev a lasting grudge.

During 1871-72 *The Russian Herald* was serializing *The Possessed*. In this work, which he took some four years to write, Dostoevsky, whose rage was cumulative, allowed himself to caricature Turgenev in the character of Karmazinov. The object of the lampoon immediately recognized himself in this Russian author who railed against Russia and praised Europe, especially Germany; who was ignored by the revolutionary youth he courted—the very name (*cramoisi;* crimson) hinted at its bearer's secret sympathy with the Reds; who had such a devoted public and yet was forever laying down his pen and talking about the time when death would close his eyes; who took such tender care of his own person; who prized his aristocratic connections beyond everything; who betrayed the fears and foibles, spoke with the shrill voice and moved with the mincing gait of a spoiled woman. (Turgenev's detractors disliked his walk, which looked affected, but was conditioned by the fact that his legs were too short and thin to bear the weight of his huge torso.)

The general public was not slow to discover that Karmazinov flaunted the mannerisms and the mufflers, the waistcoats and the Eau de Cologne, the Westernism and the aestheticism of the dean of Russian letters. There were a few who read into one passage a reference to Turgenev's life in Baden by the side of Pauline Viardot. And every one had a laugh over Karmazinov's remark: "I felt that the problem of the Karlsruhe water supply was dearer and closer to my heart than all the problems of my precious Fatherland throughout the period of the so-called reforms." At first reading Turgenev laughed too, and spoke of the Aristophanesque humor of the caricature. But he was for a long time indignant with the author for having represented him as fawning upon the extreme radicals because they were to inherit the earth. He did cultivate the Nihilists and the radical youth generally, but he certainly did not believe that the future lay in their hands.

Not content with ridiculing Turgenev's person, Dostoevsky took occasion to poke fun at his literary manner, and the novel contains parodies of several of his writings, among them the piece which originally appeared in Dostoevsky's review. It also has a veiled allusion to the old gossip about Turgenev's youthful cowardice when the ship took fire at sea, combined with a derogatory reference to his account of a public execution, which was published the year before *The Possessed* appeared in print. On the night of January 19, 1870, Turgenev "supp'd full of horrors," as he wrote Annenkov. He spent it in the company of a privileged group of French journalists and men of letters at the La Roquette prison in Paris, so as to be present at the last toilette and guillotining of a certain Traupmann, a notorious murderer who had massacred a family of eight. Turgenev agreed to go, as he told the Herzens, because refusals came so hard to him, but it was a devastating experience, and as a penance for his weakness and curiosity, he made himself write down everything he had witnessed and felt.

His discomfort began even before he reached the prison, with the gamins mistaking his enormous shape for that of the executioner. Turgenev's account is a marvel of reportage. He notes every detail: the remarkable whiteness of the condemned man's beautiful hands, the childlike gesture with which he helped the guards to take off his prison shirt, the aspect of the executioner, who looked like a diplomat or a protestant minister. It seemed to this witness that every one was participating not in an act of justice, but in a murder, and that the only innocent creatures were the policemen's horses in the crowded streets outside, chewing oats in their nose bags. What he felt chiefly was a sense of guilt, but this was wiped out by sheer terror when the two attendants jumped at the condemned, so that he fell head forward on the guillotine and his heels kicked. At that moment Turgenev turned away and for a few seconds lost consciousness. The narrative, which is a dry, straightforward, and immensely effective piece, closes: "I shall be satisfied and forgive myself my misplaced curiosity if my story will add something to the arguments of those who would abolish capital punishment, or, at least, abolish its public character."

Dostoevsky, who himself had stood upon the scaffold awaiting execution, which he escaped only by a last minute reprieve, was infuriated by this cruelly weak conclusion. What further disgusted him was Turgenev's faint-heartedness at the final moment and, in addition, his emphasis on his own reactions to the drama. To Dostoevsky's way of thinking, a human being has no right to turn his eyes away from such a scene: only by taking it in, by feeling it in the marrow of his bones, can he prove his spiritual maturity. And that Turgenev should consider his own peace of mind when another man was losing his head, was to Dostoevsky abomination.

A weird piece of gossip clings to the name of Turgenev's antagonist. One version of the story found its way, some years ago, into print. According to this account, Dostoevsky, with his usual interest in criminal cases, followed the trial of a man accused of having raped a child, and became so obsessed by it that he gradually began to identify himself with the defendant. When the little girl left the courtroom at the end of the trial, the novelist was drawn after her and made her his victim in turn. Tortured by agonies of remorse, he finally unburdened himself to a confessor, who counseled him, as penance, to avow his crime to the person whom he despised most. This tale has all the earmarks of a legend. But neither its veracity, nor its bearing upon the obscure problem of the novelist's perverse impulses is here in question. The point is that the man named in the story as having been sought out by Dostoevsky, the man to whom he must confess his crime because he despised him most, was—Turgenev.

30

THIRTY DEVONSHIRE PLACE

If *Smoke* was instrumental in causing the rupture between Turgenev and Dostoevsky, the same novel also played the part of a peace offering. Since some of the argumentative passages in the book harked back to the author's discussions with Herzen, he felt that it was in order for him to send a copy of it to this antagonist. He was anxious to make up with Herzen. As he grew older, he clung more and more closely to the companions of his youth, and he was not one to allow differences of opinon to come between him and men whom he happened to like.

For more reasons than one, he suspected Herzen would be antagonized by the novel. He had warned Turgenev not to meddle with politics, and there he was at it again, with a vengeance. Turgenev was, however, heartened by the thought that the distance between them had been reduced, since the younger émigrés had relegated the editor of *The Bell* to the ranks of the reactionaries. The letter, dated May 17, 1867, that preceded the copy of the novel said as much.

The very day that Turgenev was penning this conciliatory letter Herzen in a note to a friend made a scurrilous remark about the novel. He had previously given it a brief, contemptuous notice in *The Bell,* which he was issuing in Geneva where he had settled after leaving London. This did not prevent him from taking the hand that the novelist reached out to him and offering to wipe the slate clean.

They agreed to let bygones be bygones and resumed their friendly relations with the tacit assumption that they would avoid controversial matters. Yet before long Turgenev dug up the old bone of contention. On looking into *The Bell* he found there variations on Herzen's familiar theme. "In my opinion," he wrote to the publicist on December 12, "Europe

is not as old, nor is Russia as young as you claim: we are in
the same bag, and we Russians are not going to utter anything in the nature of a new word. But may the Lord let
you live a hundred years and you will die the last Slavophil."
Could there be anything more irrelevant than Russia's special
mission, he went on, to the real problem of the age: the
conflict between science and religion? Herzen retorted that
science would not save the world. Russia was clearly uttering
a new word. And he repeated his theme song on the decline
of Europe.

Turgenev was not impressed. Writing on Christmas Day,
1867, he told Herzen that his faith in the Russian folk was a
kind of religion, and that futhermore the democratic and
socialist instincts attributed by gentlemen to the peasant masses
were totally alien to them. And then the line of Goethe's that
he had quoted to Pauline Viardot nearly a score of years
earlier came tripping to his pen: "Man is not born to be free."
Perhaps human society was destined to parallel the caste organization of the bees. As for Russians, left to themselves
they would turn into sectarians, with all the tyranny and darkness that fanaticism engenders. Then, making an abrupt
about-face, he went on to offer a remedy for the situation:
the homeopathy of science and civilization, applied little by
little. Everything else was quackery. "It appears," he concluded equably, "that each of us is asking himself how the
other fellow does not see what seems so clear to him."

The correspondence lapsed shortly afterward for a period
of a little more than a year. It was revived just after Herzen
had silenced *The Bell,* which for some months he had been
publishing in French to enlighten Western public opinion on
the subject of Russia, and Turgenev wrote to say that the
cessation of the journal was a good thing. "Do the French
need to know the truth about anything, let alone Russia?"
Herzen responded cordially enough and went so far as to
ask a favor of his correspondent, namely, to help kill the rumor
that he was seeking to be repatriated at the price of abject
recantation. About this time Turgenev read the text of a
speech of Bakunin's in which the anarchist declared himself
an atheist. So Michel had executed another volte-face! At
their last meeting, which had occurred seven years earlier, as

they walked under a London moon he had deplored Herzen's disbelief in a personal God. Recalling the scene in a letter to Herzen, Turgenev went on: "Well, why not open people's eyes to the truth? But, I wonder, is such a public pronouncement of any practical use? There may be one advantage to it: if there is no strong government in the universe, how can such a government exist under socialism? And if it can't, what is left of socialism?" Not that he cared particularly, for he saw in socialism a denial of man's rights and energies. He would remain "an individualist to the end," he concluded.

Herzen was now living in France in the oppressive atmosphere of the approaching war, a man repudiated by his spiritual heirs and out of sympathy with them, a man ignored by the strangers among whom he had pitched his tent, and pursued by private troubles, of which the least was a considerable financial loss caused by the sale of his United States securities. He could not forgive himself this step, not so much because of the money, as because he had doubted for a moment "the success of so noble a cause as the abolition of slavery. And where? In a country as healthy and organically sound as the American Republic." Chancing to be in Paris in January, 1870, Turgenev went to see the expatriate, and found him, across the lunch table, in excellent conversational form. The next day Herzen, who was a diabetic, came down with pneumonia, and it was soon clear that he would not recover.

Turgenev wrote to Annenkov that he had visited the family daily, but if Herzen's daughter is to believed, he only looked in for a moment on January 19, the day of his departure for Baden, "in order," she wrote, "to make sure that the funeral would not delay him." It is certain that he did not stay to bid his dying friend a last farewell two days later and to see him buried at Père Lachaise. He avoided here what he had been spared in the case of Stankevich and Belinsky and his mother: the spectacle of the personal finale. He read with wet eyes the news that another old comrade was gone, and wrote sadly to Annenkov: "In Russia they will probably say that Herzen should have died earlier because he survived himself. But what do these words mean, what does our so-called activity mean, before this dumb abyss which swallows us? As though to live and keep on living were not the most important thing!"

Turgenev's last talk with Herzen must have at least touched upon the prospect of war. Like most people, he was inclined to overestimate the strength of French arms. Before he moved from his Baden lodgings into the villa he had built himself, he joked that perhaps the first one to occupy the house would be a general of the French army of invasion. Just about the time that he was uttering this pleasantry, the Chief of the French General Staff was remarking to Bismarck that though he loved and admired Prussia, they would have to cross swords in the end, for they were both cocks, and neither could allow any one to crow better than himself. The July day on which France declared war, Turgenev chanced to be in Berlin. Dining in a restaurant, he caught a glimpse, at the table opposite, of von Moltke, whose cool bearing and professorial brow strongly impressed him and raised his hopes of a German victory. Turgenev was then on his way from Russia to Baden, and when he reached his destination he found the inhabitants trembling in expectation of the arrival of the Turcos and the transient population gone. Baden was "a city of the dead," as Clara Schumann wrote in her diary.

Weeks of anxiety followed. The church bells announced the news of Sedan, and a republic was declared in France. Lying in bed at night, Turgenev heard through the closed window the faint booming of the guns that were bombarding the half-burned city of Strasbourg. The fall of Metz was marked for him by the collapse of a chimney on the villa he occupied, and he recalled that when he had criticized it in the building, the architect, a Parisian, had proudly declared: "These chimneys are as solid as France."

In September he was writing to Ludwig Pietsch: "We work for the wounded, we have music, we read, and so the hours pass. The fall of the French Empire was a great satisfaction to poor Viardot. Now his heart is bleeding." He shared Louis Viardot's disgust with "the abominable empire" and he loathed Napoleon III. "To be fed to the lice in Cayenne," he wrote to the same friend, "that is what he deserves." He had seen the Imperial couple at the opera in Paris and found the Emperor repulsive and the Empress looking like an aging cocotte.

Turgenev set down some of his observations and reflections on the war in a series of letters that he contributed to a Petersburg daily for August and September. He constrasted the bungling of the French generals with the brilliance and intelligence of the German command. Disclaiming any malice, he expressed the hope that the French would get the lesson they sorely needed. While their press was savagely mendacious, he wrote, the German bulletins and official proclamations were remarkable for their sober candor and dignified tone. The French were too hypocritical to care for truth even in literature: they had no Gogol, no Thackeray, they ignored Flaubert. He noted the decent treatment accorded the prisoners of war whom he had watched marching in endless columns along the road to Rastadt.

In August Turgenev was writing a professor of the University of Koenigsberg that the bombardment of Strasbourg was "very painful and sad, but necessary," and that Germany represented civilization fighting against barbarism. "I am, as you know, completely pro-German," he assured Pietsch the next month. "The victory of France would have meant the end of liberty. Only you shouldn't have burned Strasbourg." His sympathy with the German cause did not, however, long remain whole-hearted. "Before our eyes the star role of history," he wrote to Polonsky, "is passing from the Latin to the Teutonic race . . . But I do not conceal from myself the fact that the greed for conquest which has possessed all of Germany is not a reassuring spectacle." In one of his letters to the daily he decried the German plan to annex Alsace and Lorraine, and he told Annenkov that he could not approve of Germany's desire to saddle itself with another Poland: the Alsatians had become completely French, just as the Pomeranians, once Slavs, were now Prussians. Referring to Germany's annexationist appetite, he wrote to Paul Heyse: "I no longer understand and I fear I shall soon cease to recognize my once beloved Germans." By December he regarded the war as a threat to the existence of France, the republic, freedom. At the Cologne railway station, on his way to Russia, he saw strapping German soldiers, "fat, pink-cheeked, as though the French blood they were about to shed had already colored their cheeks." They were terrible to see, he wrote to Pauline on February 18, 1871. When the disastrous peace came, he pitied "poor, unhappy France." Nevertheless, a year later he was agreeing with Annenkov that if the Germans had obligingly allowed themselves to be beaten, "it would have been simply impossible to live in Europe."

The war deprived the Viardots of much of their income. Now Turgenev could extend to them the assistance that they had given him more than once. Incidentally, he used his good offices in the matter of the sale of a Rembrandt that they owned to Grand Duchess Yelena Pavlovna. In his letter, dated August 28, to the Petersburg daily he pointed out how well the French families settled in Baden were treated both by the authorities and the local population. Before long, however, the burghers showed hostility toward the Viardots. There was *Katzenmusik* under their windows and they were otherwise molested. For patriotic reasons, too, they could not stay on in Germany. Fet threw out the suggestion that the whole contingent should translate itself to Spasskoye and live there off the fat of the land. But this extreme expedient proved unnecessary: there was still a country where Mme. Viardot could give concerts and get as much as twenty-five francs a lesson. That was England. She had a following not only in the capital but throughout the provinces. And so in October the family removed to London, and a little later Turgenev joined them.

The Viardots lodged at 30 Devonshire Place, and he managed to be near them, living first at 4 Bentinck Street, Manchester Square, a few doors from where Gibbon had written a great part of *The Decline and Fall,* and later at 16 Beaumont Street, Marylebone. Louis Viardot's dejection weighed upon Turgenev's naturally low spirits, and the uncertainty of the family's position was another source of unease. Sometimes it seemed to him that the war might touch off a general European conflict. "What would then become of civilization and freedom?" he asked. "If only Russia keeps out!"

The passing years had only strengthened his feeling for

Pauline Viardot. His fervor is not tempered by long association. On December 5 he writes to her when she is on a concert tour: "Your absence causes me a kind of physical fear, as though I didn't have enough air. It is a secret anguish of which I cannot rid myself and which it is impossible to dispel. When you are with me, I experience a tranquil joy, I feel at ease, at home (the last phrase is in English), I want nothing more." Their relationship is twenty-seven years old; he must guard this treasure carefully. "It will be with us," he concludes, "as with Burns' *John Anderson, my Jo*: we shall totter down the hill together. Dear, dear friend, may all the good angels have you in their keeping. I kiss your hands, very, very tenderly."

The latter part of that winter Turgenev interrupted his stay in London to go to Russia, as he had done the previous summer before the outbreak of the war. Stopping off overnight in Baden, he prepares to go to bed with the feeling of being "an apparition" in his own room. He wonders how he can be there "body and bones" and not at Devonshire Place. "I said 'body and bones,'" he writes to Pauline on February 20, "because I know where my soul is. All the time I am asking myself what they are doing there in London; I see you, Didie, Marianne, Viardot, Paul; one more effort and I shall hear your voices." He reaches Russia, and there are almost daily letters from Petersburg and Moscow, reporting to Pauline his *faits et gestes*: dinners, concerts, an hour and a half with Grand Duchess Yelena Pavlovna, sittings for two portraits, a visit to the Hermitage, where he stood before a little sphinx that he wished Louis Viardot could see; a meeting with Mark Antokolsky, an obscure, poverty-stricken young sculptor (Turgenev was so impressed by his statue of Ivan the Terrible that he immediately wrote an article about it for a Petersburg daily, ending with an appeal for contributions so that the ailing artist might go to Italy for his health).

He had many callers. "It is obvious," he writes, "that if certain individuals consider me dead and wonder why I don't have myself buried, others have preserved their friendship for me." He gives a public reading of an excerpt from *A Sportsman's Sketches,* and is amazed by the ovations. Discovering how popular he is in Petersburg, he comments:

"Public taste is fickle." He is glad of this dip in the native waters. At the same time he feels himself a stranger at home. He helps form a club to unite the artistic and literary intelligences of the capital, but confesses that he has not the slightest interest in the enterprise, since, he writes on March 11: "I don't live in Russia . . ." He goes on in the vein to which he has long since accustomed Pauline: "The Petersburg whirl into which I have fallen and from which I intend to withdraw very speedily does not for a moment let me forget either London or my return or all I love in the world—now more than ever. I shall be happy only when I cross the threshold of 30 Devonshire Place."

He was in Moscow when the news of the insurrection of the Paris Commune reached him. So France was in the throes of civil war! He was horrified. It was as though the uprising of June 1848 had triumphed. He repeated the remark a banker had made to him that France was "a sinking ship." He wrote to Pauline on March 25: "What is particularly sad about the latest events is that they destroy the Europeans' sympathy for France and play into the hands of the enemies of freedom. 'You see what those famous principles of 1789 lead to!' they exclaim." He kept asking himself anxiously: what will become of France, and of the securities, the properties that the Viardots owned? He lay awake nights thinking of them all, of their unhappy country, the horrors people perpetrate, "the eternal problem of death." The events in Paris appalled him. Is Marquis de Gallifet, "the scoundrel" who ordered the execution of scores of Communards chosen at random, any better than "the beasts" who shot the archbishop, he asked in a letter to Annenkov, dated June 8, adding: "And what will the future be like with such a decay of morality?"

He had braved the rigors of the Russian winter chiefly in order to replenish his purse. Just then his finances were in a lamentable state. Although the streets of Petersburg were very muddy he could not permit himself the luxury of a cab. His son-in-law's affairs had been going from bad to worse, and the war brought him to the verge of ruin. Paulinette's letters were full of requests for money, and he was loath to leave her in the lurch. The previous summer he had attempted to sell some of his land but failed. Now he tried again, and he was also considering a plan to farm out some of his estates. Arrangements were made for him to meet a number of interested people, and he pictured them beforehand as a flock of ravens waiting for their prey with beaks agape. This *assemblée générale,* to use his own phrase, apparently did not materialize.

He had not been in the capital more than two weeks when cholera broke out. Seized with panic, he fled to Moscow, which was free from the disease, and soon crossed the frontier. "I could laugh when I think of how frightened I was," he wrote to a Russian friend. "But should cholera break out again, I shall again have my tail between my legs." Stopping off in Berlin on his way to England, he wrote to his daughter that he had not yet completed the sale of any land and so could send her only 5,000 francs, since he had also failed to secure a loan from his brother. He omitted to say that he had bought 17,500 francs' worth of Russian railroad stock for Claudie Viardot, thus raising her *dot* to the tidy sum of 80,000 francs.

Early in April he tasted peace at the side of Pauline Viardot in London. At the end of the month the papers printed a report of her death. On reading the notice, Flaubert observed that he pitied Turgenev deeply. "I love you too much," the French novelist wrote him on May 1, "to try and offer you banal phrases. But I am very sad and I embrace you." Turgenev thanked him, saying: "Fortunately, my dear friend, fortunately the news is completely false. . . . Had the news been true, I don't think I could have answered you." To another message of condolence he replied: "There is no doubt that if the report were true, all interest in life would have ceased for me. Fortunately, her health is very good and she will, of course, survive me."

This was the first time he had been in England for more than a flying visit. He found life there "cheerless but interesting," as he wrote to Fet. Speaking to Henry James some years later, he mentioned "a visit to a bishopess surrounded by her daughters" and described the cookery at his lodgings. The American concluded that Turgenev had spent a "lugubrious" winter in London. "No Englishman," Turgenev observed to Pietsch, "has the slightest inkling of what art is. His nature is anti-artistic (*Sein Urnaturel ist urantikünstlerisch*). That is an uncontrovertible axiom. Naturally, I do not speak of literature, poetry." To Flaubert he wrote that the English were not without good qualities, but that all of them, even the most intelligent, led a hard life to which you have to get used, as to their climate. The constant activity of these English, so different from the indolence of people in Petersburg and Moscow, impressed and somewhat dismayed him. He was struck, too, by their phenomenal sang-froid. Just before the suppression of the Paris Commune he was visiting Cambridge and dined at Trinity. That same evening a debate was scheduled at the Union on the question: "Do the French Communards deserve the sympathy of Englishmen?" "Turgenev was so anxious to hear the debate and witness the stormy scene," one of his companions, his English translator, W. R. S. Ralston, recalled, "that he kept asking if it wasn't time to start. After having observed with what calm and respectful attention the young men who crowded the hall listened to the arguments and voted all but unanimously dead against the motion, Turgenev turned to me and said 'Now at last I understand why you English aren't afraid of a revolution.' "

He remained in London through the spring and part of the summer, and attended the Walter Scott centennial which was being celebrated in Edinburgh on August 9. There was a pageant of Scott's characters through the hot, sunlit streets, and then a frugal banquet of wine, fruit, and cake in the glass-roofed hall of the Corn Exchange. According to the account in *The Scotsman* the next day, "the noble Chairman," the Lord of Dalkeith, proposed the health of the visitors, among whom there was an American, Dr. Beets, and "Mr. Torqueneff, a distinguished Russian novelist." "Mr. Torqueneff" had learned by heart the speech which he had prepared with the aid of an English friend, and, as he wrote to Fet, only stumbled once, thereby winning a round of applause. "All of our best writers," he said, among other things, "have been sincere admirers, some of them have been imitators of your great master of romance."

From Edinburgh he traveled to the Highlands to shoot grouse. The weather was fine and so was the breakfast on the moors, but the sport was rather monotonous and very strenuous: at the end of the first day, spent in the company of an athletic native, he was ready to cry with fatigue. He preferred, he wrote to Pauline Viardot, hunting around Baden, where one is not attached to "a madman with the legs of a deer, who shouts, 'Come on, come on,' every time you stop to draw breath." It was a joy to breathe the air of northern Scotland, than which, he thought, there was nothing finer in the world; but the company, like the grouse shooting, was wearisome, and this though it included a vigorous, white-bearded man with a strident voice and a handshake like an electric shock, who answered to the name of Robert Browning. The English poet was staying with his friends the Benzons, at Little Milton, in the hills above Loch Tummel, at the time when Turgenev was dating his letters Allan House, Pitlochry, a village nearby. The poet failed to make an impression upon him. "Mr. Browning came again last night," he wrote to Pauline on August 13. "He seemed dull to me, but I was so sleepy with fatigue, I could hardly keep on my feet." That was all he found to say of the author of *The Ring and the Book*.

Although Turgenev injured his foot his first day out hunting, he was too much of a sportsman not to try again. The second time he was on horseback and had other companions. "I was with Mr. Benzon, who," he wrote to Pauline "reminds one less of a hunter than of a marmot, and Mr. Browning's son, who wishes to look like one (a hunter, not a marmot), but is nevertheless merely an insignificant little simpleton, with a perpetually red wart on his nose." In the evening there was music, and Mrs. Benzon, Turgenev remarks uncharitably, "squeaked Schubert and Schumann *Lieder* with a false voice and true feeling." He was, however, pleased by the memories that the singing called up.

Browning had just then published "Balaustion's Adventure," which includes a translation from Euripides, and was at pains to go over from Little Milton to Tummel Bridge to see Jowett and consult with him about the rendering of a Greek phrase. Stopping with Jowett at that time was Algernon Charles Swinburne. There is no indication that Turgenev met him then, but it is noteworthy that Swinburne was the only one of the literary men of the period who won a good word from him. He wrote to Fet that he would tell him when they got together about the most recent English poetry, of which no one, or virtually no one, in Russia had any idea. "The subject is not agreeable, but interesting, and there is a very great lyrical talent: Swinburne." Earlier in the year at a Moscow gathering he had commented on the degeneration of English literary taste, especially in poetry. "The English these days," he said, "admire the verse of Rossetti, a nonentity without a trace of talent." Over a twelvemonth later he was writing on the same subject in the same terms to Polonsky: "The newest English poets, all these Rossettis, etc., are dreadfully affected; in Swinburne alone there are flashes of indubitable talent. He is an imitator of Victor Hugo, but he has true passion and fire, while in Hugo all this is invented. Get his *Songs Before Sunrise*."

If Turgenev was out of sympathy with the trend of literature in England, neither was he pleased with what the young writers in Russia were doing. He found their work without grace and without strength, smelling of trouser bottoms. And they were proud of their lack of invention, believing that this gave them a firmer hold on the truth! They did not understand that if art needs truth as a plant needs air, like a plant it cannot live on air alone.

31

THE FRENCH HOME

Leaving their Baden home in the midst of the war, the Viardots did not wind up their affairs there. The summer of 1871 they returned to settle matters by disposing of their property. Turgenev joined them there after his week in Scotland, only to be put on his back by gout. It was a dreary autumn for him, what with being ill in dismantled rooms—the villa he occupied had been sold to a Moscow banker—and the prospect of an imminent moving. With the Viardots away and himself left in charge of the young people, his was a lonely fifty-third birthday.

It was certainly a downhill plunge now, he was writing to Pietsch in November: "The brake! The brake! For the love of God!" What a pleasure—and a contrast—it had been, three months before, to see Mme. Viardot celebrating her fiftieth birthday—he never missed these anniversaries—in the best of health and the highest spirits!

Pauline was in Paris with her husband, looking for a suitable house, since they had decided to settle in what was left of that much battered city. After all, France, as George Sand had once written to Louis Viardot, was something to come back to, if only to measure the changes in one's own life by the transformation the country had undergone. Their decision automatically fixed Turgenev's place of residence. Where else should he rest his gouty old carcass? "If the family moved to Australia," he confessed, "I would follow them there." By the end of November they were all reunited at 48 (later renumbered 50), rue de Douai in the Montmartre section.

It was with no particular pleasure that he went to make his home in the French capital. His visits to the prosperous Paris of Napoleon III had always left a bad taste in his mouth. He had found the many new houses one uglier than

the other. The freshly ornamented façade of the Grand Opéra
had looked to him like "the dream of a cocotte." The opera
itself had degenerated. The streets had seemed to be full of
repulsive people with dirty faces. The unhappy atmosphere
of the Paris to which he now came was not calculated to
make him any more comfortable. Every one, including Thiers
himself, the president of the Republic, despised it, and yet
saw no way to anything better. The hatred of the Germans
was colossal; "the only colossal thing there is here," Turgenev
wrote.

In the beginning the immediate concern of getting settled
in the new home and the writing he had in hand took his
mind off the political situation. A visitor found him engrossed
with the weighty business of placing the furniture and choos-
ing the portières and curtains. He was frequently seen with
rolls of fabric under his arm, on his way to or from the up-
holsterer's, or traveling through the shopping district. One
guesses that the family took advantage of the leisured and
obliging man. His four rooms on the second floor—bedroom,
study, library, and living room—had not been designed for
a giant, and the modest apartment was rather stuffy, being,
to Alphonse Daudet's eye at least, "as crowded as a boudoir."
His green den contained the inevitable divan toward which
he naturally gravitated, and among other things on the walls
were a Rousseau landscape and a Corot, while between the
windows hung a marble bas-relief of Pauline Viardot in profile, and beneath it also in marble a sculpture of her exquisite
hand.

For a decade these rooms saw a multitude of foreign faces,
mostly young, and often troubled. Penniless Russian students
came to ask if the great novelist could not find work for
them. He claimed that the armchair in his study had been
worn out by his unemployed compatriots. He penned endless
letters of recommendation; he had, so he said, a gift for this
kind of writing. He arranged, with Pauline's aid, musical
matinées for their benefit. As often as not he dug into his
own pocket. His generosity was a byword: it rained upon
deserving and undeserving alike. One petitioner suggested in
a letter that the novelist spend a day or two on a story for
a magazine which was offering a prize, and since he would

surely win it, send the cash to the letter-writer, who was in need. Turgenev did not write the story, but he did look up the beggar and gave him money. He would send a sick girl to a medical celebrity for treatment, and assuring her that the fee was a small one, quietly foot the large bill. Toward the end, when he was mortally ill, he arranged a "sad little comedy" to assist a countryman who was too proud to accept the help he desperately needed. Turgenev dispatched a story which the man had translated to a Russian editor, and begged him to write a letter of acceptance stating that he was remitting two hundred francs as advance payment, though the money was really to come out of Turgenev's purse.

He was never without a special favorite whom he kept under his wing. He would listen to young men ardently urging upon him the imminence of the revolution, and looking quite placid in his gray Caucasian jacket with red lapels, he would furnish a quiet interlude by telling irrelevant if exquisite anecdotes. He was at the mercy of all manner of people who unloaded their troubles on his big shoulders. Women came to ask for an introduction to Mme. Viardot, for help in securing entrée to the theatrical world, in bringing a debtor to terms, in getting rid of a bad husband. He acted as secretary of the Paris Society of Russian Painters, arranged for exhibitions of their work, looked out for Mme. Viardot's Russian pupils. Indeed, it was said that there was hardly a countryman of his in Paris concerned with writing, painting, or music, who didn't, at one time or another, get help from this "ambassador of the Russian intelligentsia," as he came to be called. Of course, would-be authors flocked for advice and assistance. He offered them money, took their manuscripts, read them, entered into correspondence with possible publishers, and even with the aspirant's friends and relatives. He never had the courage to tell a hopeful writer that his work was worthless, and there was always a crow or two that he was hailing as a peacock. Years previously, a wag, making a collection of facetious dream interpretations, had included this one: to see Turgenev in a dream signified that you had the ability to dig up a talent where none existed.

He was, and enjoyed being, father confessor, mentor, guide, and friend. In a sense these protégés and postulants were closer to him than his own "family," for unlike the Viardots, these people, being Russians themselves, were interested in the same matters and excited by the same problems that agitated him. His visitors were in the way of being a substitute, however poor, for Russia. He scrutinized them closely, sometimes to their displeasure, as if in order to refute the accusation so often leveled at him that he was ignorant of the younger generation. Of course, he was examining them with the eye of a novelist. He was lavish with warnings against following his own bad example of expatriation. "I was better fitted than you for life abroad," he told one of his young friends, "and even I vegetate here and keep waiting for something, knowing that I have nothing to wait for any more."

His callers, on their way upstairs, often overheard the sound of the piano or the voice of one of Mme. Viardot's pupils. Her music room was directly under Turgenev's study, a circumstance in which he rejoiced, though a jealous compatriot interpreted it as another instance of the neglect he was suffering. Indeed, he had a special speaking tube installed so that he could hear the music more distinctly. He dined belowstairs, and after dinner they would all gather around the fireplace, where, falling into a doze, "Tourguel," as the girls called him, would wake to the sound of a duo or a quartet. To all intents and purposes he was as completely identified with the family as old Viardot himself. He went back to Vergil and Ovid, partly because he loved the classics, but chiefly to help Paul with his Latin. The boy was unmannerly and sometimes insufferable, but he was developing into a remarkable violinist. He watched with paternal solicitude the progress of Didie's affair with young Georges Chamerot, which ended in her betrothal to him. They were married in March, 1874. Turgenev considered him "a splendid, capable, high-minded fellow"; otherwise, he told Pietsch, he would never have consented to the match. "I have never seen anything more charming," he wrote of the pair. "All of us, so-called writers, are blind botchers and *à-peu-près-Macher** in these things. Fortunately I don't write any more, so I am saved from the temptation of trying to reproduce this spectacle. . . . But I am swallowing everything, everything." He told Fet that the young man

---

* People who don't quite hit the mark.

was beyond all praise, but could not say that he was worthy of Claudie, for in his eyes no man was that. The happiness that the young couple radiated was something to thank God for, but he could not feel grateful to a Providence that would not restore his own youth, and all else was "dust and vanity." In good time came the anxious days preceding Didie's confinement and the grandfatherly joy in the little Jeanne Edmée —the baby, like his own granddaughter, born in July, 1872, having been named for him.

Not surprisingly, vulgar gossip had it that the three-cornered establishment was a *mariage à trois*. Three years after Turgenev's death the wife of the notorious Austrian novelist Leopold von Sacher-Masoch, speaking in her memoirs of her lover's suggestion that he, she and her husband live together, quotes him as saying: "There will be one more *mariage à trois* in Paris, and what of it? Did not Turgenev live with the Viardots? All Paris knew it, and what harm did it do them?"

A regular feature of his life on rue de Douai was the Viardots' Thursdays and Sundays. George Sand described one of the Thursday musicales given soon after her darling Pauline moved to Paris: the bare, spacious room, furnished only with a piano, an organ, and chairs; the great jars of poppies and cornflowers on the steps leading up to the adjacent picture gallery; the violin playing of young Paul and the singing of Claudie and Marianne to their mother's accompaniment; and the miracle of that voice which she had not heard for twenty years, and which, carrying the melodies of Gluck, had the power to obliterate for a moment the smoking ruins of France, the miseries of the present and the uncertainties of the future. Flaubert, too, when he heard Mme. Viardot singing Gluck, declared that the emotions her art aroused consoled one for the malignity of life. What Flaubert was saying, his friend Turgenev must not seldom have felt. One of his "Poems in Prose," dated 1879, celebrates the triumphant moment when, her last note uttered, she stands transfigured by the beauty she has just expressed, and becomes, although but a handful of dust, the radiant incarnation of immortality. His admiration for the artist altered less with the years than his passion for the woman.

She continued to delight her friends, and occasionally even the general public, when there was only one octave left to her voice. Thus, as late as 1876, beginning somewhat rustily, she yet made her audience shudder as, rubbing together her perfect white hands, she sang to Verdi's music, Shakespeare's words: "All the perfumes of Arabia will not sweeten this little hand." The same evening she showed her versatility by singing "Erlkönig," with Saint-Saens at the piano, and then, with a Spanish tenor who was present, doing a comic love duet. Af fifty-five, in spite of her bulging, near-sighted eyes, thick lips, and bad figure, this supple-bodied woman in the black lace gown exercised over the guests seated on her white-lacquered, silk-upholstered chairs a spell that put into eclipse her two young daughters.

The Sundays were less serious occasions, what with charades, games of forfeits, and other parlor amusements. Turgenev, who had always relished this sort of thing, Saint-Saens, and Paul Viardot were the principal actors. On one occasion Turgenev took the part of a professor of medicine, while the musician, in pink tights, was the corpse, and at the grand finale Paul, the chief machinist, held up a white china plate to represent the moon. Fat old Renan, with his paunch on his right side, was made to jump over a handkerchief, to the great glee of the company, especially "the perfidious young." Again, he powdered his vast face all over, trying with his lips to lift a ring from the top of a flour pyramid. Turgenev's first impulse, when in 1868 he was offered an introduction to this "exquisite seminarist," as he called Renan, had been to decline it. Was it that he felt an instinctive dislike for the man who was to pronounce the funeral oration over his body, when the coffin, on its way to Russia, rested at the Gare du Nord?

The apartment on the rue de Douai was Turgenev's winter quarters. The first summer away from Baden he spent partly at home in Russia, partly with the Viardots in the country, at Valéry-sur-Somme, which he described as "a charming seaside town." The following year he summered with them in a suburb of Paris, Bougival. There was everything to recommend the place: it was within forty-five minutes of the city; it was pleasantly situated on a forested hill overlooking the Seine; and—cholera had never been known there! And so in 1874 Turgenev, in partnership with Viardot, purchased a fine property there at the price of one hundred and eighty thousand francs. There was some suggestion of a Russian manorial estate about *Les Frênes*. The place was so called because of the ash-trees surrounding the house. Had he known, Turgenev would have found a melancholy propriety in the fact that his last home should be named for the tree of whose wood his coffin was to be made. With its spacious grounds, its springing fountains, its moss-covered statues, its river view, this was an estate fit for gentlemen. Thirty paces from the main house he built himself a comfortable chalet in the Swiss style, but with incongruous ornaments intended to remind the owner of his far-away Scythia. The last tile was placed on the roof in 1875, but he did not move in until the spring of the next year. Henry James found it "a little un-sunned."

In the eight summers that remained to him, *Les Frênes* was the counterpart of his Baden nest. There were the same faces, the same domestic diversions, the same sporadic, half-acknowledged unease. The Viardots' married children summered there, too, and the whole family would gather as of old around the lunch table, to which the samovar was regularly brought, the one Russian feature in Turgenev's French home. In the afternoon they would fill his study, which was on the second floor of the chalet and furnished richly in crimson and black, Mme. Viardot with some handwork, Claudie at her easel in the big bow window, Louise reading aloud from some French or English book, and he at his desk over his correspondence, interrupting now and then, only to have Marianne's fingers close up his mouth: "See here, Tourguel, we want to listen!" On Sundays there was always music, with Pauline at the piano in the drawing room.

These companioned hours were matched by many lonely ones of lying abed with the gout. The disease played with him, he complained, like a cat with a mouse. At any moment it was ready to pounce on him and send his best-laid schemes a-gley. "Man proposes," he paraphrased the old proverb, "and Gout disposes." The very first year in Paris was particularly trying in this respect. On his fifty-fourth anniversary he suffered the twelfth spell in six months, and cursed the day of his birth. His visits home usually ended in an attack, and it was Mme. Viardot's contention, with which he agreed, that the famous Russian hospitality was to blame. He suffered cruelly in 1877 and 1878, but thereafter he was able to lay his crutches aside and actually mounted a horse—Didie maintaining that he looked like a retired Württemberg general. As in Baden, except for these attacks, he enjoyed fairly good health. At the age of sixty he was able to enjoy hunting, although his pulse was no longer one hundred and eighty when he saw his hound pointing. Two or three times he crossed the Channel to shoot partridge on the estate of a friend who boasted the best preserves in Engand, although confessing that it was rather shameful for such an old fellow as he to go to all that trouble merely to riddle poor birds with lead. He complained that he was hard put to it to follow the sport in France, because he had neither dogs nor legs, and besides, only millionaires could engage in hunting there.

He was farther than ever from being a millionaire. Sometimes he was in severe straits. When he reached Petersburg in 1876, for example, he had to borrow a hundred rubles to get to Spasskoye. He was sure of about seven thousand rubles annually from the sale of his books, and he eked out his income by selling pieces of land. His estates brought him relatively little; Kiszinski, the manager whom he had installed with so much difficulty, was no improvement on poor Uncle Nikolay. When Turgenev asked his advice on important matters, the only thing he did was to wag his magnificent beard and show his false teeth. If the man had at least been honest! Turgenev had been foolish enough to trust him for nearly ten years, but his eyes were opened when a large sum of money vanished, obviously into Kiszinski's pocket. On June 3, 1876, Turgenev wrote from Moscow that he had decided to effect a coup d'état and "overthrow this Abdul-Aziz"—the deposition of the sultan of Turkey was then the topic of the day. He kept his word, and when the ordeal was over, went to his study and watched from a window the carts being loaded with the scoundrel's belongings, preparatory to his departure. Among the goods the master of Spasskoye recognized some of his own possessions, but made no attempt to interfere. Only when the caravan was on the road, he dashed out, shook his fist at it, cursed the thief vigorously, and having thus relieved his feelings, went in to write his ladies an account of the proceedings in his best humorous vein.

He appointed a new manager, and leased him Spasskoye for a period of twelve years, retaining the privilege of selling it. Thanks to Kiszinski's depredations, he was, he wrote, "a ruined man." *Virgin Soil* brought in several thousand rubles. Thereafter he did so little writing that his literary income came almost entirely from the previously published works. The Russo-Turkish War (1877–78) resulted in a lowered rate of exchange. (He had not shared the pro-Slav ardor that the Russian public exhibited briefly in 1876, and had doubted that the government would declare war, what with the lamentable state of the Treasury and the Russians being "strongly inclined to thieving," as he wrote to Polonsky. When the armed conflict did break out, he deplored it: he feared that it would further impoverish the country and delay internal reforms.) At the same time his financial obligations had increased. He was finally forced to recognize that he had grievously erred in his generous estimate of his son-in-law. Gaston Bruère had sunk his wife's entire dowry in his factory, and when he was faced with bankruptcy, Turgenev got himself into debt to avert the disaster but succeeded only in postponing it. The fellow was even worse as a husband than as a businessman. He drank, there were scenes between him and his wife, and he went as far as to threaten her with a revolver. His parents added to her unhappiness: they had believed Turgenev to be wealthier than he was, and did not hide their disappointment. Things came to such a pass that she was forced to run away from her husband and go into hiding in Switzerland. With her two children Paulinette remained a charge upon Turgenev to the end.

One of his creditors was his own brother, who had lent him fifteen thousand rubles at nine per cent interest. Nikolay had taken to augmenting his large fortune by usury. In 1878, Turgenev, finding himself unable to make a payment, offered Nikolay one of his canvases instead. The usurer refused the substitute, and Turgenev, what with other monetary obligations, was forced to put on the market his collection of pictures. Since his settlement in Paris he had developed the collector's hobby. He declared that he was known at the auction rooms as "*le grand gogo russe*," the great Russian sucker. He owned forty-eight canvases, nearly one third of them old masters, including a fine Teniers; and among the landscapes, of which he had many, the productions of the Barbizon school predominated. He sold the lot, except his Rousseau, at a great loss. Antokolsky, the sculptor, who came in to see him the day after the first sale, which took place April 20, 1878, found him sprawling on his ugly green rep divan and repeating dejectedly, "What a Waterloo! What a Waterloo!" He had forseen the loss; the same thing had happened on other occasions. But, as he wrote to his brother, his one consolation was that he was now too old to make many more mistakes.

That year he turned sixty. He who had cried wolf so many times needlessly, now had the wolf at his throat. There were moments, rare enough, when he could find an ambiguous virtue in old age: it simplified life, and, when neither gout nor spleen tormented him, he had hours of feeling reasonably well off. But if he had had his periodic depressions before this, he was now come to a time when, like Prospero's, his every third thought must be his grave. The letters to his intimates abound in half humorous and often wholly pathetic lamentations. He is going down-hill: there she waits, the blind, dumb, gray, cold, stupid, voracious, eternal Night. Why should he regret the disarrangement of his plans by illness? That feeling does not befit the dead. He hopes his correspondent will remember kindly the cadaver named Turgenev. He is an overripe fruit, hanging heavily on its rotten branch. His mood is gray, with yellowish spots. He is swinging like a pendulum between aversion to life and fear of death. *The Atlantic Monthly* had called him a genius; pshaw! he would give up, not only his own reputation, such as it is, but the fame of a real genius, to have a few weeks of foolish youth again, and spend them hunting partridge, ten hours on end. He is cooling and growing a film, like a pot of rendered fat placed out in the frost. He would be glad of any excitement, but the spirit cannot be aroused any more. Strange, when you're old, life goes so much faster. But you get nothing done, and there's really nothing to do. In old age one feels the thorns of the rose one picked—or didn't pick—when one was young. One draws on one's patience, a bitter herb, which heals as little as do all the other medicines.

In a letter to Polonsky he quotes an entry in his diary for March 17, 1877, in which he appears to attribute to Pauline Viardot his own misery: "Midnight. I am again at my desk. . . . Downstairs my poor friend is singing something in her completely cracked voice. . . . And a darkness blacker than night is in my soul. It is as though the grave were in a hurry to swallow me: the day, empty, aimless, colorless, flits by like a moment. Before you turn around, it is time to fall into bed again. I have neither the right nor the desire to live; there is nothing more to do, nothing to expect, nothing even to wish for." And he adds, referring to himself and Pauline: "My dear fellow, the two of us are just two potsherds of a broken vessel."

32

VIRGIN SOIL

Coming to Paris to stay, in the late autumn of 1871, Turgenev brought with him the manuscript of a novel, completed except for minor details. He had managed to write *Spring Freshets* between trains, as it were, and in spite of the miseries of moving. Annenkov, to whom, as a matter of course, the manuscript went first for criticism, wrote back enthusiastically that his friend was still at the zenith of his creative powers. Thus sanctioned, the novel, like several short things that immediately preceded it, came out in the great liberal review, *Vestnik Yevropy* (*The Herald of Europe*). *Smoke* had been his last major work to be printed in *The Russian Herald*. Once a fairly progressive publication, Katkov's magazine had become extremely retrograde after the Polish rebellion, and the fact that his writings appeared in its pages troubled Turgenev's conscience. His withdrawal as a contributor earned him the editor's implacable enmity, which he fully reciprocated. He even nicknamed his gout *Katkovka,* and on October 9, 1874, was writing to Fet: "All that remains of my hatred and contempt is directed against Katkov, the vilest and most dangerous man in Russia."

He had transcribed *Spring Freshets* three times and when the clean copy was ready he made, as he wrote to the editor, a surprising discovery: he had thought of his work as full of blue sky and the song of larks, but it proved to be a poisonous toadstool. "So immoral," he said, "I have never been." He repeated this self-accusation in a letter to Pietsch. The reference was to the fact that his hero could appreciate stainless beauty and betray it ignominiously by yielding to lust. The situation here parallels that of *Smoke,* only the man is younger, his bride is not a plain Russian girl but a ravishing Italian maiden, and instead of resisting the scarlet woman after a momentary lapse, he trails after his siren, no less shameful than her other lovers or than the gluttonous husband whom she amuses with her conquests. The remark of Potugin in *Smoke*: "Man is weak, woman is strong, Chance is all-powerful," is better exemplified in *Spring Freshets* than in any of Turgenev's other novels.

Annenkov suggested that Sanin, the central character, should have been made to run away from both women, horrified and puzzled by himself, so as to counteract the impression that he is capable of "savoring divine ambrosia and devouring raw meat like a Kalmuck with equal relish." And immediately after publication, the author wrote that he was disgusted with his production: if he had only considered it before it went into print, he would at least have altered the end, have had Sanin flee his enchantress, have allowed him another interview with Gemma, his bride, would have had her reject him, and so forth. But now he was done with it, and he was not going to touch his abortion again. As a matter of fact, he need have had no qualms about the ethical import of his story: if it conveys any lesson at all, it is that the wages of sin is death—death not of the body, but of the spirit.

While one may put aside Annenkov's scruples as to the moral implications of the tale, one can share his admiration for it as a piece of writing. The characters live—not only the weak-willed Sanin, and the woman who seduces him, but also the girl's mother, and the excellent Pantaleone, old friend and majordomo of the little Italian household, as well as the German shopman who is the epitome of Philistinism. Through this character Turgenev was working off a grudge against the fatuousness of postwar Germany. Gemma, like so many of his enchanting virgins, is too much the incarnation of man's wistful dream to be quite human.

The story, according to Turgenev, was based in part on a sentimental episode of his early manhood, when, passing through Frankfort in 1840, he was smitten by a beautiful Jewish girl. The impulse that worked itself out in the tale was clearly an effort to recapture the spirit of youth. Life to him was like one of those fruits of Oriental legend, "all sweetness on one side, all bitterness on the other." And as he munched, wry-faced, the bitter half that was age, he kept trying to recall the taste of the sweet half that had been consumed.

Spring Freshets is related as the reminiscence of a middle-aged man who, at two o'clock in the morning, after an evening spent with charming women and distinguished men, flings himself into his armchair and covers his face with his hands, overcome by a disgust with life. If this lonely man stretched beside his empty fireplace and meditating on "the vanity, the uselessness, the stale falsity of everything human," on the suddenness of old age, on the gnawing fear of death—if this man were to take his hands from his face, would he not uncover the very features of his creator? And this image of the sea of life, smooth and transparent "even to its very dark bottom," this sea on which a man floats in a small cranky boat, while "on that dark slimy bottom horrible monsters, like huge fishes, are dimly visible—all the ills of life, sicknesses, woes, madness, poverty, blindness . . . ," monsters that move, and rise, and threaten, and sink again, barely moving their gills, only biding their time till one of them shall inevitably "capsize the boat,"—does not this image convey the essence of Turgenev's private laments?

The novel had a tremendous success, especially with women. The issue of the magazine in which it appeared went into a second printing, an unheard-of thing. But all this did not hearten the writer. For one thing, the critics, finding in the novel no food for their homiletics, were inclined to dismiss it as light literature. Their dissatisfaction with the work because of its lack of social import was in a sense an indirect reproach to the expatriate for exiling himself from the scene which it was his duty to represent. Turgenev was all too ready to admit that this reproach was justified, although occasionally he protested that the novelist was not obligated to deal with matters of public interest and point a moral.

In the years that followed, he published very little. What could he write about? He had once spoken of his Muse as a hen which he must summon coaxingly with "Here, chick, chick, chick." Just now the hen was shy; or, to change the metaphor, there was "rust on the wheels." He confessed in March, 1873, that if it hadn't been for promises he had made to two editors, he would joyfully have thrown down his pen. "And, of course," he added, "once these obligations are discharged, I shall never touch my pen again. Here is my solemn oath on it." It would be a pleasure to watch the literary scene with the serenity of one who had retired.

Of course, his literary impulse was not dead, but it was certainly dormant. Such writing as he did was done under compulsion. When there was no demand for his rye, the remittance in payment for some tale or other was welcome. At a loss for suitable subjects, he found himself rummaging in his portfolios and turning up yellow sheets which contained drafts jotted down at least a quarter of a century earlier. Most of these notes had gone to the making of *A Sportsman's Sketches*. But some of the material which had remained unused looked as though it could be put in shape for publication. By September, 1872, he had turned out a sequel ("The End of Chertopkhanov") to one of these sketches, and was planning to salvage four more pieces. In two minds as to the wisdom of such a step, he put the matter up to Annenkov: should he write them or not?

Annenkov said no. *A Sportsman's Sketches* was not only a milestone in the career of its author but also a monument to a completed phase of Russian culture, and it would be vandalism to tamper with the book at this date. "On the anniversary of the Poltava victory," he wrote, "Peter wore his old bullet-ridden hat, but he didn't deck it out with peacock feathers." Turgenev replied by cheerfully quoting Julian the Apostate, "Thou hast conquered, Galilean," and decided to leave well enough alone. In 1874 he did augment *A Sportsman's Sketches* by one more tale, the little classic, "Living Relics." This sketch, which came out in French immediately on publication and brought Turgenev an enthusiastic letter from George Sand, he had originally put aside as too dull to waste time on.

The same year "Punin and Baburin" appeared. Because of its central character, a humble clerk of independent spirit and republican convictions, who, implicated in the Petrashevsky "conspiracy," is exiled to Siberia, this partly autobiographical tale may be regarded as a preliminary sketch for the larger canvas that Turgenev was planning at the time.

Nearly two years later he offered his public another reminiscential story, "The Watch." When he sent it to the editor of
The Herald of Europe, he stipulated, with that lack of self-
assurance which he never outgrew, that should the piece be
found wanting in merit, it should be consigned to the flames.
He hoped that the critics would not say, "Mr. Turgenev's
watch is slow: he still imagines himself a writer!" It was
quite in character for him to concede on occasion that he
was in truth no writer. All his life, he said, he had spent with
people who took no interest in his work; his nearest and
dearest didn't even know the language in which he wrote;
for months, for years, he would forget that he had any business
with a pen.

He might deny the writer in himself as often as the cock
crew, but his literary instinct was as strong as ever. Nor, in
spite of his residence abroad, had he resigned the function of
the author who, in tracing the lives of his characters, fills out
the wider contours of the contemporary scene, the writer
who seeks to show the very age and body of his time, its form
and pressure—in short, the function of historian to his day.
"I myself understand that I should produce something bigger
and closer to the present [than 'The End of Chertopkhanov'],"
he wrote on January 3, 1873. And he went on to confess
that he had "the subject and plan for a novel all ready."
(As a matter of fact, the germ of it dates back to the summer
of 1870.) Two of his twelve characters, however, had "not
been studied on the spot, not been caught alive," he said.
As he was not the man to rely on invention, it was necessary
for him to "saturate" himself with his material. To do that
he had to live in Russia, which was out of the question. So
he would try to remedy the situation by staying there occasionally. "But will these visits be sufficient?" he asked. "My
literary conscience will tell me that. If so, I'll write the novel,
if not—amen!" While in Russia during the summer of 1874
he was able to send Flaubert word that he had found the
information he needed.

That very spring and summer something unprecedented
was taking place in quite a few Russian villages. Young men
and women, mostly students, disguised as farm hands, itinerant
artisans, day laborers, peddlers, were traveling from one rural

community to another, leaving in their wake subversive tracts and memories of queer talk. Previously there had been sporadic efforts to carry the gospel of rebellion to the masses. This year was marked by a small-scale crusade, a children's crusade, lacking organization and utterly futile. The crusaders were idealistic young people who, having left lecture halls and ballrooms behind them, or given up army commissions, "went to the people," to use Herzen's phrase. Some of them, holding with Bakunin that the Russian folk were socialists by instinct and revolutionaries by nature, were out to rouse the peasantry to immediate revolt. Others followed Peter Lavrov in believing that the people must first be enlightened, and saw their task as peaceful propaganda for the new order. The members of both factions shared a quasi-religious faith in a social revolution which would abolish economic inequality and political oppression. They were acting on the conviction that to be effective, an agitator belonging to the privileged classes must shed his identity and become at one with the masses, the People, living, thinking, feeling as they did. It was with this phase of Russian militant Populism that Turgenev's novel dealt.

Its gestation was long and difficult. As usual, the novelist worked up his subject carefully. An admirer, Anna Filosofova, provided him with the diaries and letters of several young radicals of her acquaintance. Living abroad, as he did, he had the advantage of free access to the underground literature which was being printed, chiefly in Geneva, for clandestine distribution at home. Some of his models, too, were to be found right there in Paris. Not a few of the young compatriots who turned to him for help were political émigrés who starved and plotted in the attics of the Latin Quarter. The circle of his acquaintances included not only the rank and file, but also notable revolutionary figures. Such was Hermann Lopatin, "our indestructible youth," as Turgenev called him, who was one of the first to "go to the people" and one of the few Russians admired by Karl Marx. The novelist was also in touch with Lavrov and during 1874–76 contributed 500 francs annually to the support of the revolutionary organ that this former professor of mathematics issued from a London press after first publishing it in Zürich. For a short time that Swiss city was a center of Russian radicalism. The University and Polytechnic there attracted many youths expelled for political reasons from the schools of higher learning at home and an even larger number of girls to whom the doors of those institutions were still closed. Some of the young people were followers of Lavrov, others swore by Bakunin, the schism leading to a bitter feud. Turgenev was on the point of going to Zürich in order to have a glimpse of the Russian colony there, but was apparently dissuaded by Lavrov, who feared that the author of *Fathers and Children* and *Smoke* would get a hostile reception.

He picked up his novel several times, only to drop it again. He had promised it long before its completion to *The Herald of Europe*. In order to force himself to get ahead with it, he had the editor, Stasulevich, advance him money of which he had no need at the moment, so that his indebtedness would spur him on to fresh efforts. While he was working on the book, he was insisting that he had nothing more to say and desired to say nothing more, that living away from Russia as he did, his art was no better fed than a hibernating bear who sucks his own paw. At the same time he was not unaware that he was hatching an important piece of work. On January 3, 1876, he wrote to the earnest and caustic Saltykov that he didn't want to disappear from the face of the earth before he had finished his big novel, which, he thought would remove many misunderstandings about him. He begged the great satirist not to be annoyed with him because, to keep his hand in, he was writing trivial things. "Who knows?" he added. "Perhaps I am yet destined to kindle the hearts of men!"

He finally wrote the novel "at one stroke," as he said, in the summer of 1876 when he was again at Spasskoye in the throes of difficulties connected with the administration of his estates. In a surprisingly cheerful letter to Flaubert he wrote that he was spending white nights bent over his desk. He was possessed by what, with his wonted modesty, he described as the "illusion" that if he could not say a new word, he could at least say an old one in a new way. "My devil of a novel," he wrote, "has gotten hold of me in a ravaging fashion in spite of everything." In the middle of July he completed the manuscript under Belinsky's eyes—the portrait of his old friend hung above his desk. It was October, and he was back at Bougival, in his recently built chalet, which smelled of new furniture, when he set "Finis" to his clean copy. The manuscript was forthwith sent by messenger to Annenkov, who was just then staying in Baden. Turgenev was overjoyed by his friend's warm reception of the book and obediently followed his advice as to alterations and omissions. Annenkov was highly enthusiastic. Here, once more, he wrote was a novel which was an event. The Danube guns—the preamble to the Russo-Turkish War was then in progress—might drown out the book, but not for long. Turgenev need not worry about the success of *Virgin Soil*; such works leave broken pavements behind them, like Krupp cannon.

Turgenev explained his conception of the novel to Stasulevich as follows:

"I decided to choose the middle road [between maligning and idealizing the revolutionaries] and thus get closer to the truth; to take young people, most of them good and honorable, and to show that in spite of their honesty, their very cause is so false and remote from life that it cannot but end in a complete fiasco. . . . At any rate, the young people cannot say that it is an enemy who has undertaken to depict them; on the contrary, they must feel the sympathy I have, if not for their cause, then at least for their personalities."

Since *Virgin Soil* trod on dangerous ground, Turgenev was careful to leave much unsaid. Nevertheless he suffered some anxiety as to how the book would fare at the hands of the censor. He wrote to Henry James that he kept wondering if what he put down on paper would be permitted to reach his public. At first the prospect was not unfavorable. But on December 6, 1876, a crowd of students, emerging from the Kazan Cathedral, where they had ordered a prayer for the health of Chernyshevsky, marched down the Nevsky shouting: "Long live the People! Death to the czars!" and carrying a red flag with the inscription: "Land and Liberty." The slogan long survived the underground organization of that name which originated the same year. Both Turgenev and his publisher despaired: surely the authorities would consider untimely the publication of a novel that dared to deal with revolution. Nevertheless, the first part of the work passed unchallenged and appeared in *The Herald of Europe* for January, 1877. The second part got by with some difficulty, half of the members of the censorship committee voting against it. The novel appeared in book form the following year and by that time it was accessible in nine languages.

The authorities had reason to look askance at *Virgin Soil*. The pillars of the existing order, while not caricatured like their counterparts in *Smoke*, are nevertheless held up to pitiless scorn. On the other hand, the author's attitude to the small band of conspirators is one of almost friendly irony. The cause they serve is presented as chimerical and hopeless; they include misfits and sheeplike souls, but, except for a pusillanimous fellow traveler, they are sincere idealists moved by a genuine love of the people. When their preparations for an uprising meet disaster, they do not betray each other or recant. Solomin, obviously the author's spokesman, sympathizes with the ends of the revolutionaries even though he resolutely rejects their means. The word "sober" is written in large letters at the head of the sheet on which Turgenev first sketched out this character's biography. The reader is left with the impression that the future of the country rests on the broad plebeian shoulders of such men as this hardheaded engineer, whose English technical training is successfully grafted on the native shrewdness of the Great Russian. Certain that the peasantry is in a state of torpor which will defeat all the efforts of the Populists, he cannot believe in the possibility of an agrarian revolution. He foresees the utter decay of the landowning nobility, but his satisfaction with that eventuality is clouded by the conviction that the masses would gain nothing from the rise of an equally predacious bourgeoisie. A man of firm purpose and democratic temper, he is dedicated to the achievement of a just social order, but he sees no other way to it than the slow, incremental, peaceful process of education and reform. Like his author, he is a gradualist, but "a gradualist from below," that is, from the base of the social pyramid.

If Solomin is Turgenev's mouthpiece, the novel's central character is Nezhdanov. He is a student who, having joined the thin ranks of the revolutionaries, is ready to merge with the people and devote his life to their interests. Taken on as a tutor in the home of a high government official, he meets there his employer's dependent niece, a recalcitrant young girl deeply resentful of her humiliating position in the household. The two are drawn to each other largely by a community of ideals, for she, too, is eager to dedicate herself to the oppressed masses, and they flee the house together in order to "go to the people." Marianna is one of Turgenev's finest achievements in portraiture. She is a Yelena who has found her work and, in the end, her mate at home. But Nezhdanov is no Insarov. A sensitive, introspective youth, bitten by skepticism, torn by contradictory impulses, he is a house divided against itself, a fact partly accounted for by his birth: he is the illegitimate son of an aristocrat and his daughters' governess. Here is the familiar contrast between the faltering, inadequate man and the strong, completely integrated woman. A Hamlet in the role of a Don Quixote, Nezhdanov takes part in an abortive effort to rouse the peasants. The result is self-disgust and literal nausea, because he cannot carry the raw vodka that his potential proselytes force down his throat. The young man is entangled in a tragic coil. He is reluctant to sacrifice himself for a cause in which, he discovers, he does not really believe, and he decides that he is unworthy of Marianna. He solves his problem by putting a bullet through his heart.

The author points the moral of his tale by giving Marianna in marriage to Solomin. They go off to the Urals to start a factory on a cooperative basis.

Peasants and factory hands appear dimly in the background. Writing to Konstantin Kavelin, the historian, Turgenev admitted that he should have delineated the workman Pavel, Solomin's factotum, "the people's revolutionary of the future," in greater detail. "Some day," he added, "this type will become the central figure of a new novel (of course, not from my pen—for that I am too old and I have lived too long outside Russia)."

The counsel offered to the younger generation by *Virgin Soil*, the most unmistakably political of Turgenev's novels, is in essence the same as the lesson of *Smoke*: work patiently and steadily at the small task; advance by inches; serve the people humbly that they may be ready for a future leader. The epigraph to the book is a quotation from an agricultural manual to the effect that virgin soil must be worked with a plow that cuts deep. The author assured his publisher that what he meant was "not revolution but enlightenment."

Before *Virgin Soil* took definite shape Turgenev had expected that its publication would dispel the cloud of disapproval by the radicals which had enveloped him since the appearance of *Fathers and Children*. By the time the novel was in proof he had lost that confidence and was saying with pretended cynicism that he didn't care what happened to the book as long as he got the cash for it. Not unnaturally, he found himself under fire from the right. But he was even more severely attacked from the left. He was denounced for having defamed the insurgent youth as Dostoevsky had in *The Possessed,* and accused of being generally incompetent to deal with the subject. Saltykov, in a letter to Annenkov, wrote scathingly about the way Turgenev portrayed "the new men." Lavrov's charge was that the novel confused the conspiratorial attempts of the late sixties (the action of *Virgin Soil* is laid in 1868) with the "going to the people," which took place in the middle seventies. Yet, for an outsider, the novelist acquitted himself creditably in representing the incipient revolutionary movement. The critics had accused him of having invented Marianna, he wrote to a friend, yet in the trial of fifty propagandists, which took place while the novel was being serialized, eighteen of the defendants were women not unlike his heroine. Events were to justify his view of the nature and prospects of militant Populism.

As usual, hostile criticism carried great weight with him. Shortly after the appearance of the novel he wrote on the same day in almost identical terms to his brother and to his publisher, crying *mea culpa* and announcing his final abdication as a writer. His eyes had been opened, he declared: *Virgin Soil* was a fiasco. Surely the entire press had not entered into a conspiracy against the book. Furthermore, all that the critics said was true; in his heart he agreed with them. No, you could not write about Russia without living there. He had taken upon himself a task to which he was unequal and had fallen down under it. He should have stopped writing several years previously. To Stasulevich he said: "There has been something tragic about the fate of every Russian writer who has been at all prominent; with me it is absenteeism, the causes of which it would take too long to search out, but the influence of which is incontestably manifest in my last—I mean last—work."

33

A MARRIAGE OF SOULS

Life in Paris had its compensatory features. In spite of his prejudice against France, Turgenev had moments of feeling that nowhere else could one live so comfortably and freely. For one thing, there were highly stimulating contacts. His was an uneasiness of spirit which might have crabbed and soured another, and a habit of narrowly observing his companions, which few of them relished. But he had, too, the savoir-faire of a man of the world, the novelist's interest in his fellows, a boy's love of fun, and the approachability of an abjectly modest man—all of which made for smooth and generous social intercourse. On his previous visits to Paris he had come to know virtually everybody worth knowing. By the time he came to make his home there, some of those old acquaintances were gone: Prosper Mérimée, one of his translators, whom, on his death in 1870, he had eulogized in a Petersburg daily, Sainte-Beuve, who, during their last encounter in 1868, had drawn the location of his supposed cancer for his guest.

Of the old guard there remained, among others, "Mother Sand." Although he had known her for many years through the Viardots, it was only now that he was entering the circle of her familiars. As a young man he had, like the rest of Belinsky's group, thrilled to her championship of caged emotions, the oppressed sex, the downtrodden People. Belinsky himself had called her "the Joan of Arc of our time." In his maturity Turgenev was inclined to dismiss her writings as tiresome garrulities. But now, seeing her intimately and ignoring, as most good friends had to do, her novels, he succumbed completely to her charm. For her part, she had long known and admired his work: he wrote simply and sincerely where her compatriots, she contended, either posed or wallowed.

She praised him to his face, and he showed himself "as surprised as a child." She said the same kind things in print when she dedicated to him a sketch published in *Le Temps* in October, 1872.

There was more than one exchange of courtesies. He sent her his kill, and in default of game, a barrel of oysters for her lunch; she presented him with a pair of cuff links. She begged their common friend Gustave Flaubert to prepare him for abduction: she must see him at Nohant. And, indeed, after he settled in Paris, he made more than one trip there, generally along with the Viardots. He arrived, usually after several postponements, occasioned sometimes by gout, sometimes by his habit of letting himself be waylaid. "That's what it means," he apologized on April 12, 1873 to his prospective hostess, "to have a short thumb—the sign of a weak will."

Not these latter-day visits, but rather the memory of his youthful admiration, led him to canonize her after her death in 1876. "George Sand," he concluded his obituary note, "is one of our saints." And yet his final estimate of her owed not a little to this friendly intercourse at the end. Certainly it was rare refreshment to spend a day with this plump, soft-voiced, soft-footed old lady, who, with her fine brow under a mass of curly hair, looked like a Jewess, he observed, and who was always trailing cigarette smoke and an atmosphere of benevolence and generosity. She lived at Nohant, her ancestral estate, companioned by her son, his wife, and their two little daughters. Here was an idyllic epilogue to a life dangerously crowded with loves and labors. Her guests were treated to hunting in the morning, bathing in the afternoon, and music or marionettes in the evening. Maurice Sand modeled the dolls' heads and his mother made their dresses; like Voltaire and Goethe before her, she was devoted to her puppets. And amid these preoccupations, "the dear lazy soul of a Turgenev," as she called him, was sure to find time to tell fairy tales to her favorite grandchild, their "delicious Lolo."

In March, 1873, she invited him and Flaubert to Nohant for a "mid-Lent fantasy." She even promised the giant Norman a costume; she had heard he was "very good as a pastry cook at Pauline's." Flaubert replied that Turgenev seemed to him "to enjoy very little liberty," but that he had

finally succeeded in making him swear to go to Mme. Sand's
on Easter Eve. It was after this visit that the two men, sitting
in the carriage which took them to the railway station, spoke
enviously of young Sand, who, in addition to being happily
married and the father of two charming children, had this
jewel of a mother. Flaubert, whose attachment to his own
mother had verged on the morbid, had only recently lost
her, and Turgenev must have contrasted the good Mme.
Sand with his erratic maternal parent. In the train Flaubert
felt heavy and sad, and consoled himself with his companion's
excellent cognac. Turgenev could well sympathize with the
giant Norman, who had the shoulders of an ox, the mustaches
of a Viking, the complexion Gautier had likened to brandied
cherries fallen into the fire, and who concealed the spirit of a
shy boy behind his roaring vehemence.

They had met for the first time on February 23, 1863, at one
of the fortnightly literary dinners held in Magny's restaurant
on the left bank, and they took an instant liking to each other.
They were to go on exchanging opinions on life and letters
across a variety of dinner tables as long as Flaubert lived.
On receiving two volumes of Turgenev's stories, the Frenchman responded enthusiastically. "For a long time now" he
wrote, "I have regarded you as a master." He went on to
extol the Russian's art as at once vehement and restrained,
particular and general, an amalgam of "tenderness, irony,
observation and color." On April 18 Turgenev invited Flaubert to visit him in Baden, offering as one inducement its
giant trees: to sit in their shade, he wrote, was to borrow a
little of their sap.

Although Flaubert did not accept the invitation and there
was apparently no contact between them for the next five
years, they continued to have a warm regard for one another.
In 1868, having read *Smoke* in translation, the French novelist wrote to his confrère, and in his reply "*le bon Moscove*"
observed that his correspondent was one of the few men with
whom he felt completely at ease and at the same time wide-
awake. "And besides," he added, "we are two moles tunneling
in the same direction." Late that very year he went to see
Flaubert for the first time in his lair, an old house overlooking
the Seine, in the village of Croisset near Rouen. On his

departure his host sent after him a native cheese, which he took with him to Baden, assuring the sender that at every mouthful he would remember the day at Croisset. A few months later, at Easter time, they dined together in Paris.

At the outbreak of the Franco-Prussian War Flaubert was telling George Sand that she and Turgenev were the only people to whom he could talk freely of the things closest to his heart. The two men were out of touch during the hostilities. Their correspondence was resumed with Flaubert's message of condolence, mentioned earlier, on the occasion of the false report of Pauline Viardot's death. In his response, written shortly before the signing of the peace treaty, Turgenev invited his friend to join him in his Baden mole burrow, and inquired how he had stood the storm. "We have some hard times to live through," he observed, "we others, born spectators." As a matter of fact, the maître, who had always lived in an ivory tower and abominated the patriotism of the mob, had been so aroused by the invasion that he wanted to take arms against "Hegel's compatriots" and swore he would never set eyes on another one of "these cannibals" bent on destroying Paris because it was beautiful. When the fighting was over, he was so disgusted by the dishonorable conduct of his countrymen in the war that he said in bitter jest that he was going to ask Turgenev what he must do to become a Russian subject.

Flaubert turned down the invitation to come to Baden and intimated that it was incumbent upon Russia to avenge France. Obviously he was not aware of his correspondent's pro-German bias. "I understand your repugnance to setting foot on German soil," Turgenev replied on June 13. As for what he thought about France, they would talk about it at length when they saw each other again. "You must find my hatred of Prussia very silly," Flaubert wrote three days later. "What I have against that nation especially is that it has given me the sentiments of a twelfth-century brute. Do you believe that in any other age the *literati*, the learned, behaved like savages?"

What the two men found to say to each other about the war when they met, two years later, is not a matter of record. Turgenev must have avoided stressing his pro-German sympathies. As for Flaubert, his animus was now directed less against the enemy than against his own countrymen. A week in Paris just after the suppression of the Commune filled him with profound disgust and with a sadness that penetrated to the marrow of his bones, as he phrased it. "There are more lamentable things than [the city's] ruins; it's the *mental* state of its inhabitants. You navigate between cretinism and raving madness," he wrote to Turgenev. As the months went by, matters did not improve. "Never have the interests of the spirit counted less. Never has hatred of grandeur, disdain of beauty, abhorrence of literature been so manifest." Thus Flaubert to his friend on November 13, 1872. He felt like a fourth century Roman patrician. The armed conflict, he held, had revealed all the rottenness of the French nation. Such wholesome self-criticism was just what Turgenev had hoped would result from the defeat. In any event, his friendship with Flaubert did not shatter on the rock of the war. It grew stronger with the years.

They saw much of each other in Paris, where they both wintered. Flaubert occasionally attended the Viardots' Thursdays and Sundays, and Turgenev thought nothing of spending the day with him, only to return after dinner and remain until one in the morning. There would also be, after many delays, a visit to Croisset now and then. That is, when Flaubert could tear Turgenev away from the Viardots, of whom he was not a little jealous: "Turgenev would like to come, but the Viardots want to take him elsewhere, and he is afraid to face their wrath." But it was not easy for Flaubert to make him comfortable when he came. Before one prospective visit the host was much exercised as to whether or not his guest could be accommodated on the bed in the spare room. He wrote from Paris to the niece who kept house for him, asking her to measure the couch, and saying that he would give up his own bed. Turgenev presented his friend with a dressing gown, plunging him into what he called "dreams of absolutism and lust," and regaled him with such Russian products as Tolstoy's *War and Peace* and caviar. They were both gourmets, especially the Frenchman. He won ten bottles of champagne from the Muscovite by wagering that hot roast chicken is eaten with mustard. The famous chef, Pellé, was consulted and rendered this decision: "It is done, and even often, but it is not according to the rules of good cooking."

The notes Turgenev wrote to Flaubert, addressing him as *"mon cher vieux"* or *"mon vieux féroce,"* are among the most charming of his letters and are, indeed, more felicitously worded than those he wrote in Russian. There is a considerable amount of shop talk in these messages. When, in the summer of 1875, Flaubert was taking a rest in a Swiss resort, Turgenev asked if he was inventing "something passionate, torrid, incandescent, in his icebox at Righi," and wished that his hyperemic friend would come back "pale and monochrome as a line by Lamartine." Often the letters carry a strain of fraternal solicitude. It expressed itself practically in an effort, which proved futile, to obtain for the pinched Flaubert a sinecure at the Bibliothèque Mazarine.

"I am a soft pear and an old rag, but I love you and embrace you," one letter concludes. Flaubert, in a moment of exasperation at the Muscovite's *mollasserie* (spinelessness), had dubbed him "a soft pear," and the nickname stuck—a fact which Turgenev accepted with the heartiest good humor. Hadn't he reproached himself years earlier, in a letter to Herzen, with what he called "my sheep-like nature"? Besides, there was the gout. Flaubert could not understand this disease; the procrastination it caused made him dizzy.

The letters from his "Patmos," as Turgenev called Spasskoye, had to make up to Flaubert for the visit that never materialized. He described the rustic old garden with its odors and birds and the pattern of sunlight and shade; the sense of "grave and immense stupor, in which there is at once something of life, of the beast, and of God"; the warm pallor of earth and sky in a landscape that would be merely pretty were it not for the large sweep, the great uniform spaces which lend it dignity; the old wooden mansion, with its ivy-clad veranda and green iron roof; his study, with its soporific sofa, and an ancient Byzantine icon frowning darkly from the corner, nothing but an immense face, black, lugubrious, rigid, framed in silver—a rather annoying companion, which he dare not remove, lest his servants think him a pagan. According to legend, it had been presented to a Lutovinov by Ivan the Terrible. One evening, Turgenev wrote, he sat on the balcony while some sixty peasant women, nearly all in red and all ugly, except one, were dancing like she-bears and singing in harsh if true voices. It was one of the little fêtes he was in the habit of arranging, and which cost him only a couple of pails of vodka, some cakes, and nuts. And then, too, it cost him some heartache. Watching their awkward gambols, he felt "terribly sad."

It was scarcely an unusual thing for him to be sad. True, sometimes he tried to cheer up his correspondent, who was in sore need of cheering, especially in his last years, when he was contending with genteel poverty and was in the midst of the excruciating labors on his last novel. Shortly before his death, Flaubert complained that he was liquefying like an old Camembert. All too often Turgenev allowed himself the luxury of detailing the minutiae of his own liquefaction and general wretchedness. "Infirmities, slow and chill disgust, the painful agitation of useless memories—that's, *mon bon vieux,* the prospect that offers itself to a man past fifty." At the writing, they are both past that age. Turgenev is indisposed: Mme. Death has left a visiting card to show that she has not forgotten him. His days at Bougival run out, like water, like sand—the reading of the second canto of Byron's *Don Juan* making "a luminous streak across the grayness." People who walk on crutches seem to him "heroic." He feels old, gray, dull, useless and stupid, and even his attack of gout was abortive, like everything else. He has no sorrow, but neither has he any joy, like a shadow in the Elysian fields of Gluck's *Orphée.* He turns sixty: "This is the beginning of life's tail." When existence becomes absolutely personal and on the defensive against death, it loses interest, even for the individual concerned. A year later, he feels "impotent, old, forlorn, gouty, with two sores instead of legs," but even though he keeps to his room like an old crab in his damp hole, he will make an effort to drag himself to Flaubert's lodging on the morrow.

Flaubert was the first to surrender the fort. Turgenev was in the depths of Scythia when, in May, 1880, his friend died at Croisset. Four years earlier, condoling with that very friend on the death of George Sand, he had written that this "good fellow" and "good woman," with all her charm and valor, had disappeared into a horrible hole that didn't even know what it had devoured. And now the insatiable hole had claimed another rare and doughty spirit. To the woman who had guarded Flaubert in those last clouded years Turgenev wrote: "The death of your uncle is one of the greatest sorrows I have experienced in my life, and I can't get used to the thought that I shall not see him again. . . . It's one of those griefs that one wishes to remain inconsolable." And he offered her his services in connection with the publication of *Bouvard et Pécuchet,* the novel which had "killed" his friend. "Flaubert was one of the men I loved most in the world," he declared to Zola. With this friend and Victor Hugo, he served on the committee for the erection of a monument to the novelist, and even solicited subscriptions for it at home, exposing himself to a great deal of abuse.

Daudet, who saw much of the two men, and often when they were together, speaks of their relation as "a marriage of souls." It appears, to the outside observer, one of those unaccountable marriages. True, they were "tunneling in the same direction," in Turgenev's phrase already quoted. Both were intent on making the novel a transparent vessel which would at once show the true color of life and give it shape. They also had a high regard for each other's work and critical judgment. Turgenev held that Flaubert alone could dispute with Tolstoy the title of the foremost contemporary writer, and *Flaubertus dixit* was to him the last word. While the Frenchman was more reserved, he had the highest opinion of his friend both as novelist and critic, *Jugeur* and *Producteur.* "Nothing escapes him," he wrote to George Sand, after having read to Turgenev a part of the manuscript of *La Tentation de Saint-Antoine.* "At the end of a hundred lines he remembers one weak epithet. He made two or three excellent suggestions . . ."

Aside from their work, they had much in common. They were close contemporaries, Flaubert being Turgenev's junior by three years. Both knew the freedoms and the infelicities of bachelordom. Each abominated the class into which he was born and the respective characteristics which he to some degree exemplified. Like Turgenev, Flaubert was acutely aware of what he called "the Machiavellism of Nature." His pet idea of basing politics on science and making government a section of the Academy was in line with Turgenev's thinking, and he shared the Russian's dislike of socialism. Both men abominated the political régime of the Third Republic.

But if Flaubert, like Turgenev, was a realist committed to the objective method, his work shows a pull toward romantic frenzy and exoticism that was alien to Turgenev's sober temperament. The disciple of Gautier was far more indifferent to the moral implications of art than the pupil of Belinsky could ever be. The author of *Salammbô,* unlike the author of *Fathers and Children,* did not feel the compulsion to bear witness to his own time. Flaubert's interest was mainly in form, manner, technique. Turgenev, although he scolded his compatriots for their churlish neglect of these matters, was for his own part never so deeply concerned with them as his friend. He could not see the virtues of Chateaubriand's style, much to the distress of Flaubert, who considered it the fountainhead of French prose. Flaubert idolized Hugo, Turgenev on occasion violently rejected him. The appearance of *Les Chansons des Rues et des Bois* moved him to this outburst: "God, to what lengths can the vileness and abomination of decay go! Can any emetic compare to this? An age in which such reptiles crawl into the light can have no place for art." He conceded, in a letter to Henry James, that there were incomparably magnificent lines in the second series of *La Légende des Siècles,* but found the poet's incessant trumpeting "horribly tiresome." He is said to have spoken of Hugo as "a bombastic rhetorician."

There were all these differences between the truculent Norman and his soft-spoken confrère from the steppes, and in addition, the immutable fact that one was French and the other Russian, a circumstance the implications of which forced themselves increasingly upon Turgenev's attention. Yet the union was a real one; indeed, some of their differences drew them together. One senses in Turgenev's attitude something of the quality of his affection for Belinsky, some shadow of his feeling for Stankevich. Like those friends of his youth, Flaubert possessed a passionate integrity, a strength of will, which found expression in his monkish devotion to his work.

The "soft pear" admired and loved this tenacity, if he could not imitate it. Daudet tells us that in this union Turgenev played the feminine part. "In the factory which turns out human beings," he adds, "there is such confusion that a masculine soul sometimes gets into a female body and a feminine soul into the carcass of a cyclops."

34

PARIS:

FRIENDS AND STRANGERS

The routine of Turgenev's life in Paris included Sunday afternoons at Flaubert's. He had to limp up three flights of stairs to the apartment overlooking the lawns and trees of Parc Monceau. Generally the first of the company to arrive, he would exchange fraternal embraces with his host, and either curl up on the divan "like a boa" or sink into an armchair in genial anticipation of hours of palaver. Before long, others would assemble. The host sometimes lent to the otherwise conventional scene an exotic note. Mme. Daudet, coming to fetch her husband one evening, found Flaubert presiding over the gathering, clad in a kind of Arab blouse decorated with an ancient frill, and wearing a red Algerian cap.

Turgenev might bring with him a volume of Goethe to translate for the company, and at least one of his listeners felt that it was like hearing Goethe himself read and speak. Once he tried to introduce them to Swinburne. But readings were incidental. The late afternoon hours, when twilight was thickening the shadows in the smoky room, loosed the spirit of talk among these quick and well-stocked intelligences, and Turgenev, for whom conversation was as natural a medium as writing, basked and soared in his element. All manner of subjects were touched upon: the sciences as well as the arts, food as well as philosophy. A young stranger from the States, one Henry James, came to some of these Sunday gatherings as a half-worshipful, half-critical apprentice.

By that time the impoverished Flaubert had removed to a more modest apartment just under the roof of a house on rue Murillo at the end of the Faubourg St.-Honoré, a place which James describes as looking "rather bare and provisional." The substance of the discussion in "that little smoke-clouded room" was, he tells us, "chiefly questions of taste, questions of art and form; and the speakers, for the most part, were in aesthetic matters radicals of the deepest dye. . . . The conviction that held them together was the conviction that art and morality are two utterly different things, and that the former has no more to do with the latter than it has with astronomy or embryology. The only duty of a novel was to be well written; that merit included every other of which it was capable." If Turgenev recalled how, twenty years previously, he had disdained French writers for their want of aesthetic principles, he could only have remarked how times had changed. There was nothing now that they had in greater abundance. Henry James observed that Turgenev had "reservations and discriminations" which set him apart from these companions and kept him from being "all there, as the phrase is." But the American admitted that the Russian "so far as he was on the spot . . . was an element of pure sociability."

It was at Flaubert's that Turgenev met for the first time Alphonse Daudet, the little man with the big head that seemed to belong to another body, and Emile Zola. Both were then in their thirties; Daudet was already fairly well established in the literary world, but Zola was still struggling along. Turgenev gave his ready friendship to both, especially to the one who most needed befriending. He had long known Edmond de Goncourt, whose sharp-featured face he also saw here frequently. The four of them formed the group of Flaubert's "faithful." Turgenev was very much one of them and found all doors open to him. Daudet's son recalls how, as a little boy, at the age for fairy tales, seeing Turgenev and Flaubert enter the house, he exclaimed: "Are they giants?"

The Goncourt "attic" was another haunt of the Muscovite's. From 1872 on, the Goncourt Journals are sprinkled with references to "the gentle giant . . . with white hair falling into his eyes and a deep furrow across his forehead." The collector's passion which the two Goncourts had shared, as they had shared everything, had turned their old house in the vicinity of the Bois de Boulogne into something of a museum. The study, which smelt pleasantly of old books and glowed with the gold of the bindings, held a monument to the strange intellectual symbiosis of the brothers in the shape of an immense desk built for two. It was here, one morning in 1877, that Turgenev came to hear Edmond Goncourt read aloud the first novel he had set pen to since his brother's death. Flaubert was absent, being laid up with a broken leg and, by Daudet's account, shaking the air of Normandy with formidable Carthaginian oaths. But his "faithful," along with the publisher Charpentier, were all there.

And of course Turgenev was seen in the distinguished crowd that packed Victor Hugo's large salon, presided over by the David bust. The aged dean of French letters, a little deaf, somewhat absent-minded and withdrawn, throned it at the head of the dining table, his neck swathed in a white foulard scarf, his arms folded over his chest, his body buttoned into a frock coat and leaning back slightly. Edmond de Goncourt describes his manner of toying with and caressing the words he spoke in a slow, rather flat voice, his eyes half closed, his face, with the dark warmth of a Rembrandt syndic, "playing dead" but crossed by strange feline expressions. And hovering about was his friend, Mme. Drouet, the quondam Juliette of the Gaieté, now a white-haired old lady. Turgenev, who liked to regale his friends at home with anecdotes about the French, took away from these visits more than one to illustrate the demigod's ignorance and vanity. One of them has Hugo say: "What is Goethe? What did he write? Nothing but *Wallenstein*." "But, maître!" Turgenev remonstrates, "*Wallenstein* was written by Schiller." "Yes, yes," the master grumbles, "it makes no difference, he might have written it." According to another story, when an admirer prophesies that some day not a Paris street but the city itself will be proud to bear the name of the great poet, Hugo remarks wistfully: "*Ca viendra, mon cher, ça viendra.*"

Generally speaking, Turgenev had only sneers for French verse. In 1873 he recommended Leconte de Lisle to Fet with the comment: "Although a Frenchman, he's a true poet."

The members of the little group with which Turgenev fell in, occasionally dined together at the home of one or another, but more often at some café. Gautier died too soon after Turgenev's settlement in Paris for the novelist to see much of him, but he appeared at least once at these restaurant gatherings, and so did Mère Sand, whom Edmond de Goncourt ungallantly described as getting more and more mummified. In 1874, at a dinner at Café Riche, it was decided to hold these refections once a month. They came to be known as "the dinners of the Five"—Turgenev, Flaubert, Edmond de Goncourt, Zola, and Daudet—or "the dinners of the hooted authors." Each of the four Frenchmen laid claim to the title by reason of a recent failure, and Turgenev assured them that he was hooted at home, a statement which they accepted on faith, since they had too far to travel to verify it. For misprized writers, they were very exclusive, refusing, for example, to admit to their circle Emile de Girardin, because he was only a journalist.

The Five were hard to suit and often changed restaurants, going from Café Riche to Adolphe and Pellé, behind the Opera, or to the tavern on the corner of rue Favart, known for its bouillabaisse, or to Voisin, whose cellar "met all requirements and conciliated all appetites," as Daudet put it. Every one of the diners was something of a gourmet with strong preferences in food as in literature. Flaubert had to have Normandy cheese and Rouen duck *à l'estouffade;* Turgenev demanded caviar. On one occasion Zola, flush with money, ordered a dinner consisting of green rye soup, Lapland reindeer tongues, gray mullet *à la provençale,* and guinea fowl with truffles. The general custom was to start at seven in the evening and remain at table till two in the morning. Flaubert, vest unbuttoned, presided with Rabelaisian verve. Zola dined in shirt sleeves, Turgenev reclined on a sofa.

The conversation was even more important to the company than the food. The Goncourt Journals evoke the atmosphere of these symposia. The Muscovite's childlike voice would begin to charm his companions as soon as the soup was on the table. They talked shop, they gossiped, they reminisced. The inaugural dinner opened with a dissertation on the difference between constipated and diarrhetic writers, and from there the talk drifted to the mechanism of the French language. It was likely to drift to almost any topic. Turgenev must have relished Edmond de Goncourt's observation that every revolution is simply a change of residence, with the same ambitions, corruptions and villainies furnishing the new lodging

—"and all involving much breakage and expense." Conversation touched upon things weighty and trivial, personalities and ideas, contemporaries and classics. Once, the Goncourts report, Turgenev, "his lips wet with desire," cried that he would give anything for *The Wine Flask,* the lost comedy of that old drunkard Cratinus, which won the Athenian prize over Aristophanes' *Clouds.* As they grew more expansive, Zola would complain of his poverty and Daudet strike up a Provençal song. Each brought a *mélange* of impressions and opinions to share with the others. At one of the last dinners conviviality was broken by moans and laments over the wretched literary trade, *"notre chien de métier."*

There were two subjects of which the company never tired: love and death. The cynicism with which these Parisians discoursed on the major passion must have been almost as disconcerting to Turgenev as it was to that other stranger within their gates, Henry James. They told salacious stories which it was hard for him to match, although, being a sociable sort, he did his best, and they alluded casually to perversities which merely puzzled him. They must have listened with amusement to his declaration that the eyes of the first woman he had ever loved seemed to him discarnate. And he must have taken in with embarrassed bewilderment Flaubert's stories of his amorous experiences in Egypt.

When Flaubert and Goncourt maintained that love had no bearing on a writer's work, he simply let his arms drop. Nothing, he confessed, could take the place of women for him. Love alone could produce that exquisite unfolding of the whole being which so stimulates the artist. Zola observing that love had no specific qualities to distinguish it from other emotions, Turgenev insisted that it had a color peculiarly its own, that it produced an effect unlike the effect of any other feeling. But then, Flaubert, Goncourt and Zola all admitted that they had never been seriously in love. He himself approached a woman with respect, with agitation, with surprise at the happiness which the encounter gave him. These men seemed to know only physical sensations. When the talk was of death Turgenev was on firmer ground. A dinner would begin gaily enough, and end in a minor key. On one of these occasions he impressed the company with a nightmare he had

had, in which he had identified a brown stain on the wall in front of his bed with death itself. Sooner or later the "black subject" was bound to crop up. After Flaubert's death the dinners grew rare. A vacant chair was left for the deceased.

Turgenev's friendship for these men was not merely a matter of intellectual traffic and social courtesies. He begged off when Guy de Maupassant wanted to begin a series of literary appreciations with an essay on him. He had a horror, he pleaded, of *réclame amicale*. But he himself indulged in friendly puffery without stint. He taxed himself to promote his friends' interests. He tried to introduce them to foreign audiences, using his connections on the Continent and in England to that end. He wrote, or at least promised to write, prefaces; he revised; he translated. Occasionally he advanced money to the author on expected sales. He worked for the French, as he worked for the Germans, as he worked for his own countrymen. In his last decade he turned himself into a kind of international literary agent, an earnest, eager, not always efficient go-between, giving his services freely and sometimes to his own cost. He did this partly because of his love for literature, partly out of pure generosity—there was not a spark of jealousy in him—partly out of his inability to refuse anyone anything.

He confessed to a Russian publisher that his encomiums were often due to an amiable weakness. They finally agreed that his recommendations should be disregarded unless he volunteered to read proof. There was not a little of vicarious fatherly affection in Turgenev's treatment of struggling authors, as in his anxious running about and fussing over the scores of his young compatriots who presented themselves to him in Paris for assistance in one way or another.

Zola especially was in his debt—Zola, whom, according to Edmond de Goncourt, he treated with "paternal irony." Turgenev took him under his wing in the days when, by his own account, he was starving. He placed Zola's novels with Russian publishers; indeed, *La Faute de l'Abbé Mouret* made its first appearance in a Russian translation. He arranged to have him contribute to Petersburg reviews, and even told him what to write about. He passed on his complaints to the editor. He passed on the editor's explanations. He remitted payments. One of Zola's ways of requiting these attentions was to give a reading at a matinée which Turgenev arranged for the benefit of needy Russian students. The wild man, whom Turgenev described as something like "an intelligent, somewhat awkward and baggy Parisian working man," was altogether *comme il faut,* even to white gloves, and having stayed awake three nights over the worry of this, his first public appearance, was unable for a scandalous length of time to utter a syllable.

Turgenev also took steps to interest Russian publishers in the works of the Goncourts and Taine, and particularly of young Maupassant, the flower of Flaubert's little flock. When his efforts to get a translation of *Une Vie* published in Russia —a translation at which he personally had worked—proved vain, he paid the author a thousand francs out of his own pocket: "To present four hundred rubles to a man of talent, who is, moreover, my friend—my means permit that." As for Flaubert himself, Turgenev could not do too much for him. He translated "La Légende de St. Julien l'Hospitalier" and "Hérodias," lavishing on them all his skill as a stylist, and flattering himself that Russian had not come off so badly in this pitting of his native tongue against the French. He refused to take any payment for his pains, turning over all the proceeds to the author who was then in straitened circumstances. He had also arranged for the translation of *La Tentation de Saint-Antoine,* but the censorship barred it. He offered to send copies of the book to competent critics in England, and trumpeted the author's praises to friends in Germany.

Not that he was whole-heartedly in sympathy with the work of his French confrères, Flaubert excepted. He had the highest respect for "the gay, fresh, and healthy" talent of Guy de Maupassant, and he did not deny that the others were gifted: he recognized the originality of the Goncourts, the charm of Daudet, the solidity of Zola. He appreciated their understanding of their craft. If only their concentration upon their work had not blunted their sense of life and its values! Everything these arrant *littérateurs* handled turned to literature, as everything Midas touched turned to gold, and in both cases the gift was a curse. The works of the Goncourts and Zola stank of literature, he observed to Saltykov.

He found Zola's method essentially "vicious." On looking into *L'Assomoir* in 1876, when the novel was appearing serially, he wrote to Flaubert that it showed talent, but—"this strictly *entre nous*—it was heavy and made too much of the chamber pot." He told Henry James in a letter that the novel was not immoral, but "devilishly filthy," adding that if he were a cartoonist for *Punch,* he would draw Queen Victoria reading *L'Assomoir.* Having beer with George Moore at the Elysée Montmartre one rainy evening, he had a good word to say for the book, but added that the author's desire to tell what the heroine "felt rather than what she thought" spoiled the work. "What difference does it make to me," he asked, "if she perspires in the middle of the back or under the arms?" Zola's emphasis upon the animal processes of existence, his obscenity, his scientific pretensions, were a weariness and an irritation to Turgenev. He confessed that *Nana* bored him. He was afraid that Zola had never read Shakespeare. His own instincts were all in the direction of an art speaking with the tongues of men and of angels in the accents of reason and beauty.

He broke bread with these men, he sat at their firesides, he wrote them cordial letters, he exerted himself in their behalf, but now and then the malicious youth whose sharp tongue had delighted Belinsky cropped out in this sexagenarian, and he allowed himself unkind observations on his foreign friends. Even his most ill-natured remarks were often the result of a good-natured weakness, and he would have been scandalized by his own words had he heard them repeated. He made his comments before those who were apt to savor them—Russians intensely jealous of the strangers who had annexed their Turgenev. His malice occasionally enlivened the gatherings of the Five. Sitting at dinner with them one night, he said of one of their prominent colleagues: "The comparison is not noble, but allow me, gentlemen, to liken Taine to a hound I once owned. He searched, he pointed, he went through all the motions of a hunting dog in the most admirable fashion, but I was forced to sell him: he had no nose." Turgenev was on friendly terms with the critic and indeed recommended one of his books for translation into Russian. The French must have appreciated another remark of his to the effect that, aside from music, the Germans had no feeling for art. Apparently he found it hard to refrain from telling people what he thought they would like to hear.

Four years afer Turgenev's death Isaac Pavlovsky, a young Russian émigré living in Paris, published his reminiscences of the novelist in which he attributed to the deceased some very uncomplimentary remarks about his French friends. Thus, Turgenev was said to have spoken of Daudet as a nonentity, a mere imitator of Dickens, a very wily and very practical southerner, a disingenuous *bon enfant*. The book made not a little stir. Daudet expressed in print his pained surprise at his late friend's duplicity. Edmond de Goncourt made an entry in his journal to the effect that, after all, Turgenev's work lacked the primitive vigor of his race, and that his characters seemed to have been drawn by a Russian who had ended his days at the court of Louis XIV. He was, when all was said, a foreigner, Goncourt explained, and so, having no key to the subtleties of Parisian irony, gave vent to the irritation he could not help feeling. Daudet went farther and called in question the Muscovite's grasp of the genius of the French language, though Taine is said to have likened Turgenev's French to that spoken in the eighteenth-century Paris salons.

Indeed, at bottom, Turgenev was a stranger, though in a familiar land. His point of view was fundamentally Russian, and his affectionate respect for the West was that of an outsider, naturally distrustful, curious, amused, and a shade censorious. He was of course aware that his French colleagues held him in high regard, except for such a soured, venomous spirit as Huysmans, who dismissed him as "a tap of tepid water," and "the silliest of men." Daudet placed him on an "ivory throne" in his private heaven, and Edmond de Goncourt did reverence to his "immense and cosmopolitan knowledge." But admiration centered rather about his person than around his work. He was to them the lovable barbarian, the seductive Slav, the huge snow-man with the feline smile, the colossus with eyebrows of tow, the titan of the North, the silver-haired giant with the head of the Heavenly Father and the timid gestures of a child. The very homage they paid him betrayed their feeling that here was a prodigy, a curiosity, an alien—attractive and congenial enough, but *au fond* not one of their own.

True, being men of penetration, they grasped some of the essentials of his character. Flaubert spoke of him as an *homme mené,* a man in leading-strings. And Daudet perfectly understood, though somewhat late in the day, that Turgenev was a fretted spirit, a man dissatisfied, especially with himself; a man who had never conducted his life as he wished. The Russian, Daudet said, was like one who is badly bedded and who turns about and about restlessly in the twisted folds of his sheets.

In his last years the dissimilarity between the Russians and the West Europeans, particularly the French, was constantly in Turgenev's mind. He developed a theory the gist of which was that each race has its own morality. Indeed, this was to be embodied in the last big work which he planned. He spoke to several of his friends about it, and their various accounts all point to the conclusion that his theme was the gulf between the Russian and the Westerner, more particularly, the contrast between the Russian revolutionist's search for a millennial ideal and the French socialist's pursuit of narrow, class interests. Turgenev's English friend and translator, W. R. S. Ralston, who had hoped to stay with him at Spasskoye in the summer of 1882 and to translate, under his supervision, the novel as it came from his pen, thus sums up the plot:

A Russian girl who has accepted the ideas held by the Nihilists, leaves her native country and settles in Paris. There she meets and eventually marries a young French socialist. For some time all goes well in the household, which is united by a common hatred of all laws and ceremonies. But at length the young wife meets and has much confidential talk with one of her own countrymen, who tells her about all that the Russian socialists are thinking and saying and doing in the land of her birth. She recognizes to her horror that the ends and aims, the aspirations and yearnings of the Russian revolutionists are widely different from those of the French and German socialists, and that a great abyss divides her, so far as her thoughts and feelings are concerned, from the husband with whom she used to fancy herself entirely in accord.

In his reminiscences Pavlovsky asserted that the tale had actually been written and expressed the opinion that some day the manuscript would be found (it has not come to light). His version of the plot differs somewhat from Ralston's and runs as follows. A cultivated young Russian of "very advanced views" makes the acquaintance in Paris of a compatriot who is married to a noted French radical whose attitude toward marriage is typically French. He cannot conceive of his wife enjoying the liberties to which a Russian woman is accustomed. Gradually the two become estranged. The woman comes to see her husband as a narrow-minded person incapable of living up to her ideals. He turns jealous without cause and behaves in an ugly fashion. It all ends by the wife falling in love with her compatriot.

According to another informant, one of the leading characters of the novel was to be a Russian who seeks salvation in a religious variety of socialism. He was apparently modeled on Nikolay Chaikovsky, a former student who had given up the cause of revolution to join a newly-founded religious sect that preached non-resistance to evil and the communism of the primitive Church. He and his wife spent some three years in the United States, first in a Kansas communist settlement and then in a New York Shaker community. He was befriended by Turgenev when he returned to Europe in 1879 and stayed in the vicinity of Paris.* The novelist described him as "the (more or less) notable founder of a new religion in America."

It was almost as though in old age, when many undergo religious conversion, Turgenev grazed the danger of succumbing to what he had long rejected: Slavophil nationalism. The French, he is reported to have asserted, had exhausted their spiritual energy and reached a level of dead uniformity of tastes and aspirations, moral and legal concepts and ideals; the Russians, with their variety of cultural types, were in the growing stage, spiritually on the move, seeking new ways of thinking and living. A Frenchman, even if he was a freethinker, observed the forms of faith; ritualism was alien to the Russian. Outwardly a materialist, he was at heart an idealist with an indestructible belief in human perfectibility.

---

* Chaikovsky returned to Russia in 1907, and eventually headed the anti-Soviet Government of Northern Russia. With its collapse in 1919, he left Archangel for Paris and died, an exile, in 1926.

The French were so avid to express themselves beautifully that, unlike the Russians, they did not think things through to the end. Such observations might better have fallen from the lips of a Herzen.

At the dinners of the Five, too, Turgenev touched now and then on the contrast between the two nations. The Latins, he said, were *hommes de la loi,* in whose veins ran the milk of the Roman she-wolf, sticklers for the conventions, conformers to a code, martyrs to an artificial sense of honor. The Russians, on the contrary, though ruthlessly autocratized, were *hommes de l'humanité,* possessed of a warmer social consciousness, irreverent toward man-made rules, rooting for absolutes, unafraid of the bare, the crude, the simple. They were liars because for centuries they had been slaves, but they loved reality and truth.

35

"AU REVOIR IN AMERICA!"

Germany was Turgenev's second fatherland. France came to be his adoptive if somewhat uncongenial home at which he grumbled with filial freedom. In England he was always a visitor. He had a sound knowledge of English literature, both old and new: Shakespeare, who, he said, must be studied, like nature herself, by everyone, he had by heart; Burns he wanted to introduce to his compatriots; he prized Swinburne; Dickens delighted him immeasurably. He considered the English political system a model one and would gladly have seen Russia follow it. He loved grouse shooting in Cambridgeshire sufficiently to cross the Channel for it several times. On one of these occasions George Eliot, who, according to her husband, preferred Turgenev's society above that of any other literary man she knew, made a special trip to Six Mile Bottom to see him.

He seems not to have met Dickens, although the Viardots were acquainted with him, but attended three of his readings in Paris in 1863, and was reduced to what he called "the ecstacies of a calf." He wrote in his reminiscences that Dickens combined "in one person several first-rate actors who make you laugh and cry in turn." Carlyle had conveyed the same impression when he described Dickens' readings as "a whole tragic, comic, heroic theatre visible performing under one hat." Turgenev had some commerce with this fellow enthusiast, with whom he appears to have been in serious disagreement on more controversial subjects. He was received at the homes of men like Dante Gabriel Rossetti, Ford Madox Brown, the Pre-Raphaelite painter, and William Spottiswoode the mathematician, who in his youth had traveled in Russia. He met Tennyson, and though he did not feel completely at home in the poet's tongue and used a quaint bookish turn of speech absent from his ready French and German, he held his own happily in the conversation. Yet his personal connections with the British remained tenuous. He described to Fet the impressions he carried away from his visit in 1878 in these terms: "Marvelous, queer, grandiose, stupid, all in one, but chiefly something wholly alien to us."

The one Englishman with whom he was on terms of close acquaintance was his translator, W. R. S. Ralston. He seems to have been the only one of Turgenev's foreign friends who visited him at Spasskoye. This was in the summer of 1870. Ralston had an inquisitive, scholarly turn of mind. On being shown about the village and taken into the peasant cottages, he asked about the names and uses of the objects he saw there and carefully wrote the information down in the notebook he carried around with him. After Ralston's departure Turgenev received a deputation of peasants who wanted to know when they were to go to England. They had conceived the notion that the Englishman had taken an inventory with a view to transporting them and their household goods to his own country. It took Turgenev a long time, by his own account, to disabuse them of this idea. He did not allow his guest to depart without arranging in his honor a village fête. Fet, responding to a rhymed invitation, was also present, and left a description of the festival, which appears to have ended in a scarcely bucolic fashion. The tipsy peasants kept clamoring for more vodka, and when colored ribbons were distributed among the women, the crowd became so hilarious that Turgenev, his neighbor, and the amazed Englishman had to run for safety to the balcony of the manor house.

Ralston may have conceived the idea of having Oxford University confer an honorary degree on Turgenev. Early in 1874 the latter wrote to his translator: "I would be very much flattered to have a degree conferred upon me by the illustrious University of Oxford, but is it not too ambitious, and would not the public ask: Who is this man, and wherefore this honor?" The degree was conferred five years later. On June 14, 1879, Turgenev was writing to Stasulevich: "Miracles will happen. Tomorrow I am going to Oxford, for the University there decided to confer upon me the degree of . . . Doctor of Common Law." It was thus that he misinterpreted the initials D.C.L. "The honor," he concluded, "is as great as it is unexpected." He must have forgotten the earlier mention of the matter; he had a bad memory for such marks of esteem as were shown him.

He had been made much of at Oxford the previous year, when he was the guest of Max Müller. The scholar was rather doubtful as to whether it was proper for him as a Regius Professor to entertain a man who had publicly shown disrespect to her Majesty the Queen. In the summer of 1876, when the papers were full of the Bulgarian atrocities, Turgenev, spending a sleepless night on the train between Moscow and Petersburg, composed a fantasy in verse which held up to scorn Queen Victoria's pro-Turkish policy. The ladies at Windsor are playing the then fashionable game of croquet under the eyes of the queen, who is horrified to see the balls turn into bloodied heads. Retiring to her castle, she finds the hem of her gown soaked in gore, and implores the rivers of England to clean it, only to be told by the poet that no waters will wash out the stain of that innocent blood. "Croquet at Windsor," as he called this execrable piece, though barred by the censorship, was widely circulated, being recited even at the parties of the heir apparent, and was translated into German, French, and English. Not, be it noted, that Turgenev was swept off his feet by the wave of patriotism which seized the country on the eve of the Russo-Turkish conflict. Indeed, deeply as he felt for the Bulgars, he was one of the few people who were out of sympathy with the war. He had little feeling of racial solidarity with the other Slavs, and did not consider Islam inferior to Christianity.

When he came to Oxford to get his degree, feeling against Russia was still running high in England, and he feared that there might be some unfriendly demonstration against him as a Russian. But nothing untoward occurred. James Bryce, Regius Professor of Civil Law, who introduced Turgenev to the Vice-Chancellor of the University, seated on a velvet armchair, is said by *The Oxford Journal* to have spoken of "Mr. I. Turgenev's wonderful genius which was shown in his romances, and his description of Russian life, which had led to the emancipation of the serfs." At the same time a like honor was conferred upon John Ruskin, Sir Frederick Leighton, the ambassador at St. Petersburg, and the Governor of Fiji.

Turgenev's broad shoulders carried the gorgeous gown with dignity, but he could not help a private chuckle at the notion that he was now a Doctor of Law—he was a little hazy as to whether it was common or natural, and as a matter of fact it was civil law—he who was unable to transact the simplest ordinary business. "As a sign of special regard, the professors made me a present of my cap and gown," he wrote to a Russian journalist, concluding a description of the ceremony, "and now, if I should have to play in a charade, I can show off my doctoral attire." Two months later the French Government similarly honored him by making him an Officer of Public Instruction. "It appears," he wrote, in thanking Mme. Commanville, Flaubert's niece, for her congratulations, "that this gives one the right to wear a violet ribbon—violet, mind you, not red. I'll pin it on the doctoral gown I got at Oxford, which is a very bright red; the two colors will match perfectly."

Turgenev's interest in the Anglo-Saxon world was not confined to England. "I have a great sympathy for all that is American," he wrote, in English, to Henry James on August 4, 1874, "and a great desire to see your country. I ought to have indulged it earlier in life—I am falling in the 'sere and yellow leaf'—and that is not the best time for traveling. Still I do not altogether abandon the idea." It was probably a polite exaggeration when he told an American visitor in Paris that it was an *idée fixe* with him to visit the United States and see the great republic for himself, but the New World did touch his imagination. From the end of the sixties on, not a few Russians found an extraordinary attraction in American life and institutions, and a handful crossed the Atlantic with the notion of settling in the States, there to lead the good life which political restrictions made impossible at home. These so-called "Americans" planned to live on the land, work with their hands, and eschew the evils of private property. Turgenev's interest in the country was of a different order. What he admired was the industrial activities of the practical-minded citizenry and their democratic institutions which seemed to him the best insurance of the liberty of the individual. To such Americans as came to pay their respects to him in Paris—by the time he had settled there his name was beginning to be familiar to readers in Boston and New York—he was the friendliest of hosts. One of these visitors was Hjalmar H. Boyesen, later Professor of Germanic Languages and Literatures at Columbia University. During the summer of 1873 he came several times to the apartment on rue de Douai, in a spirit of awe and admiration, and set down his talks with Turgenev in some detail.

America was a great topic with them. The youthful guest, referring to Dickens' first trip to Yankee-Doodeldom, observed that if Turgenev carried out his intention of going there, he might react to the States in the same adverse way. Where there was freedom of thought and speech, Turgenev replied, abuses were bound to appear on the surface and it was easy to discover them, but his own prejudice was all in America's favor. He went on to mention a talk he had had with Carlyle and how the Scot had thundered against democracy and expressed "very unreserved . . . sympathy with Russia and her emperor." It was wearisome, Carlyle had said, to see how in a country like Great Britain "every petty individual could thrust forth his head like a frog and quack away at his contemptible sentiment as long as anybody had a mind to listen to him." Turgenev had wished that Carlyle might spend a month or two in one of the interior provinces of Russia. Why, the very value of American institutions was the wide scope they offered to "individual development."

Ibsen's name was mentioned in the course of this conversation and Boyesen observed that it was because of his pessimism that the playwright was no democrat: a true democrat "must have perfect faith in his kind." Lacking that faith, Ibsen could say that he would lose his self-respect if he were to find himself with the crowd in any vital matter. "I should say," countered Turgenev, "that there is always the possibility that the minority may be in the right. But that is an exception rather than the rule."

Turgenev surprised Boyesen by his familiarity with American literature, of which they had much to say to each other. He was ready to recognize Longfellow's merit as a poet, but "failed to discover the distinctly American character of his writings." Hawthorne he considered "the first literary representative of the New World." *The Scarlet Letter* and *Twice-told Tales* had the flavor of the soil and spoke of a new civilization. He had compliments for James Russell Lowell, whom he had recently met, and his guest had to mention Howells but once, to find on his next visit a copy of *Venetian Life* lying on Turgenev's desk. Turgenev touched on Bret Harte, too, a writer of sterling qualities whom, he feared, prosperity had spoilt. And he spoke with warmth of Walt Whitman; there was good grain to be found in all that chaff, he said. He seems to have discovered the poet the previous year. Having promised to send a short piece to *The Week* (*Nedelya*), and having nothing on hand, he decided to give the editor, as he wrote to Annenkov, "several translations of lyrical poems by the remarkable American poet, Walt Whitman (have you heard of him?), with a little introduction. You cannot imagine anything more striking." Annenkov became interested and wanted to see the material, but illness interfered, the translations were "stranded on a sandbank," and in the end nothing came of the project.

About his own work Turgenev spoke with his usual expansiveness. "I never try to improve on life"; he said, "I merely try to see and understand it. . . . Every line I have written has been inspired by something that has actually happened to me or come within my observation." Of course, he seldom found "a pure type"; his protagonists were like composite photographs. And how they dogged him, until he had them in hand! If he was reading, they would whisper their opinions into his ear; if he was promenading, they would criticize every one he met and all he saw and heard. He lacked, as he said Boyesen must have noticed, a "philosophical mind." He saw, and drew conclusions from what he saw. Abstractions suggested themselves to him as concrete pictures; when he could reduce his idea to such a picture, he felt himself master of it. These images became the essence of reality.

"Europe, for instance," he told his visitor, "I often think of as a large, dimly lighted temple, richly and magnificently decorated, but with the dusk hovering beneath its arched ceilings. America presents itself to my thoughts as a vast fertile prairie, at first sight somewhat barren, but with a glorious dawn breaking on its horizon."

"Au revoir in America!" were the words with which he speeded his parting guest on his way home. Turgenev never got to America. He had to content himself with the stray visitors from the United States who waited upon him in Paris. When Emerson was in the French capital they were engaged to dine together, but gout intervened. In 1878 he met the abolitionist, Thomas Wentworth Higginson, who was a delegate to the International Literary Congress, over which Turgenev presided with much embarrassment. He spoke warmly to him of his compatriots, naming Emma Lazarus, with whom he had had some correspondence, in addition to Boyesen. Mr. Higginson was charmed by this genial Russian, who "united the fine benignant head of Longfellow with the figure of Thackeray" and whose "winning sweetness of manner . . . surpassed even that of Longfellow." He was disappointed, on looking for a photograph of Turgenev in the Paris shops, to discover that "his name proved totally unfamiliar." These pilgrims from beyond the ocean were apt to regard him with a reverence which must have struck him as oddly unlike the treatment he was used to at home.

Another of his American devotees was Henry Holt. Having published an English translation of several of his works, he not only wrote a very friendly letter to his Russian author, but sent him a check. Turgenev, who had never received or expected to receive anything tangible for translations of his work, was overwhelmed. He wrote to Ralston forthwith, asking him to translate a short piece of his ("Living Relics") which he wished to send to "this phoenix of an editor," together with his photograph, "as a token and a proof of gratitude." America, he added, was "decidedly the land of eccentricities." Of the letter "with the included check" he wrote to Mr. Holt: "Seldom or never has anything during all my literary career given me such unmitigated pleasure. The deep sympathy I always felt for America and the Americans has been accrued by it; and the appreciation of your countrymen, testified by your amiable letter, makes me proud and happy. . . ."

This interchange occurred in the winter of 1874. Five years later Mr. Holt was spending the summer in Paris, and Turgenev invited him to his apartment. The publisher's reminiscences give a brief account of that meeting, with Turgenev leaning over the rail of the circular staircase to greet the young friend from the States, who felt, looking up at that "full-bearded, strong, kind face," as though he were "ascending to a prophet." The one remark the American cherished was Turgenev's "I am no puritan."

The publisher was also received at Bougival and made very much at home there. "He spoke English," Mr. Holt remarks, "better than I did." After a session with the samovar, they went into the novelist's bedroom, the windows of which gave on a fine view. His visitor commenting on the landscape, Turgenev replied that it made no impression on him. The visitor expostulated: didn't every one of the great scenes in his novels have an appropriate natural background? "Well," he said, "I hadn't realized it. So far as I know myself, if all being were arranged in an orderly progression from inanimate matter up to the highest thought and feeling, my interest would begin where conscious life begins."

There was an American with whom Turgenev's contacts were less casual than passing acquaintance—an apprentice to the craft, Henry James. When he came to Paris in 1875 it may have been chiefly to meet the Russian novelist, of whom he had written a glowing appreciation the previous year. He presented himself to the master on November 22 at the latter's apartment on rue de Douai. Here, he quickly came to feel, was no less than the platonic pattern of the writer. In his diary he described Turgenev as "the most delightful and lovable of men." Writing to his aunt, Catherine Walsh, on December 3, 1875, he said of the novelist: "I took an unprecedented fancy to him, and his whole aspect and temperament are of a larger and manlier kind than I have ever yet encountered in a scribbler."

A rather different note is sounded in his letter to his father written on December 20, 1875, less than a month after he met Turgenev: ". . . the poor man is a slave—the slave of Mme. Viardot. She has made him her property, is excessively jealous, keeps him to herself, etc. She, her husband and her children (of one of whom Turgenev is supposed to be papa) keep him as a sort of *vache à lait,* use him, spend his money, etc. Such is the tale, and I am told his friends greatly deplore his situation, and it is certainly an odd one all round. Mme. Viardot is old and ugly, but, I believe, very agreeable. Tourgueneff strikes me as a man with something pressing upon him and making him unhappy more than he knows."

On February 3, 1876 he was writing to Howells: "Yes, I see a good deal of Tourguéneff and am excellent friends with him. . . . He is everything that one could desire—robust, sympathetic, modest, simple, intelligent, profound, naïf, in fine, angelic."

The young man did not particularly impress the paragon. His graciousness had a touch of condescension. In a letter to Ralston of January 22, 1877, Turgenev urged his translator to make friends with James, whom he described as "a very amiable, sensible and gifted man, with a tendency towards *tristesse,* which will not frighten you." Five years later, again writing to Ralston, he said that he had had a visit from James, who was "as amiable as ever, but has grown very fat." Turgenev found that some of James's pages were written *de main de maître,* but the American was probably justified in fearing that his fiction struck the Russian as being "not quite meat for men," overdecorated (*tarabiscoté*), "having on the surface too many little flowers and knots of ribbon."

More than once he visited Turgenev in his "little green sitting room" on rue de Douai. What he noted here particularly was the divan, so huge that smaller persons than his host "had to lie upon it rather than sit," and a few choice specimens of French painting, notably a fine Rousseau. He attended several of the Viardots' Sundays and found them "rather dingy." On April 11, 1876, he wrote to his father: "It is both strange and sweet to see poor Tourguéneff acting charades of the most extravagant descriptions, dressed in old shawls and masks, going on all fours, etc." There were also visits to that "very pretty domain," Bougival. Of a Sunday afternoon they would meet as well at Flaubert's, where, James says, "Turgenev's beautiful faculty of talk showed at its best." It clarified for the younger man his view of the "most approachable, most practicable, least unsafe man of genius," it was his fortune to meet. "Our Anglo-Saxon, Protestant, moralistic, conventional standards were far away from him," he was to observe later. But at the time in that company he could not help feeling that the Russian, like himself, was somewhat distressed by the so differently oriented standards of the French school as regards the art that all of them were practicing. The best memories, perhaps, were of the Parisian *déjeuners* in cafés, where the two men would sit talking from noon till late dusk. At least once they lunched at Bignou's, which, according to a restaurant guide, must not be entered except with the intention of "dining seriously." At one of these repasts, James recalled, "Turgenev talked almost exclusively about Russia, the Nihilists, the remarkable figures that came to light among them, the curious visits he received, the dark prospects of his native land."

His eulogy of Turgenev is not free from such hollow phrases as "Slav genius," "Slav imagination," "Slav languor." There are other indications that in writing about his idol he spun things out of his reverent fancy. Yet he showed a penetrating insight into Turgenev's character and work. "To describe him in the fewest terms," James wrote shrewdly even before they met, "he is a storyteller who has taken notes. . . . If we are not mistaken, he notes down an idiosyncrasy of character, a fragment of talk, an attitude, a feature, a gesture, and keeps it, if need be, for twenty years, till just the moment for using it comes." And again: "He has no recognition of unembodied ideas; an idea, with him, is such and such an individual, with such and such a nose and chin, such and such a hat and waistcoat, bearing the same relation to it as the look of a printed word does to its meaning." This is just what Turgenev said of himself. Moreover, like Flaubert and the other "grandsons of Balzac," the Russian was a votary of realism. But James seems to have felt that although he was an artist who looked at life steadily, he could not help gagging when he thought of swallowing it whole. He was inclined to leave the difficult, tawdry, sordid aspects of things out of the picture. James comprehended, too, Turgenev's attitude towards his distant, repellent, seductive native land.

The two writers had much in common. Turgenev was in

his grave when James was writing to Stevenson: "I want to leave a multitude of pictures of my time—so that the number may constitute a total having a certain value as observation and testimony." This had been Turgenev's intention. Further, they shared the tendency to *tristesse* which the Russian had found in the American. James, like Turgenev, was, in the phrase of Edmund Gosse, "essentially a homeless man." Both felt that the native scene was fading from them, and that, as James has it, they "could trust [it] for effect no longer." Both had seen themselves, in the home newspapers, lampooned as renegades. But Turgenev's expatriation came too late in life to orphan his work. He did not "attempt to project himself into an atmosphere" in which he had no "transmitted and inherited property," to use James's words. He might for a time hang up his harp on a willow tree in a strange land, but he did not forget Jerusalem, and his right hand never forgot its cunning.

36

THE RETURN

OF THE NATIVE

The lesson learned from the failure of *Virgin Soil,* Turgenev wrote to his brother, would not be lost on him: his literary career had come to its final end; his name would never again appear on any original work. "Diderot," he observed, "said somewhere that 'before death one attends one's own funeral several times'; so I too have been reduced to walking behind my literary coffin. I will find some other occupation for myself, and then the last of old age will come, and the daily petty cares connected with the preservation of life will absorb all other interests." Even before his entire novel appeared in print he had begun the avowals of abdication which came in the wake of each of his books. He had done his bell-ringing, and it was time for him to climb down from the belfry. "Enough!" In the spring of 1877 he was getting ready for a trip to Russia. "I foresee that I shall not stay long in Petersburg," he was writing on May 27. "There everything smells to me of literature; and I have conceived a sufficient disgust for it lately." He had no desire to write. It seems strange for him to think that he had once been a man of letters.

While he was thus protesting, two new stories appeared over his name, one of which, "The Story of Father Alexey," was written after *Virgin Soil.* Thereafter he held his peace for nearly four years. When he did take up his pen again, it was not to resume the chronicling of his times. Out of the cedar chests of memory he drew the materials for two character sketches, "Old Portraits" (1881) and "A Reckless Character" (1882). The first belongs with the best of his pages. It is a sober evocation of the days when serfdom was in flower. While conveying all the charm of the patriarchal past, the story refuses to gloss over its horrors. Its excellence is in sharp contrast with the shoddiness of another piece published the same year, "A Song of Triumphant Love," which is a clumsy fantasy described by the author as an "Italian pasticcio." The year before his death he attempted a Poesque theme in the story "Clara Milich," and reluctantly handed to his avid publisher a sheaf of papers, dating from the years 1877–1882, which he called "Senilia." These sheets, varying in size and color, corresponded, he explained, to the cartoons an artist sketches for a large canvas, and he was surrendering them as a sign that he had given up all thought of writing, and with some idea of posthumous publication. He was, however, persuaded to allow fifty-one of them to appear at once, refusing payment for them.

The manuscript of "Senilia" included a short sketch entitled "The Threshold," but at the last moment, after it had already been set up, the author withdrew it. The piece is about a Russian girl who stands on a threshold beyond which lies a darkness that promises, as she well knows, only an anonymous martyrdom, lonely and perhaps futile. Crossing that threshold, she is hailed by two voices, one crying "Fool!", the other: "Saint!" The sketch, dated May, 1878, was apparently inspired by the trial of Vera Zasulich, who fired a shot at the Petersburg chief of police in January of that year. It was first printed secretly by The People's Will, appended to a leaflet which these revolutionists distributed on the day of Turgenev's funeral. Since the date of its composition was not given, the impression arose that it had been written in memory of Sophia Perovskaya, the young woman who paid with her life for her part in the assassination of Alexander II. "The Threshold" was published openly in 1905; thirty more "poems in prose" appeared in Paris in 1930.

The title bestowed on the collection by the editor of *The Messenger of Europe,* in which they appeared (issue of December, 1882), is not a happy one. Most of the pieces lack the pitch and pattern of poetry. The personal, lyrical quality which some of them possess is generally blighted by a weakness for the allegorical and the sententious. A few read like leaves from a novelist's notebook, but even those, though not lacking in excellent touches, wear gratuitous moral tags.

Several of them are transcriptions of actual experiences. Such a one is the piece about an evening party at which the guests' faces are suddenly transformed into death's-heads. Turgenev told a friend that he had suffered from a similar hallucination for months.

He described these anecdotes and character sketches, these parables and maxims, day-dreams and nightmares, as "the last groans of an old man." And while not all of them answer to this description, many of them revolve about such themes as the inevitability and horror of extinction, nature's indifference to human values and individual lives, the fragile immortality bestowed by art, the bitterness of a homeless old age, nostalgia for lost youth, liberty at the mercy of necessity and force. The wisdom of renunciation and self-forgetfulness, the enigma of Russia, the abyss between her masses and her intellectuals, are among other familiar motifs. There are ironical thrusts at Slavophils, critics, journalists, slanderers. The prevalent tone is one of dejection, but now and then a cheerful or defiant note is sounded. The sight of a sparrow chirping saucily and swaggering down the road with the air of a conqueror, though a hawk is circling overhead, works a magic transformation in Turgenev's mood. His despondency vanishes and his heart is flooded with courage and the will to live. "Let *my* hawk circle over me . . ." he writes, "We'll do a little fighting yet, devil take it!" In another piece the song of a blackbird at dawn after a gloomy sleepless night for a moment lifts "a dead weight" from his heart. A third "poem in prose" concludes: "Love, I thought, is stronger than death and the fear of death. Only by it, only by love, does life maintain itself and go on." The series, published during the author's lifetime, opens with a sketch of the village after emancipation which is unexpectedly idyllic, and ends with a little hymn to "the great, mighty, candid and free Russian language."

What kept him from writing was not so much the invectives of the critics and the indifference of the public, nor even his blunted responsiveness to new impressions, but rather, he repeated, the fact that living abroad almost constantly as he did, he was "unable to make diligent and close observations of Russian life, which, besides, was getting more and more complicated with every year." As a matter of fact, the tangle of Russian affairs was just then being resolved into a clearly drawn conflict. "Going to the people" having failed of its purpose, the revolutionists adopted the tactics of terrorism. At first their acts of violence were committed in self-defense or in revenge for the harsh treatment accorded their comrades. But soon, flies turning into hornets, as one of the activists put it, they began to use the revolver, the dagger, the bomb, as weapons of offense against individuals in high places for political ends. They hoped either to frighten the Government into granting concessions or to throw such confusion into the enemy's ranks as to be enabled to seize power. The warfare between the terrorists and the Government was initiated with the shot fired by Vera Zasulich and culminated in the assassination of the Czar on March 1, 1881.

Turgenev watched this new turn of events with absorption. His residence abroad was a real help to him here. He could entertain some sort of relations with the revolutionists without compromising himself. Of course, neither their views nor their program met with his approval, and he shuddered at their acts. When back in 1866 an apparently unbalanced youthful terrorist made an unsuccessful attempt on the life of Alexander II, Turgenev wrote to Annenkov: "One cannot help trembling at the thought of what would have become of Russia if the evil deed had succeeded." A Laodicean spirit heavy with skepticism, he was nevertheless drawn to these men and women prepared to undergo martyrdom for their beliefs. He continued to associate with those who came his way in Paris. Occasionally he gave them aid and comfort, even advising them how to make their propaganda literature more effective. He helped to find a French publisher for a novel by a Russian emigré, which blamed the authorities' repressive measures for the rise of terrorism. He kept up his contacts with Lavrov and followed Lopatin's career with interest. When, in the winter of 1877–78, Peter Kropotkin, the future anarchist, arrived in Paris after escaping from a Petersburg prison hospital, Turgenev suggested that the event be celebrated with a dinner. He took Kropotkin to Antokolsky's studio to see the newly finished statue of Christ Before the People, and insisted he get up on a ladder to view the sculpture from above, so that he could note the strength, the scorn and the hatred in this Messiah. "He must see it," he cried, "he is a revolutionary!" It is said that he kept in his desk the pictures of executed terrorists and kissed the photographs of the heroic women condemned in the Trial of Fifty (March, 1877), the flesh-and-blood sisters of his Yelena and Marianna. The French police regarded the novelist, whom they nicknamed "the white wolf," as "the queen bee of the Nihilist hive," to use his own words, and kept a sharp eye on him.

From 1876 till 1882 not a year passed without his spending part of it in Russia. He took advantage of these visits to study the latest phase of the social movement. He attended at least one political trial in the capital. He was apparently revolving in his mind the idea of a new novel—he would not be done with writing until he was done with living. It is not clear if this was to be the tale mentioned by Ralston, Pavlovsky and others, or a sequel to *Virgin Soil*. It is said that he intended to do justice in the latter to a revolutionary bearing no trace of Nezhdanov's Hamletism, a "nameless man" who gave himself to the cause with complete self-abnegation. It is also reported, however, that in his opinion the assassination of Alexander II had wholly isolated the revolutionaries and rendered them incapable of action. Hearing that the news of his projected novel had got into the French and German newspapers, he wrote to Polonsky's wife on November 9, 1881, that he was not seriously thinking of it, adding wistfully: "Can it be that new leaves and even branches will spring from the old, dry tree?"

He did not always return to the great steppes for what Henry James enviously described as "a strengthening bath," and what he himself spoke of as a dip in "potent waters." His trip of 1879, for example, was undertaken for the purpose of obtaining the legacy bequeathed him by his lately deceased brother. Nikolay died early in the year. It was not a bereavement that affected Turgenev vitally: they had had nothing in common, had seen each other rarely, and their letters had for the most part been either catalogues of their respective ailments or accounts of financial affairs. And yet, as Turgenev wrote to Flaubert, "a brother may be less than a friend, but he represents something different, something less strong and more intimate." Now there was no one left with whom to share the memories of their common childhood. Besides, the passing of a person, who, however uncongenial to him, was bound to him by the ties of blood, was a pointed intimation of his own mortality. And so his sorrow was "retrospective and personal." Nikolay had left him a hundred thousand rubles, willing the remainder of his large fortune to his relatives-in-law. Since they were "a thievish sort," Turgenev thought he had to be on the spot if he was to get his inheritance. As a matter of fact, he got no more than sixty thousand.

His brother's death was merely a contributing cause to his depression. He was, as he told Flaubert, leading the retired life of a mole, alone, quite alone, and idle. In February he was in Petersburg, and for once a friendly Fate surprised him. Coming from the shadow of the sad Parisian winter to claim his share of his brother's fortune, he suddenly found himself in the warm sunlight of public favor. He rejoiced in it all the more because it took him by surprise. He had always been inclined to exaggerate his unpopularity at home, and by the same token had ignored the signs of the growth of his reputation. In 1874 his name was familiar even to the attendant who served him in the public baths, and the same year two young artisans came up to him while he was waiting for a train and, having assured themselves that he was the author of *A Sportsman's Sketches,* bared their heads, bowed from the waist, and thanked him in the name of the Russian people, disappearing before the astounded man could find his voice. His novels, in the words of a Russian critic, had become fashion magazines which set the style in manners and morals, and, as another observes, the conversation in them was for several decades the conversation in every Russian dining room, bedroom and study.

His eight weeks' visit to the two capitals was in the nature of a triumph. He passed from the arms of one group of enthusiasts to those of another. He was dined and wined and crowned, figuratively, with laurel wreaths. He gave readings from his works, and even when he mumbled and stumbled the audience acclaimed him with repeated plaudits. One young woman broke a window pane in her eagerness to catch a glimpse of him, and at the end of another public appearance he had to be rescued from a cheering mob of students by a police officer, who, all the while that he was pulling the novelist away from them, kept assuring the crowd that he was an ardent admirer of his talent. The very girls who, six months earlier, had anathematized him for *Virgin Soil,* now "shrieked like jackdaws at dusk," as an eye-witness observed, in delight over an autographed copy of the novel.

At a session of the Lovers of Russian Literature in Moscow a university student greeted Turgenev in the name of young Russia. He said that in doing homage to the novelist the rising generation was paying a tribute to its "spiritual predecessors." Turgenev was moved to tears when, at a banquet, he was toasted as "the beloved and forbearing mentor of the youth." Addressing himself chiefly to the young people, he said, in an after-dinner speech, that he was being honored, he felt certain, not so much as a writer, but rather as an old *liberal.* The term, he went on, denoted protest against darkness and oppression, respect for science and education, love of the arts, and, above all, love of the folk.

He was fêted in Petersburg, too. His rooms at the Hotel d'Europe were like a public thoroughfare, what with the coming and going of all manner of people. Speaking at the banquet tendered him by the academic and literary world, he went so far as to mention "the crowning of the edifice," and Dostoevsky scandalized the company by rising to ask what the phrase meant. Like everyone else, he knew, of course, that the reference was to a constitution limiting the Czar's power. The report was circulated and later recorded in an underground journal that Turgenev was appealed to by a group of students of the Mining Institute as the one man who could unite and give shape to all the forces of the opposition, whom both fathers and children would heed, and that he virtually agreed to assume the burden, since, he said, there were no younger shoulders to carry it. The alarmed authorities made it known to him that his presence in the capital was officially frowned upon. Early in April he was back in Paris.

He appreciated that the meetings in his honor had been in effect disguised political demonstrations by the liberal segment of the public. Just then the constitutional movement, after having remained in a state of suspended animation for over a dozen years, was showing signs of life. Russian arms had secured the Bulgarians a representative regime. Could the Czar do less for his own people, who had borne the brunt of the war? Even in certain radical circles the prospects of the liberal cause were regarded rather optimistically. Shortly before Turgenev went to Russia Lavrov had visited him in his lodgings. Shaking his great beard, he cried that the constitutionalists had only to proclaim their program "with firmness" and the Government was bound to yield. After what the novelist saw and heard in Moscow and Petersburg, this belief must have seemed to him less unreasonable than the other views of the elderly revolutionary. One evening soon after his return to Paris, in the presence of Prince von Hohenlohe, German ambassador to France, Turgenev set forth the program of the constitutionalists, arguing that it was the sole means of preventing "a total catastrophe." The ambassador wrote in his diary that if he were Alexander II he would entrust the formation of a cabinet to the novelist.

The Russian banqueting having played havoc with his digestion, Turgenev, on arriving in Paris, was disabled with gout. But otherwise he was refreshed. It seemed to him that he had succeeded in making peace with the educated public, whose chronicler he was content to be, and that, furthermore, the rising generation was at last lending an ear to the counsels of moderation which he had so long been offering it. He promptly discovered that he was mistaken about the temper of young Russia. On April 2, five shots were fired at Alexander II as he was taking his morning walk. "The latest abominable news," the novelist wrote to Polonsky, kept him awake two successive nights. "I foresee that some people will use this mad attempt to harm the party which, precisely because of its liberal convictions, prizes the sovereign's life most because it expects vital reforms from him alone: a reform in Russia which does not come from above is unthinkable."

Before the year was out he said the same thing publicly. The Paris *Temps* of November 12 carried an account of his prison experiences by Pavlovsky, which Turgenev provided with a brief cautiously phrased foreword. He recommended the piece as an argument against solitary confinement and as proof that the Nihilists were "neither so black nor so callow as they are represented." This caused a storm in Russian reactionary circles. Commenting in a letter to Polonsky on the rumor that he might be forbidden to reenter Russia, he repeated what he had said about his political convictions in the communication just cited, adding: "I have a good opinion of our rulers and their intelligence and sense of justice." Katkov's newspaper printed a translation of the foreword and accused Turgenev of currying favor with the youth by apologizing for the revolutionaries. He responded with an open letter to the editor of *The Herald of Europe* which was printed by another Petersburg daily. "In the eyes of our youth," he wrote, "I have always been a gradualist, an old-fashioned liberal in the English, dynastic sense, a man expecting reforms from above, on principle opposed to revolutions, not to mention the recent abominations. The youth are right in their estimate of me, and I would have considered it unworthy of both them and me to represent myself in a different light."

Turgenev could not take his mind off affairs at home. He was no sooner back in Paris than he complained of "the burden of living abroad." A man couldn't straddle two countries, with one foot in each. He would have to return to Russia for good. In August he was telling Flaubert that he had decided to go home, not to work, but simply to breathe the native air. "This decision," he wrote, "had cured me of the nervous exasperation which has been consuming me. Laugh if you please, but the idea of plunging into that morass up to my neck has calmed me." The end of the year found his determination unshaken. Now at the age of sixty-two, he was going to his native country for the first time, he wrote to Tolstoy, without thinking of when he would return to Paris, and indeed not wishing to return soon.

The visit that he made in 1880 was indeed of extraordinary duration. He reached Petersburg early in February and did not leave Russia until nearly the middle of July. During these months he went through the usual course of public dinners, attacks of gout, and reading for charity. Of political activity there is scarcely a trace. The nearest approach to it was his effort to make some contact with the extreme left in the confraternity of letters. (It had not escaped his attention that the leftists had no hand in fêting him the previous year.) He braved the snow and three flights of stairs to meet a group of Populist writers who were publishing coöperatively a radical review (*Russkoye bogatstvo*). He arrived late, as usual, and found them having tea. The company included an inventor in a working-blouse stained with acids.

Turgenev tried to be agreeable, but the frost was not all on the windows. His companions were likely to recall the open letter in which he described himself as "a dynastic liberal" and referred to the terrorist activities as "abominations." They were acutely aware of a gap between him and them, and couldn't help making him feel it. They were commoners, who from the start had had to struggle for a living. He had lived richly by the labor of thousands of slaves. Their hair was black, but under his silver mop his face seemed fresher than their careworn faces. His mere physical bulk made them feel like pygmies; even seated, he towered head and shoulders above them, so that his genial talk seemed to flow down as from a height, and his great gestures threatened to push apart the walls of the narrow room.

In the chilly air, he gave himself over to reminiscence, until a nineteen-year-old boy, his voice trembling with eagerness, rose to put the bold question: "What do you think of the state of affairs in our country? Aren't we on the eve of a revolution? Isn't there a striking resemblance between present-day Russia and pre-revolutionary France?" This young man, like not a few others, was somewhat uncertain as to whether the real Government was in the Winter Palace or in the secret headquarters of the People's Will (the terrorist party). Turgenev answered by quietly laying the future on the lap of the gods, and added that a revolution seemed unlikely because the opposition was not united. His opponent retorted that the "extreme progressivists," as Turgenev euphemistically called the revolutionists, were all united, and were indeed the only ones to be reckoned with. Then he launched into an attack on the liberals. The novelist observed with a smile that for really concerted feeling he would have to look back to the forties and fifties, when everyone had been against serfdom. From the question of serfdom it was easy to pass to *A Sportsman's Sketches,* and thence to hunting. It happened that the inventor in the stained blouse was a passionate hunter. The dangerous topic was not referred to again.

There was another gathering in the palatial mansion of a wealthy sympathizer with the radical cause (he was to die a destitute *émigré* from Soviet Russia). On this occasion Turgenev was asked point-blank whether one should join the terrorists or "go to the people." "I see," he said after a moment's pause, "that young people are still pre-occupied with the question of what's to be done. It's for them to decide, I fancy. As for me, I only visit Russia now and then, and I don't undertake to solve complicated political problems." Already the prodigal had ceased to think of his return as permanent. "But," he ventured, "it seems obvious that 'going to the people' has been a failure." The abstractions of socialism, he observed, could have no meaning for the peasant, who lived in a world of simple, concrete things.

Of the events that occurred during these months in Russia what stood out most sharply were the festivities that opened with the unveiling of a statue of Pushkin on Strastnaya (Passion, now Pushkin) Square in Moscow. Three crowded June days were dedicated to the memory of the writer who had fathered Russian literature. The occasion incidentally made for homage to Turgenev as the master's spiritual heir, one whose work carried on the Pushkin tradition of light, grace, reason.* He was the first to place a wreath at the monument after the unveiling. The previous year the Kiev University had elected him an honorary member of its council. This time the University of Moscow honored him similarly, and when the Minister of Education embraced him on the platform of the great hall of the institution, there was wild applause. In the evening he recited a poem of Pushkin's at a gathering in the dazzling White Hall of the Noblemen's Assembly (where forty-three years later Lenin's body was to lie in

---

* Among the objects exhibited in connection with the Pushkin festival were a lock of the poet's hair and his signet ring. Both had been loaned by Turgenev, to whom the ring had reputedly been passed on by the son of the poet, Zhukovsky. It was inherited by Pauline Viardot, who presented it to the Pushkin Museum attached to the Lyceum that the poet had attended.

state). After he had crowned Pushkin's bust with a laurel wreath, the novelist Pisemsky, a heavy man with the clumsy look of a peasant, took the wreath and made a gesture as though to place it on Turgenev's head, and once more the public thundered approval.

Next morning at a session of the Society of Lovers of Russian Literature the audience rustled into silence to hear Turgenev read his speech in praise of Pushkin. It was the work of a man who loved the poet this side idolatry, a writer who regarded him as an unattainable model, but it was also a sober, discerning performance innocent of patriotic bombast. What he stressed was the virility of Pushkin's language, the simplicity, the candor, the liberating, and hence moral, power of his poetry. He paid high tribute to him and, incidentally, to his foremost interpreter, Belinsky, but questioned the appropriateness of placing him on the level of Shakespeare, Goethe, Homer, as a national poet of universal significance, reserving that glorious distinction for some future genius who would surpass his master, Pushkin. And he hailed the homage offered the latter as a sign that after some decades of neglect poetry was again assuming "its rightful place among other manifestations of social life." The response of the public was rather lukewarm. How far Turgenev fell short he realized when, the following day, the speaker was Dostoevsky. He took his hearers by storm. Even Turgenev, inimical as ever to his confrère's ideas, and slightly humbled by this demonstration, was swept off his feet and embraced the speaker with tears in his eyes. In the evening, after more reading from Pushkin, laurel wreaths were given to both Dostoevsky and Turgenev. Five days later he wrote to the editor of *The Herald of Europe* that Dostoevsky's passionate harangue was based on a falsehood flattering to Russian *amour-propre*.

At the conclusion of the exercises a number of people came up to Turgenev to press his hand. Some of them begged him to remain in Russia. He did not. Early in July he was back in his apartment on rue de Douai, and did not return to his homeland until the following spring, after having given his blessing to Marianne Viardot's union with a pianist named Duvernoy. He was therefore in Paris when, on March 1, 1881, Alexander II was assassinated. "If the new Czar too

THE RETURN OF THE NATIVE **359**

is attacked," he was writing to Annenkov several days later, "it will be necessary to run to the ends of the earth, or a peasant noose will tighten around your civilized gullet. Apparently the firebrands don't care if Russia drops into an abyss and breaks its neck." He had conceived the idea that the revolutionaries were people driven to despair, a threat to themselves and to the nation.

Under the impact of the appalling news he rushed into print with an article entitled "Alexander III," which appeared anonymously on March 26 in the Paris *Revue politique et littéraire.* He had met the new Czar, then the heir apparent, and his consort two years previously at a reception given by the Russian ambassador in Paris, and he had written to Polonsky that to his "great joy" he found him to be "frank, honest and kind" and his spouse "very amiable." To Lavrov he had spoken of Alexander's "limited outlook, ignorance and awkwardness," and he had reported that the future Empress of all the Russias deplored the fact that he wrote his novels in Russian. In his article Turgenev pointed out that Alexander III, being a man of "a broad and enlightened spirit," would perceive that certain modestly liberal reforms, including freedom of the press, had become necessary, and that, far from shaking his throne, they would make it more stable. While limiting the monarch's authority was out of the question for the present, he wrote, there was no reason why the political life of the Russian people should not rest upon the same constitutional base as that of their European neighbors. It is said, by the way, that Gambetta, whom Turgenev called "the new Pericles," approached him on the subject of France's future relations with Russia.

When, at the end of April, Turgenev arrived in Petersburg, people in high places did not hasten to invite him into the councils of state. Quite the contrary. Pobedonostzev, procurator of the Holy Synod, who wielded great power at court, wrote to Polonsky requesting him to advise Turgenev that he should not tarry in the capital, since this was no time for speeches and ovations. Although the message did not reach his ears, Polonsky having declined to transmit it, the novelist had the uneasy conviction that he was under police surveillance here as he had been in France. He did not feel safe in

the capital, he told his friends only half in jest. But at Spasskoye he was hardly better off. The previous year a rumor
circulated among his former serfs that, as a result of the
explosion in the Winter Palace, the Czar had ordered him
immured in a stone pillar with a twelve-pound pig iron hat
on his head. In the confusion prevailing after the assassination of the Emperor almost anything, he thought, could
happen. A practical joker might send a written order to the
local authorities: "Please hang the landowner, Ivan Sergeyevich Turgenev." And forthwith he would be hanged by his
own peasants. The droll idea seems to have taken hold of him.
He elaborated it with gusto to Polonsky, who reported it as a
daydream of Turgenev's:

> We sit on the balcony one fine morning and quietly sip our tea,
> and suddenly we notice a crowd of local peasants coming toward us
> from the church across the garden. As usual they take off their caps
> and bow, and when I ask, "What do you want, brothers?" they reply:
> "Don't be angry at us, little father, we are not to blame. You're a
> good master and we're very well satisfied. Still, whether we like it or
> not, we shall have to hang you. And while we're at it, we might as
> well hang him, too," pointing to Polonsky. "What?" "Yes, quite so.
> Those are the orders, little father. We have the rope ready, too.
> You'd better say your prayers now. We're no murderers, you know;
> we're human beings. We can wait a little."

Most of the four months of 1881 that he was in Russia
Turgenev spent at Spasskoye. The Polonskys were staying
with him; he entertained other guests, and managed to do
a little work. By August he was writing to a friend: "Although
in the flesh I am still here, mentally I am already in Paris,
and I feel that a French skin is growing under my Russian
skin, which is beginning to slough off. In the spring, the
process will be reversed." Two more springs were left him
for the Russian skin to renew itself. But when he saw the
green roof of the old manor house melt, as he drove off, into
the green of the August landscape, it was for the last time.
Nor did he ever see again the colored cupolas of Moscow, or
again hobble through the giddy parade on the Nevsky.

37

RECONCILIATION

One May day in 1878 Turgenev received a letter addressed in a handwriting which he had not seen for seventeen years. It was a note in which Tolstoy held out the olive branch. Having just passed through a moral crisis, and feeling himself, since seven times seven years had gone over his head, a new man, he desired reconciliation in a spirit of Christian good will with all whom he had offended or from whom he had suffered offense. He was certain, he wrote, that so kind a man as Turgenev had forestalled him in forgetting their old enmity, and he concluded by declaring his indebtedness to his senior for such fame as he had by then achieved.

This last statement was a gesture of exaggerated humility, and yet Turgenev had done more than Tolstoy perhaps realized to make him known in the West. As the self-appointed promoter of Russian letters abroad, he had interested himself particularly in pushing Tolstoy's work, in spite of his break with the author. When he was informed that the Paris *Temps* would welcome a contribution from him, he offered the daily a manuscript translation of Tolstoy's *Sebastopol Tales,* saying that he wasn't worthy to unloose the latchet of this writer's shoes.

Not that his admiration for Tolstoy was unqualified. When the first instalment of *War and Peace* appeared, he found it dry and dull, the product of a memory that fastened on small, irrelevant details, and full of petty psychologizing which was out of place in a work of epic proportions. The historical element in the novel he characterized as "charlatanry" and "hocus-pocus." By the time the third volume was out he was ready to concede that the book contained passages which would live as long as the Russian language and, indeed, that therewith Tolstoy had moved up to the first place among contemporary writers. The genre pictures gave him "the chills and fever of ecstasy," but the passages in which Tolstoy sat awkwardly enough on his philosophical hobbyhorse irritated and angered Turgenev beyond measure. The man had fashioned for himself a system of philosophy, "at once mystical, infantile and bumptious," he wrote to Flaubert. For all its defects, the thing "smelled of life." *Anna Karenina* had in it things of the first order, he thought, but it presented the spectacle of the most gifted writer in Europe stuck in the native swamp of barbarism, and it showed the influence of the author's isolation and "lack of real artistic freedom." He was always finding in Tolstoy's writings and behavior signs of hostility to the intellect. That tendency, he believed, accounted for Tolstoy's siding with the French in the conflict of 1870: the opinionated wretch abhorred Gallic phrasemongering, but he hated even more the system, the science, the rationality for which the Germans stood. If only, Turgenev sighed, a mature intelligence were added to this rare talent.

Reconciliation was naturally welcome to Turgenev. Many years had passed since he had said that they were to each other as the Montecchi to the Capuletti, and the edge of that feeling had long since worn off. He eagerly accepted the outstretched hand. Three months after Tolstoy's letter reached him, being then on one of his trips to Russia, he made a point of stopping off at Yasnaya Polyana. He followed up this visit with another a month later. Several members of the company he found there, including the Countess Tolstoy and the eldest son of the house, Sergey, who was then fifteen, recorded their impressions of the guest.

The boy was struck by the man's gigantic bulk, which dwarfed that of his father, and the yellowish-white hair contrasting with his father's, in which there wasn't a gray thread. He recalled the flabby legs and the wide-toed soft leather boots of a victim of gout, and the velvet jacket and waistcoat, in each pocket of which reposed a marvelous watch. The giant was very proud of them and kept consulting both of them to see if they agreed. Not that he, being after all a Russian, was ever on time. In another pocket he kept an exquisite snuffbox, which, he confessed, his ladies in Paris would not suffer him to use, and he had long since given up smoking because two young girls of whom he was fond refused kisses that smelled of tobacco. He was reduced to smelling salts as a substitute. Relieving all this velvet was a silk shirt and silk cravat, above which blue eyes beamed kindly from a ruddy face.

The Countess found Turgenev aged, gray and meek, and exhibiting a childish weakness of character. She was charmed, like every one else, by his conversational verve, observing: "He described a statue of Christ by Antokolsky so that we actually saw it, and afterwards told us about his favorite dog, Pegasus, with equal vividness." At table he led the talk, making everybody laugh by mimicking a chicken in the soup and by other parlor tricks. He spoke slightingly of the French people and of the Parisian argot, and took occasion to compliment the young ladies present by contrasting the Russian girl favorably with the French miss. They did not know that two years previously he had described the Russian woman to his French friends as "a *mélange* of simplicity, tenderness, and unconscious depravity." Later he beat his host at chess. His skill with one figure had won him the title of "the chevalier of the bishop."

When the talk turned to literature, he urged Tolstoy to read young Garshin, Guy de Maupassant, and a certain Lubov Stechkina, his literary protégée of the moment, upon whom, as usual, he was wasting his enthusiasm. He was also heard quoting Pushkin at his host, in defense of poetry. Tolstoy confessed to a weakness for Pushkin, but persisted in maintaining that one could express oneself plainly and freely only in prose. But for the most part, Turgenev avoided contentious subjects. He was much with the young people—the house was full of them—and showed himself, for a gouty sexagenarian, singularly spry. Sergey reports that once when his father and the guest were out of doors they found near the house a board balanced on a log, and seating themselves on the ends, began to seesaw as unconcernedly as schoolboys.

Upon reaching Spasskoye after this reunion, he effected another reconciliation, with Fet. The poet was a virulent reactionary and obscurant, who is said to have spat every time he drove past the University of Moscow. Turgenev had long ignored the politics of his old neighbor and hunting companion at whose table he had eaten excellent dinners and whose verse he had read with gusto. But late in 1874 he had decided to break with the man: Fet, he discovered, had spread a report that he, Turgenev, had engaged in revolutionary propaganda. In announcing his decision to his former friend he added: "I cannot see what there can be in common between me and a justice of the peace [Fet held that office] who seriously reproaches brawny peasants for not having used the end of a shaft-bow to knock the daylights out of a thief they had caught." And now Fet followed Tolstoy's example and made a friendly overture in a charming but not very clear letter, adorned with quotations from Kant. Again Turgenev responded warmly, although he never got back to a very secure footing in his further relations with the poet. As in the case of Tolstoy, he was happy over the closing of the breach, but well aware that the old differences had not been conjured away.

After the second visit to Yasnaya Polyana, Tolstoy was writing to a friend: "Turgenev was here again, and was just as charming and brilliant. But, *entre nous,* he is a little like a fountain spouting imported water, and one is always afraid that the jet may be exhausted and the fountain cease playing." To Fet he wrote at the same time: "He [Turgenev] is the same as ever, and we know the degree of intimacy that is possible between us." The two men wisely refrained from an attempt to exceed this measure, and thereby the relation was saved.

The letter which Tolstoy sent after his departed guest was very affectionate, but it included a request never to refer to his writings—perhaps the only thing about him in which Turgenev was genuinely interested. "God knows, when I reread my work or hear it mentioned," Tolstoy wrote, "I get a complicated feeling the chief elements of which are shame and the fear that people are laughing at me. . . . Much as I love you and firmly as I believe you well disposed toward me, still it seems to me that you are making fun of me." If at the time seeking the good life was his private concern, he did not presume to enjoin Turgenev to do likewise. "Everyone has his own way of blowing his nose," he continued. He only wished his friend the happiness of work that he would find worth-while. And he concluded: "I don't for a minute believe that you have given up writing, because, like an open bottle that has been swung round too quickly to spill, you still hold most of what filled you. The thing is to find an angle at which the fluid can run out quietly; that is what I wish for you as for myself."

To this Turgenev replied:

Although you asked me not to speak of your writings, I cannot refrain from stating that I never laughed at you, even the least little bit. Some of your works please me a great deal, others I don't like at all. But why should I laugh? I thought that you had long since got rid of such feelings. Why do only men of letters know them, and not painters, musicians, and other artists? Perhaps because there enters into a literary work more of that part of the soul which it isn't comfortable to show to everyone.

As for his own work, he wrote, he had given it up because he was not living at home. "At least," he added shrewdly, "I account for my inaction by my residing abroad."

The relations between the two men remained to all intents and purposes cordial. In May, 1880, Turgenev came to Yasnaya Polyana again and stayed three days. One object of his visit was to persuade Tolstoy to take part in the coming Pushkin celebration at Moscow, but he pooh-poohed the idea. Turgenev's final visit to Yasnaya was on his last trip to Russia, in June of the following year. As usual he found a houseful of young people, with whom he made merry. On one occasion the members of the party amused themselves by relating in turn their happiest moments in love. Turgenev, being pressed for his, made a contribution which differed substantially from the story which he had told his French friends when the same topic was under discussion. He had, he said, been in love with a girl who, as he thought, did not return his affection, but once he glanced at her and catching her eyes on him, knew that she did. After that the boys and girls kept glancing at one another. As on his previous visits, he talked about his experiences abroad, mentioning, among other things, an evening spent with Jules Verne, whom he found to be a stay-at-home and a frightful bore. He delighted the company by dancing a cancan with a twelve-year-old girl—not the vulgar steps of the café chantant, but the old-fashioned, stately measure. Tolstoy noted in his diary: "Turgenev—cancan. Sad."

Turgenev further irritated his host by making fun of one of the master's potential disciples, who discussed the opening of the fourth Gospel with such vehemence that he fell off his chair. The visitor was no great reader of the New Testament and cared least for St. John. When he confessed as much to a pious second cousin of Tolstoy's, the good old soul could only sigh: "You will never be anything but the most likable of pagans." There were thirteen at table and pleasantries were made about the ominous significance of the number. "All who are afraid of death," cried Turgenev, "raise hands," and lifted his own. Only Tolstoy followed suit.

A month later, while he was on a two-day visit to Spasskoye, Tolstoy heard his host again declare the fear that haunted him. "How can it be that Turgenev is not afraid to be afraid of death?" Tolstoy commented, in a letter referring to the matter. He himself knew the chill of that terror well enough. It had led him—blessed with genius and health and children and chattels—to the brink of suicide one night in an Arzamas tavern. This fear was perhaps the very root of the unease from which he had found refuge in the faith and the way of life of the masses. In fact, he had come to Spasskoye fresh from a pilgrimage which he had made on foot, so that he might the better identify himself with the common folk. As he stood at Turgenev's door, paying the coachman who had brought him there, they looked like two peasants. The visit over, Tolstoy made this entry in his diary: "Turgenev fears the name of God, but acknowledges Him. . . . Lives in luxury and idleness."

During one of Turgenev's visits to Yasnaya Polyana the master of the house showed him some of his most recent writings. Having found a faith to rest in, Tolstoy was then busy shelling out the clean kernel of ethical Christianity from the husks of theology and mysticism. Speaking to an acquaintance in the summer of 1881, Turgenev said that he simply did not understand the stuff, and yet Tolstoy attributed the greatest importance to it. What a pity, Turgenev lamented, that a talent unequalled in European literature should be wasted on ethico-religious tracts. And he recalled how one day the two of them, strolling through a meadow, had come upon an old nag at grass, and how Tolstoy had gone up to it, stroked it and talked to it gently, showing clearly that he knew just what the creature was thinking and feeling, until his companion exclaimed: "Lev Nikolayevich, you must once have been a horse yourself!" That was the sort of thing Tolstoy should be busy with, Turgenev felt, instead of climbing into the pulpit.

In September 1882, already seriously ill, he asked Tolstoy for a copy of his *Confession,* the edition of which had been confiscated by the police. He received the work, the first fruits of its author's conversion, toward the end of the year, and prudently avoided expressing his opinion of it for fear of "falling into an argumentative tone," as he wrote in his letter of acknowledgment. If they could meet, he added, he would have much to say about it, not to prove his case, but in his turn to make confession to a man he loved. And he urged his old friend to resume his literary labors, implying that a work like *Confession* was outside literature. He did not mince words in speaking of the book to others. "I have read it with great interest," he wrote to Grigorovich, "the thing is remarkable for its sincerity, truthfulness, force of conviction. But it is all built on false premises and in the end leads to a most gloomy negation of human life. This, too, is a kind of Nihilism. . . . Nevertheless, Tolstoy is perhaps the most remarkable man in contemporary Russia."

To the end the two men remained incompatible. What was real and precious to the one was unreal and worthless to the other. Turgenev could not breathe comfortably in Tolstoy's moral universe, and Tolstoy felt that Turgenev had no moral universe to breathe in. The one would have had the flesh follow on the leash of the spirit. The other, being of less abundant vitality, was generally able to keep his natural impulses within the bounds of the good taste which was part of his make-up, and so accepted them fearlessly. Faced with the problem of personal extinction, one worked out his salvation by submitting his ego to the group consciousness, by stepping back into the sheltering warmth of huddled, primitive humanity. The other, as jealous of his distinct, separate individuality as he was sure of its annihilation, could find no such refuge. "Non-existence is a black abyss; impersonal immortality is a white abyss," he is said to have observed. And so the small flame of his fortitude was blown upon by every passing wind.

That Turgenev was uncomfortable in his unbelief is certain. In his early forties he wrote to Countess Lambert on the occasion of her son's death: "He who has faith has everything and cannot lose anything, and he who doesn't have faith has nothing; and I feel this the more acutely because I belong to the have-nots. But I am not losing hope." In another letter of condolence written to the same lady a month later he observed that the naturalness of death was far more terrible than its suddenness or strangeness. "Religion alone could conquer this terror. But religion itself," he concluded, "must become a natural need in man; and who does not have it can only turn away his eyes frivolously or stoically (it is really the same)." Fifteen years later he expressed virtually the same sentiment when he wrote to Pisemsky:

My observations of recent years have led me to the conviction that spleen, melancholy, hypochondria are nothing but forms of the fear of death. Of course, with every year it's bound to grow. There is no radical cure for it, but there are palliatives. If the religious feeling is, as you say, beginning to grow upon you, I congratulate you on this precious acquisition. It is a sure remedy, only it's not within everybody's reach.

He fashioned for himself no staff of faith to lean upon. While he sympathized with Louis Viardot's anti-clericalism, he was not an atheist. He told Herzen that he shared Faust's attitude towards God:

> Who dare name Him,
> And who declare:
> I believe in Him?
> Who, feeling,
> Would hazard saying:
> I do not believe in Him?

What aroused his deepest aversion was any rigid set of dogmas, such as Tolstoy erected for himself. The nearest approach to a credo that he formulated was a statement which dates from the year 1875 and which has already been mentioned. It reads as follows:

I shall say briefly that in the main I am a realist, and above all interested in the living truth of the human face; to everything supernatural I am indifferent, I do not believe in absolutes and systems; I love freedom more than anything, and so far as I can judge I am sensitive to poetry. Everything human is dear to me, Slavophilism is alien, as is every orthodoxy.

It was only after death ended the intercourse between the two men that the survivor became truly reconciled to the man from whom he so radically diverged. Tolstoy continued to feel that there had been no body to their personal relations; Turgenev, he submitted, had loved no one except the women with whom he had been in love. At the same time he acknowledged Turgenev's implicit faith in goodness, and the candor which led him to "turn his soul inside out" in his books. He understood then the worth of the work which was Turgenev's enduring residue. Where a Dostoevsky, so Tolstoy wrote to a friend, was like a valuable racer, but of a skittish temper and with a secret fault that must sooner or later land his rider in a ditch, a Turgenev was like a stout, sound horse that could be depended upon to get you to your destination.

38

PHOENIX LOVE

Turgenev might prolong his visits home and even entertain the thought of settling there, but in the end he always
returned to France. His periodic excursions into Russia were
merely leaves of absence from the Viardots. They were to
him "his own people," apart from whom he could not live.
Away from them, he talked of them often and wrote to them
regularly. As the girls grew into matrons and had children
of their own, he became increasingly attached to them through
his grandfatherly interest in their offspring. He found a bul-
letin about the health of Didie's little girl better reading, so
he said, than the most absorbing magazine article. As for
the child's grandmother, he had long since ceased to be
swayed by the passion for her which had once made him
unwilling to alter by a single dot her homely, fascinating face.
But he was bound to her by that network of cumulative
habit, residual sentiment, and accepted obligation which his
unofficial, incomplete marriage, had, like most marriages, in
the end become.

It was a strong bond. Polonsky even spoke of Turgenev's
subjection as that of a hypnotic. Otherwise, how could the
man, summering contentedly at Spasskoye, exclaim appre-
hensively: "What if Mme. Viardot should call me? Then I
would have to go, I could not help it." One report had it
that Turgenev himself regarded her as literally a "sorceress."
People believed that she mistreated and exploited him. In
saying that Turgenev was the Viardots' "milch cow," Henry
James was undoubtedly repeating the gossip current among the
novelist's countrymen in Paris. It was said that when Pauline
was cross with him, she would make him don a fool's cap
with bells and put him in a corner, and when he spoke
Russian in her presence would scream: *"Assez de votre langue*

barbare!" Even his Russian friends, who could laugh at such absurd gossip, were naturally jealous of this foreigner who had ravished their great man. Knowing how they felt, he could not resist teasing them a little on occasion. If he had to choose, he said, between being the greatest literary genius in the world but not seeing the Viardots, and being their porter, he would choose the place of the porter.

If Pauline was a careless housekeeper and failed to make him comfortable, he was the last to notice it. In the fall of 1879 a Russian acquaintance, coming to the rue de Douai to take him out to lunch, found his bedroom in disorder at two o'clock and the bed not yet made. In the study, "a layer of thick dust covered the small closed piano and the music upon it. One end of the shade was torn from the roller and hung lopsided, and apparently had been thus a long time, since a layer of dust was in its folds." On another occasion Turgenev remarked that dust was "as natural on curtains as dew on grass." This was in a Petersburg hotel room; he had not noticed that they were dusty, and said that his people in Paris would not have noticed it either. The visitor observed that Turgenev himself showed signs of neglect. "He wanted to button his coat . . . and he felt for the button; not finding it, he moved his hand to the next buttonhole, but the corresponding button hung by a thread attached to the lining, which was peeking through a hole. He smiled good-humoredly, threw up his hands and wrapped the coat around himself." On the way downstairs they passed a door from behind which came a strong contralto. Turgenev seized his friend below the elbow and cried, "What a voice—still!" They had their lunch and the novelist was gay and interesting, chattering of Daudet and Zola, and only dropping to a grave tone on the subject of matrimony. But suddenly he was all eagerness to get away: "Mme. Viardot's daughter is ill in bed. Perhaps I am needed to fetch the doctor or to run to the chemist."

Now and then he did chafe under the chain. On one occasion he wrote that "unofficial" marriages could sometimes be "more venomous" than the conventional ones, adding: "If I haven't touched upon them in my literary attempts, it is simply because I have always avoided themes that are too subjective: they embarrass me." There were moments, he submitted, when he would give up all his fame in exchange for having someone to scold him for being late when he returned to his rooms. As a matter of fact, a dinner party attended by Henry James, Turgenev and two other Russians in May, 1876, broke up rather early because, as the American wrote to his mother, "Mme. Viardot does not let him [Turgenev] stay out later than 9:30 o'clock."

He was unable to shake off the spell of Pauline's personality. He would sometimes hold up his large plump hand, sparsely covered with black hairs, and stick up his short thumb: could a man with so weak a will as this brief member signified, divorce himself from such an old association? But if he could not bring himself to break away completely, he did stray afield now and then. Aside from casual flirtations with women dazzled by his fame, there were in the last decade two affairs which played havoc with his unwearied old heart.

In June, 1874, when he was laid up with gout at Spasskoye, a certain Baroness Julia Vrevskaya, an attractive widow in her early thirties, came to spend five days with the invalid. He had become acquainted with her about a year previously, and although her eagerness to show kindness to people in need of it must have come to his notice before this, her acceptance of his invitation was something of a pleasant surprise. The visit, he wrote to her, had deeply impressed him and made him feel that she had become a part of his life. Back in Bougival, he did not forget those days. "I keep thinking," he wrote to her from there, "that if we had met when we were young, inexperienced and above all, free— end the sentence for yourself." An exchange of letters followed. There was something, he insisted, that tied the two of them together. He had liked her at first glance, then there was a temporary quiescence, and after that came her visit to tighten the bond. He wrote her:

And don't you get it into your head to cut or untie the knot. What for? Alas, no harm can come of it, either to me, or, for that matter, to you. . . . I'd like to spend a few hours with you in your room, sipping tea and looking at the patterns on the frosted windows—but what nonsense! looking, of course, into your eyes, which are very beautiful, and now and then kissing your hands, which are also very beautiful, although large. But I like such hands.

They must arrange a meeting shortly: if they don't come together soon, they will only do so when they are old and it's all over with them. She must remember that if she is thirty-three, he is fifty-seven. A month earlier he had suggested that they meet in Karlsbad, *im wunderschönen Monat Mai,* a romantic season, if taking the waters was a prosy business. It would seem that they did have a reunion at the spa, and when he returned to Bougival, he informed her that he had found all "the ladies who owned him" in fine fettle. "I am well, I do nothing," he wrote to her on September 9, 1875, "but I have begun aging terribly, so that at this rate within a year I shall turn into a moral mushroom. A physical one I have been for a long time." And some weeks later: "I feel that I am getting old—'as I have often said in jest,' to quote the poet—and it's no cheerful prospect. Quite the contrary. I do awfully wish, before the end of everything, that I might have my fling; will you help me?"

She did not help him. Although the baroness was a restless, adventurous spirit, with an unconventional way of obeying her generous impulses, she held to the moral standards of her world. Besides, she was just then seriously contemplating a trip to the East, of which she had been dreaming for some time. She was a woman with a taste for the exotic, rare in her generation. Turgenev had no desire to see her vanish into the dangerous distance. He admitted that it might be interesting to go to India at that time, when the Prince of Wales was on his way there too, but he begged her to resist the temptation and remain near him. His fears were groundless. The baroness's circumstances having changed, she found herself settled on the Neva instead of wandering up and down the Ganges. And by June, 1876, he was again sitting with her in her Oriental drawing room in Petersburg. Soon after their meeting there he wrote to her:

And you still consider it necessary to soothe me and beg me not to be afraid, and you promise not to get me into trouble. I assure you that there is as little in common between me and Joseph as there is between you and Potiphar's wife. What I am afraid of is cholera, and not charming women, especially when they are as kind as you. Alas! I cannot be compromised, nor can I compromise any more, if I ever could.

But the serenity of their relation was occasionally ruffled for him, he confessed, by the teasing and futile realization that she was a young, pretty woman.

Feeling that a frank statement of his position was in order, he gave it in a letter written eight months later:

> When I first met you, I loved you as a friend, and at the same time I had the persistent desire to possess you. This, however, was not so irresistible—I was no longer young—as to make me ask for your hand. Besides, there were further reasons which stood in my way. At the same time I knew very well that you would not agree to what the French call *une passade* [a brief love affair]. That explains my behavior.

That the "further reasons" had had to do with Pauline Viardot is hardly to be doubted. Having thus made matters plain to the lady, he went on to say that he looked forward to a deep friendship, untroubled by any carnal fret, as soon as his years allowed him to regard her as a person, rather than as a woman. "But now," he submitted, "I still get hot and somewhat frightened at the thought: and what if she should press me to her heart in an unsisterly fashion?"

A fortnight passes, and he writes: "There is no doubt that some time ago, if only you had wished—but alas! now the time is gone, and all that is necessary is to endure the transitional period before sailing into the haven of old age." Sixteen years earlier he had said the identical thing in almost the identical words, and as far as tranquil friendship with a woman was concerned, the haven of old age was as distant now as it had been then. In the same letter he mentions two bits of gossip: one, about Count Sollogub, the casual companion of his youth, a man four years his senior who now, in his repulsive old age, has deserted wife and children for a young woman; the other concerning a certain marquise who is living her own life. He is far from condemning either. "Ah," he concludes, with the wistfulness that companioned his fear of life, "if only we had had the courage . . . a few years ago!"

On April 19, 1877, he was informing the baroness that he hoped to see her in Petersburg within two weeks. Before the fortnight was over, Russia had declared war on Turkey and, gout interfering, he was afraid he might not find her when he got there: she was going to the front as a nurse. He did manage to see her once that spring. He never saw her again. She died of typhus on February 5, 1878, in Bulgaria. *The Poems in Prose* include a tribute to her memory, sincere and flat.

Turgenev wrote this piece in September, 1878. Half a year later he was at the Alexandrinsky Theater in Petersburg watching a performance of his play, *A Month in the Country*. The leading lady, Mme. Maria Savina, was a woman of twenty-five, who, like Pauline Viardot, had black eyes and hair and beautiful hands, and, like her, had been virtually born on, and certainly to, the stage. The revival of this piece was a triumph, much to the amazement of the author, who was convinced that the play was "impossible," theatrically speaking. The playwright received thundering ovations as he stood bowing from his box: he refused to appear before the curtain, because, as he said, he didn't want to be thought of as a dramatist. The next day he went to call on the actress. She was flattered by his admiration, but hurt when he showed himself surprised that such fine acting should be done by a Russian and by an unschooled, self-taught woman at that.

His enthusiasm for her art—he compared her to Rachel—was soon complicated by another sentiment, which he described in a letter dated November, 1879, from Bougival, as "that tender, half-fatherly, half . . . other feeling." In his subsequent letters, of which there were many, he kept referring after his usual manner to her "dear, pretty hands," and kissed them very tenderly and very long. During his next visit to Petersburg, in 1880, he made a point of seeing her again, and after his departure for Moscow he wrote to her: "I feel now that you have become something in my life from which I shall never part." And three days later: "I think of you often, oftener than I should. . . . I love you." On March 30, her birthday, he gave her a gold bracelet.

In May the actress traveled to Odessa for an engagement. Turgenev, who was then at Spasskoye, had hoped to see her there, but was only permitted to accompany her in the train for a short time, leaving her at the Oryol station. On returning to his lonely house he sent her long letters, in which he reviewed the incidents of their brief trip together and embroidered humorously upon his impulse to snatch her from the train at Oryol. For that hour in her compartment this white-bearded man of sixty-two had felt "like a boy of twenty." But, he admitted ruefully, in a phrase that was one of his private clichés, this was "the last flare of the lamp." Alas! he would never be, as she put it, "her sin." He couldn't explain even to himself the feeling this warm-lipped laughing girl aroused in him. "Am I in love with you? I don't know. Formerly it was different with me. This insurmountable impulse toward union, toward complete self-surrender, where everything earthly is lost in some fine fire. . . . I probably talk rot, but I would have been unutterably happy if . . . if . . ." But he felt that now such thoughts were vain. The door that so short a time back had seemed to him half open, with "something marvelous and mysterious behind it," was now banged shut forever.

During the summer they saw each other in Paris. But as she was accompanied by a man who was soon to become her second husband, even the ghost of their old intimacy was absent. He wrote to a friend: "I wish her every success, but she no longer exists for me." She was, however, a woman who could not easily forego the admiration of so great a celebrity as Turgenev, and she gave him a certain amount of encouragement. He continued, in his letters, to kiss her "intelligent" hands lingeringly and to tell her that he loved her. Indeed, with arrant disloyalty to the ladies who "owned" him, he assured her, "I know of no hands pleasanter to kiss than yours." She sent him, at his request, a cast of one of them.

And then, when he went back to Russia for what was to be his last visit, he had the happiness, not granted him by Pauline Viardot, of welcoming the lady to Spasskoye. She saw, as Pauline never did, the alleys of the old park, which he evoked in his letters with its "rural odors and bird notes, its sleepy sunlight and shadow and two hundred acres of rye waving all around." His friends, the Polonskys, who were spending the summer on his estate, had never seen the host in such a flutter of happy excitement and hospitable activity as during the seven July days she was with them. He arranged a village festival, and the dancing of the peasant girls soon drew the spectators, including the actress, and even the master, into the jig. One warm night, when the garden was heavy with fragrance, he sat on the balcony with his guests and read them "A Song of Triumphant Love," which he had just completed. The moved voice of the reader, the majesty of the night, the dance of moths lured to the candles from the dark fields, lent this hour a palpable enchantment. On another evening, after a late supper, as the guest of honor recalls, they all wandered out into the park to listen, at the host's invitation, to "the voices of the night."

One day he took her into his study, seated her in an armchair, and read her one of his "poems in prose." It was a piece which he had not included among those to be published; indeed he said he would burn it, not wishing to utter a reproach from beyond the gates of death. It was entitled "To Her," and was an apostrophe to a woman loved for a lifetime with a love she never understood. "You, who have plucked all my flowers," ran one vapid phrase which remained in the listener's memory, "you will never come to visit my grave."

Turgenev's attachment to the actress was strengthened by her visit to him. His happiest memory connected with it was of the dinner served on the balcony to celebrate the wedding anniversary of the Polonskys, when, after the champagne, she gave him "a radiant and burning kiss." It "nearly singed him," he said, and the thought of it made his head swim. When Mme. Savina required it, he slipped readily enough into the part of her "best friend," becoming her confidant and advising her in her rather confused and hectic affairs of the heart. He also counselled her on matters of diction, as he had been wont to advise Pauline Viardot on her acting. Sometimes, however, he allowed his fantasy to paint him in a more personal role. He imagined the two of them drifting down a canal through the mild Venetian October, or sauntering arm in arm through the streets of Rome, visiting galleries, churches, gardens, dining vis-à-vis, sitting side by side at the play, and then . . . "there my imagination halts respectfully. Is it because what follows must be kept secret, or because there is nothing to keep secret?" There are passages in these communications which recall his early love letters, but there is also the old man's resignation to the fact that youth calls to youth.

The spring of 1882 found him incurably ill, and when, in those gray days, he received a letter from the actress, it was to him "like a petal fallen upon the surface of a muddy stream." He saw her that season in Paris, but he didn't expect to see her again. He was, he wrote to her, in the position of old Lemm in his novel, *A Nest of Gentlefolk,* the worn and wasted musician who in the evening of his days cherished an unconfessed devotion to the exquisite young Liza. Mme. Savina's second marriage took place that summer, and he sent her his blessing. At the same time he insisted that she insure her freedom to pursue her stage career.

He wrote to her almost to the end, and even though he was a ruin of a man and reduced by his weakness to mere penciled scrawls, he wrote with ardor. He recalled regretfully the fact that it had been Polonsky and not himself who, on her visit to Spasskoye, when she was bathing in the pond, had involuntarily played for a moment the part of the elders spying upon Susannah. He placed the recollection of those few days at Spasskoye upon the best shelf of the archives of his memory. In his final letter, written February, 1883, he chided her for forgetting him, and said he would cherish the same feeling for her to the last.

Eleven years earlier this man had heard Gautier, who was to die shortly, complain that he felt like one already dead. Turgenev had commented that he himself was conscious of an imperceptible odor of decay that clung to him as a faint odor of musk sometimes haunts a room. He gave as the reason for this the fact that love was no longer possible for him. In the course of his visit to Yasnaya Polyana in May, 1880, he confessed to his hostess that he had stopped writing because he could only work when he was in love, and since those days were over, the days of his writing were over, too. He made a similar confession to Tolstoy. As a matter of fact, he went on writing to the very end, and likewise kept to the end youth's prerogative of falling in love. The man was still capable of feeling the fine frenzy, and the artist was curiously drawn to it, as one leans closer to warm himself at a dying fire. Indeed, "Clara Milich," his last literary work, has for its single theme the force of love.

This narrative is based on the story of a Russian actress,

the victim of unrequited love, who, in November, 1881, poisoned herself on stage, and of a young scientist who, hearing of this, fell in love with the dead woman. Eventually he recovered sufficiently from his morbid passion to get married. As Turgenev tells the story, Clara, a young actress, falls in love with a monkish youth and, repulsed by him, kills herself on the boards. After her death he falls morbidly in love with her and, indeed, dies, "a blissful smile on his lips," that he may be eternally united with his spectral bride. "Love is stronger than death," are among his last words.

39

"TIME TO TAKE LEAVE"

If you juggle the figures in 1818, the year of Turgenev's birth, you get 1881. Seeing an omen in this, he believed the prediction, which, in a dream he had once, his mother had made, that death would come to him on October 1, 1881. As a matter of fact, in the latter part of that year he was feeling, by his own account, "as well as a fish," and even doing a little work. In collaboration with Pauline Viardot he translated "The Song of Triumphant Love" into French and wrote the story, "A Reckless Character." His letters were rather cheerful and full of lively comment on sundry subjects, including Sarah Bernhardt, who was being acclaimed by the Petersburg public and whom he violently detested.

In the autumn he crossed the English Channel. This was his last visit to England. "I had a fine time hunting," he wrote from Bougival to Polonsky on October 20, "that is, I saw a great deal of game, but my shooting was terrible. It seems that I have to give up that, too." On this occasion Ralston improvised a dinner in his honor which was attended by Trollope, Walter Besant, James Payn and other novelists and journalists. Ralston exerted himself "partly out of sympathy with me," Turgenev wrote, "but *mostly* (as he confessed to me) in order to become the chief authority on matters Russian in the eyes of the English public. . . . I was very glad when it was all over. Ralston even wants to arrange a big banquet (!!?), but I'd rather cut off my nose than agree to such nonsense! Why a banquet to me in England?"

The new year began pleasantly, but by February he was entering a cloud of troubles. For one thing, his darling Marianne had a belated confinement which proved very difficult. Then old Viardot, whom he considered as solid as a granite rock, and who, so he said, was taken for his son when they went walking together, old Viardot came down with a stroke. Furthermore, his own daughter with her two children ran away from her husband and threw herself upon her father's mercies for protection. He had to conceal her whereabouts from the rascally Bruère and engage in long and costly legal proceedings, with the result that he was forced to sell his precious Rousseau and his horse and carriage. His life, he sighed, was in the yellow leaf. The political situation in Russia, which he followed closely, could not but intensify his depression. Contrary to his prediction, the new reign turned out to be one of black reaction. Lavrov mentions a visit he had paid Turgenev in January. In the course of the conversation the host said that he had lost faith in reforms from above, without gaining any confidence in the prospects of the revolutionary movement.

As for his health, it was remarkably good, what with the mitigation of the gout. Only his hernia gave him trouble now and then and occasionally irregularity of the heartbeat reminded him that he was mortal. On March 6 he dined with Edmond de Goncourt, Zola and Daudet. In spite of themselves, they kept returning to the topic of death all through the evening. Turgenev surprised them by taking a rather unusual position. Yes, death was a familiar thought, he admitted, but when it came he thrust it aside, like this—and he waved his hand in a gesture of dismissal. It seemed as if, drawing closer to the end he had so long envisaged, he was learning to put the idea from him.

In mid-April he was attacked, without warning, by a serious illness that the great Charcot diagnosed as angina pectoris. The patient described his ailment in letters as *angine pectorale goutteuse* or *cardialgie névralgique goutteuse*. He summoned Annenkov from Baden for help in the final disposition of his literary property. As once before, that faithful friend, instead of being received by a moribund invalid, found Turgenev in full possession of his faculties, indeed showing his "usual playfulness of mind," as Annenkov put it, so that it seemed as though the calamity were a nightmare of the doctors and the patient. But it was harsh reality. Turgenev was unable to walk, stand up, lie in a certain position without severe pain, and to sleep he often had to resort to chloral or injections of morphine. He appointed Annenkov his literary executor and dictated instructions for the sale of his works. Early in May he wrote to Pietsch that it was all over with him as a person.

When the Viardots moved to *Les Frênes* for the summer, Turgenev was taken there, but any more extensive traveling was out of the question. Illness had clamped the irons of expatriation on him permanently, and all he could have of Spasskoye was a spray of lilac enclosed in a letter. At Bougival he grew worse. The weeks rolled by and still he lay abed, "a motionless Something," "the patriarch of the mollusks," as he called himself. His condition made it impossible for him to carry out his expressed intention to write an article condemning the anti-Jewish riots that had followed the assassination of Alexander II. He had, besides, the feeling that the piece would be a futile gesture. The Czar's word alone could stop "these hideous things," he wrote to a correspondent on June 8, but the Czar chose not to speak, and so, "all you can do (especially here in Europe) is to blush for yourself, your country, your people—and hold your peace." He was no Zola.

In July he was put on a milk diet, and on August 2 he decided to follow this regimen with the utmost strictness. That Wednesday he started a daily record of the course of his illness. His first entry read: "In the morning pain in the chest; it returned at 5 o'clock and lasted until 10—not very bad. When walking, pain in the collarbone. At night two severe attacks at 1 o'clock and half past 4. Applied cotton. Cold came back. Drank 9 glasses of milk. A cup of bouillon at dinner." The diet did him some good and incidentally, he said, made him more virtuous than he was by nature. He was able to travel to Paris to consult a doctor, and there were moments when a trip to Russia the following winter seemed to him a possibility. He instructed Polonsky, who with his family was summering at Spasskoye, to pour the Bordeaux he had ordered from the cask into clean bottles with new corks and have the cellar dried out, so that the wine should not spoil—perhaps he would yet have a glass of it. He read omnivorously and, as before, kept up a lively correspondence (456 of his letters, dated 1882, are extant). In response to a collective missive from the Spasskoye peasants, he sent them a fatherly letter that was at once kindly and somewhat hortatory, and, as on previous years, he made them a present of a piece of woodland. He occupied himself with preparing a new edition of his works, and he wrote "Beyond Death," the story that was to be published early in 1883 under the title "Clara Milich."

The "slight" and even "noticeable" improvements in his condition, which he recorded, attributing them to his diet, were ephemeral. On October 25, the eighty-fifth day since he had begun to live on milk and a little bouillon, he wrote: "I have given up making entries. It isn't worth while. My illness has established itself for good. . . . To the end of my life." Early in November a doctor "from beyond the Mississippi" sent him a prescription for a medicine, which, the American stated, in three days cured a lady who for five years had suffered from the same illness as Turgenev. The patient must have smiled wryly when he enclosed it with one of his reports to a physician in Russia.

He looked forward to years of vegetative existence and worked out a philosophy based on "cheerful despair." He compared himself to a man stone-deaf or completely blind, who, being without hope, was secure from disappointment. If he could not budge, at least he could sometimes sleep at night, and, after all, why should one move? Don't oysters live? In a letter to Polonsky he set forth these precepts (which he honored more in the breach than the observance): "One should meditate on the past, satisfy the demands of the present, and *never* think of the future. To live in peace, one must *never* undertake anything, never propose anything, trust nothing and fear nothing." In the evening there was whist and sometimes a little music. That was something to anticipate during the long, empty hours of the day. And then there were Didie's two little girls and Marianne's baby to relieve the gloom that now hung about *Les Frênes*, where Louis Viardot was dying and he lay ill. He had the best of care, as he assured his Russian friends, adding that his ladies would be insulted by an offer of outside assistance.

The summer was a wet and unusually chilly one, and the autumn was worse, the sky looking "like badly washed linen." He spent his sixty-fourth birthday in "the family circle," and on November 18 followed the Viardots to Paris. He was driven there, "not being able to bear the railway," as was noted by Henry James, who had happened to visit him that day and to whom the invalid gave a seat in the carriage. "For an hour and a half," the American wrote, "he constantly talked and never better. When we got into the city, I alighted on the Boulevard extérieur, as we were going in different directions. I bade him goodbye at the carriage window and never saw him again."

In the city Turgenev's condition worsened. Despairing of a cure, he gave up all medication and discarded the electrical belt he wore occasionally and the metal frame intended to enable him to walk a few steps, but he stuck to the milk diet. He told his friends that he was satisfied with his lot and had even lost the desire for relief. Preparing the texts for the new edition of his works furnished him with a steady occupation.

Somehow the days went by, and 1883 was ushered in. Early in the new year he was operated on for a neuroma in the abdomen, which he nicknamed Feoktistov, after the chief censor. The operation was performed without general anaesthesia, and he told Alphonse Daudet that as he lay on the table he kept trying to find the right words to describe his sensations when the blade entered the flesh: it was "like a knife cutting a banana." He might lose the use of his limbs and forgo all hope, but his literary instinct, which he had so often disavowed, was indestructible. The wound healed within two weeks, but his old illness, he wrote, "was in full bloom." Pain in the chest and back was now ceaseless, he could not stand up even for a moment, he could not sleep without injections of morphine, and using a pen was becoming difficult.

By March he was in the grip of inhuman agonies, which were only posthumously recognized as due to cancer of the spinal cord. What with the tortures he had to endure, and the morphine he was given to dull the pain, he became deranged. He screamed so that he was heard in the street. He wanted to die. He wanted to kill. He pleaded for poison. He complained that all these people around him were "conspirators," plotting to put him out of the way. Pauline told Annenkov that the patient called her "a terrible woman who outdid

Lady Macbeth." He dictated irrational telegrams which betrayed his persecution mania. "Why do you put chains on me?" he asked the Russian ambassador as he stood at his bedside. He confided in Charcot, his physician, that he was being attacked by Assyrian soldiers. One night he pulled his bell rope so hard that several members of the household ran in to him, and when he saw Pauline he tore off the heavy brass ball of the bell and hurled it at her, crying out, "Ah, there is Lady Macbeth!"

While he was tossing from one crest of suffering to another, old Viardot breathed his last. Turgenev mourned him less than he envied him. After the funeral the family took their remaining patient back to *Les Frênes* with them for the summer. It was now May. For a while he had relief. He had survived the tempest, but it was the mere shell of his former self that came to shore. Seeing Annenkov, he began to cry, and Annenkov had to struggle to keep back his own tears. The details of his delirium had bitten like acid into his memory, and the inveterate littérateur promised himself to put his experiences into writing, if he ever took up his pen again. "I was at the bottom of the sea," he told Annenkov, "and I saw monsters and foul creatures tangled together which nobody has as yet described because nobody has survived the spectacle."

He hated himself for the way he tormented his ladies when he was in pain. Mme. Viardot was so good, so patient. One day he begged her to throw him out of the window.

"But my dear Turgenev," she remonstrated, "You are too large, and too heavy, and besides, it would hurt you."

He could not help smiling at that. As soon as he drew a free breath his sense of humor revived. He mimicked with all his old vivacity the righteous indignation of the old-fashioned Russian woman doctor of whom, among others, he had begged poison. Nor did he lose interest in his literary protégés.

The new edition of his works continued to be his chief preoccupation during these months. He astonished Stasulevich, who came to consult with him on the matter in August, by the practicality of his judgment and an unwonted firmness. Having taken care of his literary remains, he arranged for the disposal of his poor bones. He wished, he said, that he might lie at the feet of his master, Pushkin, but that he did not deserve, just as none of his works had deserved to be dedicated to the poet's memory. Let them lay him beside his old friend and teacher, Belinsky. Stasulevich tried to dismiss the matter with a joke. He pointed out that the Volkov cemetery in Petersburg (the Russian counterpart of Père Lachaise), where Belinsky was buried, was in very bad condition and might be condemned, in which case Turgenev would have to resume his travels even in his coffin.

He had previously deposited with the Viardots certain securities, the interest on which was to go to his daughter's maintenance. All his possessions, including his papers and the income from the sale of his books, he bequeathed to Pauline Viardot, and he left an instruction that his estates should be sold and the proceeds turned over to her, since, being inherited property, the land could not, according to Russian law, be willed to anyone outside the family. But because of the testator's habitual procrastination or what Henry James called Turgenev's "comprehensive indecision," his instruction proved invalid, for his signature was not duly notarized. As a result, after his death his real estate in Russia became the property of relatives.* The will was eventually contested by his daughter and her husband, but without success.

The novelist's condition was one of the topics of the day in Russia. His reputation there had been hurt by "The Song of Triumphant Love." It was taken as evidence of his complete alienation from life at home. In the eyes of the radicals he rehabilitated himself with "The Threshold" which circulated in manuscript copies. There were conflicting bulletins in the newspapers about the progress of his illness and more than the usual amount of gossip about how he was neglected by his foreign friends. It is true that he lacked the atmosphere of intense public sympathy, which would have braced and heartened him had he been in Russia. But, as a matter of fact, the "old carcass," as his trained nurse referred to him, had the best of care.

---

* After the October Revolution Spasskoye became a *sovkhoz* (State farm) and later a *kolkhoz* (collective farm). It was pillaged by the German invaders during the last war.

Early in May 1882, he received an affectionate letter from Tolstoy:

The news of your illness . . . distressed me terribly when I became convinced that it was serious. I realized how much I loved you. I felt that if you should die before me, it would deeply hurt me. The latest newspaper notices are reassuring. Perhaps it's all hypochondria and the lies of the doctors, and we shall yet see each other again at Yasnaya and at Spasskoye, please God. When I first came to believe, I hope without cause, that you were dangerously ill, I had the idea of going to Paris to see you. Write or have someone write me definitely and in detail about your condition. I will be very grateful. I want to know for sure. I embrace you, my dear and cherished old friend.

In reply Turgenev managed to send Tolstoy half a dozen friendly messages. The last one was a penciled scrawl in his own hand, dating from mid-July, 1883. It reads as follows:

Dear and beloved Lev Nikolayevich, I haven't written to you for a long time, as I was and, to speak frankly, am now on my deathbed. I can't recover, and there's no use thinking of it. I am writing just to tell you how glad I have been to be your contemporary and to make my last, sincere request of you. My friend, return to literary work! That gift comes to you from the same source as all else. Oh, how happy I should be if I could believe that my entreaty would influence you!! As for me, I am done for—the doctors don't even know what to call my complaint, *Névralgie stomacale goutteuse*. I can neither walk, nor eat, nor sleep! It's even boring to repeat all this! My friend, great writer of the Russian land, heed my request! Let me know if you receive this scrap of paper, and permit me once more closely to embrace you, your wife and all yours, I can no more, I am tired.

This, his last letter, was widely circulated, and the title "great writer of the Russian land" was always to shadow Tolstoy, to his displeasure.

During these tortured final months, when the once ample contours of Turgenev's personal life shrank and withered, his fundamental devotion to writing came to the surface like the bones in an emaciated face. During a respite, which occurred in June, he dictated to Pauline in French a piece which recalled in detail one of the most vivid, if not most glorious, experiences of his youth: the fire on the boat that was taking him from Russia to Germany, when he was nineteen. And then, a fortnight before the end, as Mme. Viardot related at

length in a letter, he called her to his bedside and with tears in
his eyes—he cried easily now—asked her to do him a favor
which no one else could render.

"I'd like to write a story which I have in my head, but
that would tire me too much; I couldn't do it."

"Well—" she understood him at once—"dictate it to me.
I don't write Russian fast, but still I think that with a little
patience on your part, I shall be able to manage."

"No, no," he said. "If I dictate it in Russian, I shall stop
at every word, every phrase, to choose my expression, and
I don't feel capable of so exhausting an effort. No, what I
would like to do is to dictate the story to you in the various
languages that we both know, using the expressions that come
to me most readily, and you put it into French."

They set to work according to this plan, and after a few
sessions, she showed him her final version, with which he was
delighted. This French text was translated into Russian a few
years later by his friend Grigorovich. It is the story of the
degenerate scion of a noble Russian family gone to seed, who
becomes a horse thief. On one occasion the wretch is nearly
torn to pieces by incensed peasants, a lynching, the author
observes, which would not have had "the excuse of the sentiment of justice which is, in some measure, in the heart of
every American." The tale concludes with the narrator coming
upon the mutilated corpse of the wellborn rogue, and the
piece is with double fitness entitled, "An End." In thus ex-
emplifying the decline of the class to which he himself belonged, Turgenev seemed to be saying to the new social order,
Morituri te salutamus. It is appropriate, too, that his last
story should suggest, as far as such an unauthentic product
could, his first manner, that of *A Sportsman's Sketches.* It
was as though his art had described a full circle, and returned
again to its origins.

And yet even now his thoughts were not wholly retrospective. He kept returning to his plan for another big novel. He
was so well pleased with the collaboration on the short story
that he suggested to Pauline that they begin preparatory work
on the large piece. "But alas!" she concludes, "his condition
grew worse, and he could do no more than dictate the names
of the characters."

His sufferings had a certain compensatory feature: their cumulative effect was to destroy in him his ancient fear of death. In February, hearing that the author of *Meistersinger* had died, he was writing: "That Wagner should make his escape upon the first attack of an incurable illness, is another sign of his unfailing luck. I know people who envy him." He wrote to Polonsky in May: "My thirst for death is growing, and all that's left for me is to beg that you on your part should desire the granting of your unhappy friend's wish." He told the painter Vereshchagin that he called upon death a hundred times a day, and was not afraid to face it. He begged Maupassant, who came to see him five days before the end, to prove his friendship by giving him a revolver; none of the family would consent to let him have one. Physically, the giant had shriveled to a thin waxen image of his old self. His eyes were sunken, his limbs were sticks. "How can one live," he asked, "with legs like a grasshopper's?" The tenement was no longer habitable, and he was ready to abandon his lease.

Often, just before waking consciousness is blotted out, the drowsy mind leans for a moment upon a single image, which is like a stile on the borders of sleep. And it may well be that before all consciousness ceases, the mind turns its back on nothingness and rests briefly upon such a soothing image. If this was Turgenev's experience, what detained his fading awareness? Was it some scene of these latter days, or some quiet memory floating out of the past: his mother's bonneted head nodding over her game of patience; under the gray and green-gold lindens of Oryol a path overgrown with silken grass and wild strawberries; Stankevich's gnarled fingers beside Chouchou's at the piano; a little red Moscow church with green cupolas; the corner house on the Nevsky where he had first met Pauline Viardot; Didie in the bow-window at her easel; a sunburnt old peasant woman holding a pot of unskimmed milk, beaded with dew; Tolstoy astride a log, bobbing gravely up and down; the broken rusty prow of the old galley in the museum at Ventnor, with the inscription *Giovane Speranza?* He had asked a similar question in one of his prose poems: "What shall I be thinking of when I come to die?" Would it be of how he had let the years go by, taking the least of their gifts, and seeing their scorn too late? Would it be of the rare good hours, the few loved faces? Would old mistakes and misdeeds foreclose upon his last moments? Or would he be wondering what, if anything, awaits the dead? No, he concluded, rather would his mind take up some trivial thing, as if trying to look away from the advancing dark.

On the last day of August, a Friday, Louise came into his sickroom, and he seemed to recognize her, but his mind was badly befogged.

"Look, Louise!" he exclaimed; "look, how strange: my leg is suspended over there in the corner. The room is full of coffins. But," he added, with a sly glance, "they have given me three days to live."

It fell out that he spoke the truth. Toward the end he was unconscious most of the time. On Sunday he came to himself, and began to talk. But it was only a compatriot who chanced to be at his bedside and, in some measure, Pauline Viardot, who understood him, for the words he spoke were neither in the language of his "second Fatherland" nor in that of his adopted family, but in the language of his wet-nurse and the serf who had first chanted verse to him in the Spasskoye park. At one point he turned to Didie's husband and assured him repeatedly that he loved him.

"You must believe me," he said. "Kiss me in token of it. I believe you; you have such a fine Russian—yes—Russian face."

To Marianne, who knelt beside his bed, he spoke of her son. Neither Chamerot nor Marianne understood a syllable of what he was saying. For a moment he seemed to recognize Pauline as she bent over him, and became alert. "There's the queen of queens," he said. "How much good she has done!" He reached out as though in an effort to embrace them all, his eyes moving from face to face. "Come nearer, nearer . . ." he faltered, "Let me feel you close to me. . . . The time has come to take leave. . . . Like the Russian czars . . ."

The words of the common folk began to come to his lips. It was as if he imagined himself a dying peasant, bidding his household farewell. Then his speech became more and more broken, and finally ceased. Early Monday afternoon he began to breathe heavily. His hands were warm to the touch. He lay quiet. It was two o'clock. He stretched out his arms for the last time.

"Ach, my friend," Pauline Viardot was writing to Ludwig Pietsch before the week was over, "it's too much, too much suffering for one heart! I do not understand how mine hasn't broken! Our beloved friend almost completely lost consciousness two days before the end. . . . The first day [after his death] the frown left by his suffering, together with the immobility of his features, gave him a severe and energetic look. The second day he resumed his kind and gentle appearance—at moments one would have said that he was going to smile . . ." And she concluded: "Now I shall have enough to mourn over for the rest of my life."

Turgenev's final journal was a slow one. The coffin did not reach Petersburg until September 27. It was accompanied by Claudie and Marianne together with their husbands. Their mother remained behind. She poured out her grief in letters. To the composer Ambroise Thomas she wrote on September 8: "I have lost the dearest of my friends. . . . His end resembled the death of my ardently beloved husband, and so I felt a double agony." A fortnight later she was writing to Ludwig Pietsch: "I am so lonely, so sad, so wretched! So endlessly alone! My children are so good and affectionate that I must make a terrible effort to hide my grief from them. . . . I long for solitude with my beloved dead."

Public mourning for Turgenev was limited by the authorities as far as lay within their power. The Russian Government was at pains to prevent the obsequies from becoming a political demonstration. Nevertheless large crowds gathered at the stations along the route followed by the coffin, and the funeral cortege on its way to the Volkov cemetery stretched for miles. Scores of delegations from all kinds of literary, educational, and civic institutions marched in the procession. Among the countless wreathes was one from the Society for the Prevention of Cruelty to Animals, inscribed "To the author of 'Moomoo'." The eulogies, as a matter of course, paid tribute to the literary genius of the dead and his devotion to the art that he had practiced for forty years. His sense of moral beauty, love of freedom, compassionate and understanding heart, his temperate habit of mind, allegiance to reason, faith in enlightenment—all were duly acknowledged, and it was pointed out further that his writings, far from lulling the public, had pricked its civic conscience. All but the most reactionary sector of the press honored him as the glory of the nation. The clandestine leaflet distributed by The People's Will, which was mentioned earlier, declared that Turgenev, though a member of the privileged class by birth and a gradualist by conviction, had sympathized with, and indeed served, the cause of revolution by celebrating the idealism of the insurgent youth.

BIBLIOGRAPHICAL NOTE

The best edition of Turgenev's writings is the one brought out in 1954-58 under a Moscow imprint in twelve volumes. Prepared with much care and nearly complete, it is provided with explanatory notes and ample commentaries offering critical estimates and factual data on the composition, publication and reception of each work. The old translations of the stories, novels, "Poems in Prose" by Isabel F. Hapgood and Constance Garnett, leave much to be desired. In recent years the novels, except for *Virgin Soil,* have been re-translated, three different renderings of *On the Eve,* and of *Fathers and Children* appearing in London and New York in 1948-51. There is also a new translation of *A Sportsman's Sketches* and of several of the stories. The plays were not translated until 1924 (by M. S. Mandell); three of them, including "A Month in the Country," were rendered into English by Constance Garnett; this was also translated by George R. Noyes. Turgenev's "Recollections of Life and Letters" have become accessible in English through the publication of his *Literary Reminiscences and Autobiographical Fragments,* translated by David Magarshack, with a preface by Edmund Wilson, New York, 1958. There is also a translation (by Robert Nichols, London, 1930) of the essay "Hamlet and Don Quixote." Turgenev's verse is not available in English.

There is at present no comprehensive collection of Turgenev's letters. An annotated selection from them forms the last volume of the edition mentioned at the beginning of this Note. The novelist did not think that they were worth preserving, and as far as possible he destroyed them. The Institute of Russian Literature, which is part of the Soviet Academy of Sciences, is preparing a complete edition of his polyglot correspondence, and has been able to locate nearly 6,000 of his letters, addressed to 450 persons. By the early thirties upward of 5,000 were in print. Couched in Russian, French, German and, in the case of a few, English, they are scattered in numerous books and periodicals. These are listed in M. Kleman, *Letopis zhizni i tvorchestva Turgeneva,* Moscow, 1932, a useful compilation in the nature of a detailed chronological outline of the novelist's life.

His letters to Pauline Viardot, though by no means all of them, have long been available both in the original French (latest edition of *Lettres à Mme. Viardot*: Paris, 1926) and in Russian translation. It is uncertain if any of her communications to him are in existence and, in any event, none of them has been published. This lends added interest to her correspondence with Julius Rietz, printed in *The Musical Quarterly,* New York, July 1915—January 1916. The epistolary material that has come out within the last quarter of a century includes the novelist's letters to his daughter. Edited by E. K. Séméneoff, a part of the collection was serialized in *Mercure de France,* Paris, November 15, 1931 and February 1, 1932, and it was published in full under the title, *La vie douloureuse d'Ivan Tourguéneff,* Paris, 1933. Other additions are a number of communications to Du Camp, Flaubert, and Edmond de Goncourt (supplementing the volume, *Ivan Tourguéneff d'après sa corespondance avec ses amis Français,* Paris, 1901; there is an English translation), in *Literaturnoe nasledstvo,* Moscow, v. 31-32, 1937; several notes to Victor Hugo, in *Revue des études slaves,* v. 27, 1951, and to Henry James, in *Comparative Literature,* Eugene, Oregon, v. 1, no. 3, 1949; 5 missives from 13-year-old Ivan to his uncle, in *Zapiski* of the Ms. Division of the Lenin Library, Moscow, v. 18, 1956; many letters to Russian friends in *Zvenya,* Moscow, v. 5, 1935, in two miscellanies, ed. by N. Brodsky, published in 1940, one in Oryol, the other in Moscow; in *Literaturnyi arkhiv,* Moscow, v. 4, 1953, and *Voprosy literatury,* Moscow, 1957, 2.

Of considerable interest are Annenkov's letters to Turgenev, in *Trudy* of the Lenin Library, v. 3, 1934, and the novelist's correspondence with the Polonskys in *Zvenya,* v. 8, 1950. Flaubert's many missives, with the Russian's summarized replies, are collected in *Lettres inédites à Tourguéneff,* Monaco, 1946, and Maurice Parturier, *Une amitié littéraire,* Paris, 1952, contains 95 notes addressed to the novelist by Prosper Mérimée. The letters to Turgenev from his mother, which the present writer consulted in ms. during the winter of 1923-24 in the Leningrad Public Library, have not as yet been published, only excerpts from them having been printed back in 1915.

Turgenev kept a diary, which, as he wrote to Grigorovich on December 15, 1882, was "intended for destruction." It is apparently not extant.

There is no general Turgenev bibliography, but partial lists are not lacking. Most of the memoir literature is noted in A. Ostrovsky's compilation of passages from what the novelist's contemporaries wrote about him from personal knowledge (*Turgenev v zapiskakh sovremennikov,* Leningrad, 1929). One such source of information, the reminiscences of Turgenev's foster-sister, originally published in 1884, became available in English with the publication of *The Turgenev Family,* by V. Zhitova, London, 1947. Detailed bibliographical references are furnished in the anthology of Russian criticism of Turgenev, edited by K. Bonetzky, Moscow, 1953, which opens with a few pages from Lenin's pen. Contributions to Turgenev scholarship during the Soviet period down to 1954 are recorded and ably discussed by Peter Brang in *Zeitschrift für slavische Philologie,* v. 24, Heidelberg, 1956. The most ample list of Turgeneviana, including French and German books on the novelist's times, is to be found in Henri Granjard, *Ivan Tourguénev et les courants politiques et sociaux de son temps,* Paris, 1953, 507 pp. This is a scrupulously documented, masterly synthesis, resting on the solid foundation of much of the Turgenev literature which has accumulated over the years.

One special study may be cited: *Turgenev in England and America,* by R. A. Gettmann (*Illinois Studies in Language and Literature,* v. 27, no. 2, Urbana, 1941). Turgenev the playwright is the subject of a substantial essay by G. Berdnikov which introduces his edition of the plays (Moscow, 1953). The catalogue of Turgenev's papers preserved by Mme. Viardot's granddaughters, which is mentioned in the Preface to the first edition of the present book as in preparation, appeared under the title, *Manuscrits parisiens d'Ivan Tourguénev,* by André Mazon, Paris, 1930. The Paris documents, published previously by Professor Mazon (in *Revue des études slaves,* v. 5, 1925) consist of dossiers for "First Love," *On the Eve, Smoke* and *Virgin Soil.* Two other texts brought to light more recently by the same editor, in volumes 30, 1953, and 31, 1954, of *Revue des études slaves* respectively are: "The Temptation of Saint Anthony," 1842, and "Two Sisters," 1844, both unfinished one-acters.

The history of the relations between Turgenev and Pauline Viardot is traced in I. Grevs, *Istoriya odnoi lyubvi,* Moscow, 1927; revised ed., 1928. It is the subject of Alja Rachmanowa, *Die Liebe eines Lebens,* Frauenfeld, 1952, a novel translated from the Russian ms. Among the recent general works about Turgenev mention should be made of the compact biography by the émigré, Boris Zavtzev, Paris, 1932, and the "sketch" of the novelist's life and art by M. Kleman, Leningrad, 1936, a distinctly Soviet-oriented treatment of the subject. A full-size sensitive study of the man and his work, taking account of all that is known about both, is still to be written in the novelist's own tongue.

CHRONOLOGY

The dates in this table, as throughout the book, are Old Style for events taking place in Russia and New Style for events occurring elsewhere. In the nineteenth century the two calendars differed by twelve days, so that, for instance, March 1 (O.S.) was March 13 (N.S.). The date of a title is that of first publication. Practically all of Turgenev's writings first appeared in periodicals.

1818 Ivan Sergeyevich Turgenev born in the city of Oryol, central Russia, October 28.

1819-27 Reared on the ancestral estate at Spasskoye.

1827-34 With the family in Moscow, summering in the country. Attends two boarding schools, 1827-29. Is tutored at home, 1830-33. Matriculates at the University of Moscow, September 20, 1833.

1834 Transfers to the University of Petersburg, autumn. Father dies, October 30.

1837 Graduates from the University of Petersburg, June 24.

1838 Embarks for Germany, May 15. Enters University of Berlin, October.

1839-41 Studies, chiefly philosophy. Travels. Friendship with Stankevich and Bakunin. Returns to Russia, May 21, 1841. Beginning of affair with Tatyana Bakunina, October, 1841.

1842-47 Lives in Petersburg, visiting Moscow and spending weeks at Spasskoye in summer and autumn. Goes abroad, January, 1847.

1842 Illegitimate daughter Pelageya (Pauline) born, April 26. Examined at the University of Petersburg for the degree of Master of Philosophy, April-May.

1843 Meets Belinsky, February, and before long the two are on friendly terms. *Parasha,* April. Obtains minor post in the Ministry of the Interior, June. Beginning of lifelong friendship with Annenkov, autumn. Makes the acquaintance of Pauline Viardot, end of October.

1845 Retires from the service, April.

1846 Becomes closely associated with *Sovremennik* (*The Contemporary*), a monthly dominated by Belinsky.

1847-50 Summers on the Viardots' estate at Courtavenel, winters in Paris. "Khor and Kalinych," opening story of *A Sportsman's Sketches,* January 1847. Witnesses the February Revolution in Paris. Finishes *A Month in the Country,* March 22, 1850. Returns to Russia, June 1850. Mother dies, November 16, 1850, and he comes into a large inheritance.

1850-52   In Petersburg. Under arrest, April 16-May 15, 1852.

1852-53   Confined to Spasskoye under police surveillance, May 1852-November 1853. *A Sportsman's Sketches,* August 1852. Back in the capital, December 1853.

1854   "Moomoo," March.

1855   "A Month in the Country," January. *Rudin* written, June 5-July 24. Beginning of friendship with Countess Lambert, winter.

1856   *Rudin,* January-February. Goes abroad, July 21. At Courtavenel, summer. Taken ill in Paris, November.

1857   Pauline Viardot gives birth to Paul, allegedly Turgenev's son, June 20. At Courtavenel, summer. Travels to Italy, October.

1858   "Asya," January. Leaves Italy, March. Arrives in Petersburg, June.

1859   *A Nest of Gentlefolk,* January. At Courtavenel, July-August. Writes *On the Eve,* June 28-October 25.

1860   *On the Eve,* January. "First Love," March. The charge of plagiarism leveled at him by Goncharov is arbitrated, March 29. Arrives in Paris, May. At Courtavenel, July. Conceives the idea of *Fathers and Children* on the Isle of Wight, August. Severs his connection with *The Contemporary,* October 1. Winters in Paris.

1861   Returns to Russia, April 27. Quarrels with Tolstoy, May 27. Breaks off relations with his old friend Nekrasov. Finishes *Fathers and Children* at Spasskoye, July 30. At Courtavenel, September. Winters in Paris.

1862   *Fathers and Children,* February. Sees Bakunin in London for the last time, May 14. Back in Petersburg, May 26. In Baden, August-October. Spends the winter in Paris. Engages in a debate with Herzen, which ends in a rift between them.

1863   Summoned to appear before a senatorial committee in Petersburg to answer the charge of aiding the London group of expatriates headed by Herzen, February. Meets Flaubert at a literary dinner in Paris, February 23. Arrives in Baden, where the Viardots have taken up residence, May 3. Settles there, paying six visits to Russia in 1864-71.

1864   Appears before the senatorial committee, January 7 and 13. Exonerated, January 28, and permitted to leave Russia. Returns to Baden, March 11. Buys land for villa there, June.

1865   Daughter married, February 25. Begins writing *Smoke,* November 18.

1867   *Smoke,* March. Renews contact with Herzen, May. Quarrels with Dostoevsky, July 10.

1868   "The Brigadier," January. Because of financial straits sells newly built villa and moves into it as a tenant, April 17. Prepares edition of his collected works.

1869   "Reminiscences of Belinsky," April.

1870   At Spasskoye, June. Originates the plan for *Virgin Soil,* July. "King Lear of the Steppes," October. Arrives in London, where the Viardots are staying, November 13. Spends part of the winter in England.

1871   In Russia, February-March. Returns to London, April 7. In Scotland, attending the Walter Scott centenary, and shooting, August 9-15. Arrives in Baden, August 21. Finishes *Spring Freshets,* November. Leaves Baden for Paris, November 19. Settles there, sharing a house with the Viardots.

1872   *Spring Freshets,* January. "A Month in the Country" first staged (in Moscow), January 13. In Russia, May-June. Granddaughter born, July 18. Plan for *Virgin Soil* ready.

1873   Meets Baroness Vrevskaya, December.

1874   "Punin and Baburin," April. At Spasskoye, June.

1875   Jointly with the Viardots buys an estate at Bougival, near Paris, and builds a chalet on the property, spring. Second grandchild born, September.

1876   "The Watch," January. In Russia, June-July. Writes *Virgin Soil,* April-October.

1877   *Virgin Soil,* January-February. In Russia, May-June.

1878   Makes peace with Tolstoy, May. Visits Yasnaya Polyana, August 8-9, September 2-4.

1879   His brother Nikolay dies, January 7. Feted by the liberals during his stay in Petersburg and Moscow, February-March. Meets Maria Savina, on her appearance in the Petersburg premiere of "A Month in the Country," January 17. Awarded honorary degree of DCL by the University of Oxford, June 16 (?). Prepares a new edition of his collected works.

1880   In Russia, February-June. At Yasnaya Polyana, May 2-4. Takes part in the Pushkin festival, June 6-8.

1881   "Old Portraits," January. Last visit to Russia, May-August. At Yasnaya Polyana, ca. June 10. Tolstoy at Spasskoye, July 9-10. Maria Savina at Spasskoye, July 14-18.

1882   Is taken seriously ill, April. Has his ups and downs, but by the end of the year his condition is worse. Writes "Clara Milich," August. Begins to prepare a new edition of his collected works, December. "Poems in Prose," December.

1883   Continues to occupy himself with the new edition of his works. "Clara Milich," January. Becomes critically ill, February. Dictates "Fire at Sea," June, "The End," August. Dies at Bougival, September 3.

1910   Pauline Viardot dies at the age of 89, May 18.

INDEX